Anglo-Jewry since 1066

MANCHESTER
1824

Manchester University Press

For Ben and in memory of Cissie Ribeiro

Anglo-Jewry since 1066

Place, locality and memory

Tony Kushner

Manchester University Press

Manchester and New York

distributed in the United States exclusively by Palgrave Macmillan

Published by Manchester University Press
Oxford Road, Manchester M13 9NR, UK
and Room 400, 175 Fifth Avenue, New York, NY 10010, USA
www.manchesteruniversitypress.co.uk

Distributed in the United States exclusively by
Palgrave Macmillan, 175 Fifth Avenue,
New York, NY 10010, USA

Distributed in Canada exclusively by
UBC Press, University of British Columbia, 2029 West Mall,
Vancouver, BC, Canada V6T 1Z2

British Library Cataloguing-in-Publication Data is available

Library of Congress Cataloging-in-Publication Data is available

ISBN 978 0 7190 8598 7 paperback

First published by Manchester University Press in hardback 2009

This paperback edition first published 2011

The publisher has no responsibility for the persistence or accuracy of URLs for any external or third-party internet websites referred to in this book, and does not guarantee that any content on such websites is, or will remain, accurate or appropriate.

Printed by Lightning Source

Contents

Preface and acknowledgements

The barmitzvah of my son, Jack, took place a few weeks before this project was completed. The ceremony was held in the fifteenth-century Tudor Merchant's Hall in what was the heart of medieval Southampton. It is unlikely that any Jewish event had taken place in this building before, although Jews have had a connection to Southampton since the twelfth century. I have lived in Southampton for over twenty years, longer than anywhere else. We are members of the South Hampshire Reform Jewish Community, established in 1983. Its members have diasporic roots and connections to many parts of the world, as shown in the cover illustration reproducing a silk screen artwork that we have created ourselves. The Jewish connection to the locality is, however, much deeper and I have developed a fascination in the history of Jews and others who settled or passed through it. This book reflects this interest, charting the history and memory of Anglo-Jewry from medieval through to modern times through the prism of the county of Hampshire, relating the concept of the 'local' to those of the 'national' and the 'global'. It has also grown out of opportunities provided by the 'Port Jew' project of the ARHC Parkes Research Centre for the Study of Jewish/non-Jewish relations at the University of Southampton. Through a series of conferences held at both Southampton and its partner, the Kaplan Centre at the University of Cape Town, I was able to give papers that formed the very early forms of some of the later chapters of this study. I would like to thank all those involved with the Port Jew project, including its director, David Cesarani, for the encouragement to develop my work in this area further. The British Academy enabled visits to conferences at Cape Town and I am grateful for its support and to Milton Shain and Janine Blumberg in making these visits so memorable and stimulating.

The research for this project has required extensive research and I would like to thank the archivists, librarians and museum workers at the British Library, Central Zionist Archives (Jerusalem), Hampshire Record Office,

Manchester Central Reference Library, Manchester Jewish Museum, National Archives (London), National Archives (Washington, DC), Portsmouth City Library, Portsmouth Archives and Museum, Southampton City Art Gallery, Southampton Local Studies Library, Southampton Oral History Unit, Southampton City Record Office, University of Cape Town Archives and Winchester City Library. Special praise is due to all at the University of Southampton Special Collections. Chris Woolgar and Karen Robson have facilitated my research over many years. Jenny Ruthven was especially supportive by helping not only with the Parkes Library but also one of the hidden treasures of the University's Hartley Library – the Cope collection. Both were of central importance in researching this project. Jewish communities and individuals in the region have also been cooperative and supportive and I would like to thank them for their interest in and help with this project. I am also grateful to those who have shared their memories of the migrants and others who passed through the region.

Colleagues in the History Department and the Parkes Institute at the University of Southampton have provided a supportive and stimulating environment to carry out this project. Sarah Pearce in particular deserves special mention for her collegiality, wisdom and friendship which is deeply appreciated. I would like to express my particular gratitude to my good friends and colleagues who generously read and commented on this material in draft form, including Mark Levene, John Oldfield, Mark Stoyle, Colin Richmond and Greg Walker. Discussions over many years with Colin Richmond concerning the importance of particular places have prompted much of this study and I feel privileged to have his comradeship. As Colin states: 'It is essential for the historian to "be there"'. James Jordan helped with research concerning Atlantic Hotel and has taken a keen interest in this project throughout and Sue Bartlet was an inspiration and tremendously generous with regard to the Jews of medieval Winchester. Alas, Sue died in the last stages of this project. I am also grateful to Nadia Valman for her support with literary sources. I have also gained much from discussing this project with Tobias Brinkmann, Aimée Bunting (to whom Chapter 1 on 'the local' is dedicated), Nick Evans, Lloyd Gartner, Colin Holmes, Tom Lawson, Stuart Olesker, Gemma Romain, Trish Skinner and Miles Taylor, as well as audiences, academic and public, who commented on lectures and talks linked to it. I have also benefited from discussing it with the person who has inspired so much of the new wave of British Jewish history, Bill Williams, who continues to write such pathbreaking work. I hope this work meets with his approval of what British Jewish studies should be about and how it should be approached.

The Cavaliers Cricket Club continue in what is now their twenty-first sea-son with their unique blend of the sublime and the ridiculous. I am grateful for the opportunity to play in a team in which anything is possible and nothing is expected. Finally, my family have, as ever, provided love and support throughout. Mag, Jack and Sam have accepted more than their fair share of topographical wanderings linked to this book, mainly with tolerance and good humour. Mag deserves additional praise for producing the index. My brother Mike, mother and grandmother always make trips to the place of my birth, Manchester, special. In this respect, I would like to mention my eldest brother, Ben, to whom this book is co-dedicated. Apparently through his mistake in a primary school playground nearly half a century ago, my family ended up supporting Manchester City rather than their rivals. Over thirty years without a major trophy now is the ongoing price we (including now Jack and Sam) are paying for that schoolboy error. Because of the support Ben provided in my early studies and subsequently I can forgive him and wish him the happiest of quasi-retirements in his new role as a 'West Country artist'.

Sadly as this book was being revised, my grandmother, Cissie Ribeiro, passed away, six days short of her hundredth birthday. Her parents were Galician Jews and she was the only one of their seven children born in England. From an impoverished and unhappy childhood, she strove through hard work and tenacity to make a loving and secure home for her family. Grandma was proud of my achievements but she was rightly suspicious of any academic pomposity or snobbery. She was to me and to so many others, a truly inspirational figure and we will miss her beyond words. I hope this book, which I dedicate also to her, in some tiny way does justice to the struggles and achievements of those, like Cissie, who came to Britain, or were born here, with so little.

TK
Southampton

1

Placing the 'local'

Introduction

In 1920, the philosopher, John Dewey, contrasted perspectives of the United States as an entity from the outside with that presented by an American small-town newspaper:

> Then one gets a momentary shock. One is brought back to earth. And the earth is just what it used to be. It is a loose collection of houses, of streets, of neighbor-hoods, villages, farms, towns. Each of these has an intense consciousness of what is going on within itself in the way of fires, burglaries, murders, family jars, wed-dings, and banquets to esteemed fellow citizens, and a languid drooping interest in the rest of the spacious land.

Was this inward-looking journalistic vision of the world not very provincial, asked Dewey, to which he responded, 'No, not at all. Just local, just human, just at home, just where they live.'[1] Dewey was convinced after the First World War and the growing movement in the United States for 'Americanization' that 'We are discovering that the locality is the only universal. Even the suns and stars have their own times as well as their own places.'[2] Some fifty years later, the poet William Stafford came to the same conclusion: 'All events and experiences are local, somewhere. And all human enhancements of events and experiences – all the arts – are regional in the sense that they derive from immediate relation to felt life.' It was such immediacy, suggested Stafford, that distinguished art, and 'paradoxically the more local the feeling in art, the more people can share it; for that vivid encounter with the stuff of the world is our common ground'.[3]

Dewey and Stafford were convinced that only by intense engagement with the local – whether living in, passing through or simply by thinking of places – could communication between different peoples become universal. Such commitment to and faith in the 'local' contrasts with the dominant associa-tions of the concept as parochial, insular, and, ultimately, narrow-minded.

At very best in such thinking, the 'local' acts as a retreat and a defence or refuge from the rest of the world. W. G. Hoskins, the founder of the 'Leicester school' of English local history, answering why there was a growth in interest in his subject after 1945, suggested that it

> may be that with the growing complexity of life, and the growth in size of every organisation with which we have to deal nowadays, not to mention the fact that so much of the past is visibly perishing before our eyes, more and more people have been led to take an interest in a particular place and to find out all about it.

Anticipating that such an interest might be labelled 'escapism', Hoskins rejected the charge and added that 'the fact is that we are not born internationalists and there comes a time when the complexity and size of modern politics leaves us cold'. In contrast to the perspective offered by Dewey and Stafford, Hoskins had no universal vision for identifying with the 'local': 'We belong to a particular place and the bigger and more incomprehensible the modern world grows the more will people turn to study something of which they can grasp the scale and in which they can find a personal and individual meaning.'[4] Hoskins, as Christopher Parker suggests, 'portrayed local historians in a distinctly romantic and nostalgic way, mapping their villages or their country towns in the shortening days of autumn, studying in county parsonages, writing in humble school exercise books and so on'. As Parker concludes, in spite of Hoskins's denial, 'one has to say this looks very escapist'.[5]

Hoskins devoted only four pages of his *Local History in England* (1959 and 1972) to the 'mobility of population', although he did acknowledge that one of the most deeply held but 'false ideas about English social history is that the majority of our population were rooted to the soil in one place until quite recent times'.[6] Even then the emphasis was placed on internal migration rather than the world beyond the nation state represented by the presence of immigrants. Rather than diversity, it was the continuity of families and customs that dominated the work of the first academic local historians in Britain after the Second World War. Rejecting the bias of earlier antiquarian studies with their focus on the manorial system, the task of these new 'professional' historians was to locate and document the existence of local *communities*. While the leaders of the 'Leicester school' reflected, indeed agonised, on what constituted the geographical scale and definition of the 'local', they failed to problematise the idea and manifestation of 'community'. In his inaugural lecture at Leicester in 1970, for example, Alan Everitt returned to the questions raised by his predecessors, W. G. Hoskins and H. P. Finberg: what was local history, and how should it be approached? To Everitt,

> It means in the first place that ... we should study the *whole* local community, and not merely a single class or industry or section of it. Secondly, it means that

we study the *structure* of the local community, as an organism, so to speak, with a more or less distinct and continuous life of its own.[7]

To the 'Leicester school', formalised in the late 1940s, the existence of community was taken for granted. 'Community' was natural like the specific landscape around it which was so intricately connected to the making of local uniqueness. There is, however benign the intention, a *volkisch* potential in the pursuit of what Hoskins called the revealing of 'a true society of men, women, and children, gathered together in one place'.[8] As Felix Driver and Raphael Samuel warned in 1995, 'The idea that places have fixed identities or personalities, the product of continuous and inward-looking histories stretching back for generations, is a fantasy which might in some circumstances be comforting; in others, as in what is left of the former Yugoslavia, it is patently disastrous.'[9]

At a popular cultural level, the correlation between the 'local' and exclusionary prejudice and reaction has been parodied acutely by the *League of Gentlemen* in radio, television, film and print. Set in the fictional Peak District village of Royston Vasey, the grotesque creations in this darkest of comedies include Tubbs, who helps, along with her husband, to run the 'local shop for local people'. They kidnap, sexually abuse, murder and then burn any 'strangers' who stumble across their premises, giving menace to the village's seemingly innocent tourist slogan, 'Once discovered, never forgotten'. The outside world is utterly alien to Royston Vasey, but its danger is represented within through the presence of dangerous 'others' such as Herr Lipp, the paedophile German; Papa Lazarou, an Italian version of 'Black Peter' (a demonic representation of the black man)[10] who steals men 'to be his wife' through his 'Pandemonium Carnival'; and, finally, more covert references throughout their work to Jewish blood libel/cannibalism as exemplified by Hilary Briss, the village's family butcher with his 'special' [i.e. human] meat.[11]

It is no doubt easier within the liberal, if superficial, commitment in the twenty-first century to the concept of the 'global village' to highlight the backward looking and discriminatory tendencies of the 'local', rather than to imagine its universal potential. Thus those involved in local studies have 'generally been regarded by the world at large with a certain well-meaning condescension, not unmingled with a little kindly amusement', especially within the historical profession.[12] Returning to Royston Vasey, the semi-literate Tubbs's parochialism is manifested in a local pride and imagination that takes 'Leicester school' ideas and praxis to their logical absurdity: 'I am keen on local history, and one day hope to write a book about it. You can learn a lot of things about people by what they throw away … beautifl things I Haf collected from the moors about local Things about local people who are Local.'[13] The warped, monstrous and introverted local *Weltanschauung* of Tubbs, albeit in less concentrated form, is not purely a postmodern comic invention, as will become apparent throughout this study. It is especially manifested in Chapter 3 and the anthropological exploration of Jewish ritual murder narratives in medieval England and their later legacies. Nevertheless, *Anglo-Jewry since 1066* will include examples that put into practice the universalist aspirations of the local as envisioned by John Dewey and William Stafford. This book will thus both reflect on the nature of local studies and explore the key question raised by Driver and Samuel of whether it is 'possible to maintain a sense of the uniqueness of localities, and the singularity of our attachments to them, without falling prey to introverted (and ultimately exclusionary) visions of the essence or spirit of places?'[14]

The 'local' and minority studies

In a study of 'discourses in local history', George and Yanina Sheeran point out how class and gender analyses, and more recent work on black history, through specific English urban case studies have undermined the concept of 'community' as put forward by the 'Leicester school'.[15] Research revealing the existence of class conflict, sex inequality and racism has attempted to undermine the myth of consensus and harmony at the level of the local. Yet within the specific historiography of 'ethnic and racial studies', while prejudice, discrimination and violence have not been ignored, an equal if not greater energy has been expended on showing the sheer *presence* of minorities in specific localities. The desire to reveal rootedness and longevity has at least partly been inspired to counter the assumptions of 'ethnic' homogeneity in Britain, a national mythology, which aside from associations made with 'untypical' areas such as the East End of London and 'Tiger Bay' in Cardiff, is even more pronounced in imagining the local. To highlight further the exceptionality of the East End and 'Tiger Bay', both have been portrayed and perceived through their inhabitants as morally dangerous and essentially other, 'a race apart' representing the results of degeneration. Less menacingly, but no less fancifully with regard to their everyday normality, they have been pictured and experienced as exotic and enticing islands of cosmopolitanism in more mundane seas of sameness.[16] Chapter 8 of this book, on the street between the docks and the town in Southampton known as 'The Ditches', will show such processes at work in a less nationally notorious, but equally revealing, case study as will an earlier example of the 'sailortown' district of Portsmouth, explored in Chapter 4.

Against the dominant trend of ignoring past and present diversity (or the sub-theme of presenting it as a freak show or theme park and, there-fore, essentially alien), two extended photographic essays – *Black Londoners 1880–1990* (1998) and *Asian Leicester* (2002) – illustrate neatly the desire to integrate minority history into local history.[17] They are typical of a genre of historical literature in Britain which emerged in the last quarter of the twentieth century. This new writing revealed a growing consciousness of the black experience and melded populist and academic approaches in work intended, with an explicit pedagogic purpose, to reach a wide audience. It would empower local minority communities by providing evidence of their 'roots of the future'[18] and serve an educational purpose in the cause of anti-racism and multi-culturalism.

In *Black Londoners*, Susan Okokon states that her aim was 'to remind readers of the contribution of Black Londoners to the twentieth century, as we embark upon the twenty-first'. She adds that while 'White British people are discovering African ancestry from the waves of immigration centuries ago ... Black people must also lay claim to this past. A multicultural commu-nity must, by definition, make all its members proud and confident about the achievements of its Black citizens, both nationally and internationally, wherever they are found.'[19] Yet the desire, on the one hand, to show achieve-ment and contribution and, on the other, her geographical focus on London, leads to an interesting tension within Okokon's book. Okokon is aware of the complexities, confusions and contradictions created by the interplay of lo-cal, diasporic and transnational identities as represented by many of her case studies. While most of her chapters are simply ways of dividing the black contribution into neat packages – for example, 'arts, entertainment & sport'; 'military'; 'civic & political' – one is entitled 'London International'. At this point, Okokon acknowledges that 'Throughout this book an attempt has been made to broaden the concept of what it is to be a "Londoner" in order to include those who themselves may not immediately perceive themselves as such.'[20]

In *The Peopling of London* (1993), the most extensive exhibition on im-migration held in a British heritage centre during the twentieth century, the Museum of London played on the myth of the capital's ethnic homogeneity by 'ethnicising' Herbert Gregg's 1944 'Cockney' anthem 'Maybe It's Because I'm a Londoner'. The Museum used the song as background to its displays relating to 'Fifteen Thousand Years of Settlement from Overseas', but gave the tune an 'Indian' or 'Chinese' accent, so repetitively that some visitors felt that they 'were somewhat over-exposed to the strain in various guise'.[21] The mes-sage was clear: even if the visitor was an immigrant or of immigrant back-ground, they too could still be a 'true' Londoner. Moreover, the contrived twangs added to the song only highlighted the artifice of the stereotypical (non-immigrant or minority) Cockney. Okokon is anxious to go further, however: 'It may be contended that instead of sticking rigidly to birth or length of residence, it may be more useful to assess Black Londoners' "credentials" by more complex notions, such as contribution, sense of belonging, impact upon a wider community, and international consciousness.'[22] 'London International' focuses especially on diplomats from Africa, and yet having raised the possibility of black diasporic identities, or what Paul Gilroy has labelled the 'Black Atlantic',[23] Okokon falls back upon a London-centric perspective: 'When one's children have been raised and educated in London and one's everyday existence is living and working in the capital, who can say that one is not a Black Londoner at the end of diplomatic mission when it is time to be called "home"?'[24]

Okokon's narrative structure is pulled in two directions. She recognises that 'Nationality and our sense of place are often constrained by the notion of a world in which populations remain within a single geographical region, and the notion of one's national loyalty is fixed and simple.' Against this '"Black Londoners" ... have been part of a shifting population, in which movement has occurred to and from Africa and the West Indies, not just among individuals, but among different generations of the same family.'[25] Her emphasis on the identification with and influence of the local, even if one's presence is temporary, is also perceptive, and will have strong resonance with Chapter 7 of this study, which focuses on the dynamics of transmigrancy in relation to ideas of 'place'. As will be illustrated, if historians and others have had difficulties accepting the role of immigration at the local level, this has been even more pronounced if such movements have been impermanent and settlement temporary – a fluidity which has been the norm, rather than the exception in modern population movements. Nevertheless, the more apologetic and defensive nature of *Black Londoners*, and especially the focus on contribution and rootedness, partially undermines Okokon's more critical reading based on her understanding of individuals', families' and groups' multi-layered identities and the centrality of flux in the diasporic experience.

Highlighting achievement and presence, especially under the frequent adversity resulting from racism and poverty, provides a valuable societal function in a world in which such exclusion is still prevalent and damaging to minority and majority alike. Indeed, 'ethnic cheerleading' to counter outside hostility has been a central feature of much immigrant and minority historiography from the nineteenth century onwards – including that within the Huguenot, Jewish, Italian, Irish, as well as black and Asian communities. Faced, for example, with a contemporary historiography, which bled into the political arena, that portrayed medieval Jews in England as alien and malevolent, the pioneer late nineteenth-century Jewish scholar, Joseph Jacobs, writing exactly a hundred years before the Museum of London's landmark exhibition, contrasted the rootedness of two figures, the second of whom was a relentless antisemite:

> it is absurd to call Jacob fil Mosse, an Oxford Jew, whose ancestors we can trace in London and Bristol for seven preceding generations, more of an alien or foreigner than Simon de Montfort, whose ancestors were, indeed, Earls of Leicester, but only visited England on sporadic occasions.[26]

In a similar vein, David Kahn, Director of the Brooklyn Historical Society, pointed out how in the permanent exhibition in this New York suburb 'we state that black people have lived in Brooklyn since the seventeenth century, the earliest period of European settlement. Functionally, that piece of information serves the same purpose as the statement in the Museum of London's *Peopling* exhibition that blacks have lived in London since the early sixteenth century.' Kahn's hopes for the impact of such historicity replicated that of Joseph's a century earlier: 'These are not throwaway, merely interesting or curious, pieces of information. These are myth-shattering weapons that undermine popular notions of otherness, and rootlessness, of people of color.' History, he adds, 'is being used to confirm legitimacy'.[27]

But while assertive minority history – as envisioned by the founders of the Jewish Historical Society of England in the late nineteenth century and those promoting black historical consciousness on both sides of the Atlantic in the late twentieth – can act as a form of politico-cultural resistance against the exclusionary potential of the local, such writing can also inhibit engagement with its universal possibilities. This book has, as its focus, the southern English county of Hampshire, the construction of which will be explored in Chapter 2. It is through the prism of Hampshire that Anglo-Jewish history from medieval to modern will be viewed, enabling a close and detailed understanding of the inter-relationship between the local, national and global. As we will see, it is hard, if not impossible, to separate the local, national and global, as the following example illustrates. In the lifestyle magazine, *Hampshire View*, first published in 2003, the editor, Rosemary Staal, reflects on the rise of 'localness', what she describes as 'the best way of describing what so many of us yearn for in this age of global everything'. Staal argues that the 'antithesis of this alien culture [of the global] is localness, something that is becoming more and more desirable in the struggle against the creeping corporate takeover of our lives. Localness means, in its simplest sense, making best use of what is on our doorsteps.' Some thirty pages later, however, Staal extols the virtues of an Italian restaurant in Southampton. To her 'It simply doesn't matter that [the Greek owner] isn't Italian, nor that the cooks and the rest of the staff are French, Spanish, Moroccan, Chinese, Latvian – and Italian.' Indeed, she concludes that 'This is definitely a place that flies an international flag, and with a flourish.'[28] Even then, Staal fails to point out that much of the food and drink on offer would have similarly global origins. Whether at the level of ideas, people or products, restraining the local to the locality can only be achieved at the level of mythology. And while this 'truth' about the local may be more blatant in the world of twenty-first century globalisation and instant communication, it is no less true of the totality of human experience in which trade and movement of peoples and ideas have been ever constant. Rather than limiting its scope, the Hampshire case studies within *Anglo-Jewry since 1066* will confirm this analysis of global flux and interchange.

Returning to the two historiographical case studies, *Asian Leicester* reveals the tendency to emphasise the local, at the expense of the universal, doing so largely without the (uneven) self-awareness evident in Okokon's text in *Black Londoners*. Martin and Singh's city is thus praised as 'a model of civic multiculturalism' and it is 'the work and efforts of local Asians that are the root of Leicester's success'. Evidence for this economic achievement is provided by 'the emergence of a very competitive Asian business sector in retailing, hosiery and garment manufacturing. There are over 10,000 registered Asian businesses [in Leicester].'[29] While there is space within this narrative to emphasise the international trading connections of 'Asian Leicester', such commercial expertise is highlighted more to show contribution and success rather than to explore the nature of complex, diasporic networks at work. The kernel of the book, not surprisingly, is Leicester, but the city becomes a centrifugal force, sucking up the rest of the Asian world rather than acting in reciprocal relationship to it. Local patriotism is represented through 'The growing self-confidence of Asians in Leicester and their attachment to the city'. Martin and Singh thus aim to provide a 'record of the contribution of Asians to the modern development of [Leicester]'. But Leicester is also, the authors claim, 'the centre of Asian cultural life in Britain', with new arrivals from the rest of the country as well as South Africa, Malawi and Tanzania. Only occasionally do loyalties elsewhere receive passing mention, as with a photograph of a visiting Indian politician and the acknowledgement that the Bharatiya Janta Party 'has a strong following among Leicester's Gujurati population'.[30]

Civic pride in constructing a narrative of an 'Asian Leicester [that] is likely to remain an outstanding example of diversity and ethnic plurality' is understandable, especially in a city whose council in 1972 advised Ugandan Asians to 'not come to Leicester'.[31] *Asian Leicester* and many other examples of local ethnic history writing have been produced within (and against) a wider context of political, social and concomitant historiographical exclusion over many centuries. It is ironic, for example, that Leicester, 'today internationally recognized as a model of civic multiculturalism',[32] was an English town that was amongst the first, in 1253, through the efforts of Simon de Montfort, to expel its Jewish population – an early civic example of what would in the late twentieth century be given the seemingly benign title of 'ethnic cleansing'. As Colin Richmond has pointed out, Jack Simmons, one of the great local historians in post-war Britain, in his 1974 popular history of Leicester, noted how de Montfort 'is much commemorated in Leicester – a square, a street, and a concert hall are named after him [and] his statue adorns the Clock Tower'. Yet as Richmond adds, 'Jews (and their expulsion) are not mentioned' in Simmons's narrative of the city.[33]

Shortly after the publication of Richmond's critique of Englishness and Jewishness in 1992, Leicester's second university was named after Simon de Montfort.[34] As will be explored in Chapter 3, it is antisemites and antisemitism, rather than the Jewish experience in the medieval period, that tends to be commemorated, even celebrated, at a local level in modern Britain. Indeed, the exclusionary tendencies of history and heritage nationally have a particular acuteness when translated to the local level. Leicester has been the focal point of English local studies since 1945. It is telling, therefore, that the many layers of immigrant movement and settlement (and, as with the Jews, opposition to them) in this city have been ignored by its leading practitioners. It has been left to minority 'specialists' to write more inclusive and critical histories of a place that will probably be the first urban locality in Britain to have a non-white majority. Such tendencies were replicated at a national level: the *Victoria History of the Counties of England*, whose first volume was published in 1900, hardly mentioned the presence of *recent* immigrant groups as opposed to those that settled before the modern era. Instead, its purpose was to 'trace, county by county, the story of England's growth from its prehistoric condition, through the barbarous age, the settlement of alien peoples, and the gradual welding of many races into a nation which is now the greatest on the globe'.[35]

'Race', community and local studies

H. P. Finberg, in a 1962 essay on 'Local History', defined 'community' as a 'set of people occupying an area with defined territorial limits and so far united in thought and action as to feel a sense of belonging together, in contradistinction from the many outsiders who do not belong'.[36] Tying topography to 'local' identities and definitions of 'insiderdom' and 'outsiderdom' has been a longstanding occupation of local historians. Changing concepts of 'race' and nation, and later ethnicity, have been utilised extensively in determining belonging and exclusion. As Charles Phythian-Adams, who developed 'Leicester school' theoretical perspectives to their most sophisticated level in the late 1980s and 1990s, summarises, in England the 'most fertile stages in the development of serious local history were ... periods when broader inquiries into matters of *national* identity were afoot'. Pythian-Adams identifies two periods:

> The first, in late Tudor England, saw the systematic disinternment of evidence for the Anglo-Saxons – their church, their language and their law-codes; the second, in Victorian times, witnessed that national search for the genius of English free institutions which discovered its origins in the law and polity of the early Teutonic peasantry. At both periods the links between national and local history were simultaneously racial and institutional.

County history, with its origins in Tudor times, 'was related to the perceived early racial divisions of the country: the British in Cornwall and Wales, with the shires south of the Tees under West-Saxon, Mercian or Danish law respectively'. In the Victorian era, however, 'it was the Germanic "village community", with its equitably divided and communally regulated fields, that was related to an Anglo-Saxon east as opposed to a Celtic-dominated west'.[37]

Pythian-Adams set himself the 'quest for the peoples of England' which would be to 'identify and to disentangle the structures and fortunes of the many regional or local societies of which the nation is composed. These societies represent the "peoples" of England'. He then added that it would be 'more appropriate to treat them ... in ethnic rather than racial terms'.[38] In 1935, a group of (mainly) progressive anthropologists, sociologists and scientists published *We Europeans*, a popular study which attempted to show the dangers of racist politics, as practised by Nazi Germany, and, more generally, the failure of science to identify meaningfully racial differences amongst humans. Its authors, whilst not totally abandoning the possibility of a legitimate 'race science' in the future, concluded that attempts to define races so far were essentially subjective. Caught between their desire to maintain the idea of difference and their profound distress at the politicisation of 'race', the authors of *We Europeans* replaced it with the term 'ethnic'.[39] Since the Second World War, in which 'race' thinking was even more discredited, use of 'ethnicity' has grown further, yet meanings associated with it have been as loose, if not looser, than those connected to 'race' in the pre-war era. For many, ethnicity is simply used as a substitute for 'race' given the dubious associations of the latter. Pythian-Adams's work, and that of much post-war local history, falls into this category, although the term 'race' has continued to be used to describe and differentiate local population groups well beyond

1945. Moreover, a close reading of Pythian-Adams's attempts at 're-thinking English local history' reveal the interchangable use of 'race' and 'ethnicity'.

Defining membership of a community, Pythian-Adams has suggested that in a given area 'there well may emerge comparatively dense networks of blood relationships, the perpetuation of which in one form or another over generations will be likely to engender traditionalized modes of local self-identification and hence, in cultural terms, some sense of local exclusiveness'.[40] Here, definitions of belonging linked to 'race', based on genetic blood relations, are melded with those of ethnicity, based on culture. Within such a framework of analysis, the existence of a homogeneous local culture is taken for granted as illustrated by Pythian-Adams's use of a league table of the 'most indigenously populated counties' based on mid-nineteenth-century census returns. The statistics are 'unambiguous' and 'by definition' show the counties which have 'suffered least from the diluting effects of recent immigration'.[41] As *Anglo-Jewry since 1066* will explore, one of the ironies of such essentialist readings of 'community' is that immigrants or newcomers as a whole have often been at the forefront of constructing and representing what is allegedly distinctive about the 'local'.

More worrying still is Pythian-Adams's uncritical acceptance of modern genetic research on 'hereditary traits' enabling the differentiation of 'neighbouring sets of people today' in order to justify his belief in separate regional cultures. Dealing with the borders of Britain, for example, he notes that 'south of [the England–Scotland] national boundary the mapping of blood groups in Northumberland today still shows a genetic divide between two separate groups, the one on Tyneside and the other occupying the less hospitable upland regions running up to the Scottish border'. The Herefordshire England–Wales boundary similarly 'separates two blood groups'.[42]

The continuation and, indeed, the revival of 'racial' analysis in defining community in local historical studies stands in stark contrast to recent developments within the discipline of geography. In the inter-war period, leading British geographers such as H. J. Fleure (Aberystwyth and Manchester) and P. M. Roxby (Liverpool) developed the concept of regional studies. They were convinced that 'racial geography' would help explain differences in the outlook of populations and, with such insights, promote greater understandings between peoples and nations. The scholarship of Fleure and Roxby had both an academic and a popular appeal: 'In the 1920s and later [their] work on race fascinated many students of geography'. Yet reflecting on this inter-war approach to regional studies in his history of the discipline in Britain, T. W. Freeman commented in 1980 that 'Little [now] is generally said of racial characteristics in modern geography teaching, and ascription of particular mental characteristics to actual or supposed racial types, however

11

cautious and tentative, is fraught with social danger.'[43] Since Freeman, social geographers have gone further and have been at the forefront of deconstructing notions of 'race, place and nation'. In moving 'beyond essentialism' there has been, as Peter Jackson notes, been 'a growing insistence on problematizing the very idea of "race" within geography'.[44]

The example of Cornish studies

Before moving in the next chapter to the specific subject matter of this study – Jewish migration and settlement – and its geographical focus – Hampshire – it will be valuable to explore the evolution of what is the most developed (and institutionalised) example of 'local' studies in Britain, that of Cornwall. The evolution of Cornish studies reveals many of the tendencies previously outlined in this chapter, including the dilemmas involved in defining the 'local', especially through concepts of 'race' and 'ethnicity'. It is, however, the increasing sophistication and self-reflexivity of Cornish studies, its multidisciplinary and inter-disciplinary nature and willingness to engage with new approaches, that make it especially worthy of engagement.

In 1993, launching the second series of its annual journal, the director of the Institute of Cornish Studies, Philip Payton, was clear about its mission. The articles in its first issue placed an

> emphasis on a Cornish 'difference' which finds its expression in everything from political behaviour to the natural environment. When all is said and done, it is this Cornish 'difference' that is at root the *raison d'etre* of Cornish studies as an area of academic inquiry.

Yet anticipating the critique of local studies previously outlined, Payton added that 'It is a "difference" that exists not in parochial isolation but is an integral part of that wider pattern of European cultural and territorial diversity.' *Cornish Studies* should thus be seen 'as a reflection of that diversity, a window into the life of one small but (we like to believe) unique part of the Atlantic periphery of Britain and Europe'.[45] Moreover, each successive issue of the annual has developed its ambitions further. Bernard Deacon especially has championed the idea of 'new' Cornish studies. Through incorporating migration and concepts of diaspora, Deacon argues that 'we move to another, global, scale that links Cornwall and its people to other peoples and to places around the world', as well as to theoretical perspectives drawn from 'the broad theory of postcolonialism'.[46] Emphasising heterogeneity, Deacon has articulated the difference between what he views as 'old' and 'new' Cornish studies. The former highlighted an essentialised 'Cornwall' whereas the latter believe in the existence of 'Cornwalls' and varieties of Cornishness.[47] Finally, in outlining the possibilities of 'Critical Cornish Studies', Deacon has introduced discourse analysis in the constructing, de-constructing and contesting of Cornishness. 'From the rebellious periphery of the sixteenth century [through to] the tourist-business-induced imagery and romantic novelists of the twentieth century, Cornwall has been awash with metaphors and buffeted by a veritable storm of signifiers.' Deacon concludes that

> Both Cornwall and the Cornish people have been and are being discursively constructed in a number of often conflicting ways. The result is a confusing kaleidoscope through which 'real' Cornwalls are glimpsed only hazily and intermittently.[48]

In Deacon's vision for Cornish studies, we are a long way removed from the racial certainties of nineteenth- and twentieth-century outsiders (and some insiders) in defining Cornishness, and equally distanced from the antiquarianism of early Cornish scholarship as exemplified by the work of the Royal Institution of Cornwall (1818) or the Royal Geological Society of Cornwall (1814).[49] Nevertheless, as Deacon, the major proponent of new approaches, acknowledges, there are 'gaps between the rhetoric of claims and the substance of achievements'. Furthermore, assessing the achievements of the first decade of *Cornish Studies*, he concluded that 'rather than a sharp discontinuity between "old" and "new" Cornish Studies, we might detect a continuum between them'.[50] As we will see, this includes the application of 'race science' in identifying Cornish distinctiveness.

In 1885, John Beddoe published *The Races of Britain*, subtitled 'A Contribution to the Anthropology of Western Europe'.[51] This work had a popular appeal and remained the standard authority on its subject matter for many decades, even though most of its findings were based, as has later been noted, on 'commonplace bigotry'.[52] In essence, Beddoe divided the 'races' of Britain into Saxon/Teutonic and Celtic (or British) types, classifying individuals according to levels of 'nigrescence' through eye and hair colouring identified by personal observation. Beddoe concluded that 'The Cornish are generally dark in hair and often in eye: they are decidedly the darkest people in England proper'. With the arrogant certainty and sheer idiosyncrasy that exemplified racial ethnography of the late Victorian era, Beddoe concluded that 'All the British types … occur in Cornwall, and the most characteristic is … Iberian with a dash of the Semitic'.[53] It has been claimed that Beddoe's work was simply 'naive' and, ultimately, innocent because in Britain 'race had no direct political implication, in contrast, for instance, to the United States or Germany'.[54] In fact, the 'science' of Beddoe and others was used 'to bolster assumptions about the contrast between superior, fair Saxons and inferior, dark Celts'.[55] While, as Simon Trezise illustrates, Victorian authors with West Country connections such as the Reverends Sabine Baring-Gould and Charles Kingsley attempted to subvert 'the opposition of Saxon superiority and Celtic weakness', they did so within the confines of race science and their belief in the essential difference of the Cornish.[56]

The tendency to think 'racially' in Britain from the mid-nineteenth century onwards was deep even if such a *Weltanschauung* was far from homogeneous and consistent. It was also persistent, and although increasingly challenged after 1918, 'race thinking' continued well into the twentieth century. The leading nature writer, W. H. Hudson (1841–1922), was perhaps unusual in his obsessive desire to ethnographically place, through racial discourse, the various people he experienced in his English travels. Furthermore, Hudson's classification of 'racial types' was somewhat peculiar and random, even within the inherent eccentricities of contemporary 'race science'. Yet incorporating such utterly subjective ways of thinking into a variety of literary as well as scientific genres was far from uncommon in the Victorian era and beyond.

Hudson has particular significance for this study as the reception of his *Hampshire Days* (1903) will form the framework for much of the analysis in the following chapter. As we will see, from 1874, when he first arrived in England at the port of Southampton from the country of his birth, Argentina, Hudson became deeply attached to the county of Hampshire. It was not until 1905 that he paid his first visit to Cornwall, publishing *The Land's End* in 1908. Hudson was fascinated by Hampshire because he believed that, of all English counties, 'the divergence of racial types [was] greatest' there.[57] In contrast, Cornwall 'because of its isolation, or remoteness, from Saxon England … remained longest unchanged': it was the 'most un-English county'.[58] Cornwall was inhabited by 'a Celtic people with an Iberian strain'. Even then, its racial strain was unique amongst British Celts, accounting for the Cornishman's inherent lack of an indigenous humour coming from 'the soil and race', as well as the strange mixture of cruelty and sobriety that was manifest by the Cornish racial type. Hudson was pleased to locate in his travels in Cornwall several 'specimens' which he believed represented pure 'aboriginal' and the 'very ancient type' of Cornishman, including a 'small, dark peppery man' who was 'chattering, screeching and gesticulating more like a frenzied monkey than a human being'.[59]

Beddoe based his measurements of 'nigrescence' on hair and eye to which Hudson, distrustful of the 'recognised authorities' within such anthropology, substituted observations on skin colouring.[60] H. J. Fleure, in *The Races of England and Wales* (1923), was more willing to accept Beddoe's research, adding to it a belief in craniology. Fleure concluded from the existing research that Cornwall had 'the darkest population in England with dark longheads widely distributed, but also the stalwart dark broad-heads, who are found in nearly all the fishing harbours'.[61] Fleure, a progressive internationalist, was aware of the dangers of 'race science' in the wrong hands. The reader, he warned, should be on guard 'against the common political statements against the Latin race, Teutonic race, Anglo-Saxon race, Celtic race, and the like'. Yet although he did not believe in the existence of 'pure' races because of the mixing of populations, he equally argued against the 'extreme views of impermanence of race-types' as proposed by Franz Boas in America. Fleure's 'middle ground' position is neatly illustrated by returning to his use of the Cornish example. On the one hand, he argued that 'the distinction between English and Welsh, or English and Cornish, is hardly a racial one'. On the other, he suggested that 'The south-west would well repay closer investigation of its physical types.'[62]

Fleure, however, in spite of his warnings to the contrary, by providing scientific and academic legitimacy to racial thinking, only encouraged popular belief in racial difference. Within Britain and elsewhere such 'difference' was often interpreted hierarchically with assumptions of Saxon superiority and Celtic inferiority. The melding and mutual reinforcement of race science, ethnographic anthropology and travel writing was revealed in a short article in *Man*, the monthly journal of the Royal Anthropological Institute of Great Britain and Ireland, entitled the 'Cornish Fisherman Type'. It was published in September 1921 alongside ruminations on West African, Indian and Fijian ethnography. Drawing upon his own observations as well as those of Fleure, Baring-Gould and Beddoe, T. H. Andrew identified 'a swarthy type with very persistent characteristics'. Exposing the surety of inter-war race thinking and the ability of those articulating it to convince themselves of anything, Andrew concluded that the Cornish fisherman type had previously been 'confused with the long-headed, small-boned, and grey-eyed survivors of the west country Neolithic aborigines; but it is clear that there is nothing in common between them, except that both have dark complexions and are generally of medium height'.[63]

Furthermore, 'outsiders' wanting to identify with Cornwall were forced to use the discourse of race to show that they belonged, just as Baring-Gould and Kingsley had attempted to invert racial notions of Celtic inferiority. Thus the novelist, Daphne du Maurier, Home Counties born, but with Cornwall as her adopted home and literary inspiration, exploited the flexibility of what Paul Gilroy has termed 'raciology'[64] to fashion a mystical sense of local place identification. In her *Vanishing Cornwall* (1967) she identified three racial influences in the making of the unique Cornish character and physical characteristics – Iberian, Celtic and Breton: 'As an outsider, with Breton forebears, I like to think that the two races [Cornish and Breton], facing an Atlantic seaboard blown by identical gales, washed by the same driving mists, share a common ancestry'.[65] Concepts of Cornishness, whether defined by 'outsiders' wishing either to prove its inferiority or a common ancestry, or 'insiders' desiring to demonstrate commonality or to challenge the idea of subordinacy, have been subject to powerful forces of racialisation.

More specifically within the genre of local studies, the acceptance of Hudson's belief, and that of others, such as S. P. B. Mais, that while Devon was 'unmistakably an English county', the Duchy of Cornwall was 'in every respect un-English', had a wide and durable currency.[66] Writing in 1978, Jack Simmons, in his overview of the historiography of English counties, separates Cornwall from the other thirty-nine in providing a justification of its separate study. Tellingly he does so as much as by *race* as by geography. Only Cornwall, he argues,

> can properly be regarded as a separate physical entity: a triangular mass of land, bounded on its two long sides by the sea and for almost the whole length of the third by the River Tamar; *a land, too, divided quite sharply by differences that may be called racial from its neighbour, Devon.*[67] [My emphasis]

More recently, by moving beyond the unit of the county to that of geographical regions, Charles Phythian-Adams, as has been noted, has developed an ethno-racial analysis of difference within England, replicating, to some extent, the inter-war work of Fleure and Roxby. Using this approach, Cornwall and Devon, with their high percentage of 'local born' in the mid-nineteenth century, would be suitable cases for treatment using genetic research on local populations living approximate to natural and political boundaries. Indeed, from the 1980s onwards, detailed research has taken place to 'prove' Cornish genetic difference and to revive, using scientific techniques, the concept of the *essential* difference of the Cornish as postulated/assumed by Beddoe, Fleure and others.

Published sixty-five years after Andrew's article, and in the same journal, *Man*, scholars from the British Museum and the Universities of Durham and Oxford (hereafter Harvey et al.), combined to produce a study asking 'how Celtic are the Cornish?' If Andrews had focused on head shape and skin, hair and eye colouring, Harvey et al. highlighted blood group systems that 'comprise the genetically determined characteristics' of local populations. Nevertheless, 'head size, hair and eye colour' data were also used in this research to determine biological difference: remarkably, Beddoe's earlier data were incorporated into the investigation. The survival and exploitation of the racial categories 'Anglo-Saxon' and 'Celtic' – at the analytical heart of this project – amongst leading British scholars in the final quarter of the twentieth century is deeply disturbing, as was the support and encouragement given to the research by Charles Thomas, then director of the Institute of Cornish Studies.[68]

In contrast, Thomas's successor, Philip Payton, warned in 1993 that 're-search in the area of genetics had led discussions of Cornish ethnicity into the arid and potentially dangerous area of spurious racial theories'.[69] In 1997, as editor of *Cornish Studies*, Payton added that it was 'Clearly … foolish to try to analyse (let alone judge the "validity" of) modern ethnic identities by recourse to genetic data'.[70] In this volume of *Cornish Studies*, an article by Dick Cole debunked the findings of Harvey et al., especially highlight-ing that 'Celtic' was a social construct and not a biological reality. Cole also pointed out their 'similar inability to deal adequately with that other value-laden term, "Anglo-Saxon"'.[71]

Responding to Cole, Malcolm Smith, one of the authors of the 1986 *Man* survey, conceded some weaknesses in their original approach. It remained, however, that while there was no 'reason to expect the Celtic populations to have either genetic affinities with each other or differences from the popula-tions of England, for the most part they actually do'. Here there was a circu-larity of definition and proof that replicated the earlier racial certainties of scholars and writers such as Beddoe and Hudson. Smith also defended the value of the 1986 article 'not least through attracting some public interest in what is a difficult debate'.[72] In this respect, Philip Payton has commented on the use of genetic data in determining Cornishness, that, paradoxically, whatever the dangers and limitations, 'myths of origin may be of extreme significance to those ethnic identities themselves'.[73] For those determined, inside or outside, that the Cornish are essentially different, the very fact that academic scholars such as Smith had carried out such genetic research as late as the 1990s, regardless of the flawed assumptions of their work, provides a false legitimacy and justification for an insular and exclusive definition of lo-cal identities. By the twenty-first century those involved with Cornish studies have largely abandoned the 'arid and potentially dangerous' area of racial-genetic research. Nevertheless, there has been a general acceptance within the field that the Cornish do, in fact, represent an ethnic or ethno-national group. While there is an awareness that ethnicity is a social and cultural con-struct, the concept of ethnicity has not, so far, been as problematised as that of 'race'.

If there is less of a danger of 'essentialising' Cornish difference through the idea of ethnicity, as opposed to 'race', there is still a danger of overemphasis-ing homogeneity in culture at the expense of divisions based on class, gender, politics, locality and so on. Moreover, past migration and diversity can be ignored in the desire to show regional distinctiveness. It is thus not acciden-tal that while much effort has been made within Cornish studies to produce an increasingly nuanced understanding of emigration and the creation of a

Cornish diaspora, there has been little or no work on immigration – recent or distant – into the county. Philip Payton's magisterial *Cornwall: A History* (1996 and 2004), has only a handful of brief references to immigration and yet he recognises that in the medieval period 'many of the inhabitants of Cornish towns were foreigners – Dutch, Irish, Flemings, French, English, Bretons'. He adds that these ports and towns were 'multicultural communities where Cornish, Latin, French and English would have co-existed with a smattering of other European languages such as Breton, Flemish and Irish'.[74] There is no mention, however, in his narrative (or for that matter within the volumes of *Cornish Studies*) of groups and individuals such as, and amongst many others, the German engineers who developed mining in Cornwall in the early modern period, or the Jews who settled from the late eighteenth century onwards, through to modern immigrants, including the south and east European immigrants who, after 1945, provided much of the labour for the increasingly ailing tin-mining industry. As will be explored in the following chapter, there has been a historiography of Cornish Jewry since at least the 1930s. The ignoring of this work in 'mainstream' Cornish studies (partially) justifies the title of a collection published in 2000, *The Lost Jews of Cornwall*.[75]

Mark Stoyle, widely accepted as the most sophisticated modern historian of Cornwall, has noted that 'None of the key works of the new British historiography deal with Cornwall in any depth ... while the prevailing scholarly attitude toward Cornwall and its inhabitants is well summed up by a recent comment that Cornish history is "best accommodated within the traditional 'national' framework"'.[76] It must be added that recent attempts with 'four nations' history to undermine Anglocentric tendencies in British historiography have failed to provide space for regional studies, including that of Cornwall or, for that matter, immigrant and ethnic minority studies as a whole. The tendency towards local/regional studies marginality, even in the 'distinctive' case of Cornwall, is thus ongoing and powerful, no matter how impressive recent scholarship has become. There is a danger, however, that promoting Cornish studies as a form of 'ethnic studies' could lead to its own silences. It is significant that Bernard Deacon, who has produced the most complex and reflexive approach to Cornish studies, has been most critical of the turn towards ethnicity as an overarching analytical devise in his subject area. In promoting a vision of the 'New Cornish Studies', Deacon argues that it will have

> to embrace the more fragmentary, fluid and heteregeneous accounts of society that have become fashionable in many academic circles. These offer the opportunity to re-think the very ways we imagine Cornwall and, by implication, ourselves. As

the practitioners of Cornish Studies, through helping to construct differences and identities, we are inevitably 'forced to confront the construction of ourselves'.

Moving away from the essentialised readings of Cornwall by 'insiders' and 'outsiders', Deacon concludes that to 'adopt this more reflective approach is to accept that the New Cornish Studies may be *place-based, but it is not place-bounded*.'[77] [My emphasis]

From such a perspective, how Jewish and local studies could be profitably combined has been illustrated by Paul Manning in an article published in *Cornish Studies* in 2005. Manning explores why the mythical character of the Jew appears so regularly in histories and other representations of the Cornish mines from late sixteenth century onwards. He concludes that

> The figure of the Jew ... sums up and condenses the opposition between a 'Christian' natural economy, consisting primarily of diverse agricultural and pastoral labour processes ... over and against an equally various set of 'Jewish' labour processes that are each performed not for use-values but as part of exchange.[78]

Manning suggests that the persistence of the 'Cornish Jew' until the nineteenth century and even beyond owes much to superstitious belief at a local level. To this we can add the writings of those who constructed the Cornish in racial terms, such as Sabine Baring-Gould. In his *A Book of Cornwall* (1899), Baring-Gould stated without any hint of doubt that 'In King John's time the tin mines were farmed by the Jews'. His evidence was that 'Old smelting-houses in the peninsula are still called "Jews' houses", and, judging by certain noses and lips that one comes across occasionally in the Duchy, they left their half-breeds behind them.'[79]

At a popular level, an understanding that Cornishness is, in some form, a construct has at least enabled the inclusion of the Penzance-born Jewish rum businessman, Lemon Hart (1768–1845), in *101 Cornish Lives* (2006). Its author, Maurice Smelt, asks whether anyone can be 'Cornish and Jewish?' Smelt's answer, while not the most subtle, ultimately allows for this possibility:

> If being Cornish means being Cornish and nothing else (least of all English, of course) then Lemon Hart would be out. But so would every other entry in this book, for if home and birthplace count for nothing and pedigree matters, could anyone trace a pure bloodline from some Cornish Adam and Eve?[80]

Returning to the work of Deacon, the Cornish studies theorist was building on an earlier collection of essays *Cornwall: The Cultural Construction of Place* (1997) which recognised that 'Ideas of place are persuasive ideological forces' and that 'We all construct the places we inhabit, work in or remember: they are, to a large extent, imaginary.'[81] Through such an approach, a fluid, open and inclusive approach to Cornish studies is enabled. As Amy Hale argues, 'Cornwall does not contain a homogenous mass of people. It never has and there are a number of hybrid Cornish identities which could profitably be researched. Hale has in mind 'the various ethnicities residing in the peninsula' as well as 'gender groupings, class groupings, religious groupings, industry-based groupings and sexual identities all of which overlap and combine', in conflict, one might add, as well as in cooperation.[82]

While not all of Cornish studies is as self-reflexive and innovative as those who promote it through interdisciplinary forms of micro-history, at its most sophisticated it provides a challenging model for the study of the 'local'. This overview of the development of Cornish studies and its quest to explore 'Cornish difference' has revealed the pitfalls of essentialist readings of the 'local' as well as the potential, if not yet fully realised, of analysing the making of multi-layered and contested 'Cornwalls'. It has been through acknowledging 'place as text'[83] that the 'new Cornish studies' has freed itself from antiquarianism on the one hand and ethnic and racial certainties on the other. Similarly, in *Anglo-Jewry since 1066* the focus will be on the social and cultural construction of place identity, teasing out the interplay between the 'local' and the 'global'. But before moving on to its specific subject matter and geographical focus, the notion of place, especially in relation to concepts of race and ethnicity, and memory and identity, requires further consideration.

Conclusion: the importance of 'place'

In *Locating English Identity* in the nineteenth and twentieth centuries, Ian Baucom argues that 'Englishness has been *generally* understood to reside with some type of imaginary, abstract, or actual locale, and to mark itself upon that locale's familiars'. Only in the last decades of the twentieth century has a 'racial narrative of what it means to be English … begun to displace … the localist narrative'. From Enoch Powell's interjections from the late 1960s onwards, Baucom concludes, there has been a 'turn from place to race'.[84] It will be already apparent from the overview of Cornish studies in the previous section that rather than exist as separate, indeed alternative, entities, concepts of 'race' and 'place' have informed one another: place identity has been subject to processes of racialisation and raciology has often been place-specific. At certain times and places 'race' has mattered more than at others. Moreover, as geographer Peter Jackson suggests, 'particular notions of "race" and nation are articulated by different groups of people at different times and at different spatial scales, from the global to the local'.[85]

The study of 'race' and its relationship to place is still in its infancy. As Jan Penrose and Peter Jackson acknowledge in their conclusion to their important volume, *Constructions of Race, Place and Nation* (1993), 'Ironically, for a collection of geographical essays, we may have achieved greater sophistication in our theorization of "race" and nation than we have collectively achieved in theorizing the significance of place.' They add that their collection demonstrates 'the scope for further research on place by highlighting its centrality in understanding the relationship between "race" and nation'.[86] *Anglo-Jewry since 1066* is part of that process, fundamentally querying the oppositional model of place and 'race' posited by Baucom in his study of Englishness.

The chapters that follow explore the construction of the local identities in relation to the 'other' and especially Jewish migrants and settlers. They are equally concerned with how minority identities have been constructed in relation to the 'local'. From both perspectives, there is potential, following the example of Cornish studies, for inclusive and exclusive visions of the 'local'. As Michael Keith and Steve Pile argue:

> Politically, there is a reactionary vocabulary of both the identity politics of place and a spatialized politics of identity grounded in particular notions of space. It is the rhetoric of origins, of exclusion, of boundary-marking, of invasion and succession, of purity and contamination; the glossary of ethnic cleansing. But there are also more progressive formulations [such as diasporic identities] which become meaningless deprived of the metaphors of spatiality.[87]

Either way, a sense of place, and notions of 'home', clearly matter.

Beyond the first two chapters of this study, those following are ordered with apparent chronological simplicity, moving from the medieval through the early modern through to the late modern and finally the contemporary. In relation to the subject matter, this is indeed the case, following the pattern of the entry and expulsion of medieval Jews in England; their readmission in the seventeenth century and subsequent waves of immigration, settlement and subsequent movement. Yet rather than 'just' being a study of the whole gamut of Anglo-Jewish presence (and absence) through the local, or history, as one of Alan Bennett's characters puts it in *The History Boys*, being 'just one f … ing thing after another',[88] the chronology is challenged throughout by the complicating factor of memory. *Anglo-Jewry since 1066* is thus as much about 'then' (when the events explored in this study happened) as 'now' (when they were remembered and re-remembered). Combining history with the analysis of memory work, and then exploring the relationship between them, concepts of time and chronology will be problematised but certainly not abandoned in this study.

In *Social Memory* (1992), James Fentress and Chris Wickham defend their title from the criticism that if it is 'individuals who actually do the remembering, what is social about it?'. The essential answer, they respond, is that 'much memory is attached to membership of social groups of one kind or another'.[89] The potential of studying memory for social historians is articulated neatly by Fentress and Wickham:

> When we remember, we represent ourselves to ourselves and to those around us. To the extent that our 'nature' – that which we truly are – can be revealed in articulation, we are what we remember. If this is the case, then a study of the way we remember – the personal and collective identities through our memories, the way we order and structure our ideas in our memories, and the way we transmit these memories to others – is the study of the way we are.[90]

In similar mode, Penrose and Jackson conclude that in 'exploring constructions of "race", place and nation, we have been forced to confront the construction of ourselves'.[91] *Anglo-Jewry since 1066* is intended as a part of that reflexive exploration and opening up of the meanings and memories of place. It also provides, following Paul Gilroy's work on diaspora, an 'alternative to the metaphysics of "race", nation and bounded culture coded into the body … disrupt[ing] the fundamental power of territory to determine identity by breaking the simple sequence of explanatory links between place, location and consciousness'.[92] This book is thus, in its small way, intended as a work of scholarship *and* 'resistance'.[93]

Notes

1   Jo Ann Boydston (ed.), *John Dewey: The Middle Works, 1899–1924* vol. 12 (Carbondale & Edwardsville: Southern Illinois University Press, 1988), p. 12, originally published in *The Dial*, 1920.
2   Ibid., pp. 15–16.
3   William Stafford, 'On Being Local', *Northwest Review* vol. 13 no. 3 (1973), p. 92.
4   W. G. Hoskins, *Local History in England* (2nd edn London: Longman, 1972 [1959]), pp. 7–8.
5   Christopher Parker, *The English Historical Tradition* (Edinburgh: John Donald, 1990), p. 235.
6   Hoskins, *Local History in England*, pp. 179–82, esp. p. 179.
7   Alan Everitt, *New Avenues in English Local History* (Leicester: Leicester University Press, 1970), p. 6.
8   Hoskins, *Local History in England*, p. 15.
9   Felix Driver and Raphael Samuel, 'Rethinking the Idea of Place', *History Workshop* no. 39 (Spring 1995), p. vi.
10   See Jan Nederveen Pieterse, *White on Black: Images of Africa and Blacks in Western Popular Culture* (New Haven: Yale University Press, 1992), pp. 163–5.
11   See, for example, The League of Gentlemen, *A Local Book for Local People* (London: Fourth

Estate, 2000).

12 Everitt, *New Avenues in English Local History*, p. 3.

13 League of Gentlemen, *A Local Book*, n.p.

14 Driver and Samuel, 'Rethinking the Idea of Place', p. vi.

15 George and Yanina Sheeran, 'Discourses in Local History', *Rethinking History* vol. 2 no. 1 (1998), pp. 70, 76.

16 See, for example, Ross Cameron, '"The Most Colourful Extravaganza in the World": Images of Tiger Bay, 1845–1970', *Patterns of Prejudice* vol. 31 no. 2 (1997), pp. 59–90; Peter Keating, 'Fact and Fiction in the East End', in H. J. Dyos and Michael Wolff (eds), *The Victorian City: Images and Realities* vol. 2 (London: Routledge & Kegan Paul, 1973), pp. 585–602.

17 Susan Okokon, *Black Londoners 1880–1990* (Stroud: Alan Sutton, 1998); John Martin and Gurharpal Singh, *Asian Leicester* (Stroud: Alan Sutton, 2002).

18 Mayerlene Frow, *Roots of the Future: Ethnic Diversity in the Making of Britain* (London: Commission for Racial Equality, 1996).

19 Okokon, *Black Londoners*, pp. 7–8.

20 Ibid., p. 75.

21 The exhibition opened in November 1993. See Nick Merriman (ed.), *The Peopling of London: Fifteeen Thousand Years of Settlement from Overseas* (London: Museum of London, 1993); visitor comment in 'Green Book', Museum of London files.

22 Okokon, *Black Londoners*, p. 75.

23 Paul Gilroy, *The Black Atlantic: Modernity and Double Consciousness* (Boston: Harvard University Press, 1993).

24 Okokon, *Black Londoners*, p. 76.

25 Ibid., p. 75.

26 Joseph Jacobs, 'The Jews in England', in H. D. Traill (ed.), *Social England* vol. 1 (London: Cassell, 1898 [1893]), p. 480.

27 David Kahn, 'Diversity and the Museum of London', *Curator: The Museum Journal* vol. 37 no. 4 (1994), p. 247.

28 *Hampshire View*, June 2006.

29 Martin and Singh, *Asian Leicester*, pp. 7, 13.

30 Ibid., pp. 14, 118 and back cover.

31 Ibid., pp. 14, 26 and *Ugandan Argus*, 17 September 1972.

32 Martin and Singh, *Asian Leicester*, p. 7.

33 Colin Richmond, 'Englishness and Medieval Anglo-Jewry', in Tony Kushner (ed.), *The Jewish Heritage in British History: Englishness and Jewishness* (London: Frank Cass, 1992), p. 48.

34 See *Times Higher Educational Supplement*, 8 May 1992.

35 General advertisement for the series in *The Victoria History of the Counties of England: Hampshire and the Isle of Wight* (London: Constable, 1900), vol. 1, p. vii.

36 H. P. Finberg, 'Local History', in H. P. Finberg and V. Skipp, *Local History: Objective and Pursuit* (Newton Abbot: David & Charles, 1967), p. 33.

37 Charles Phythian-Adams, 'Local History and National History', *Rural History* vol. 2 no. 1 (1991), p. 2.

38 Ibid., p. 3.

39 Julian Huxley and A. C. Haddon, *We Europeans* (London: Jonathan Cape, 1935), written with the aid of Charles Singer and Charles Seligman. For an astute analysis of this text, see Elazar Barkan, *The Retreat of Scientific Racism: Changing Concepts of Race in Britain and the United States Between the World Wars* (Cambridge: Cambridge University Press, 1992),

Chapter 6.

40   Charles Phythian-Adams, *Re-thinking English Local History* (Leicester: Leicester University Press, 1987), p. 27.

41   Ibid., pp. 28–9.

42   Ibid., pp. 27, 43.

43   T. W. Freeman, *A History of Modern British Geography* (London: Longman, 1980), p. 112.

44   Peter Jackson, 'Introduction', in Peter Jackson and Jan Penrose (eds), *Constructions of Race, Place and Nation* (London: UCL Press, 1993), p. 13.

45   Philip Payton, 'Introduction', *Cornish Studies* vol. 1 (1993), pp. 1–2.

46   Bernard Deacon, 'The Spatial Dimension and Cornish Studies', *Cornish Studies* vol. 8 (2000), p. 223.

47   Bernard Deacon, 'New Cornish Studies: New Discipline or Rhetorically Defined Space?', *Cornish Studies* vol. 10 (2002), pp. 24–43.

48   Bernard Deacon, 'From"Cornish Studies" to"Critical Cornish Studies": Reflections on Methodology', *Cornish Studies* vol. 12 (2004), pp. 26–7.

49   Philip Payton, *Cornwall: A History* (Fowey: Cornwall Editions, 2004 [1996]), p. 195.

50   Deacon, 'New Cornish Studies', p. 25.

51   John Beddoe, *The Races of Britain: A Contribution to the Anthropology of Western Europe* (Bristol: Arrowsmith, 1885).

52   Barkan, *The Retreat of Scientific Racism*, p. 23.

53   Beddoe, *The Races of Britain*, pp. 258–9.

54   Barkan, *The Retreat of Scientific Racism*, pp. 22–3.

55   Simon Trezise, 'The Celt, the Saxon and the Cornishman: Stereotypes and Counter-Stereotypes of the Victorian Period', *Cornish Studies* vol. 8 (2000), p. 57.

56   Ibid., pp. 62–7.

57   Robert Hamilton, *W. H. Hudson: The Vision of the Earth* (London: J. M. Dent, 1946), p. 85.

58   W. H. Hudson, *The Land's End: A Naturalist's Impressions in West Cornwall* (London: Hutchinson, 1908), pp. 39, 59–60.

59   Ibid., pp. 60, 104, 153.

60   Ibid., p. 105.

61   H. J. Fleure, *The Races of England and Wales: A Survey of Recent Research* (London: Benn Brothers, 1923), p. 102.

62   Ibid., pp. 18, 84, 102, 105.

63   T. H. Andrew, 'The "Cornish Fisherman Type"', *Man* vol. 21 no. 9 (September 1921), pp. 137–9.

64   Paul Gilroy, *Between Camps: Nations, Cultures and the Allure of Race* (London: Allen Lane, 2000), p. 12.

65   Daphne du Maurier, *Vanishing Cornwall: The Spirit and History of Cornwall* (Harmondsworth: Penguin, 1972 [1967]), p. 11.

66   S. P. B. Mais, *The Cornish Riviera* (London: Great Western Railway Company, 1928), p. 9.

67   Jack Simmons, 'The Writing of English County History', in Jack Simmons (ed.), *English County Historians* (Wakefield: E. P. Publishing, 1978), p. 2.

68   R. G. Harvey, M. T. Smith and S. Sherren et al., 'How Celtic are the Cornish? A Study of Biological Affinities', *Man* vol. 21 (1986), pp. 177–201.

69   Philip Payton, 'Post-War Cornwall: A Suitable Case for Treatment?', in Philip Payton (ed.), *Cornwall Since the War* (Redruth: Dyllansow Truran, 1993), p. 13.

70   Philip Payton, 'Introduction', *Cornish Studies* vol. 5 (1997), p. 2.

71 Dick Cole, 'The Cornish: Identity and Genetics – An Alternative View', *Cornish Studies* vol. 5 (1997), pp. 21–9, esp. 25.

72 Malcolm Smith, 'Genetic Variation and Celtic Population History', *Cornish Studies* vol. 6 (1998), pp. 9, 19.

73 Payton, 'Introduction', *Cornish Studies* vol. 5, p. 2.

74 Payton, *Cornwall: A History*, pp. 83, 92.

75 Keith Pearce and Helen Fry (eds), *The Lost Jews of Cornwall* (Bristol: Redcliffe Press, 2000).

76 Mark Stoyle, 'The Dissidence of Despair: Rebellion and Identity in Early Modern Cornwall', *Journal of British Studies* vol. 38 (October 1999), p. 425 and quoting John Morrill.

77 Deacon, 'New Cornish Studies', pp. 11–13, 38.

78 Paul Manning, 'Jewish Ghosts, Knackers, Tommyknockers, and Other Sprites of Capitalism in the Cornish Mines', *Cornish Studies* vol. 13 (2005), p. 229.

79 S. Baring-Gould, *A Book of Cornwall* (London: Methuen, 1925 [1899]), p. 59.

80 Maurice Smelt, *101 Cornish Lives* (Penzance: Alison Hodge, 2006), pp. 116–17.

81 Ella Westland, 'Introduction', in Ella Westland (ed.), *Cornwall: The Cultural Construction of Place* (Penzance: Patten Press, 1997), p. 1.

82 Amy Hale, 'Cornish Studies and Cornish Culture(s): Valuations and Directions', *Cornish Studies* vol. 10 (2002), p. 249.

83 Ibid., p. 248.

84 Ian Baucom, *Out of Place: Englishness, Empire and the Locations of Identity* (Princeton: Princeton University Press, 1999), pp. 4–5.

85 Jackson, 'Introduction', p. 13.

86 Jan Penrose and Peter Jackson, 'Conclusion: identity and the politics of difference', in Jackson and Penrose (eds), *Constructions of Race*, p. 207.

87 Michael Keith and Steve Pile, 'Introduction: The Politics of Place' in Michael Keith and Steve Pile (eds), *Place and the Politics of Identity* (London: Routledge, 1993), p. 20.

88 *The History Boys* (Twentieth Century Fox, 2006, director Nicholas Hytner) based on the 2004 Alan Bennett play.

89 James Fentress and Chris Wickham, *Social Memory* (Oxford: Blackwell, 1992), p. ix.

90 Ibid., p. 7.

91 Penrose and Jackson, 'Conclusion', p. 209.

92 Gilroy, *Between Camps*, p. 123.

93 See similarly the comments in Penrose and Jackson, 'Conclusion', p. 209.

2

Wessex tales/Yiddisher spiels

Introduction

In his general history of the county, published in the 1860s, B. B. Woodward pointed out that in its 1672 square miles, and bordered by Berkshire, Dorset, Surrey, Sussex and Wiltshire, 'Hampshire has no natural boundaries except the sea-coast'.[1] Some thirty years earlier, in a multi-volume 'historico-topographic' survey, Robert Mudie warned more generally against county histories. 'Hampshire especially,' he suggested,

> notwithstanding the very important place which it holds in the early history of England, and its modern beauty, agricultural richness, and salubrious climate, has no individual or detached history, even for a short period of time.

If 'history' was to be the basis of 'our Description of Hampshire', he added, then the 'attempt would be a failure' and the 'results of our labours would be, like that of most works of similar title, a collection of scraps, without any connecting principle, or general lesson of instruction'.[2]

Lacking either the unifying force of geographical cohesion or historical identity, the concept of 'Hampshire studies', therefore, appears unpromising. Indeed, its historiography has remained relatively undeveloped and was slow in evolving. The Hampshire Field Club was founded in 1885, 'somewhat belatedly by the standards of neighbouring counties'.[3] The authors of the Victoria County History of Hampshire pondered 'Why a district so intimately connected with the history of the country should have been so neglected it is difficult to understand … [especially as] early in our history … its capital was for a long period of time the seat of national government'.[4] For those working in Cornish studies, the explanation for Hampshire's historiographical marginality is straightforward. In Cornwall, even after the Second World War and 'the apparent evidence of homogenenisation … the reality was that Cornwall had not only remained "different" but was in fact asserting that difference with renewed vigour'. Such distinctiveness, they argue, is not located elsewhere. Indeed, Philip Payton makes the direct comparison between the two counties, referring to 'the small minority of newspaper correspondents who, with calculated malevolence, responded to expressions of Cornish distinctiveness in angry retorts that insisted that Cornwall was no different to a Hants or a Herts'. Payton continues that 'Little did such correspondents realise that their vitriol itself bore witness to such distinctiveness: they protested too much.'[5] Not surprisingly, Hampshire appears several times in Payton's narrative of Cornish history as a typical, but undistinctive, *English* county, acting as a counter-example to the self-contained ethno-nationalist region that is his subject matter. It is thus implied that whereas Hampshire can be studied within general national history without disturbing narrative cohesion, Cornwall should not. The early history of England, Payton suggests, is often simplified to a 'succession of invasions – Celts, Romans, Anglo-Saxons, Vikings, Normans. This is the approach of the so-called National Curriculum, the staple diet of schoolchildren in Cornwall as much as it is in Sussex or Hampshire, one that leaves pupils in many Cornish schools with little idea of the reality'.[6] Turning to the early modern period, Payton remarks that it is 'no coincidence that most European languages have their own word for Cornwall (but never for Hampshire or Rutland), as though it were a Scotland or a Wales'.[7]

The previous chapter, however, has shown how Cornwall and Cornishness have been constantly invented. While the Tamar has acted as a natural boundary from neighbouring Devon (even then with 'various territorial anomolies along the [river] border')[8] and far more dominated by the coast, Cornwall possesses as many geographical variations and multiple, competing histories as does Hampshire. Furthermore, until recently Cornish historiography, broadly defined, was equally limited and antiquarian. Cornish distinctiveness has been constructed and re-constructed from inside and outside and rests, ultimately, as Payton argues, on the belief in, rather than necessarily on the reality of, difference. Yet even if the process has not been as profound, attempts *have* been made to distinguish the history and people of Hampshire both from within and without. That a county so lacking 'natural' borders and with at most a diverse or, as Mudie argued, an incoherent history, should be so often particularised, indeed essentialised, shows the power of discourse when imagining 'local' distinctiveness.

As has been noted in Chapter 1, the authors of the classic anti-racist tract, *We Europeans* (1935), attacked the politicisation of 'race' but maintained, through the loose classification of 'ethnicity', a belief in the general difference of groups according to region and nation. Within Britain, their views were exemplified in comments designed to show the variation in population types, thereby revealing assumptions of local ethnic/racial particularity. In

its introductory sections, *We Europeans* noted that the 'superficial anthropological observer from Mars who had landed in some corner of North Wales
might easily imagine himself among a Mediterranean people' whilst

> A traveller who lands at Liverpool and carefully explores the neighbourhood of
> the great industrial area by which that port is surrounded, would form a very dif-
> ferent view of the population of England from one who landed at Southampton
> and investigated agricultural Hampshire.[9]

Freed from raciology, but equally convinced of local distinctiveness, W. G.
Hoskins similarly used a north–south comparison, but removed the indus-
trial/agricultural differentiation: 'if [the local historian] is working in the
wilder parts of Yorkshire and the northern counties generally, many of his
basic problems and questions will be very different from those of the local
historian working in, say, Hampshire'.[10] But on what basis has Hampshire's
distinctiveness been constructed?

Imagining Hampshire

> He too was a stranger … [with] a certain jovial cosmopolitanism sat upon his fea-
> tures … 'And a stranger unbeknown to any of us. For my part, I don't like the look
> o' the man at all.' (Thomas Hardy, 'The Three Strangers', in *Wessex Tales*)[11]

Constructions of Cornishness have been highly racialised. Although far from
unified, it was largely assumed within raciology that the Cornish represented
a dark Celtic type, though one complicated further by 'aboriginal' blood. It
might be assumed that widescale acceptance of a precise 'local' racial type
was, within the English counties, peculiar to the exceptional Cornish case.
W. H. Hudson's comments that, in wandering round and identifying the human 'species' of Hampshire, 'one is sensible of a difference in the people',
would thus simply reflect the idiosyncratic 'race' obsessions of this naturalist
writer – especially in relation to the pseudo-precision of his place-specific
classifications. In *Hampshire Days* (1903) Hudson wrote

> Of the Hampshire people it may be said generally, as we say of the whole nation,
> that there are two types – the blond and the dark; but in this part of England there
> are districts where a larger proportion of dark blood than is common in England
> has produced a well-marked intermediate type; and this is one of my four distinct
> Hampshire types.[12]

According to Hudson, the majority were of Anglo-Saxon origin mixed with
blood 'of a distinctly different race'. It led, he believed, to women who while
not totally ugly, lacked sufficient flesh and colour to be attractive. Alongside
these 'dim and doubtful people' within Hampshire was the 'unmistakable

Saxon'. He was mentally 'rather a dull dog', and degenerate.[13] More attractive and to be found in the south of the county were the 'dark-eyed, black-haired people', mistaken for, but in fact totally different from, 'the gipsy type'. The dark types were also divided into two – first, those of small 'narrow heads' and dark skin and second, the 'oval faced' who were taller. It was the former of these types that was racially the most interesting, believed Hudson, as they reflected the survival of an 'Iberian race who inhabited Britain in the Neolithic period [who] were never absorbed by the conquerors'.[14] To Hudson, such racial observations had a deeper significance: 'Is there in us, or in some of us, very deep down, and buried out of sight … an ancient feeling of repulsion or racial antipathy between black and blonde? … [H]ere in Hampshire I have been startled at some things I have heard spoken by dark-eyed people about blondes … may it not be in Hampshire any one with bright colour in eyes, hair, and skin is also by association regarded as a foreigner?'[15]

Outside the Hampshire countryside, Hudson did not even make an attempt to categorise its people. 'There is little profit in looking at the towns'-people. The big coast towns have a population quite as heterogeneous as that of the metropolis; even in a comparatively small rural inland town, like Winchester, one would be puzzled to say what the chief characteristics of the people were.'[16] To Hudson, such diversity reflected the essential otherness of urban life, a result of modernity's intensive mongrelisation. In contrast, in the countryside and small villages he never hesitated to place individuals racially, reflecting his belief that 'racial characters are practically everlasting, that they are never wholly swamped'.[17] In visiting the Roman remains in Silchester, to the north of Hampshire, for example, Hudson revealed a sense of security and belonging enabled by an employment of localised raciology:

> Here it seems good to know, or to imagine, that the men I occasionally meet in my solitary rambles, and those I see in the scattered rustic village hard by, are of the same race, and possibly the descendants, of the people who occupied this spot in the remote past – Iberian and Celt, and Roman and Saxon and Dane … By and by, leaving the ruins, I may meet with other villagers of different features and different colour in hair, skin, and eyes, and of a pleasanter expression; and in them I may see the remote descendants of other older races of men, some who were lords here before the Romans came, and of others before them, even back to Neolithic times.[18]

The question remains: how unusual were Hudson's views? It has been suggested by Paul Rich that Hudson's was a 'mode of race classification that had become absorbed into a wider pastoral movement in English nature writing by an essentially urban-based group writing about the countryside and its people without actually being part of it'.[19] By briefly exploring Hudson's predecessors, and subsequent reception of his work and later writings on Hampshire, it will emerge that such racial imaginings of its population largely assumed that the 'true' Hampshire was, in essence, rural. While some writers were willing to contest the 'outsider' status of Hampshire's towns and cities, they, too, worked largely within a racial framework determining who did, and did not, belong.

T. W. Shore, an equally prolific writer on Hampshire as Hudson, for example, does not fit into the pastoral tradition but was more 'race' obsessed than the author of *Hampshire Days*. Founder of the Hampshire Field Club in 1885, Shore was equally at home in researching the urban as the rural. His *History of Hampshire* (1892), concluded that its 'local history is that of an agricultural county which is also a maritime county'. Shore included chapters on Winchester, Southampton and Portsmouth.[20] Shore, secretary of the Hartley Institute, the precursor of the University of Southampton, was a leading archaeological and anthropological 'authority' on race science. It is not surprising, therefore, that his history of Hampshire should contain an extensive analysis of the Anglo-Saxon and Celtic racial influences on the county, based especially on skull measurements. To Shore, Hampshire, which he regarded as 'the original Wessex', had a long-standing integrity and natural difference which could be explained by 'race'.[21] Past and present were thus intimately linked:

> The blending of races which must have taken place in Hampshire appears to have been the cause of many of the Celtic survivals in that county, for certain parts of the religion, mythology, customs, communal organization, and part of the language of the Celts, appear to have become mixed with and engrafted upon [those] of the Saxons. In no other way can I account for much that was characteristic of the Celts surviving until the present day …[22]

Hampshire/Wessex was perceived by Shore and others as distinctive. Yet in contrast to those who perceived Cornwall and the Cornish to be marked by the 'persistence of difference',[23] racially Hampshire was an integral and critical part of, and not apart from, England and Englishness. A sense of Hampshire's national belonging was typified by its county town, Winchester. To Shore, as 'long as the English race lasts, Winchester will be classic ground' and visitors to it came to see 'the cradle of those early institutions of the Anglo-Saxon race, which are their inheritance as well as ours'.[24] In the inter-war period and even beyond, travel writers and social commentators such as H. V. Morton who sought out, for the good of the future, England's past and present 'common racial heritage',[25] had a special place for Hampshire. It was 'beyond any measure of doubt the most *English* of English counties'.[26] Hampshire was 'the heart of Wessex … the stronghold of the Saxon kings and [therefore] very near the heart of England'.[27] If the 'Saxon Lands' south of the Thames were the 'cradle of our race', then Hampshire was 'the cradle of English greatness'.[28]

It remains, returning to the analysis of Paul Rich, that the areas within Hampshire singled out as having special 'racial' significance were essentially rural. In 1858, Charles Kingsley, obsessed with arresting what he perceived as racial degeneracy in England, wrote of the 'dark-haired ... ruddy and tall of bone' peasant type in his parish, Eversley, to the north-east of the county. While this peasant had his faults, he was a 'far shrewder fellow ... – owing to his dash of wild forest blood – gipsy, highwayman, and what not – than his bullet-headed, and flaxen-polled cousin, the pure South-Saxon of the Chalk-downs'.[29] The New Forest, in particular, was believed within raciology to have 'retained a primitive population'.[30] Awareness of the 'extreme difficulty of classification of race in the New Forest' did not hinder John Wise, in his classic history and topography of the area, originally published in 1862, from identifying the characteristics of the 'West-Saxon element not only in the appearance of the long-limbed Forest peasantry, with their narrow head and shoulders, and loose, shambling gait, but also in their slowness of perception'.[31]

In contrast to such racial rootedness, for many observers both inside and outside the county, and following Hudson, the large coastal towns were deemed simply not to belong to Hampshire. To Brian Vesey-Fitzgerald in *Hampshire Scene* (1940), there was 'not much Hampshire in Southampton. Voices from every corner of the globe, but few, very few from Hampshire ... I like Southampton, but it is not Hampshire. It is cosmopolitan.' Similarly Portsmouth, as with Aldershot and Farnborough and their armed forces, had a 'shifting population, a population with no roots in Hampshire'.[32] In contrast, the Roman, Saxon, Danish and Norman influence on Winchester made it part of Hampshire. It was a 'city venerable and rich in association' where 'history lives ... Indeed in great measure the past in Winchester is the present.'[33] Thus for Vesey-Fitzgerald, recent diversity of populations made certain places outside 'essential' Hampshire. Winchester, however, with its racial rootedness in English history could be included. Indeed, its stability, coming from the continuity of its population, enabled the celebration, indeed the romanticisation, of *past* cosmopolitanism as exemplified by St Giles's Fair, held outside the town from the medieval period onwards:

> here were men and women of all nations and all tongues, English, French, Irish, Scots, Venetians, Genoese, Poles, Jews, Saxons, Prussians, Danes, Muscovites, perhaps even Turks and Chinese and Moors and negroes. There was then much babble, huckstering and gesticulating. Men traded honestly in hard-bargaining with the local countrymen, with merchants from far-distant towns; and there were

ballad-singers and contortionists and jugglers; and mountebanks and thieves and beggars and murderers.

As Vesey-Fitzgerald concluded, 'The world came to St Giles's Hill six hundred years ago.'[34] Equally verging on a mystical vision of local belonging, John Arlott concluded in 'The Return of the Native', that Winchester was 'part of the enduring and characteristic Hampshire, as Aldershot, Portsmouth, Southampton and Bournemouth are not: Winchester, outside the College, *sounds* like Hampshire'. Written in 1962, and paying homage to Thomas Hardy, this was the first of many reflexive articles by Arlott in *Hampshire*, the county magazine established two years earlier.[35]

There were those who questioned such rural/urban inclusivity and exclusivity when constructing Hampshire's past and present. F. E. Stevens in *Hampshire Ways* (1934), whilst not rejecting racial categories, both accepted and praised the fact that through invasion and the nature of its history 'Hampshire folk are a mixed lot'. Indeed, they were 'proud of their mixed ancestry. It may have failed to produce an easily recognisable type, but it stands at the very heart and centre of what Mr Baldwin has called "essential Englishry"'.[36] Stevens argued that its past experience meant that 'It was not to be expected that Hampshire men could conform to type in the sense that the Cornish man and the Welshman does.' Instead, the 'spirit of Hampshire', built on the 'foundation stone' laid by King Alfred, enabled a successful later 'cosmopolitianism' [*sic*]. Thus newcomers, including those entering the army, navy and merchant fleet, 'in due time became Hampshire folk'. Even those most racialised within Hampshire, the 'Forester', while, in Stevens's view 'nearly a type', was not essentialised: 'the truth about him is that if he were transplanted to the Down country he would be an equally good downsman. He would be quite at home'.[37] Stevens's construction of local belonging was ultimately assimilatory and porous.

Stevens's 1934 vision of Hampshire fits that later constructed by Payton and others within Cornish studies of the 'normal' English county. Hampshire's history was essentially, as Lord Mottistone, Lord Lieutenant of the county, stated in the foreword to *Hampshire Ways*, 'the history of England'. What Stevens outlined were minor local variations: 'Hampshire is the county of all others in which it would have been possible to relate small happenings to the great'.[38] The poet and naturalist writer Edward Thomas could be added to those who saw rural Hampshire as quintessentially 'English' without separating it out from others. Thus Thomas, although deeply influenced and supported by Hudson, commented in *The South Country* (1909), which covered eight counties south of the Thames and east of Exmoor, including Hampshire, that it 'would need a more intellectual eye than mine to distinguish county from county by its physical character, its architecture, its people, its unique contribution of common elements, and I shall not attempt it'. In contrast, however, Thomas wrote confidently of the racial difference of the Cornish:

> In Cornwall many of the women looked less English than the men. The noticeable men were fair-haired and of fair complexion, blue-eyed and rather small-headed, upright and of good bearing. The noticeable women had black hair, pale, seldom swarthy, faces, very dark eyes. Perhaps the eyes were more foreign than anything else in them ...[39]

There were others, however, who, while accepting the integrative model of Hampshire as posited by Stevens, were anxious to define the distinctiveness of the county. In the process they became as convinced about Hampshire difference as were those insistent on the reality of the separateness of the Cornish. Although such an outlook was not as blatantly politicised as was the case with Cornish nationalists, there was a desire amongst some to define, by whatever means, the essence and integrity of Hampshire. It is a tradition that can be identified most clearly through various county magazines in Hampshire, especially after the Second World War.

Defining distinctiveness and dealing with difference

While there were short-lived journals such as *Wheeler's Hampshire and West of England Magazine*, from 1828, which aimed to be 'consistent with the *local* character', and others such as the *Hampshire Magazine* during the 1880s, little attempt was made at defining the county's distinctiveness within them.[40] Similarly, the early *Papers and Proceedings of the Hampshire Field Club* focused on local natural history, archaeology and history but did so largely without recourse to an essentialist discourse.[41] Indeed, it was not until after 1945 that a more reflexive approach to local identity emerged, especially through the *Hampshire Review* (1949–57) and *Hampshire: The County Magazine* (1960 onwards) and in other publications, including those of the Hampshire Field Club.

The mission of the *Hampshire Review* was initially relatively modest, if inclusive. It aimed to cover 'the architectural treasures of Hampshire, and the beauty of its countryside, its farms, its industries, its schools, its voluntary and youth organisations' as well as 'the story of its great men and references to many of the historical and other curiosities in which the county abounds'. Its scope was 'limited to the county of Hampshire', which the editor believed would be 'surely wide enough for interest, but compact enough for the writers to be known personally, and for the subjects to be within easy reach'.[42]

Nevertheless, in the eight years of its existence, the journal provided a forum for those who wanted to explore whether there was, in fact, a 'persistent difference' in the county and its people.

When *Hampshire Days* was published, its reviewer in the *Hampshire Chronicle* focused on Hudson's descriptions of the countryside, concluding that he had 'done excellent service to local natural history'. It was simply noted without any dissent that Hudson had devoted a chapter to 'Hampshire people' and 'their racial differences from the inhabitants of surrounding counties'.[43] Given the rudeness and peculiarity of Hudson's racialisation of the types to be found in Hampshire, it is remarkable how much his views seem to have been accepted or at least passed over. There certainly is no evidence of the hostile response that Hudson's *The Land's End*, published five years later, received in Cornwall. Invited to give a speech in Camborne, Hudson wrote to his fellow writer, Morley Roberts, that if he accepted, 'I shall have to ask you to come with your gun to back me up'.[44] Moreover, there was much more contemporary engagement with Hudson in Cornwall than in Hampshire. *The Cornishman* newspaper gave *The Land's End* coverage in five successive weeks and while there was ambiguity about its contents and the manner in which Hudson had 'put us in a book as we put things in a pasty',[45] there was also clearly excitement over the prominent author's interest in the county. This excitement and tension was not replicated in Hampshire, suggesting less local pride and anxiety was then at stake. It was not until 1976, in *Hampshire*, that it was noted that Hudson 'wrote reams on local ethnology and often ... in a condemnatory manner'.[46]

Indeed, more generally, serious reflection on *Hampshire Days* did not occur until close to half a century after its publication. It corresponded to an increasingly urgent debate about the identity of Hampshire, most blatantly in relation to its borders, planning decisions and population influx that were especially changing its urban–rural balance. Hudson's book was rediscovered and was no longer read simply for its naturalist insights but as a statement of a world worth preserving. Thus Brian Vesey-Fitzgerald, in the *Hampshire Review* (summer 1951), used Hudson's ethnographical assumption 'of a difference in the [Hampshire] people' as his starting point for an interrogation of local identity, past and present. 'Would you agree?', Vesey-Fitzgerald asked his readers, responding 'I imagine not. I imagine that now everybody would say, "Oh, well, it may have been so then, but not now; you couldn't tell any difference now."'[47]

Vesey-Fitzgerald had met Hudson who had maintained 'even so late as 1921 ... that there was a difference in Hampshire people'. Half a century later Vesey-Fitzgerald was convinced that the great naturalist writer was correct: 'There was a difference. It was not noticed only by Hudson. It was noticed by Gilbert White, by Charlotte Yonge, by Daniel Defoe, by Charles Kingsley, and by William Cobbett. All five refer directly to the difference of Hampshire people.' Moreover, what Hudson believed in his own time could 'still be said today'.[48] Hampshire's 'difference', according to Vesey-Fitzgerald, was that it was less homogeneous than its neighbouring counties, but made up, as it was in Hudson's day, 'full of little pockets of types'. Significantly, while writing well after the end of the Second World War, Vesey-Fitzgerald had no hesitation in defining these 'types' as 'racial'. Indeed, in defending the term 'race' he exposed his own 'anti-cosmopolitanism' tendencies, covertly referring to Jews and others who had shown its unscientific provenance:

> 'Race' is a word much out-of-fashion today, now that the scientists of UNESCO (themselves as mixed a bunch as you could wish to see in a day's journey round London or New York) have put it where it belongs. But, in fact, we all know what we mean by the word, and we are not, most of us, concerned at all with the political sores that fester in the minds of those who have too nice an appreciation of words and too little understanding of them. Certainly Hudson knew what he meant by racial type.[49]

Following Anthony Collett on the 'inherent' difference of the Cornish, Vesey-Fitzgerald was equally convinced of the racial distinctiveness of Hampshire people.[50]

The return of 'race science' from the late twentieth century onwards has revealed the incompleteness of the post-war UNESCO campaign at an intellectual level.[51] At a popular level, the continuation of and confusion about the use of race discourse, past and present, has been even greater. It is reflected locally in the continued use of Hudson as a reference point concerning Hampshire people – for example, his chapter on racial types in *Hampshire Days* was reproduced without comment in a popular anthology *Hampshire of One Hundred Years Ago* (1993).[52]

Hudson's direct influence can be most easily detected within *Hampshire* – in the first quarter of a century of its existence there were fourteen articles devoted to his writings on the county and many more in which he was referred to in passing. To John Arlott, who campaigned within his monthly contributions to the magazine for the maintainance of the character and integrity of Hampshire, *Hampshire Days* was 'one of the best books written about this … county'.[53] For some, including Arlott, Hudson's work became a nostalgic refuge as the battle against modernity and change was increasingly lost. In this vein, 'Hudsoneering' was thus promoted as a 'new pastime for discovering old Hampshire'.[54] To others, the battle to recognise and maintain 'Hampshire's long-established and distinct [political, cultural and geographical] identity' was ongoing.[55] Hudson's ethnography, while no longer relevant to understanding the county's present population's nature, reflected what many perceived as the reality of past difference and therefore the deep roots of its distinctiveness. In *Hampshire: A Sense of Place* (1994), for example, published by Hampshire County Council, Peter Mason accepts that 'Starting with the people themselves, it would be very difficult today, if not impossible, to distinguish Hampshire people from other English people by their looks.' Yet Mason adds that 'as recently as the beginning of the twentieth century W. H. Hudson commented that ... "one is sensible to a difference in the people"'.[56]

Mason's acceptance of Hudson's analysis is intriguing as *Hampshire: A Sense of Place* generally employs a pluralistic approach to the county's identity. Hampshire, Mason emphasises, has been

> enriched by the cultures and traditions of the Black and Asian communities and other ethnic minority groups. The main minority communities are Pakistani, Indian, Bangladeshi, Afro-Caribbean and Chinese. There are also other smaller groups including Polish, Greek, Vietnamese and Cypriots, all contributing to a multi-racial society in Hampshire.[57]

Mason, writing in a semi-official capacity, takes for granted that 'Hampshire is a geographic and historic entity' and as then County Arts Officer, hoped that he had illustrated that 'it can also be seen that it has a cultural entity – one that makes it distinct from its neighbours'.[58] Yet he is also fully aware that the local cannot be separated out from the global: 'To avoid parochialism a regional culture cannot ignore national and international trends. It will draw inspiration from a variety of places including external sources as well as its own locality and history.' This is a two-way process, however, and Mason recognises that 'Products of a regional culture will often take to the international stage.' Mason uses pop music to illustrate his point neatly: 'It could be said that Tanita Tikaram [whose parents came from Fiji and Borneo], brought up in Basingstoke, largely a post-war town, is part of Basingstoke's culture. In 1992 the group, The Trogs, acknowledged their [international/ local] roots in the title of their disc, *Athens to Andover*.'[59]

Mason thus starts from an inclusive perspective and is anxious that these popular multi-cultural 'modern examples' should be put alongside the medieval Winchester Bible, Winchester Cathedral and Portchester Castle with 'watercress soup, trout, and Brown Bread and Honey Ice Cream' in making up the 'the culture of Hampshire'.[60] There are, however, some rules of entry for 'outsiders' if they are to be included within Mason's idea of Hampshire. The first is *contribution*, requiring at least some degree of integration in the county. In this respect, one Hampshire family of refugee origin – the Portals – has been referred to regularly. Henri de Portal came to Southampton as a child, a Huguenot escaping persecution under Louis XIV, allegedly by being hidden in a barrel. Subsequently he created a papermaking business in the Hampshire countryside. Nearly three centuries on, the Portal family, as Mason adds, 'still produces watermarked paper for the Bank of England at the [Laverstoke] Mill'.[61] It was, in the words of *Hampshire*, a story of 'glorious romance' and one which the magazine returned to repeatedly.[62] Just as Mason was happy to include this refugee 'success' story within the 'personality' of the county, so *Hampshire* believed that the Portal family and its papermaking represented 'a continuous thread linking three centuries'. This family business was not only an important aspect of the 'economic development of the county' but was also part a significant 'aspect of *our* heritage' [my emphasis].[63] Generations of Portals had left their mark on church, society and army as well as commerce. They thus belonged to Hampshire.

The second element, again typified by the Portal family, that Mason requires for inclusion is *continuous presence* within Hampshire. For ethnic minorities in the county, he argues, it is the 'second generation for whom Hampshire is home'.[64] Thus even in this progressive and relatively open study of Hampshire's identity, past and present, the possibility is ruled out for those who come to the county from outside, let alone those who passed through it as transmigrants, possessing, even if only temporarily, a local sense of belonging. Rootedness, it implies, requires inter-generational presence and settlement. More generally within histories of Hampshire, there is even less inclusion of immigrant and minority settlement than in Mason's more open and imaginative account. Those whose settlement was less permanent have been neglected in the construction of Hampshire's past, either in synthetic histories or within the museum and heritage world. Typifying this antipathy, a proposal to the Hampshire Record Series, run by the County Council, on refugees in the twentieth century, was rejected because of its contemporary focus and possible '"political" slant'. It was made clear, however, that a study of earlier – that is Huguenot – refugees would have been welcomed in the series.[65] In contrast, by recognising both temporary and modern population movements to the county, the memory work within the monthly journal *Hampshire* has been exceptional.

As it moves towards its fiftieth anniversary, *Hampshire* has included, amongst others, features on past and present minorities in Hampshire. These range from individuals such as an ex-American slave in Bournemouth;[66] Eugenie, Empress of France, who finished her days in Farnborough;[67] and 'A Brazilian in 16th century Southampton'[68], to groups including Gypsies, French and Indian prisoners of war, Poles, Greeks, Hindus, Vietnamese and many others. It has also included those whose stay in Hampshire was temporary, especially transmigrants in Atlantic Park, near Eastleigh, during the

1920s (featured in Chapter 7 of this study) and Basque refugees from the Spanish Civil War.[69]

Such inclusion, on the surface, is surprising. *Hampshire* was a journal that insisted, along with John Arlott, that while 'County loyalty ... may be unjustified, administratively untidy, economically unjustified, or illogical', the fact was 'that it exists'.[70] Arlott, fearing 'the end of Hampshire' with impending boundary changes, wrote in 1969 that

> In the life of this magazine we have received many hundreds of enthusiastic letters ... from people who were born in the county but have not lived in it for many years. However far away they may be, they retain a warmth and a loyalty for the county, arbitrarily defined more than 1200 years ago, which is known as Hampshire and which has given its name and crest to emotionally integrated groups of human beings professionally engaged in many different activities, but who warmly, even proudly, announce themselves as Hampshiremen.[71]

With its 150th issue, an editorial, 'What Hampshire means to us', explained that the magazine had 'tried to define and illuminate the character of the county and its people – elusive though it often is – in the belief that it is more difficult to lose something you know you possess'.[72] If John Arlott was arguing for the existence of a Hampshire diaspora based on over a millennium of continuous history, the frequent inclusion of articles on 'outsiders', whose stay in the county was sometimes brief and tragic, suggested the possibility of other transnational movements being part of its evolving identity. Indeed, W. H. Hudson himself, the constant reference point for the magazine, while positing a racially exclusive definition of the county's difference, grew up in the Argentinian countryside and only came to know Hampshire late in his life. As a contributor to its Field Club argued, Hudson qualified as a Hampshire writer 'neither by birth, nor residence, but by adoption – his own adoption of the county'.[73]

Yet while it would be possible to write a narrative of foreign immigration to Hampshire through the pages of its county magazine, and its predecessor, the *Hampshire Review*, it remains that, as with Vesey-Fitzgerald's medieval Winchester, the acknowledgement of past and present cosmopolitanism was always secondary – indeed complementary – to its 'real' history based on settlement and continuity. In this respect, only Hampshire's Gypsies, and especially those from the New Forest, were treated by the magazine as being part of the county's 'true' landscape and history. Gypsies were largely represented romantically as part of the land and traditions of Hampshire that were being wiped out through the homogenising forces of modernity and recent population influxes, especially from the London region.[74] In contrast, individuals such as ex-American slaves or Russian Empresses were presented as intrinsically interesting because they were perceived as being literally out of place – topographically and experentially. In similar fashion, Edric Holmes's *Wanderings in Wessex* (1922) referred to the Norman church at Mottisfont and 'the alien touch in this remote corner of Hampshire' brought by the Meinertzhagen family (of Danish origin) who were currently occupying the mansion house.[75] Implicitly, past examples of cosmopolitanism were presented as being atypical – either linked to specific spaces, especially exciting and exotic 'sailortown' districts of ports, or as being intrinsically temporary such as the 'visitors from Spain' in 1937.[76]

By failing to confront, other than superficially, a *tradition* of immigration to Hampshire there is also implicit denial of the factor insisted upon by Doreen Massey that 'the local is always a product in part of "global" forces'.[77] Furthermore, the 'otherness' of certain minority groups, real or imagined, at particular points and places was emphasised in defining the 'self'; in this respect, the essence of a locality. In Chapters 3 and 4 of this study we will see this in relation to the Jews of medieval Winchester and early modern Portsmouth respectively. In both cases, post-1945 Hampshire journals continued a longstanding tradition of presenting Jews in these places as 'alien' presences. A classic example involving another group was the labelling of Gosport by neighbouring Portsmouth as 'Turktown'. On one level 'Turktown' simply referred to the arrival of roughly 500 Turkish sailors in Gosport from 1850–51, some of whom subsequently died and were buried in the local naval cemetery. On another, it was part of a boundary-making process through which place identity, in this case relating to Portsmouth, is defined 'by marking not only what/where it *is*, but also what/where it is *not*'.[78] Gosport, smaller and regarded as less sophisticated than its naval neighbour, could thus be belittled through this temporary Turkish presence, playing upon an Orientalist discourse of subordinacy, disease, dirt and danger. Within Gosport, the '500 Turkish sailors, because of their perceived foreignness, could not "belong" to the place'. Ironically, Portsmuthians 'thought of Gosport in terms of its supposed inferiority, symbolised by its association with the Turks'. Subsequently, as Margaret Marlow has illustrated, various stories have developed, all of which have created a mythological Turkish community in the town, adding an exotic element within self-construction of local place identity and, to outsiders, confirmation of Gosport's 'otherness'.[79] Within the *Hampshire Review*, for example, it was stated, in matter-of-fact manner, that 'Gosport's nick-name of "Turktown" is a reminder of the Turkish colony which *for many years* flourished in the vicinity' [my emphasis].[80]

The essentialising discourse of 'race' has hindered recognition of the heterogeneous nature of the 'local', as well as the local's inseparable links to the global. Equally, the way in which the 'local' self has been defined has involved the imagining of difference through the construction of the 'other', often in the form of a racialised minority. In the case of 'Turktown' there was at least a 'real' Turkish presence in the locality, no matter how distorted this later became. The final examples in this section, both relating to Jewishness, show how the processes of 'othering' in relation to the construction of place identity do not require foundation on any form of reality.

The first involves the Tory radical, William Cobbett. His *Rural Rides* (1821 onwards), including the many writings devoted to Hampshire, contain diatribes aimed at the 'Jews, jobbers and tax-eaters' who had, Cobbett believed, bought up and exploited local estates to the detriment of the farmer and labourer. To Cobbett, the Jews' influence extended everywhere. Travelling across Hampshire from Burghclere to Petersfield in 1825 he came across a village store 'licensed to deal in tea and tobacco'. Soon it would be necessary for ordinary country folk, he warned, to *'pay the Jews* for permission to chew tobacco, or to have a light in their dreary abodes' [original emphasis].[81] Cobbett was a man of many prejudices but, as one of his biographers notes, his 'most violent hatred ... was reserved for the Jews'. Cobbett opposed Jewish emancipation, a topic to be dealt with further in Chapter 5 of this study, and praised Edward I for expelling the medieval Jews from England in 1290, the memory of which will be explored in Chapter 3.[82] Cobbett's Jews of Hampshire were purely fanciful: they represented a means by which he expressed his rage at agricultural decline in the county and the country as a whole by blaming what was to him the personification of evil: paper money. It is revealing that he never wrote of the 'real' Jews of Hampshire, including those in the town so familiar to him, Portsmouth.[83] In this port the Jews were not the fantastically wealthy and powerful figures of Cobbett's imagination but ordinary people struggling to make a living and part of everyday local life.

The second example of extreme imaginative racialisation takes us back to W. H. Hudson. In what was the first of his local English nature books, *Nature in Downland* (1900), Hudson came across a caged owl, kept on the Sussex–Hampshire border. A lover of birds especially, Hudson was horrified by the owl's imprisonment. Having failed to buy its freedom, the bird's 'melancholy image was ... deeply ingraved in my mind – a feathered Dreyfus, Semitic features and all, the head bowed, the weary eyes closed, the hooked nose just visible amidst a wilderness of white whiskers'.[84] The melding of animal and human characteristics and physiognomy was a major feature of Hudson's nature writing and his fiction, most famously in the creation of the bird-girl figure, 'Rima', in *Green Mansions* (1904). Unlike his predecessor and hero, Cobbett, Hudson wrote little about Jews, but his Dreyfus-owl is, even within the inventive work of Hudson, a remarkable image. Both owl and Dreyfus were wrongly imprisoned. Nevertheless, the Dreyfus of Hudson's imagination is dreamed up from grotesque French antisemitic cartoons and was not based on the 'real' figure of the ordinary French Jew falsely held on charges of treachery, until 1899, on Devil's Island.[85] There is a certain irony that the memorial to Hudson in Hyde Park by Jacob Epstein, based on the character in *Green Mansions*, would be subject to a vicious xenophobic and antisemitic campaign: 'The general public know that *Rima* is hideous, unnatural, un-English, and essentially unhealthy', as one opponent proclaimed.[86] Hudson, the obsessive race thinker who was born in Argentina was commemorated by an Anglo-American Jewish artist who was deemed too cosmopolitan and racially suspect to perform the task.

The 'Jew' was a symbol, within Hampshire, to Cobbett and Hudson respectively, of finance capital and imprisoned nature. The following chapters of this study will analyse the less extreme but no less inventive memory work associated with the 'Jew'. It will explore the role this figure played in the process of constructing and reconstructing local place identities. There is a danger, however, in relating such imaginary 'Wessex tales' that the perspectives and narratives of minorities within the locality – in this case those of the Jews – might be ignored or downplayed. Indeed, it is vital to avoid treating Jews and Jewish communities as simply figments (often malign, sometimes romantic) of literary imagination or, alternatively, as passive subjects to whom (largely unpleasant) things were done. Alongside 'the Jew', this study will equally focus on Jews themselves and the contesting narratives and power struggles within the varying communities operating, as they did, at different times and locations. It will, on the one hand, be mindful of the potential pitfalls accompanying the 'enclosure of "the Jews" in inverted commas [which] effectively relegates them to the status of a questionable entity, a shadowy form, an indistinct and largely inarticulate third party'.[87] On the other hand, it will be equally aware of the power of the constructed 'enclosed Jew', through what Bryan Cheyette has termed 'semitic discourse', to act as 'a key touchstone for [drawing] the racial boundaries of European "culture"'.[88] But one further consideration is in order before moving on to the substance of this study: how has the 'local' been constructed and imagined within Jewish memory work?

Jewish memory and the 'local'

There was a storm in Sudminster, not on the waters which washed its leading Jews their living, but in the breasts of these same marine storekeepers. For a competitor had appeared in their hive of industry – an alien immigrant without roots or even relatives at Sudminister. (Israel Zangwill, 'The Sabbath Question in Sudminster', in *Ghetto Comedies*)[89]

Specific aspects of Jewish memory work will be left to individual chapters of this study. Here the focus is on how those who have written and presented the Jewish past have perceived the local context and place identity within it. Local Jewish studies, especially in Britain, face a triple marginality. First, there is the antipathy, patronisation or indifference of those working within 'mainstream' British or English history against minority studies. Second, within global Jewish studies similar attitudes towards the 'local' can be detected as within British historiography. It is intensified within Jewish studies through the perceived marginality of British Jewish history. Lacking either the religious 'giants' of the continent or the experience of the modern horror of antisemitism, particularly through the Holocaust, British Jewry is often regarded as a quiet and unimportant backwater. The leading British historian, David Cannadine has summarised the assumptions underlying these two factors in characteristically belittling tone: 'In the context of international Jewry, the history of British Jewry is neither very interesting, nor very exciting. In the context of British history, it is just not that important.'[90] Such hostile views have wide academic currency. It will be argued here, however, that they say much more about the exclusivities and prejudices of contemporary scholarship than they do about the nature of British Jewish history. Third, within British Jewish historiography and memory work more generally, reflecting power politics within the community as a whole, the provinces have been especially sidelined.

London accounted for roughly 20 per cent of the population of medieval English Jewry and up to two-thirds of the Jewish community since the eighteenth century. Nevertheless, almost all general works on British Jewry since the readmission in the mid-seventeenth century have an exclusive focus on the capital: they have worked on an assumption of 'for Britain, read London'. Indeed, the emphasis on the national has been so profound that it has tended to obscure *local* London Jewish identities and attachments to specific locations within the capital. Only recently, for example, has there been any detailed exploration of meanings attached to the 'East End' or the 'Jewish East End',[91] while the 'Jewish' suburbs of London have hardly registered in historical accounts or critical memory work.[92]

Until the 1970s, local Jewish studies in Britain mirrored those elsewhere and were designed to celebrate achievement, rootedness and longevity of presence. Lee Shai Weissbach, in his history of *Jewish Life in Small-Town America* (2005), outlines the nature of most publications chronicling their existence: 'most have taken the form of brief congregational histories … usually focused on familiar topics such as the development of hometown Jewish institutions and the biographies of locally prominent personalities'. Weissbach is critical of such accounts as 'they lack attention to context'. While this may be true from a professional historical perspective, such studies are important in themselves as expressions of local patriotism. Furthermore, although Weissbach is equally right in highlighting how few of these local histories 'have recognised that [they are] part of a larger story', his critique raises a wider question: in *which* wider context are they to be situated?[93]

Weissbach's magisterial study, which encompasses scores of communities across America, links them together and places them within an overarching framework of the modern Jewish experience. Only secondarily is it a study 'of the character of small-town America'.[94] Examining family life, religious observance and behaviour, economics and relations with non-Jews, Weissbach's analysis returns again and again to the same point: '"Place" really mattered'.[95] His conclusion will be replicated within *Anglo-Jewry since 1066*. Nevertheless, there is a tendency within Weissbach's study to homogenise the experiences he has documented and to argue that taken together 'America's smaller Jewish communities were quite unlike those of the country's large or even midsize cities'.[96] Size clearly is an important factor and Weissbach is perceptive in pointing it out. None featured in this study of Hampshire replicated the very large urban Jewish communities of say London and Manchester or even the smaller Jewish settlements in major cities of Leeds, Glasgow and Birmingham. Even so, there is variety: some, such as medieval Winchester, Portsmouth (both in the late eighteenth and early twentieth centuries) and Bournemouth after 1945 were amongst the largest within British Jewry, whereas others were amongst the smallest. But what is inevitably downplayed in Weissbach's work, given the number of case studies, is the importance of *specific* places and their impact on the formation of majority and minority identities. In this respect, an alternative model is provided within British Jewish historiography through the work of Bill Williams.

Williams's *The Making of Manchester Jewry 1740–1875* (1975) was a pathbreaking study in both urban history and modern Jewish history. A classic example of the new social history emerging from the late 1960s, articulated within Britain by the *History Workshop* movement, Williams's starting point was that

> in no sense can the Jewish community be regarded as 'alien' to Manchester. It was not a late addition to the established pattern of urban life, but an integral part of the pattern itself. Its role, like that of other minorities – the Germans, the Italians,

the Greeks, and, particularly, the Irish – was not peripheral and derivative, but central and creative, in a city which has always been cosmopolitan in character.

To Williams, his study aimed to shed light on the role of the Jewish minority 'in the life of a Victorian city'. Alongside class (a factor to the forefront of contemporary social history in the 1970s, but one almost neglected within Jewish studies), Williams focused attention on the 'more autonomous groupings which centre upon nationality and religion' – ones which had been largely ignored by scholars of the urban experience. While Williams acknowledged that the local Manchester Jewish community 'to some extent shared the changes experienced by Anglo-Jewry as a whole', the predominant context is Manchester itself and the Jews in relation to it. *The Making of Manchester Jewry* thus interrogated the 'degree of their individuality and independence, the process of their integration, their interaction both with each other and with the city as a whole, the attitudes and feelings they evoked, and the influence they exerted'. These matters, urged Williams, were all 'of concern for the urban historian'.[97] Freed from presenting the Jewish experience in isolation, but far from downplaying the role of migration and diasporic connections, Williams was able to explore the tensions and divisions within Manchester Jewry. By the early 1830s, he argued, there 'were, in effect, two communities in Manchester ..., the one increasingly anxious to live down the reputation of the other'.[98]

As Steven Zipperstein noted two years after the publication of *The Making of Manchester Jewry*, it reflected a new approach to urban Jewish history which was a late developer within Jewish studies as a whole. On the rare occasions that 'scholars studied cities they preferred Jewish urban concentration in medieval Germany or early modern Poland to the rapidly urbanizing centres that dominated contemporary Jewish life'.[99] More recent work with its 'focus on local studies', of which Zipperstein regarded Williams's as a key example, suggested that 'the large-scale comprehensive works that dominated nineteenth- and early twentieth-century Jewish historiography may no longer serve as models'.[100] Yet even Zipperstein, who was suspicious of the downplaying of Jewish 'ethnic-religious attachments' in Williams's study, ultimately downplayed the importance of the 'local' factor. 'Local history', according to Zipperstein, was a way of testing wider questions of assimilation in 'Western Jewry as a whole',[101] rather than accepting Williams's own justification for his study. Williams had argued that, alongside its own 'intrinsic importance, the development of Manchester Jewry provides the case history of a nineteenth-century urban minority'.[102]

If Williams's work was a challenge to those working in British Jewish history to take the local context and provincial communities seriously, then only limited progress has been made since *The Making of Manchester Jewry* was published. Here there is marked contrast to the increasingly sophisticated work on local Jewish studies beyond Britain. Taking the United States as an example, the quality of such work, certainly since the 1960s, has been of a higher standard than that relating to Anglo-Jewry. From 1963 solid urban studies were published in the Regional History Series under the auspices of the American Jewish History Center of the Jewish Theological Seminary of America. The goal of these publications was ambitious, calling for 'the broadest analysis of the continuing interplay between the psychological and social facets of urbanization as they relate to human aspiration in a given time and place'.[103] The achievements of these urban histories were perhaps more modest, but they were carried out with professional rigour.[104] A more interdisciplinary approach was adopted in Steven Lowenstein's *Frankfurt on the Hudson* (1989), a study of the German Jewish community of Washington Heights, in which the author 'attempted to place individual cultural traits, customs, and communal activities within an overall context'.[105]

Indeed, the impact of the social and cultural history revolution of the 1960s, and the importance of adopting interdisciplinary approaches was much greater in American Jewish studies than in its British counterpart. It can be detected in a remarkable set of essays covering history and culture, secular and religious history, and the broad area of Jewish/non-Jewish relations, *Jewish Roots in Southern Soil* (2006). Its editors, Marcie Cohen Ferris and Mark Greenberg, are unapologetic about the local focus of their volume and their justification for it is equally applicable for *Anglo-Jewry since 1066*: 'To dismiss the impact of region on Jewish identity is to underestimate the power of place.'[106] Similarly, Seth Wolitz's study of the Texan Jewish experience explores the making and remaking of identities across the generations and the complex nature of the construction of roots in relation to time and place.[107]

Outside American Jewish studies, the importance of memory has been incorporated into the understanding of the 'local'. Bea Lewkowicz's study of the Jewish community of Salonika provides an ethnological account exploring 'the intersection of history, memory and identity'.[108] A more multi-layered and fuller chronological analysis of memory and locality is provided in Nils Roemer's study of Worms. Roemer suggests that

> The popularity of a destination culture like Worms ... underpins the enduring importance of smaller communities: cities and small towns played a crucial role in modern Jewish identity formation. Alongside the production of Jewish memory in modern historiography, literature, and museums, tourism infused abstract notions of a modern Jewish heritage with local realms of memory.

His conclusion that 'This provincialized grounding of Jewish cultures operated within a geographically diverse, local, national, and transnational leisure activity, and today it provides new avenues to study German Jewish history within a national and wider Continental and Atlantic context' has a wider currency, as this book hopes to illustrate within Anglo-Jewish studies.[109]

Returning to Britain, general studies of its Jewish minority have still been London-focused,[110] and the increasing number of provincial histories have, with only a few partial exceptions, failed to engage sufficiently with the dynamics of the world around them. Williams concluded his book by insisting that the Jewish community 'grew *with* Manchester, and was to an extent a variation on urban themes, reflecting the social moods and prejudices, reacting to the changing economic fortunes, sharing the political *éclat* of the shock city of the age'.[111] Only the Birmingham Jewish History Research Group, tellingly under the influence of Williams, came close to emulating the work on Manchester Jewry. This group set off with the desire to query 'the traditionally accepted view of the origins of Birmingham Jewry', and to do so in the context of the city's evolution in the eighteenth and nineteenth centuries.[112]

Nevertheless, in spite of their historiographical limitations, the fast growth in the publication of provincial histories in the last quarter of the twentieth century and beyond is of significance in itself. Several interrelated factors have been at work in explaining this development. First, and on a general level, it is part of an intensified interest in the past in Britain, though it has been articulated more through celebration in the form of heritage rather than by critical engagement through historical analysis.[113] Second, and more specifically, provincial Jewish history has acted as memorialisation of a past or fast-disappearing world. In Chapter 1, brief reference was made to the book *The Lost Jews of Cornwall* (2000), part of a wider project that has traced the Jewish presence in the county from 'the Middle Ages to the Nineteenth Century'.[114] The history presented of Cornwall is thus firmly located in the past, leaving now only the built heritage, one that is in need of preservation. Revealingly, alongside other publications and exhibitions, *The Lost Jews* was produced in conjunction with the 'Hidden Legacy Foundation' which aims to restore the memory of Jewish communities destroyed in the Holocaust.[115] Bernard Susser's *The Jews of South-West England* (1993), covering some of the same ground, is of far higher analytical quality. What is significant here, however, is that it also employs a Hoskins/Leicester School style approach, charting 'the rise and decline of [the Jewish] medieval and modern communities'.[116] A long-standing rabbi of the Plymouth congregation, Susser dedicated his book as 'a memorial to Anglo-Jewish life in the provinces which is fast vanishing from all but a handful of cities'.[117]

The third factor at work is that of showing rootedness in and contributions to a fast-changing society, and one, as was shown in Chapter 1, that pays increasing attention, superficial or otherwise, to multiculturalism. It is noticeable that *The Lost Jews of Cornwall* and *The Jews of South-West England* both take their narratives back to 'the early settlement', exploring medieval communities and the evidence for even earlier Jewish presences. Similarly, *Eight Hundred Years* is the collective 'story of Nottingham's Jews'. It concludes that 'the community's munificent gifts to the city and to the nation at large are a lasting tribute to the generosity of spirit which informed the Jews of Nottingham'.[118] In each case the sections on 'the early settlement' are, on one level, brief and perfunctory. On another, the inclusion of the deep past shows its importance with regard to creating a local sense of belonging, no matter how brutal the treatment of medieval Jewry. The wider question of what medieval and modern, or even early and late modern, Jewish communities had in common is never raised: continuity and commonality is assumed. Within this less critical provincial Jewish historiography, the 'local' is imagined as progressive and welcoming. If there was past persecution then later treatment provides a more comforting story of acceptance and integration.

We will return to the politics relating to the 'ownership' of medieval Anglo-Jewry in Chapter 3. Before then, one final point of clarification is in order with regard to *Anglo-Jewry since 1066*. The first concerns chronology. Taking the geographically proximate urban centres of Winchester, Southampton and Portsmouth together, only London and Bristol have had the existence of similarly prominent and sizeable Jewish communities in the medieval, early modern and late modern periods.[119] This study is not primarily intended as a Hoskins-style inclusive 'rise and fall' history of all the Jewish communities and presences in Hampshire. Nevertheless, these histories – individual and collective – will be far from neglected. Its major emphasis, however, is on the construction of place identities with regard to the presence (and absence) of Jews and their role in the making of the local world. While the chapters follow an apparently logical chronological structure, it is complicated throughout by subsequent memory work. Thus Chapter 3 is equally if not more concerned with the years beyond 1290, and the expulsion of the Jews, than it is with the medieval period per se. It is as much about 'the myths we live by' as it is a study of a specific minority in a specific locality.[120] The beginnings of such work are taking place in areas of former mass immigration, asking, with regard to America, for example, 'How does the act of remembering the Lower East Side relate to its actual history and to that of New York more generally?'[121] It is important, however, that other, less notoriously 'cosmopolitan', areas are similarly interrogated, illustrating that, freed of raciology and ethnocentric thinking, concepts of the local and the universal are inseparable and not polar opposites. *Anglo-Jewry since 1066* is thus intended as a micro-history, illustrating that 'The global is everywhere and already, in one way or another, implicated in the local.'[122]

Notes

1   B. B. Woodward, *A General History of Hampshire* (London: James Virtue, 1861), p. 1.

2   Robert Mudie, *Hampshire: Its Past and Present Condition, and Future Prospects* vol. 1 (Winchester: Gilmour, 1838), pp. 2, 292.

3   Michael Hicks, 'Hampshire and the Isle of Wight', in C. Currie and C. Lewis (eds), *English County Histories: A Guide* (Stroud: Alam Sutton, 1994), p. 173.

4   *The Victoria History of the Counties of England: Hampshire and the Isle of Wight* vol. 1 (London: Constable, 1900), p. xix.

5   Philip Payton, *Cornwall: A History* (Fowey: Cornwall Editions, 2004 [1996]), pp. 272–3.

6   Ibid., p. 49.

7   Ibid., pp. 75–6. See also his *The Making of Modern Cornwall: Historical Experience and the Persistence of 'Difference'* (Redruth: Dyllansow Truran, 1993).

8   Philip Payton, 'Territory and Identity' in Philip Payton (ed.), *Cornwall Since the War* (Redruth: Dyllansow Truran, 1993), p. 227.

9   Julian Huxley and A.C. Haddon, *We Europeans* (London: Jonathan Cape, 1935), p. 26.

10   W. G. Hoskins, *Local History in England* (2nd edn, London: Longman, 1972), p. 14.

11   Thomas Hardy, 'The Three Strangers' in Thomas Hardy, *Wessex Tales* (London: Macmillan, 1952 [1888]), pp. 12, 15.

12   W. H. Hudson, *Hampshire Days* (Oxford: Oxford University Press, 1980 [1903]), pp. 173, 176.

13   Ibid., pp. 176–9.

14   Ibid., pp. 182–3, 185.

15   Ibid., pp. 183–4.

16   Ibid., p. 175.

17   W. H. Hudson, *Nature in Downland* (London: J. M. Dent, 1951 [1900]), p. 113.

18   W. H. Hudson, *Afoot in England* (London: Hutchinson, 1911), p. 81.

19   Paul Rich, *Prospero's Return? Historical Essays on Race, Culture and British Society* (London: Hansib, 1994), p. 13.

20   T. W. Shore, *A History of Hampshire including the Isle of Wight* (London: Elliot Stock, 1906), p. 274.

21   T. W. Shore, *Origins of the Anglo-Saxon Race* (London: Elliot Stock, 1906), pp. 3–4.

22   T. W. Shore, *Characteristic Survivals of the Celts in Hampshire* (London: Harrison & Sons, 1890), p. 17.

23   Payton, *The Making of Modern Cornwall*.

24   Shore, *A History of Hampshire*, p. 200.

25   H. V. Morton, *In Search of England* (London: Methuen, 1933 [1927]), p. viii.

26   Brian Vesey-Fitzgerald, *Hampshire Scene* (London: Methuen, 1940), p. vii.

27   Arthur Mee, *The King's England: Hampshire with the Isle of Wight* (London: Hodder & Stoughton, 1939), p. 3.

28   W. H. Shears, *This England: A Book of the Shires* (London: Right Book Club, 1938), pp. 157, 232.

29   Charles Kingsley, 'My Winter-Garden', *Fraser's Magazine*, January 1858 and reproduced in

Charles Kingsley, *Miscellanies* vol. 1 (London: John Parker, 1859), p. 162.

30 John Beddoe, *The Races of Britain* (Bristol: Arrowsmith, 1885), p. 257.

31 John Wise, *The New Forest: Its History and Its Scenery* (London: Gibbings, 1895 [1862]), p. 161.

32 Vesey-Fitzgerald, *Hampshire Scene*, pp. 130, 134.

33 Ibid., p. 136.

34 Ibid., p. 155.

35 John Arlott, 'The Return of the Native', *Hampshire* vol. 2 no. 7 (May 1962), p. 29.

36 F. E. Stevens, *Hampshire Ways* (London: Heath Granton, 1934), p. 93.

37 Ibid., pp. 95–6.

38 Ibid., pp. 5, 140.

39 Edward Thomas, *The South Country* (London: Dent, 1909), pp. 11, 172.

40 *Wheeler's Hampshire and West of England Magazine* vol. 1 no. 1 (January 1828), p. 4. The short-lived *Hampshire Magazine* was founded in 1884.

41 Its first volume covered the period from 1885 to 1889.

42 Paul Woodhouse, 'First Fruit of a Dream', *Hampshire Review* vol. 1 (Autumn 1949), pp. 3–4.

43 *Hampshire Chronicle*, 16 May 1903.

44 Hudson to Roberts, 16 July 1908, in Morley Roberts (ed.), *Men, Books and Birds* (London: Eveleigh Nash & Grayson, 1925), p. 98.

45 Ruth Tomalin, *W. H. Hudson: A Biography* (London: Faber and Faber, 1982), p. 189.

46 Brian Martin, 'The Forest Philosophers', *Hampshire* vol. 16 no. 10 (August 1976), p. 31.

47 Brian Vesey-Fitzgerald, 'A Different People', *Hampshire Review* no. 8 (summer 1951), p. 18.

48 Ibid., pp. 18–19.

49 Ibid., p. 20.

50 Ibid., pp. 21–2.

51 Marek Kohn, *The Race Gallery: The Return of Racial Science* (London: Vintage, 1996).

52 Barry Stapleton, *Hampshire of One Hundred Years Ago* (Stroud: Alan Sutton, 1993), pp. 36–43.

53 John Arlott, 'Hampshire Days', *Hampshire* vol. 12 no. 8 (August 1972), p. 28.

54 See Duncan Pepper's article in *Hampshire* vol. 13 no. 12 (October 1973), p. 51.

55 James Campbell, 'This is Really Hampshire', *Hampshire* vol. 34 no. 10 (August 1994), p. 18.

56 Peter Mason, *Hampshire: A Sense of Place* (Crediton: Hampshire Books, 1994), p. 107.

57 Ibid., p. 139.

58 Ibid., p. 141.

59 Ibid., p. 23.

60 Ibid.

61 Ibid., p. 21.

62 'The Romance of the Money Mills', *Hampshire* vol. 2 no. 10 (August 1962), p. 14.

63 Michael Kennett, 'Laverstoke', *Hampshire* vol. 9 no. 12 (October 1969), p. 33.

64 Mason, *Hampshire*, p. 139.

65 Letter from Hampshire Record Office, 17 November 1994, to University of Southampton.

66 B. M. Ponton, 'Remarkable Story of Thomas Johnson', *Hampshire* vol. 31 no. 2 (December 1990), p. 39.

67 Joan Martin, 'Eugenie, Empress of the French – and Farnborough', *Hampshire* vol. 16 no. 7 (May 1976), p. 47.

68 Peter Paterson, 'A Brazilian in 16th Century Southampton', *Hampshire* vol. 15 no. 6 (April 1975), p. 40.

69 Mark Phillimore, 'Basques at Stoneham', *Hampshire* vol. 19 no. 2 (December 1978), pp. 49–50; Walter Greenaway, 'Visitors from Spain, 50 Years Ago', *Hampshire* vol. 27 no. 3 (January 1987), p. 17.

70 John Arlott, 'The End of Hampshire?', *Hampshire* vol. 9 no. 10 (August 1969), p. 25.

71 Ibid.

72 *Hampshire* vol. 13 no. 6 (April 1973), p. 37.

73 C. H. Wilkinson, 'Hampshire Writers', *Papers and Proceedings of the Hampshire Field Club* vol. 18 (1953–4), p. 259.

74 See, for example, Norman Goodland, 'A Hampshire Diary', *Hampshire* vol. 7 no. 8 (June 1967), p. 31.

75 Edric Holmes, *Wanderings in Wessex* (London: Robert Scott, 1922), p. 47.

76 Greenaway, 'Visitors from Spain'.

77 Doreen Massey, 'Places and Their Pasts', *History Workshop Journal* no. 39 (spring 1995), p. 183.

78 Gillian Rose, 'Place and Identity: A Sense of Place', in Doreen Massey and Pat Jess (eds), *A Place in the World?* (Oxford: Oxford University Press, 1995), p. 103.

79 Margaret Marlow, 'Gosport: Place, Identity and Memory: From the 1770s to the Present', (unpublished MA dissertation, University of Southampton, 1998), Chapter 3. See Edgar Mann, 'Why Gosport became "Turk Town"', *Hampshire* vol. 33 no. 12 (October 1993), pp. 44–5.

80 S. E. Barrington, 'The Royal Hospital, Haslar', *Hampshire Review* no. 18 (Winter 1953/4), p. 24.

81 G. D. H. and Margaret Cole (eds), *Rural Rides* vol. 1 (London: Peter Davies, 1930), pp. 187, 320.

82 Daniel Green, *Great Cobbett: The Noblest Agitator* (London: Hodder and Stoughton, 1983), pp. 321–2.

83 William Reitzel (ed.), *The Autobiography of William Cobbett* (London: Faber and Faber, 1967), pp. 174–5 on Portsmouth Point.

84 W. H. Hudson, *Nature in Downland* (London: J. M. Dent, 1951 [1900]), p. 258.

85 For contemporary imagery, see Norman Kleeblatt (ed.), *The Dreyfus Affair: Art, Truth and Justice* (Berkeley: University of California Press, 1987).

86 Stephen Gardiner, *Epstein: Artist Against the Establishment* (London: Michael Joseph, 1992), p. 258.

87 Lionel Kochan in review of Tony Kushner and Nadia Valman, *Philosemitism, Antisemitism and 'the Jews' in English Historical Review* no. 492 (June 2006), pp. 863–4.

88 Bryan Cheyette, *Constructions of 'the Jew' in English Literature and Society: Racial Reprsentations, 1875–1945* (Cambridge: Cambridge University Press, 1993), p. 12.

89 Israel Zangwill, *Ghetto Comedies* (London: William Heinemann, 1907), p. 119.

90 David Cannadine, 'Cousinhood', *London Review of Books*, 27 July 1989.

91 See Eitan Bar-Yosef and Nadia Valman (eds), *The Jew in Late Victorian and Edwardian Culture: Between the East End and Africa* (Palgrave, forthcoming).

92 David Cesarani, 'A Funny Thing Happened on the Way to the Suburbs: Social Change in Anglo-Jewry between the Wars, 1914–1945', *Jewish Culture and History* vol. 1 no. 1 (summer 1998), pp. 5–26.

93 Lee Shai Weissbach, *Jewish Life in Small-Town America: A History* (New Haven: Yale University Press, 2005), p. 3.

94 Ibid., p. 10.

95 Ibid., p. 294.

96 Ibid., p. 155.

97 Bill Williams, *The Making of Manchester Jewry 1740–1875* (Manchester: Manchester University Press, 1975), pp. vii–iii.

98 Ibid., p. 57.

99 Steven Zipperstein, 'Jewish Historiography and the Modern City', *Jewish History* vol. 2 (1987), p. 74.

100 Ibid., p. 85.

101 Ibid., pp. 85–6.

102 Williams, *The Making of Manchester Jewry*, p. viii.

103 Moshe Davis, 'Preface', in Max Vorspan and Lloyd Gartner, *History of the Jews of Los Angeles* (Philadelphia: Jewish Publication Society of America, 1970), p. v.

104 See, for example, Lloyd Gartner, *History of the Jews of Cleveland* (Cleveland: Western Reserve Historical Society and Jewish Theological Seminary of America, 1978). Not in this series, but a fine urban history, is provided by Judith Endelman, *The Jewish Community of Indianapolis: 1849 to the Present* (Bloomington: Indiana University Press, 1984).

105 Steven Lowenstein, *Frankfurt on the Hudson* (Detroit: Wayne State University Press, 1989), p. 268.

106 Marcie Cohen Ferris and Mark Greenberg, 'Introduction', in Marcie Cohen Ferris and Mark Greenberg (eds), *Jewish Roots in Southern Soil: A New History* (Hanover: University Press of New England, 2006), p. 18.

107 Seth Wolitz, 'Bifocality in Jewish Identity in the Texas-Jewish Experience', in Sander Gilman and Milton Shain (eds), *Jewries at the Frontier* (Urbana: University of Illinois Press, 1999), pp. 185–208.

108 Bea Lewkowicz, *The Jewish Community of Salonika: History, Memory, Identity* (London: Vallentine, Mitchell, 2006), p. xvii.

109 Nils Roemer, 'The City of Worms in Modern Jewish Traveling Cultures of Remembrance', *Jewish Social Studies* vol. 11 no. 3 (2005), p. 84.

110 See, for example, Todd Endelman, *The Jews of Britain 1656 to 2000* (Berkeley: University of California Press, 2002).

111 Williams, *The Making of Manchester Jewry*, p. 340.

112 Birmingham Jewish History Research Group, *Birmingham Jewry 1749–1914* vol. 1 (Birmingham: Zoe Josephs, 1980), p. 1.

113 See David Lowenthal, *The Heritage Crusade and the Spoils of History* (Cambridge: Cambridge University Press, 1996).

114 Keith Pearce and Helen Fry (eds), *The Lost Jews of Cornwall* (Bristol: Redcliffe Press, 2000), introduction.

115 See Tony Kushner, 'Jewish Local Studies and Memory Work: A Case Study of Cornwall', *Journal of Jewish Studies* vol. 55 no. 1 (spring 2004), pp. 157–62.

116 Bernard Susser, *The Jews of South-West England* (Exeter: University of Exeter Press, 1993).

117 Ibid., p. xxii.

118 Nelsen Fisher, *Eight Hundred Years: The Story of Nottingham's Jews* (Nottingham: Nottingham Jewry Research Team, 1998), p. 167.

119 Judith Samuel, *Jews in Bristol: The History of the Jewish Community in Bristol from the Middle Ages to the Present Day* (Bristol: Redcliffe Press, 1997).

120 Raphael Samuel and Paul Thompson (eds), *The Myths We Live By* (London: Routledge, 1990).

121 Jeffrey Shandler in the introduction to Hasia Diner, Jeffrey Shandler and Beth Wenger (eds), *Remembering the Lower East Side* (Bloomington: Indiana University Press, 2000), p. 2.

122 Doreen Massey, 'Double Articulation: A Place in the World', in A. Bammer (ed.), *Displacements: Cultural Identities in Question* (Bloomington: Indiana University Press, 1994), p. 120.

3

Winchester: constructing the city of memories

Introduction

After the Norman invasion, an important and relatively sizeable Jewish community existed in Winchester until the nationwide expulsion of the Jews from England in 1290. It was one of the earliest settlements, dating from at least the 1140s, and its size and significance grew thereafter, especially from the late twelfth century onwards when Jewish business activities had to be officially recorded in *archae* (chests), leading to concentration in certain towns.[1] It was also one of the longest established Jewish presences in medieval England. Statistical evidence is partial and uncertain. Nevertheless, contemporary surveys, carried out essentially for fiscal purposes, placed Winchester Jewry between the third and sixth most wealthy of the Jewish communities in twelfth- and thirteenth-century England. It was also possibly the fifth or sixth most populous amongst medieval Anglo-Jewry. At its largest, in the thirteenth century, there were between one and two hundred Jews in Winchester (or between 1 and 2 per cent of the city's total population).[2] Of greater significance than the maximum number, however, was the fluidity of Winchester Jewry: the total population varied immensely because of internal movement within England (both forced and voluntary, including expulsion from other settlements in Hampshire), fresh immigration from France, and murderous persecution.[3] Adding to the complexity of Winchester Jewry's composition, while most were of French origin, some were from the south of Europe and another, Isaac of Russia, showed the diasporic nature of this medieval minority.[4] It is also clear from the activities of the wealthier members of the community that close links were maintained with Jewish settlements in other parts of England.[5]

While, as will emerge, the historiography of Winchester Jewry is still relatively undeveloped, memory work associated with this medieval community is rich and multifaceted, providing unique insights into the construction of local, national and imperial identities. Jews themselves have played an important role in the process of remembering, reinforcing as well as challenging wider perspectives on Winchester Jewry and adding further layers of complexity to its memory. This chapter will also consider other minority groups within Winchester's history, especially the Huguenots, in order to allow a comparative approach and to enable an analysis of whether or not the memory and representation of the Jews is unique. It should be added that such memory work associated with Winchester has a wider significance because of the momentous place the city has occupied in constructing the 'English' past.

A description of the city in 1910 proclaimed that 'in Winchester antique tradition and historic association are not a mere adjunct of picturesque accident: they are the keynote of its very existence'.[6] Its fame in this respect was global – Winchester was regularly included in book series devoted to internationally important 'historic towns' published between the late nineteenth century and the Second World War.[7] Yet Winchester's significance 'as the most historic of English cities'[8] was deemed to have gone beyond either the famous people and events associated with it or its surviving architectural treasures. Winchester, as place and symbol, has featured prominently in the construction and re-construction of Englishness over many centuries. In their 1893 guide to Winchester, A. R. Bramston and A. C. Leroy stressed that 'It is no small thing to live in a city of memories where, not here and there, but at every turn, the past is brought before us.' They continued '*Non nobis nati*, not for ourselves are we born, and Winchester, of all the cities of England, owes its greatest debt of gratitude to the Past.'[9] In the preparations leading to the King Alfred Millenary, held in Winchester during 1901, Sir Walter Besant emphasised that 'the name of Alfred's capital continues in this venerable and historic city, which yields to none in England for the monuments and the memories of the past'.[10] Writing after the event, Alfred Bowker, mayor of Winchester and one of the key organisers of the Millenary, justified the choice of the host city on explicitly racial grounds. For the English-speaking peoples of the world, 'it was felt that the memorial to the "hero of our race" should be worthy not only of the city and neighbouring counties, but also of the Anglo-Saxon race'.[11]

Moving to the literary sphere, A. G. Macdonell's classic *England, Their England* (1933) ends, in the words of Krishan Kumar, 'on a mystical note in the very English city of Winchester'.[12] Melding myth and history in this 'ancient … city of Alfred, once capital of England, perhaps even the Camelot of Arthur', Macdonell removes any distinction between past and present: time itself does 'not move'.[13] Finally, the mist clears and 'there was no longer any trace of the passing of that absurd host of kindly, laughter-loving, warrior poets', leaving 'the muted voice of grazing sheep, and the merry click of bat upon ball, and the peaceful green fields of England, and the water-meads, and the bells of the Cathedral'.[14] Writing in a similar vein before the First World War, Telford Varley wrote that Winchester was

> a city with an atmosphere – an atmosphere of the reality and range of historic things, through which the gazing eye can peer, mile after mile as it were, till it loses itself in a vaguely distant and indistinct horizon, where the mists of myth and legend blur the outline and mingle inextricably together fact and fancy, record and surmise.[15]

Winchester is a city that has inspired attempts to bolster collective memory through a powerful and deeply romanticised evocation of place. 'Winchester is, and while there are Englishmen, will be classic ground'.[16] In the construction of Jewish identities, the impulse towards memory has been equally important even if the dynamics are very different. Yosef Yerushalmi notes how 'the Hebrew Bible seems to have no hesitations in commanding memory. Its injunctions to remember are unconditional, and even when not commanded, remembrance is always pivotal.' He adds that

> As Israel is enjoined to remember, so it is adjured not to forget. Both imperatives have resounded with enduring effect among the Jews since biblical times. Indeed, in trying to understand the survival of a people that has spent most of its life in global dispersion, I would submit that the history of its memory ... may prove of some consequence.[17]

With literary license and far less restraint, the American novelist, Jonathan Safran Foer, suggests in *Everything is Illuminated* (2002) that 'Jews have six senses. Touch, taste, sight, smell, hearing ... memory. While Gentiles experience and process the world through the traditional senses, and use memory only as a second-order means of interpreting events, for Jews memory is no less primary than the prick of a pin ... The Jew is pricked by a pin and remembers other pins.'[18]

Foer's novel explores the deep scar left after the Second World War by the memory of the Holocaust on both the Jewish and non-Jewish worlds. His work is a reminder of the centrality of memory, especially that of past persecution, in the construction of secular Jewish identities as well as in the sacred sphere. Winchester has many multi-layered meanings associated with it, the result of the 'local' being shaped by, amongst others, notions of race, Christianity, nation and Empire. All these factors have influenced the memory and representation of medieval Winchester Jewry, acting as both forces for inclusion and exclusion in the construction of place identities. Moreover, the existence of many intriguing sites of memory – both physical and literary – have, as we will see, enabled a variety of readings of Winchester's past in relation to the Jewish presence.

Memory, as Yerushalmi reminds us, 'is always problematic, usually deceptive, sometimes treacherous'. If the verb *zakhar* – remember – 'appears in its
various declensions in the Bible no less than one hundred and sixty-nine
times', it does not answer the question of 'what were the Jews to remember,
and by what means?'[19] Power relations often decide who is remembered and
who is forgotten, part of what Jonathan Boyarin describes as the 'the politics
of Jewish memory'.[20] Such battles over memory are far from exclusive to the
Jewish world and the case of Winchester is no exception. As Patrick Geary argues, 'the study of historical memory is a study of propaganda, of the decisions
about what should be remembered and how it should be remembered'.[21]

In his *Lyrics of the White City* (1896), poet Herbert Powell wrote of 'A City
of Memories':

> My window looks upon the street,
> The city's voices gathered there,
> Stream in for ever, and the beat
> Incessant of incessant feet
> Pants upward through the vibrant air.
>
> A thousand cries are in the stone,
> But one note rings upon the ears;
> Change treads a measure of its own,
> But through it runs an undertone,
> The pulse of the continuous years.[22]

Powell's emphasis on the unbroken nature of Winchester's past, later highlighted in this poem through the ringing of its cathedral bells, monarchy and
college playing fields,[23] excludes from consideration the Jews whose place in
the city was, through forced removal, temporary. As we will see, the choice of
whether to include (and, if so, on what terms) or simply to exclude the Jews
in representations of Winchester and its past has been continuously contested in what now amounts to over eight hundred years of ongoing memory
work. Indeed, the story, or more accurately, stories, of Winchester Jewry, and
of other minority groups within the city, confirms the analysis of Doreen
Massey that 'The identity of places is very much bound up with the *histories*
which are told of them, *how* those histories are told, and which history turns
out to be dominant.'[Original emphasis][24]

Jewry Street

In the *Arcades Project*, his incompleted 'virtual encyclopedia of 19th-century
Parisian (and by extension, European) culture',[25] Walter Benjamin argued
that

Being past, being no more, is passionately at work in things. To this the historian trusts for his subject matter. He depends on this force, and knows things as they are at the moment of their ceasing to be. Arcades are such monuments of being-no-more ... And nothing lasts except the name: *passages* ... In the inmost recesses of these names the upheaval is working, and therefore we hold a world in the names of old streets, and to read the name of a street at night is like undergoing a transformation.[26]

Our first case study in this chapter will undertake a close reading of the worlds revealed and disguised 'in the names of old streets' in Winchester.

In the second volume of *Theatres of Memory*, Raphael Samuel argued that 'Street-names serve in some sort as almanacs, registering those personalities and events – mythic or real – which have imprinted themselves on popular consciousness.' He added that they can 'also serve as archaeological indicators of some more ancient past when there was a haymarket in St. James's, when pheasants were dressed in Poultry, loaves baked in Bread Street and flour ground in Windmill Street, Piccadilly'. In line with his belief that popular representations of the past were often inclusive in the telling of 'island stories', including the presence of immigrants and minorities, Samuel highlighted how 'Lombard Street reminds us of the time of the Bardi and the Peruzzi, when Italians replaced the Jews as the king's moneylenders.'[27] Here, using the example of Jewry Street in Winchester, it will be suggested that Samuel's analysis is far too consensual. Samuel underplays the politics and power relations involved with such street naming and the exclusion due to forgetting that almost inevitably accompanies the process of remembering. Instead, it will follow Jonathan Boyarin's work on the Lower East Side which he labels 'a place of forgetting'. Boyarin refers to the perpetuation of names in the Hasidic neighbourhoods of New York, such as the Satmar (from Hungary), Lubavitch in Lithuania and Bobov in Poland, each reflecting various rabbinic constituencies. Yet such continuity of place names 'masks the struggle of the [rabbis] and their bands of surviving followers to reassemble a new constituency in post-Holocaust America'. Boyarin concludes that

Forgetting and memory are so intermingled as to become almost one here. The point is not to separate them, but to realize the surprising point that forgetting is also sometimes a technique of the dominated, used to enable memory.[28]

In 1953, the Hampshire-born travel writer, Brian Vesey-Fitzgerald, complained that of the thousands of people who visited Winchester each year 'hardly any go to the Cathedral Library or even ask for it, probably because they do not know that it exists. The same thing applies to so many places in this very ancient city.'[29] Few, for example, 'walk up the Alley and into The Royal Oak Inn. Fewer still walk through the little garden of the inn and out into the narrow lane at the back (there are a lot of these narrow lanes, some of them no more than passages, in Winchester and all of them are worth exploring) and in to the old Jewish quarter of the city.'[30] Nevertheless, several pages later and drawing to a close the 'hidden treasure of Winchester', Vesey-Fitzgerald bemoaned the decision 'made [by] the council at the beginning of the nineteenth century [to] do away with the old [street] names. I do not think that High Street is an improvement on Cheapside'. He was particularly vexed about the loss of street names associated with specific trades: 'Lower Brook Street, which used to be Tanners' Street; Upper Brook Street, which used to be Sildworten Street (that is, the silver workers' street); St Peter Street, which used to be Flescmangers Street (that is, the Fleshmongers' or Butchers' Street)'. Parchment Street survived, which he put down to it sounding respectable, whereas to 'the Council of the day ... alter[ing] names that had stood since the twelfth century thought that Fleshmongers and Tanners [did] not ... What Winchester has lost in this matter of street names is more than just an old name, for there is also the tradition that went with it.'[31]

In fact, the street name changes occurred earlier – during the eighteenth century – and the motivation for them is not fully clear. Writing in 1892, W. H. Jacob, proprietor of the *Hampshire Chronicle* and a skilled local historian, anticipated Vesey-Fitzgerald's later irritation and lamented how the re-naming by 'the then guardians and managers of the city' had prompted amnesia of medieval trading in Winchester.[32] Yet while an act of modernisation, these name changes also harked back to greater antiquity – Southgate Street and High Street summoned up Winchester's Roman past. Moreover, while decrying the neglect of Jewry Street and the 'old Jewish quarter' it was associated with, *and* the removal of the twelfth-century street names, Vesey-Fitzgerald was ignoring the earlier dynamics of Winchester topographic nomenclature. The name Jewry Street dated only to the very early fourteenth century and replaced another that was Saxon trade-related – Scowertenestret, or Shoemakers' Street. To some extent, therefore, the forgetting of the shoemakers enabled the remembering of Winchester Jewry.

There is no doubt that the continuous existence (in name if not quite direction and scope) of Jewry Street from 1302 through to the present day, with only a brief gap from the mid-eighteenth century until 1830 as Gaol Street, acted itself as a crucial aide-memoire with regard to the presence of medieval Jewry in Winchester. As the authors of the Hampshire volumes of the Victoria History of the Counties of England (VHC) recognised in 1912, 'Apart from the freemen one other class of inhabitants must be noticed. Their memory still remains in the city in Jewry Street, where they were settled by William the Conqueror.'[33] The VHC's early modern precursor, John Leland, Antiquary Royal to Henry VIII, visited Hampshire in the 1530s and reported that 'Ther is a streate in Winchester that leadeth right from the High-strete to the Northgate, caullid the Jury, by cause the Jues did inhabit it, and had their Synagoge ther.'[34] While admittedly relegated to the 'shopping guide', a twenty-first century tourist leaflet produced by Winchester City Council at least acknowledges that as well as now providing 'numerous restaurants and lively bars', Jewry Street was 'Once the city's Jewish quarter'.[35] Another produced by the Council, 'The Winchester Walk: A Tour of King Alfred's City' (2003), traces 'Alfred's Final Journey' and along the way crosses over the street that was 'the centre of Jewish Winchester in the Middle Ages'.[36] As will emerge throughout this chapter, the treatment of the Jewish presence in such guides and descriptions of Winchester across the ages has varied immensely in depth and tone, and the few that are sustained are rarely free of prejudice or romance. Yet without the stimulation provided by the street name itself, it is certain that medieval Winchester Jewry would have been subject to even greater obscurity. In 1818, for example, Charles Bell's *An Historical Account of Winchester, with Descriptive Walks*, then the longest and most thorough guide to the city, made no mention of the medieval Jewish presence, either in the lengthy overview of its past, or in the topographies provided – it was at this point that the name Jewry Street had been abandoned. Ironically for a publication boasting that its purpose was to remove the 'ignoran[ce] of many of the important traits of its History' from both the inhabitants of and visitors to Winchester, Bell's discussion of Gaol Street focused on the prison building.[37] It was, however, the absence rather than the presence of Jews that that led to the street naming in the first place.

Walter Benjamin in the *Arcades Project* suggested that the naming of a street becomes 'like a filter that only lets through the most inner, bitter, essence of the past'.[38] This was certainly the case with Jewry Street in Winchester. In the second half of the twelfth century and throughout the thirteenth century until the expulsion, part of Scowertenestet 'was undoubtedly the Jews' main thoroughfare'.[39] Whether the re-naming in 1302 reflected either an element of local nostalgia about the absence of the recently departed Jews or satisfaction about their removal is now impossible to tell.[40] Yet, whatever the motivation, such naming did acknowledge the notable presence and impact of Winchester Jewry. Indeed, their absence was reflected in the decline of the street, and perhaps the medieval city as a whole, from the expulsion onwards.

In the fourteenth and early fifteenth centuries there are references in contemporary documents to *Vicus Judaeorum* and *Jewerye Street*.[41] Its only notable feature, however, from then onwards, was the county gaol which gradually increased in size and importance. The re-building of the prison in the mid-eighteenth century undoubtedly led to its new name, *Gaol Street*.

When, by 1816, the final extension took place, the gaol 'occupied much of the western frontage'.[42] In both nineteenth-century and recent accounts it is suggested that the removal of the gaol to a new site in 1850 prompted the return to the name Jewry Street.[43] In fact, the decision of the Winchester Pavement Commissioners to revert back to its 'ancient name', occurred exactly twenty years earlier.[44]

The name change would appear to have been prompted by the widening and paving of the street, improvements that began in 1825 and concluded in 1830.[45] Thereafter, the street became a far more respectable location, leading to the construction of a variety of shops alongside some distinguished residences and several landmark civic and religious buildings. Over a century later, John Arlott praised Jewry Street over High Street in Winchester: 'it is much less spoilt, though many of its buildings are of a substantially later date'.[46] If the nomenclature, Gaol Street, had a utilitarian function in the eighteenth and early nineteenth century, then it was undermined if the intention was to make it a desirable place to live or to pass through, given the prison's notoriety. If respectability was the key, it is significant that the return to Jewry Street was deemed acceptable, suggesting some pride in this 'ancient name', or at least an absence of embarrassment either in relation to the Jewish presence or the city's past treatment of the medieval minority. Intriguingly, in April 1856, with another spate of name changes reflecting the continued growth of mid-Victorian Winchester, an attempt was made to re-name Jewry Street as Northgate Street.[47] As with changes in the eighteenth century, the reference was to the Roman past of the city, one reflected in the recent building on the street of 'Northgate House' inhabited by the Reverend Thomas Westcomb.[48] All but two of the fifteen name changes/ new names were approved, with a decision on Jewry Street postponed as the Pavement Commissioners were divided equally – it thus came within a whisker of being lost thereafter. The chief opponent of the name change argued that modernisation had its place, 'but they would not be doing an advisable thing if for the sake of only such a theory they altered and did away with old and familiar names'. This was especially the case with Jewry Street as it had been 'applied to the locality for such a very long time'.[49] When the Pavement Commissioners met a month later they received a 'memorial by the inhabitants of Jewry Street signed against the alteration of the name-change'. It was resolved that the 'old name' was to be continued, although the reason given was that the change 'would be attended with considerable inconvenience'.[50] While the practical factor involved was clearly to the fore, it does not appear that the inhabitants themselves had major cultural antipathy to the name of the place where they lived or worked, or else they would have gone along with the Pavement Commissioners. That some of the major civic figures within Winchester, however, in their attempt to both modernise *and* hark back to a greater antiquity, were willing to obliterate reference to the medieval Jewish community is significant in itself. If the decision to revert back to Jewry Street in 1830 revealed some local pride in the connection, the debate in 1856 reflected other tendencies of local memory work in which the Jewish presence was often simply forgotten, left out, or noted without much thought. Yet alongside such rejection or superficial engagement there were also more complex, often ambivalent, identifications with Jewry Street and its past inhabitants in the nineteenth century and beyond that merit further attention.

Until the late nineteenth century, the historical treatment of Winchester Jewry was still limited. While the original edition of Thomas Warton's *Description of Winchester* (1750) made no mention of the Jews, the revised version in 1774 referred to the civil war between Henry III and his barons, leading in 1254 to the Earl of Leicester 'besieg[ing] the city, which at length surrendered: the besiegers seized every thing of value, knocked down and butchered men, women and children, among whom fell upwards of an hundred Jews'.[51] Although wrong in date (the attack was ten years later), perpetrator (the siege was carried out by the Earl's son, Simon de Montfort the younger), and scale of disaster, this reference (taken from contemporary local sources as well as medieval chronicles, especially those of Robert of Gloucester and the Mayors and Sheriffs of London)[52] formed the foundation for descriptions of Winchester Jewry for the next century. It was thus in the context of civil war, in which all of Winchester suffered because of its royalist connections, that references were made to the city's Jews.

The first extensive history of Winchester, by the local Catholic clergyman, John Milner, was published in two volumes in 1798 and 1801. While its references to the Jews follow Warton's *Description of Winchester* in focusing on the events of 1265, Milner's narrative added further dimensions to the description of this community and of local responses to them. The first volume gave an historical overview of the city and Milner put particular emphasis on the brutality following Simon de Montfort's attack on Winchester. Ill-treatment was 'particularly the hard fate of the Jews, who were then exceedingly numerous here, in consequence of the protection which they had hitherto experienced, whilst in most other cities they had been riotously assaulted and murdered'.[53] The second volume provided a 'survey of antiquities' and Milner returned to the Jewish minority. The prompt was John Leland's topographical reference to Jewry Street, enabling Milner to elaborate further on his earlier comments:

> Here a great number of Jews resided in the 12th and 13th centuries, and here they had their synagogue, until the popular commotion, so frequent in those ages,

against that devoted people, and, at last, the great slaughter of them, that was made by the barons, when they stormed and sacked Winchester, in the reign of Henry III, seem to have extirpated them out of this ancient metropolis.[54]

There are a number of points to highlight here in relation to later memory work on Winchester Jewry. First, as has been noted, the Jewish population of Winchester at its peak probably numbered 150 individuals.[55] There has been a tendency beyond Milner to use phrases such as 'a great number' that while acknowledging the presence and importance of Winchester Jewry, also suggests a larger community than was actually the case. Second, reference to the existence of the synagogue provided topographical ambiguity, torn between an emphasis on the rootedness of the Jewish community in medieval Winchester and their anthropological otherness as non-Christians. Third, the impact of anti-Jewish sentiment and action is fully recognised and condemned, although the people of Winchester are exculpated as the attacks came from those outside the city. Indeed, Winchester is praised for its earlier tolerance towards the Jews which enabled the community to flourish in the first place. This self-mythology contrasts to less differentiated, but equally lachrymose accounts of the Jewish community which occur in descriptions which, while focusing on other places, mention Winchester in passing. Thus the *Illustrated Handbook to Southampton* has a brief section on the 'city of memories', including instructions to 'Notice the Jewry [Street], which tells of bygone intolerance'.[56] Fourth, the narrative, in spite of the recognition of a functioning synagogue and a sizeable community, is dominated by the theme of persecution. Following the earlier chronicles, especially that of Robert of Gloucester, the massacre of 1265 is deemed to have destroyed Winchester Jewry – of 'All the gywes of the town ... he ne leude alive non'.[57] In fact, some of the most interesting episodes and developments within Winchester Jewry occurred after 1265, as will be explored later. Fifth, Milner glossed his account of Winchester Jewry with religious language, referring to the Jews as 'that devoted people'. Later writers on Winchester also used Christian discourse when referring to the city's Jews, but their sentiment was, more often than not, hostile and lacked Milner's philosemitic impulse.

It was not until the late nineteenth century, and the development of a more professional approach to local and Jewish historiography that a fuller picture of Winchester Jewry emerged. As late as 1868, the *New Winchester Handbook* was prompted to devote a 'separate notice' to Jewry Street because of 'its ancient associations with the nation whose name it bears'. The material included in this section was based on romantic supposition about Jewish history, owing more perhaps to *The Merchant of Venice* than to historical accuracy. Jewry Street 'remind[ed] us of a time when in England, as still at

Rome, the Jews were confined to this quarter of the city'.[58] In fact, while to some extent concentrated around this particular street, Jews were free to live where they wished in Winchester and other English towns and cities. Later accounts of Winchester Jewry continued to refer to them living in a ghetto, implying far less social and economic integration on an everyday level than would have been the case.[59] In all other respects, the 1868 guide replicated earlier descriptions, relating how 'In the 12th and 13th centuries they appear to have been numerous in Winchester, until popular commotions, and a massacre of them by the Barons of England in the reign of Henry III, reduced or extirpated them. They had a synagogue in this street.'[60]

In the mid-Victorian era, outside Winchester itself, there was little knowledge of its medieval Jewish community. Indeed, the Reverend Moses Margoliouth's *History of the Jews in Great Britain* (1851) is interesting in the respect of *not* mentioning Winchester in his list of 'streets and walks, which are distinguished by the names Jewry ... which are to be found in London, Cambridge, Canterbury, Oxford, Leicester, Suffolk [and] York'.[61] Margoliouth's account was the first extensive history of medieval Anglo-Jewry written by a British Jew, albeit an apostate. As Margoliouth acknowledged of his own account, 'From the period of the death of Henry I to the time of the expulsion of the Jews ... [a] melancholy monotony pervades the history of these two hundred years'.[62] The first generation of British Jewish novelists, especially women, were also drawn to the medieval period and the suffering of the Jews. The location of such stories, following Walter Scott's *Ivanhoe* (1819), focused on the Jews of York. In 1839, for example, aged just sixteen and eighteen, the Moss sisters, Celia and Marion, published 'an historical poem' on 'The Massacre of the Jews at York' in 1190.[63] If not York, London provided the setting for fictionalised accounts of medieval Anglo-Jewry.

Such Jewish literary work on the medieval period, aside from allowing the opportunity of highlighting the nobility of the suffering Jews, also enabled a reflection on the improvement in their subsequent treatment, especially in England. In *The King's Physician and Other Tales* (1865), a collection that focused on the medieval period, Celia Moss (now Levetus) concluded the story of Mordecai, a rabbi in thirteenth-century London, with the following reflections:

> it would be useless to harrow up the feelings of the reader by details of suffering already too well known. These scenes were reacted through every Christian land, until, at length, the progress of civilization opened the eyes of the potentates of Europe to their true interest, while the introduction of the art of printing, and the consequent dissemination of education ... brought into action the principles of religious toleration, and paved the way for an improvement of the social condition of the Jews and the acknowledgment of those rights which had been so long and so unjustly withheld from them.[64]

Celia Moss and her sister were born and brought up in the Portsmouth Jewish community, just over twenty miles from Winchester. It is significant, therefore, that the stories within Celia's collection *The King's Physician*, which focus on medieval England, do not mention Winchester Jewry. This is especially so as one of them, *Neela: A Tale of Jews in England*, is located, if loosely, in Hampshire – the county in which she had grown up and published her first works. Yet rather than being set within Winchester Jewry, the story takes place in the fictional village of Chesterton, neighbouring Southampton, where a young woman, Neela, lives with her mother and her father, a rabbi. While mention is made of the court held at Winchester, there is no reference to its Jewish community – Neela's family are the only Jews in the story. It is a tale of false ritual murder accusation, with the opponents of Neela and her family chanting 'Down with the murdering Jews! Down with the sorcerers!'. The tale takes place the year after the Jews of Lincoln, in 1255, were accused of murdering a young boy. Moss's fictional protagonists are urged to 're-member Hugh of Lincoln'.[65] Indeed, in this respect Celia Moss's short story is a rejoinder to the legacy of Chaucer's *Prioress' Tale*, with its lines

> O yonge Hugh of Lincoln, slayn also
> With cursed Jews, as it is notable,
> For it nis but a litel whyle ago …

As Gavin Langmuir suggests, some 135 years on, the 'event did not seem distant to Chaucer', adding that as late as 1821 'the traditional story of Hugh's death made Charles Lamb fearful of entering a synagogue'.[66]

That Winchester Jewry escaped the attention of writers in the mid-nineteenth century, including those such as the Moss sisters who were both Jewish and geographically proximate, reflected the relative obscurity of this medieval community. Indeed, as late as 1893, in the founding prospectus of the Jewish Historical Society of England, the aim to throw 'fresh light upon the earliest history of English towns' listed ten examples but not Winchester.[67] The fragmentary nature of historical material on Winchester Jewry, or at least the inaccessibility of relevant primary sources, and its largely subordinate place in the collective memory of Winchester itself, meant that it lost out to York, Lincoln and London in the literary and historical imagination. By the end of the nineteenth century, however, the situation had, to some extent, altered. Rich evidence became available and fascinating episodes came to light enabling a fuller and multi-layered narrative of Winchester Jewry to emerge. Moreover, this 'new' material challenged the lachrymose representation of medieval English Jewry that continued to be the dominant theme in historiography and heritage representation. It further strengthened the idea of the exceptionality of Winchester's treatment of the Jews. Most important as a stimulus to fresh memory work beyond the stimulation provided by Jewry Street itself was the editing and translation of the chronicle of Richard of Devizes, a Benedictine monk at St Swithun's, the cathedral abbey of Winchester.

Richard of Devizes, ritual murder and Winchester

Described as 'one of the most interesting historical works of the twelfth century in England', Richard of Devizes' chronicle, or *Cronicon*, covers the period from King Richard's crowning in 1189 through to 1192 and the king leaving for the Holy Land. The modern translator of the *Cronicon*, John Appleby, suggests that Richard 'probably spent at least his adult life in the cloister of the Old Minster' in Winchester. A work of satire, with only two surviving copies, it was, Appleby suggests, 'a private production written for the entertainment of the friend to whom it is dedicated and unknown outside a narrow circle of friends'.[68] In his close and sophisticated reading of the text, Anthony Bale agrees that 'it is unlikely that [it] ever achieved a large readership', but suggests that it 'would seem to have been written for the amusement of those familiar with the Winchester area, its ecclesiastical politics and personalities, the Benedictines more generally, and those without a strong or indeed particularly loyal attitude towards the monarchy'.[69] It was not until the nineteenth century that the work became better known, edited for the English Historical Society in 1838 and the Rolls Series in 1886 and translated in versions published in 1848 and 1858.

Richard of Devizes' chronicles begin with an account of the attacks on the Jews made in 1189, following the coronation of Richard I, and close with a ritual murder allegation against Winchester Jews made in 1192. Both provide an opportunity to describe the Jews of Winchester and local responses to them. As Bale suggests, Richard's ritual murder account is 'both fascinating and unique'.[70] The *Cronicon*, by drawing out the absurd nature of the accusation and the dubious motivations of the Christians behind it, do not suggest that the Jews were guilty of this demonic crime. Nevertheless, Richard's chronicles, alongside a Pipe Roll of 1193 which outlines an allegation made against Winchester Jewry, 'preserve the space for rumour and fantasy'.[71]

Richard's first mention of Winchester is in relation to the mass murder of the Jews in London after the coronation. It was a 'holocaust' that was emulated in 'other towns and cities of the country' which 'with equal devotion … dispatched their bloodsuckers bloodily to hell … Winchester alone spared its worms'. The reason given by Richard for Winchester's restraint was that its people were 'prudent and far-sighted' and it was a city that 'always behaved in a civilised manner'. He added that the people of Winchester

> never did anything over-hastily, for fear that they might repent of it later, and they looked to the end of things rather than to the beginnings. They did not want partially to vomit forth the undigested mass violently and at their peril, even though they were urged to do so, when they were not ready. They hid it in their bowels, modestly (or naturally) dissumulating their disgust meanwhile, till at an opportune time for remedies they could cast out all the morbid matter once and for all.[72]

Much later in his narrative, Richard reminds his readers that 'Winchester should not be deprived of its just praise for having kept peace with the Jews'. He then constructs an equally powerful mythology of the significance of the city to the Jews. The Jews of Winchester were 'zealous, after the Jewish fashion, for the honour of their city'. Winchester was 'the Jerusalem of the Jews; in that city alone do they enjoy perpetual peace. That city is a school for those who want to live and fare well'.[73] At first, however, it seems that Richard argues that the Jews betrayed this hospitality: they 'brought upon themselves, according to the testimony of many people, the widely known reputation of having made a martyr of a boy in Winchester'.[74] As the story unravels, however, its ludicrous nature is increasingly made clear.

The story starts with a Jew in France who sends his servant boy to England. The Jew advises him to avoid London, where the 'number of parasites is infinite'. In a passage recently re-appropriated by those wanting to show the past diversity of the capital,[75] Richard parodies London as being a city full of 'Actors, jesters, smooth-skinned lads, Moors, flatterers, pretty boys, effeminates, pederasts, singing and dancing girls, quacks, belly-dancers, sorceresses, extortioners, night-wanderers, magicians, mimes, beggars, buffoons'.[76] Richard, as Appleby reminds us, is 'a man of strong prejudices, national, local and monastic, which he airs at every opportunity'. Thus York should also be given a wide berth as it 'is full of Scotsmen, filthy and treacherous creatures scarcely men'.[77] The boy takes the Jew's advice and goes to Winchester, obtaining work, through his former master's contacts, in a 'Jew's shop' in the city. He goes missing and the boy's friend accuses the Jew he is working for of not only killing him but also of 'eat[ing] him too'. The Winchester Jew is charged with the boy's murder. He denies the charge and the 'matter was dropped', though Richard adds that 'Gold won the judges' favour'.[78]

John Appleby suggests that this 'preposterous story of the Christian boy … begins with portentous solemnity and then fizzles out in a burst of mocking laughter at the absurdity of his own tale'.[79] Similarly, in the 1886 edition of the chronicles, Richard Howlitt suggests that 'Perhaps the best introduction to Richard as a writer may be found in his ludicrous account of the alleged crucifixion of a boy by the Winchester Jews. Obviously he does not believe the story'.[80] Yet as Nancy Partner suggests, Richard 'uses the Winchester case, not to express any sincere opinion about Jews or ritual murders, but to air his amusement with the conventions of ritual-murder literature' – especially Thomas of Monmouth's history of William of Norwich, and the attempt to create a local cult out of such fictions.[81] Bale adds that 'The idea of ritual murder is not used here in order to discuss the rights and wrongs of Judaism, but to mock and critique Christian fictions and the royal crusade underway in Palestine.'[82] If Richard's chronicles were written for a small audience of like-minded Benedictines, parodying the sucess of their 'confreres at Norwich, Gloucester and Bury St Edmonds in developing and marketing child-murder martyr cults',[83] once popularly rediscovered in the nineteenth century, they would, as with Chaucer's *Prioress' Tale*, have an (after)life of their own.

Anthony Bale's sophisticated analysis of Richard's chronicles concludes that they do not 'offer a history of Winchester's Jewish community'. Rather they give 'a partial account of the concerns, desires and fictions of a Winchester monk', using the 'paradigm of the written Jew as a tool for commentary concerning monarchy, orthodoxy and national identity'.[84] In turn, it is possible to argue that the often simplistic use of this multi-layered and fundamentally ironic source, from the second half of the nineteenth century onwards, tells us much more about the identities – national, local, ethnic and religious – of those writing about Winchester than it does about its medieval Jews and responses to them.

Charles Dellheim has pointed out the 'striking paradox' that 'as England became the first industrial nation, it became increasingly fascinated by its preindustrial past and in particular its medieval inheritance'.[85] This interest was manifested especially at a local level, with, from the 1840s onwards, the formation of archaeological, historical and architectural societies in various counties, cities, towns and even suburbs. In a period of rapid social change and the increasing dominance of London, such 'Historical and archeological explorations helped Victorians to deal with these problems because they furnished them with an invaluable source of provincial pride, identity, and consciousness'.[86]

One manifestation of all these trends was the *Historic Towns* series, edited by Edward Freeman and William Hunt, published in the 1880s and 1890s. It was within the volume on Winchester, written by G. W. Kitchin, dean of the city, that the first detailed modern narrative on its Jewish community was produced.[87] Kitchin's account made use of pipe rolls which provided the detail of everyday life and interaction of Winchester Jewry and their Christian neighbours. It was underpinned, however, by Richard's chronicles – the first attempt to integrate this remarkable source into a cohesive account of the medieval city and its life of letters and learning. Indeed, Kitchin believed that 'the best view of this Winchester can be got from a story which Richard of Devizes tells against the Jews'.[88] With such a claim, it is not surprising that his reading of the chronicles tended towards the literal. Certainly the irony that ran throughout the text passed by Kitchin.

Rather than understanding the text as a subtle use of the figure of 'the Jew' to explore the nature of Christian behaviour, including in Winchester itself, as well as the actions of King Richard, Kitchin interpreted it as a direct response to the money-lending activities of the local Jews and 'the burden of debt' that St Swithun's was experiencing. In 1198 Richard had noted that 'a Lombard Jew lent the Convent twenty-one marks'. As a result of such Jewish usury it was 'No wonder that the sarcastic pen of brother Richard longed to avenge itself.'[89] The 'revenge' taken by 'good Richard' is 'by telling the old story, so beautifully woven afterwards by Chaucer into his "Prioresses Tale", of the Christian boy sacrificed by the Jews'.[90]

Kitchin thus placed Richard's chronicles firmly in the canon of English (and anti-Jewish) literature. Nevertheless, he stopped short of believing the charge of ritual murder, although he does seem to have accepted the historicity of Richard's account: 'It is pleasant to learn that the man who was said to have sacrificed the French apprentice, when brought before the itinerant judges, escaped, for the judges asked for proof of the dark tale, and none was forthcoming'.[91] Charles Dellheim has written of the social significance of the *Historic Towns* series that although the individual volumes 'testify to the power of provincialism, their author's eagerness to stress the contribution of the locality to the nation and to show that its people were the most faithful representatives of the "English character" are also symptomatic of the nationalization of provincial cultures in the 1890s'.[92] In this particular case, however, Winchester's treatment of medieval Jewry, as exemplified by Richard's chronicle, enabled Kitchin and later writers to revel in the city's supposed difference to the rest of England. Accepting that Winchester was, in fact, 'for the Jews the Jerusalem of that land; here alone they enjoy perpetual peace', Kitchin exulted that 'The kind feeling at Winchester towards the Jews is apparently almost unique.'[93]

In contrast to the treatment of medieval Jewry elsewhere in England, Kitchin's interpretation of Richard's chronicles proved to be a self-affirming 'usable past' not only for those in Winchester but also in the newly-emerging world of Anglo-Jewish heritage and historiography. Indeed, the idea of the city as a unique haven of tolerance was mutually reinforced, in the late nineteenth and early twentieth centuries, by local and Jewish historians who swapped references and disseminated each other's work in their respective journals and newspapers. It must be stressed that, while not unchallenged, this reciprocal and complementary relationship was itself unusual. The situation in Winchester diverged from other major places of earlier Jewish settlement, especially Lincoln, which, until the 1930s attempted to exploit the Little St Hugh legend in both the local heritage industry and in the cathedral itself through the shrine to the child martyr.[94]

James Picciotto's *Sketches of Anglo-Jewish History* (1875), the first synthetic account since Margoliouth's some quarter of a century earlier, made no mention at all of Winchester, reflecting a London-centric bias that is still ongoing in studies of British Jewry.[95] In other respects, however, Picciotto's use of sources and overall analysis was far more sophisticated and heralded a new professional approach to the subject matter. By the 1880s, modern Anglo-Jewish historiography and heritage preservation developed rapidly and was manifested in the 1887 Anglo-Jewish Historical Exhibition held at the Albert Hall. The stimulus for this exhibition was partly to be found abroad, especially in Germany and the development of *Wissenschaft des Judentums* (Science of Judaism).[96] Nevertheless, the national and local context was more influential. In some respects, the motivation of the exhibition's organisers was defensive. Leading British historians, especially Goldwin Smith and Edward Freeman, attacked what they saw as the malevolent Jewish influence in the contemporary world. Smith, as David Cesarani has pointed out, 'buttressed his arguments that the Jews were clannish and obsessed with money by drawing on the history of the Jews in medieval England'.[97] Freeman's pathological portrayal of Winchester Jewry will feature in the next section of this chapter. The negative instrumentalisation of the past by such prominent historians led the *Jewish Chronicle* in 1881 to chastise 'the Jews of England [who] … have made no attempt worthy of the cause to utilise the masses of documentary material relating to the English Jews of the middle ages which have within late years been freely placed at the disposal of historical studies'.[98]

There were, however, more positive elements in this new burst of enthusiasm within British Jewry for studying its own past. It reflected an ethno-religious pride in place identity and the desire to show rootedness within British society. The parallel growth in local studies helped provide evidence of Jewish presence in the British past, especially in the medieval period. One direct output of the 1887 exhibition was the publication of the first bibliographical guide to Anglo-Jewish history, compiled by Joseph Jacobs and Lucien Wolf. It is significant that much of the secondary material listed in their bibliography relating to the medieval period came from recent local publications.[99] The rise of English provincialism in the second half of the nineteenth century, as reflected in historicisation and heritage preservation, is thus an important but hitherto neglected impetus in the development of Anglo-Jewish historiography.

From the 1880s through to the First World War, both the leading newspapers of British Jewry, the *Jewish Chronicle* and the *Jewish World*, gave space to detailed articles on the Jews of medieval England. Joseph Jacobs, whose work spanned the fields of social science, folklore, anthropology and history, was one of the most energetic respondents to the *Jewish Chronicle*'s call to the Jews of Britain to take responsibility for studying its deep past. Sometimes more enthusiastic than accurate, Jacobs wrote widely on medieval Anglo-Jewry, including on the Jews of Winchester. His work on that city owed a large debt to Dean Kitchin which Jacobs acknowledged. Thus Jacobs's first article on Winchester, published in the *Jewish Chronicle* in 1889, included Kitchin's translation 'of an important document relating to the early history of the Jews in this country which has hitherto been buried in the obscurity of a local newspaper, the *Hampshire Chronicle*'. Jacobs concluded this piece by echoing, within a Jewish sphere, Kitchin's *Cronicon*-inspired belief in local uniqueness: 'Winchester formed an exception to the general rule. For Winchester was always favourable to the Jews; it was almost alone in sparing them in the massacre following Richard I's ascension, and Richard of Devizes in an amusing passage calls Winchester the Jerusalem of the English Jews.'[100] Four years later, in a collection of translated Hebrew and Latin documents on the Jews of Angevin England, Jacobs reproduced the relevant section of the *Cronicon* under the heading 'Winchester does not join in the Massacres'.[101] Substance to the exceptionalist claim had been provided by Kitchin who had discovered that in 1268 the Mayor of Winchester, Simon le Draper,

> by the counsel and assent of the Bailiffs, citizens, and entire commonality of the said city, have received our beloved and faithful friend and special neighbour, Benedict, the Jew, the son of Abraham, into the full membership of our Liberty as a co-citizen and our co-Guildman of the Merchant Guild, and to all the privileges which belong to the said Liberty.

Jacobs concluded that this acceptance of Benedict 'reflects credit both on the Winchester guild and on the Winchester Jew'.[102]

The mutuality of local and Jewish descriptions of Winchester Jewry and its favourable treatment is neatly exemplified in what was an influential historical guide to the city, first published in 1903, entitled *Winchester Illustrated*. Partly stimulated by interest in the city following the King Alfred millenary celebrations two years earlier, it covered all periods of Winchester's past from the Romans onwards and devoted a five-page chapter to its 'Jewry'.[103] The chapter was, until the 1950s, the longest treatment by far of the medieval community and was, in essence, an integration of three sources – an article,

'Early Winchester Jews', from the *Jewish World* (which was later reproduced in the *Hampshire Chronicle*), a letter-essay from Alderman W. H. Jacob from the *Hampshire Chronicle* and documents, including the *Cronicon* and 1268 guild inclusion, used or translated by Dean Kitchin.

The anonymous article, 'Early Winchester Jews', was a remarkable piece of historical re-creation. The article was accompanied by an equally outlandish plan of the 'Jewish quarter'. It indicated an abundance of 'private' synagogues on either side of the street in addition to the major, and presumably public, synagogue itself. The plan, which gave 'a fair idea of the Jewish ghetto', thereby implied that these medieval streets were something akin to the East End of London at the turn of the twentieth century as known by the *Jewish World*'s historical correspondent.[104] Indeed, a sister article, no doubt by the same author, in this weekly newspaper, outlining a legal squabble between two Winchester Jews in 1195, suggested that 'We have here – several centuries back – the precursor of what occurs pretty often at the present day, when his Honor of Whitechapel County Court ... relegates a case for the decision of the Chief Rabbi or the Beth Din'.[105] The contemporary 'aliens question' never lurked too far from the minds of those who were writing about the Jews of medieval England.

The earlier *Jewish World* article itself started by extrapolating (without foundation) from a brief statement in a thirteenth-century French rabbinic text, the *Sefer Mitzvot Gadol* (or Semag), that 'Passing over the sea leading to England by way of Dieppe occupied a single day if there was a fair wind'. This quotation from the Semag had been taken from Jacobs' and Wolf's bibliography which, in turn, they had found in a study of German Jewry published in 1880. Such 'borrowing' neatly revealed the cross-fertilisation of the burgeoning historical interest in German Jewry, Anglo-Jewry and English local studies.[106] Beyond the impressive but rather spurious citation from the Semag, the origins of the 'Early Winchester Jews' subsequently provided in the *Jewish World* were imaginary. They wrested purely, if entertainingly, on romantic conjecture:

> During the two centuries that spanned the years 1090 and 1290 a large colony of Jews found a settlement in the famous city of Winchester, the ancient capital of the kingdom. We can trace them in their wanderings. Leaving at times Rouen, Caen, Mandeville, and other spots in Normandy, they made their way seawards to Dieppe, embarked in vessels carrying produce to the English shores, and landed safely at Southampton.

The author's fantasy did not end at the arrival of these Jews in England. Indeed, the description of Winchester out-eulogised many written by local writers: 'A few short hours inland ... brought the French pilgrims to a haven of rest. Passing St. Giles's Hill, they crossed the Itchen, entered the city by the East gate, looked admiringly at the pretty meads surrounding the Cathedral, and made for the High-street, with its busy shops, stalls and shambles.' The foundation myth ended by stating that these Jews 'stopped midway in the High-street, selected a nice spot adjacent to the market, a thoroughfare known then as Scowertenstrete (Shoemakers' Row) and settled down in their new quarters'.[107]

Reference to the cathedral and to the 'French pilgrims' finding a 'haven of rest' in Winchester suggest a Christian authorship of this anonymous account and it was almost certainly the work of the Reverend Henry Paine Stokes, later the first non-Jewish president of the Jewish Historical Society of England (1914–16).[108] Undoubtedly, the positive, quasi-redemptive image of the city presented in the article – Winchester Jewry lived in 'comparative peace till the final expulsion in 1290'[109] – facilitated its prominence within *Winchester Illustrated*. Thereafter, the *Jewish World* description, alongside that in the *Cronicum*, were incorporated into general narratives of the city's history in the first decades of the twentieth century. The earlier spare and gloomy descriptions of the former inhabitants of Jewry Street and their massacre by Simon de Montfort now gave way to an embellished celebration, confirming Winchester exceptionalism. Sidney Heath's *Winchester* (1910), for example, asserted that

> 'Jewry' Street recalls to our memory the early settlement of the Jews in Winchester, for the citizens seem to have been more kindly disposed towards this persecuted race than the majority of English cities at an early period in their history. Richard of Devizes, in 1189 [*sic*], called Winchester the 'Jerusalem of the Jews', and, writing of the massacre and plunder of the Jews in London and other cities, said: 'Winchester alone, the people being prudent and circumspect and the city always acting mildly, spared its vermin'.[110]

Close to plagiarising the *Jewish World* article, Heath continued that the Jews had lived in Winchester between 1090 and 1290. Yet, unlike the text from which it was taken, no mention was made by Heath of why the latter date marked the end of the community. Instead, the focus was on its triumphant arrival and successful settlement. The Jews landed 'at Southampton and ma[de] their way up the Itchen until they came in sight of the old capital of the kingdom. Crossing the river, they entered the city by the East Gate, and finally chose as their abiding-place a site near the north walls ... The community soon could boast of a synagogue, and were the possessors of several schools'.[111]

The uncritical, and self-serving reading of Richard's *Cronicon*, augmented by the fiction of the *Jewish World* narrative and the example of Benedict the guildsman, were thus utilised by those such as Telford Varley who promoted Winchester as a 'delightful old mediaeval city'.[112] According to Varley, 'the Jews were not merely tolerated here, but actually welcomed'.[113] For Anglo-Jewish historians, a soothing counter-example against the 'almost uninterrupted record of deeds of blood and rapine'[114] that represented the medieval period was no doubt welcome, especially in a city such as Winchester with its wider national and religious significance. For local writers, such as Varley, it enabled Winchester Jewry to be presented as a quaint cosmopolitan addition to medieval life with the city being able to bask in its past benevolence.

It was left to M. D. Davis, one of the key figures to 'research and publish Anglo-Jewish history in a systematic way' from the 1870s,[115] to point out the groundless basis of this mythology:

> Certain it is that if persecution, imprisonment, and forfeitures were not rampant in Winchester, there was no *raison d'etre* for a portion of the ancient castle being styled 'Turris Judaeorum', for in this tower many a Jew pined away till freedom brought him again into the light of day, or the hand of the hangman terminated his sufferings. Winchester was not then 'the Jerusalem of the Jews in which they enjoyed perpetual peace'.

Davis's article on 'Early Winchester Jews' appeared in the *Jewish Chronicle* in September 1892 and was reproduced in the *Hampshire Chronicle* several months later.[116] Yet his grim counter-narrative of despoilation and ritual murder accusations fell on barren ground. With regard to Winchester, Davis's lachrymose history failed to provide a usable past. It was the later and romanticised article of the same title, appearing in the *Jewish World*, that served this function.

There were, however, alternative interpretations of Richard's *Cronicon* that read into it evidence of Jewish perfidy. In particular, the slipperiness of his text in general enabled some who believed in the possibility of Jewish ritual murder to use the *Cronicon* as evidence of this diabolic crime, despite its ironic intention. Davis was aware that 'Twice at least, if not more, the Jews of Winchester had to meet the accusation of having martyred Christian children in order to provide blood for their Paschal rites; and twice at least, in 1192 and again in 1232, the local community was plunged into distress through these charges'. Davis took Richard's *Cronicon* at face value and, in defensive mode, referred to a non-Jewish historian, Walter Rye, in respect of the earlier accusation, who 'in crisp language scoffs at its absurdity'.[117] Rather than paranoia, the reason behind Davis's nervousness can be explained by the persistence of belief in late nineteenth-century England that Jews *had* carried out such crimes in the medieval period. Indeed, a clear scholarly example was provided four years after his article was published.

In 1896, Augustus Jessopp and M. R. James translated and edited *The Life and Miracles of St William of Norwich by Thomas of Monmouth.*[118] Explaining the ritual murder allegation at Norwich, James, director of the Fitzwilliam Museum and Fellow and Senior Dean of King's College, Cambridge, 'hypothesized, without any respectable evidence, that some bad Jew … might have reverted to "half-forgotten practices of a darker age"'. Gavin Langmuir has labelled such interpretations by late nineteenth- and twentieth-century scholars as part of the 'historiographic crucifixion' of medieval Anglo-Jewry.[119] In his introduction to *The Life and Miracles*, published by Cambridge University Press, James's treatment of the *Cronicon* is remarkably naive and literal, especially as the translators and editors of Richard's text had underlined its ironic nature. James simply regarded it as a real martyrdom at Winchester as 'reported by Richard of Devizes'. Here was 'contemporary evidence' and the 'victim was a French boy' although the 'body was never produced'.[120]

James's analysis was not unusual for the late Victorian period. His ability to convince himself that some Jews, though not the whole community acting in conspiracy, had been responsible for such crimes in the past was inspired by both the search for a rational explanation for this common medieval accusation and a lingering influence of a discourse that imagined 'the Jew' as somehow different and dangerous. Within H. D. Traill's influential collection, *Social England* (1893), published three years earlier, the Reverend W. H. Hutton, a leading historian at St John's College, Oxford, similarly commented on ritual murder allegations that it was 'difficult to refuse all credit to stories so circumstantial and so frequent'.[121] Such mainstream scholarship was not motivated simply by antisemitism. Even if somewhat grudgingly, James acknowledged that it would be unlikely in the case of William that the 'educated Jews of Norwich *in their corporate capacity* would perpetrate this crime … [as they] would be running a quite unnecessary risk, and there is nothing to shew that the practice was a recognised one at any period of their history' [original emphasis]. Hutton also commented that 'the tales are too many for them all to be true, and most of them may be dismissed as wholly fictions'.[122] Ultimately, Colin Holmes, in a survey of the ritual murder accusation in Britain between 1880 and 1939 is correct to argue that 'A belief in the charge had an amorphous existence in British society, but its most tenacious home was in committed anti-Semitic groups whose ideology never exercised a wide appeal.'[123] Nevertheless, those whose *Weltanschauung* was shaped by sheer Jew-hatred would utilise the ambiguity found within works such as James and Traill to give legitimacy to their accounts of Jewish ritual murder. Furthermore, the case study of Winchester, where the Jewish community suffered the accusation in 1192, 1225 and 1232,[124] reveals, through local heritage production, how the work of fringe antisemitic groupuscules and individuals could percolate into wider society and help cast further doubt on past Jewish innocence.

In 1920, The Britons, the first organisation set up in Britain with the sole intention of promoting and publishing conspiratorial antisemitism, published *The Jews' Who's Who*. Within a section devoted to 'Landmarks in History', it provided a chronology of the 'Jew conquest of England' including the dates 1192 and 1232 when 'Winchester Jews [were] accused of Ritual Murder'.[125] The Britons provided the intellectual framework for a wider-based organisation led by Arnold Leese, the Imperial Fascist League, formed in 1928 and notable for its pro-Nazism and virulent racist antisemitism. Within its publications, allegations of Jewish ritual murder, past and present, were made regularly.[126] Leese acknowledged that some charges may have been trumped up 'where death may have been due to causes other than ritual murder and the Jews blamed for it; but the case of St Hugh, particularly, was juridically decided, and the Close and Patent Rolls of the Realm record definitely cases at London, Winchester and Oxford. There seems no reason to doubt that many cases of ritual murder have been unsuspected and even undiscovered.'[127] The ultimate proof for Leese was that the crime of Jewish ritual murder came out of a 'racial urge'. When it came to evidence, Leese asked his readers: 'Whom do *you* believe – the Jews or the English?'[128]

One of Leese's protégés, and a leading figure in the Imperial Fascist League during the 1930s, was John Hooper Harvey. In a 1936 article entitled 'The Jewish Horror', published in *The Fascist*, Harvey wrote that 'To those who see in past history a useful lesson for today, the existence of previous attempts by bodies of Jews to overthrow the stable government of Aryan states, must complete the chain of proof linking the Jews with present unrest.'[129] Closely monitored by the British security forces during the Second World War, Harvey wrote to Leese in 1940 that 'I don't want to be ruled by Germany or any other foreigner, but at a pinch even that is preferable to being ground to pulp under the heel of the Jew financier, and his pimps and proselytes.'[130] In the context of these statements it is perhaps surprising that Harvey, the son of a historical architect, was described after his death in 1997 in the liberal *Independent* as 'the greatest British historian of Gothic architecture of the 20th century'. He was labelled 'genius' by the journal of the British Records Association, its obituarist adding that this title still did 'no justice to a man who added an incredible breadth of learning, fluency in several languages and deep sensitivity to his powers of painstaking accuracy and analysis'.[131] It is hard to correlate such alleged research professionalism with the profound prejudice articulated, for example, in Harvey's obsessive and unchanging belief in Jewish ritual murder which was voiced most clearly in his bestselling and much reprinted textbook, *The Plantagenets* (1948). Referring to the Jews of medieval England within this text, Harvey emphasised that they were 'a highly organized community' who formed 'an exotic mass segregated from that united national body which it was [Edward I's] purpose to form'. Alongside the 'economic difficulties caused by the presence of this alien body was a series of most sinister crimes committed against Christian children, including murder (allegedly ritual) and forcible circumcision'. Harvey insisted that 'a number of instances of mysterious child-murder undoubtedly did occur in twelfth- and thirteenth-century England, at least ten being well authenticated between 1144 and 1290'. Amongst these, and following Leese closely, Harvey included the case in Winchester in 1232 which was 'mentioned in official records'. Harvey concluded that in such light 'it is difficult to doubt the statesmanship of Edward's decision [in 1290] to remove the whole Jewish community'.[132]

When Harvey published *The Plantagenets* he was consultant architect to Winchester College. From 1950 to 1964 he was the College archivist. It is evident that post-1945 Harvey was a prominent figure within the city's historical world, his work on medieval architecture, for example, included in an anthology of 'a thousand years of comment, anecdote and allusion' on Winchester Cathedral.[133] His influence in shaping the representation of medieval Jews, or their absence, in the physical heritage of Winchester will be examined in the final section of this chapter. Here his impact, alongside others who had suggested Jewish guilt with regard to the ritual murder accusation when confronting sources such as the *Cronicon*, can be detected in a publication of the Winchester Preservation Trust, *Jewry Street Winchester* (1984).

Harvey's insinuations about Jewish ritual murder were deliberate and were part of the ideological baggage that he continued to carry from his days indulging in extreme racist politics. Far more innocent, but revealing of the 'amorphous existence' of the charge in British society as referred to by Holmes, was the treatment within *Jewry Street Winchester*. Relegated to a paragraph within the booklet, the 'history of the Jews in Winchester' presented was deeply problematic and proved distressing to the Jewish community:

> Their skills in finance led them to be hated by the barons who borrowed money. Records indicate some Jews were executed in the 12th and 13th centuries for 'having martyred christian children to provide blood for paschal rites'. All Jews were to be expelled at the end of the 13th century but, as in Germany and Holland, evidence remains, in the following centuries which points to their continuing financial skill in both banking and the retail business.[134]

In response to the booklet, the *Jewish Chronicle*, in a piece entitled 'Blood libelled again', urged the Board of Deputies of British Jews 'to take the authors to task for perpetuating such *quoted* arrant nonsense'.[135] In fact, the quote concerning ritual murder was taken from Davis's 1892 article on Winchester Jewry which had, ironically, appeared originally in the *Jewish Chronicle*. What was inexcusable in the booklet was quoting Davis out of context – the pioneer Anglo-Jewish historian had made clear that these were false accusations. Indeed, Davis had only referred to the allegations of 1192 and 1232 to show the dangers of accepting uncritically the *Cronicon*'s myth of Winchester as 'Jerusalem the golden' for medieval Anglo-Jewry.[136] What the *Jewry Street Winchester* booklet had revealed was the failure of the heritage industry, however well-meaning, to deal with either the trauma inflicted and prejudices revealed from another age or the subtlety of medieval sources, such as Richard's *Cronicon*, that had parodied such superstitions.

Some historians of the Holocaust have (understandably) focused on the rescuers of Jews in order to provide relief amidst the suffering and inhumanity that was at the heart of this catastrophic event. Similarly, as Robert Levine argues, modern scholars, 'recoiling in justifiable horror at the unrelenting abuse to which medieval Jews were subjected ... have searched diligently through chronicles, histories, poems, and miscellaneous documents, to find some traces of pro-Semitic sentiments expressed within the Christian community'. In this respect, Richard's *Cronicon* has played a particularly important role.[137] Thus for Antonia Gransden, Richard's choice of a Jew 'as the vehicle for the panegyric is curious and seems to reflect pro-Jewish sentiments'. She adds that Richard was 'obviously interested in the Jewish community in Winchester – he praised the citizens of Winchester for tolerating and protecting the Jews in the city when elsewhere in England Jewish lives and property were the object of violent attack'.[138] In contrast, Colin Richmond quotes Richard's account of the 1190 massacres and his descriptions of Jews as sons of the Devil, 'bloodsuckers' and 'worms' to suggest that 'Here is the familiar temptation intellectuals fall for: the pornography of bad language. When the ideologues speak like this synagogues burn.'[139]

As this section has illustrated, Richard's *Cronicon* was the most important source during the late nineteenth and early twentieth centuries in reconstructing the place of the Jews in medieval Winchester. Coinciding with the burgeoning of Anglo-Jewish history and local studies, Richard's text was subject to a range of interpretations and a variety of uses. From those promoting the city at a time of growing provincial pride and tourist visiting, it is not surprising that the positive interpretation put forward by Gransden as late as 1974 was dominant. In contrast, no contemporaries had the later analytic insights of Colin Richmond when confronting Richard's *Cronicon*. Indeed, Richard's abusive language, especially the phrase 'Winchester alone spared its worms', was repeated frequently (and without thought for its offensiveness) in locally-produced guides to and histories of Winchester until the Second World War.

Anthony Bale has suggested with regard to the *Cronicon* that 'Anti-semitism is rarely uncomplicated and, in this case, it is more helpful to think in terms of fluid and supple boundaries rather than binarisms of philo-semitism and anti-semitism.'[140] He concludes that rather than a historical source on Winchester Jewry it only provides a (partial) insight into the 'concerns, desires and fictions of a Winchester monk'.[141] In similar vein, and moving forward eight hundred years to the late nineteenth century, one can argue that the later utilisation of the *Cronicon* tells us more about Anglo-Jewish and local Winchester identities than it does about medieval Winchester Jewry. And just as Richard's text drifts between and beyond the 'binarisms of philo-semitism and anti-semitism', so references to it in the late Victorian and Edwardian era reveal the fundamental ambivalence in British society towards the Jews. This is neatly illustrated in the final example to be explored in this section, the Reverend A. G. L'Estrange's *Royal Winchester: Wanderings in and about the Ancient Capital of England* (1889).[142]

L'Estrange's account of his eight days in Winchester in itself revealed a second phase development in the production of late Victorian guide books and topographic descriptions. It self-consciously built on the existing literature, and through a dialogue between the author and his companion, 'Mr Hertford', engaged in constant debate about the nature of Winchester's past, as reflected in its surviving heritage. With regard to the Jews, by having a guide in two voices, conflicting emotions and assumptions could be articulated in a free and revealing manner.

The first mention of the Jews in *Royal Winchester* was gratuitous. The two visitors gain permission to enter the tower of the medieval Westgate where they come across the old city treasure chest. L'Estrange explains how this huge object had 'long chains and rings by which it could be carried about like the Ark of the Israelites', prompting the following dialogue:

> 'From what we read of the propensities of the Jews', said Mr. Hertford, 'I should say they would have preferred such an ark as this to their own'.

> 'Well, some of them would, perhaps', I replied. 'Their ark carried the law and holy things, but this contained the coin, and also the gold and silver plate of the city.'[143]

Amidst the forced humour was an attempt to project the avaricious tendencies of medieval Winchester onto the Jews. Although the author queries the stereotyped money-obsessed Jew outlined by his companion, his own prejudices in this respect were revealed in the book's major treatment of Winchester Jewry. Prompted into such memory work by 'Jewry Street, the

ghetto', in a remarkable sentence L'Estrange added that it was 'a name recalling the wealth, rapacity, and persecutions of this peculiar people'.[144] Not surprisingly from this start, L'Estrange then developed a narrative of Winchester
Jewry which managed to combine and predict the lachrymose approach of
M.D.Davis with the pathological analysis of John Hooper Harvey.

According to L'Estrange's narrative, at first the Jews 'managed to obtain
property and to increase in this city'. These Jews were then 'taxed according
to their ability', had their wealth removed and finally 'At a Parliament held
here [*sic*] in 1290, the Jews were expelled from the country.' L'Estrange, as an
outsider to the city, had no imperative to defend Winchester, and he refused
to accept Richard of Devizes' claim that it alone had 'spared its vermin'. The
firm impression is given, however, that the Jews, because of their behaviour,
deserved their punishment and final expulsion. To emphasise further their
problematic nature, L'Estrange added that 'In 1232 a story was circulated
that a boy had been tortured and murdered by them.' Such a bold statement was then immediately countered, but in a backhanded and qualified
manner which further emphasised their otherness and danger to medieval
society. The allegation, suggested Mr. Hertford, was 'Invented, perhaps, by
their debtors'.[145]

Bale suggests that 'We must not think of Richard's *Cronicon* and its portrait of Winchester Jewry as "true history"'.[146] Nevertheless, if the account is
purely fictive, the impact of the ritual murder accusation on the Jews then,
and thereafter, was very real. While revising his earlier view, Colin Richmond
still warns that while 'Richard of Devizes may or may not have been an antisemite ... [a]las his mental agility seems only to have been for the amusement of a handful of fellow monks, the only ones who might have got
the point, so that the old adage of intellectuals contemplating their navels
while synagogues burn survives the challenge'.[147] In this respect, Nicholas
Vincent's study of Peter Des Roches (Bishop of Winchester) and the Jews
puts L'Estrange's cavalier treatment of the ritual murder accusation into a
sober perspective:

> At some point in 1232 a year-old boy, named Stephen, was found strangled near
> St Swithun's Priory, in Winchester. According to those who found the body, it
> had been dismembered, castrated, and its eyes and heart plucked out. The boy's
> mother promptly fled the city, but popular suspicion fixed on Abraham Pinche, a
> Jew who, it was claimed, had purchased the child from its nurse so as to carry out
> some sort of crucifixion ritual. The sheriff was forced to imprison the city's entire
> Jewry, probably as much for their own protection as for anything else.

The Jewish community was then released on payment of a fine. Pinche, who
had also been accused of such crimes in 1225, finally 'failed to escape the

citizens' retribution' and was hanged, in front of his synagogue, in 1236.[148]

Dealing with this execution, M. D. Davis in 1892 wondered about the impact it must have had on Winchester Jewry: 'Woe and lamentation seized his congregation. They implored the royal clemency in vain ... "No", thundered forth the king, "he must be hanged in his own courtyard before the Scola (Shool), and there bury him". The community had to yield, and Abraham had to rest in unconsecrated ground under the gallows. Poor Abraham Pinch!' If Davis's narrative must be regarded as literary embellishment as much as that of Richard of Devizes, it remains that the former was writing about real Jews. For Davis, Pinch was one of the '16 leading individuals swaying the destinies of the Winchester Jews 667 years ago'.[149] In contrast, for J. A. Giles, the first editor and translator of the *Cronicon*, writing in 1841, Richard's reference to blood-suckers was annotated for his earlier Victorian readership as 'Jews, so called probably from their usurious practices'.[150] The next section deals with the struggle, as outlined in these two differing Victorian engagements with the *Cronicon*, to transform the image of Winchester Jewry from undifferentiated 'rapacious' usurers to flesh and blood human beings.

From rapacious usurer to feminist heroine?

In 1960, H. G. Richardson, justifying his study of English Jewry in the period before the reign of Henry III, argued that the need for 'a corrective of current beliefs is manifest'. To illustrate his point, Richardson quoted a sentence from the medieval volume in the *Oxford History of England* (1951), written by A. L. Poole:

> The ostentation which possession of great wealth enabled the Jews to display, and their unconcealed contempt for the practices of Christianity, made them an object of universal dislike; as usurers, moreover, they had gained a strangle-hold on the recently founded monastic houses whose splendid buildings they had financed, and on many of the smaller aristocratic families ...[151]

Richardson then proceeded to demolish Poole's assertions and generalisations. Six years later, Gavin Langmuir developed Richardson's point further in a more systematic analysis of 'Majority History and Postbiblical Jews'.[152]

Langmuir highlighted how, in representing the medieval period, English historians in the nineteenth and twentieth centuries tended to exaggerate the economic role of the Jews, placing them 'in a clearly unfavorable light in the English saga'. He concluded that, in general, 'majority historiography as it relates to Jews has been marked by lack of interest and by ignorance, when it has not also been marked by derogatory attitudes'.[153] Following Langmuir, Colin Richmond refers to Sir James Holt, President of the Royal Historical

Society of England from 1980 to 1984, and his book, *The Northerners* (1961), which refers to the 'unwholesome conflict with the rapacity of the Jew'. Richmond adds, 'We are bound to inquire: what was Professor Holt thinking of?'[154] Langmuir carefully states that 'Most majority historians may not have been notably prejudiced personally, but they have been influenced by the prevailing attitudes of their society.'[155] Similarly, Richmond is not intent on particularly singling out Holt or other major British historians of the medieval period. Instead, his point is to underline how, while 'Jewish history permeates European history', its absence or distortion in the historiography of medieval England 'tells us at once a great deal about Englishness'.[156] This section, by adding the extra dimension of local identities, will explore whether historians and others have overcome the description provided in 1889 by the Reverend L'Estrange of Winchester Jewry as wealthy, rapacious and peculiar. By comparing the descriptions of Winchester Jewry by both non-Jews and Jews, it will enable an analysis of Langmuir's statement that historians of the majority, inheriting 'a historiographic tradition hostile or ignorant of Jews, or both, and writing for a society little interested in Jewish history or more or less hostile to Jews ... have been little attracted to Jewish history, little inspired even to read the work of Jewish historians, let alone study the matter for themselves'.[157]

Edward Freeman, as Regius Professor of History at Oxford University, provides a useful starting point in identifying the 'majority history' of Winchester Jewry. Hugh MacDougall in his *Racial Myth in English History* (1982), suggests that in the nineteenth century, 'Of all professions none served the cause of progress and Anglo-Saxonism more faithfully than historians.'[158] Within this group Freeman is described as a 'formidable champion of Teutonic excellence ... His firm convictions on the ethnic superiority and providential calling of the modern Anglo-Saxons led him at times to the extreme limits of racism.' MacDougall illustrates how this manifested itself particularly against the Irish and Negroes,[159] but, as David Feldman suggests, it extended also to the Jews. In the mind of Freeman, 'The Jews, their nationality underscored by religious particularity, had been shown to be unassimilable to the wider European family of Christian nations.'[160]

Freeman drew his examples for such beliefs from throughout history – in his prolific writings on the middle ages as well as mid-Victorian England. In his treatment of medieval England, rather than ignore their presence, Freeman noted that the 'Jews meet us at every turn in the twelfth and thirteenth centuries'. His narrative of Jewish arrival and activities in England in that period was pathological:

among the endless classes of adventurers whom the Conquest brought to try their luck in the conquered land, came men of a race whom Normans and Englishmen alike looked on as cut off from all national and religious fellowship. In the wake of the Conqueror the Jews of Rouen found their way to London, and before long we find settlements of the Hebrew race in the chief cities and boroughs of England, at York, Winchester, Lincoln, Bristol [and] Oxford ...

While these Jews were 'Hated, feared, and loathed', Freeman was anxious to add that they were 'too deeply feared to be scorned or oppressed, they stalked defiantly among the people of the land, on whose wants they throve'.[161] Within this picture of the privileged and exploiting Jew, the settlement at Winchester is given a particular significance by Freeman. The city, argued this prominent and highly respected historian, was, within medieval England, simply 'their Jerusalem'.[162] Here, Richard's *Cronicon* was being utilised not to pontificate on either the alleged tolerance of Winchester towards its 'virmin', or to explore the veracity of ritual murder accusations, but as evidence and proof of the malevolent, conspiratorial, alien financial presence of the 'Jew' who had come to 'own' this important medieval city.

Freeman, as an academic historian and political commentator, was well known. His writings, however, did not have the same popular appeal as our second example of majority history writing, Hilaire Belloc. If Belloc's historical writing owed more to imagination than research, he more than matched Freeman in the area of prejudice. A Catholic who was strongly influenced by the anti-Dreyfusards, Belloc shared Freeman's belief that the Jews were unassimilable and a danger to society, even if his form of racism was different to the historian's Anglo-Saxonism. In *The Old Road (From Canterbury to Winchester)*, published in 1904 and much reprinted thereafter, Belloc described the trail of ancient men 'which was at once their chief mystery and their only passage to the rest of their race – from Hampshire to the Straits of Dover'.[163] To Belloc, as to so many others, Winchester was a special place. 'It preserves, from its very decay, a full suggestion of its limitless age. Its trees, its plan, and the accent of the spoken language in its streets are old ... [T]he memory of Winchester is held close in a rigidity of frost which keeps intact the very details of the time in which it died'.[164]

Within this description of a city that 'is still half barbaric, still Norman in its general note',[165] Belloc confronted the place of the medieval Jewish community in Winchester. Describing the settlement as a 'sort of Ghetto', Belloc focused on the wealth and power of the Jews. For Belloc, who was simultaneously campaigning against what he perceived as malevolent Jewish political and economic influence in Edwardian Britain,[166] the ghetto had a significance for medieval Winchester which was both topographic and financial. Jewry Street was symbolic of the alien otherness and extreme commercial control exercised by its inhabitants:

> The whole stream of traffic which passed out from the capital to the rest of England went through the lane of the moneylenders, and we may say with certitude that the north gate, the limit of that lane, was the starting-point of the Old Road.[167]

The influence of Belloc and Freeman, and their emphasis on Jewish usury, was long-lasting. It was to be found as late as 1953 in Hugh Ross Williamson's *The Ancient Capital*, subtitled 'an historian in search of Winchester'. Williamson, a former Mosleyite and editor of the *Bookman*,[168] devoted a chapter of his study to the Jews. They are immediately described as being different: the Jews are an 'anomoly' within Winchester. Williamson, unlike Belloc, acknowledged that Winchester Jewry did not live in a ghetto, utilising the *Cronicon* to show that the tolerant and welcoming 'attitude of Winchester toward the Jews must have been unique'.[169] Yet the point of such emphasis was to indicate how this hospitality had been abused by the Jews. Williamson claimed that the 'annoyance' to the Christians caused by the Jews 'was probably less theological than economic. The lowest rate of interest the Jews charged seems to have been about 43 per cent and it was usually much higher.'[170] What is particularly revealing, however, about Williamson's narrative was his utilisation of Edward Freeman's work to justify his portrayal of the Jews as more oppressive than oppressed. 'Freeman's picture of the Jews', argued Williamson, was 'worth quoting, if only because he was writing *accurately* in the days before the current fashion of distorting past history in the interests of contemporary ideologies' [my emphasis]. The expulsion of the Jews, concluded Williamson, was directly attributable to their exploitative and damaging usury.[171]

Williamson's belief that what would later be termed 'political correctness' was standing in the way of understanding, post-Second World War, of the *real* position occupied by Jews in the medieval world, ultimately tells us more about this author, a former 'fellow travellor' of the extreme right, than it does about his subject matter. As we have seen, Holocaust-inspired sensitivity certainly was not evident in the work of major British historians such as Poole and Holt during the 1950s and 1960s. There seems little restraint on the latter when he wrote that 'Few men were unscathed by the financial operations of the Jews.'[172] Yet it would be wrong to suggest there was no self-awareness in the Nazi era and after amongst those confronting the presence of medieval Winchester Jewry. Jewish New Year in 1935 was marked by the *Hampshire Chronicle* with an article on the 'Jews in Ancient Winchester'.[173] It started by noting that 'Persecution of the Jews by the Nazi Party in Germany is the subject of frequent comment in our daily newspapers; let us, therefore, glance at Winchester's ancient history with reference to the Jewish people.'

This prompt to memory work was followed by a balanced account that high-lighted both the integration and the persecution of the Jews in Winchester and medieval England as a whole. If the focus was on the wealth of the Jews, their treatment and final expulsion was, in contrast to Williamson's later account, presented as undeserving. Nevertheless, the article ended redemp-tively: 'Happily the 19th and 20th centuries have seen England treating the Jews with the greatest possible respect, one becoming Prime Minister, and a vast number given titles and many other honours.'[174] Here, if the contrast with the medieval period was drawn explicitly, the diffence between England and Germany with regard to the Jews was also implicit.

Yet it should not be assumed that Williamson's account was, in 1953, be-yond the pale. The *Hampshire Review* greeted the *Ancient Capital* by sug-gesting that it 'should be read and savoured at leisure. It is likely to make the lover of this gracious old city think anew about many things taken for granted. This in itself is sufficient justification for the book.'[175] His chapter on the Jews was particularly singled out in this respect. But it was in the same journal, in winter 1954/55, that the most extensive treatment of Winchester Jewry, until the late twentieth century, was to appear, authored by the city's first archivist, Barbara Carpenter Turner, probably the most important fig-ure in the Winchester heritage and history world after 1945.[176] On the one hand Carpenter Turner's article maintained the tradition of 'majority histo-ry' with respect to Winchester established by Freeman by focusing on Jewish moneylending. On the other, it represented a fundamental break with the pathological approach of Freeman, Belloc and Williamson by placing Jewish financial activity in a positive light.[177]

Carpenter Turner's motivation for writing the history of Winchester Jewry is not known. There is, however, no direct or even indirect evidence of her writing as a response to what would soon be known as the Holocaust. In 1942, the Reverend Michael Adler wrote of Benedict the Gildsman, 'the only Jew in pre-Expulsion days to be highly honoured by his Christian neigh-bours', that 'the men of the city of Winchester stand out as the one com-munity of the Kingdom that showed its liberality of spirit in this exceptional way'.[178] It does not seem far-fetched to suggest that the murderous context of the continent was weighing on Adler's mind in his address to the Jewish Historical Society of England (JHSE) (most of Polish Jewry, for example, was exterminated in 1942). What Winchester was to medieval England, as outlined by Adler, was now represented by liberal Britain in relation to a world hostile to the Jews. In contrast, it would seem that Barbara Carpenter Turner's interest in medieval Jewry came out of an admiration for what she perceived as their entrepreneurial talents. Indeed, in contrast to Freeman et al., she could be described as an economic philosemite. Carpenter Turner was an independently-minded local Conservative politician, twice Mayor of Winchester. She clearly admired those in history who had showed economic innovation and initiative. As an economic liberal, Carpenter Turner believed that the English Channel, while acting as a 'vital defence' in time of war, was also, to Hampshire, 'an important means of communication, bringing to the county new production of trade and industry, new ideas, and new peoples'. Carpenter Turner thus not only wrote many times about the Jews and included them prominently in her histories of Winchester and Hampshire as a whole. She also showed similar empathy and respect for other religious minority groups such as the Huguenots. Carpenter Turner was especially interested in Henri de Portal, a Huguenot who, as noted earlier in this study, established 'One of Hampshire's most successful industries'. This was the paper-making mill near Whitchurch, opened in 1712, which was to be the foundations of a business that was to make notes for the Bank of England.[179] Her progressive views, especially when compared to many of her contemporaries in the historical world, on the place and significance of those of immigrant and refugee origin, was articulated succinctly when addressing the Winchester Historical Association in 1962. Carpenter Turner opened her lecture on the Jews of the medieval city by arguing that:

> Much of the history of our English towns is the history of minorities. The rise and decline of the Gild Merchant, the history of the Craft Gilds, even the fortunes of the very *Commune* and Corporation itself are in some ways the story of the failure or success of differing kinds of minorities.

Reflecting, perhaps, her strong Anglican faith, manifested in a devotion to the past and present heritage of Winchester Cathedral, Carpenter Turner added that 'Religious minorities are always of great interest: in Winchester the Jewish community undoubtedly played an important part in the city's development.'[180]

Superficially, it could be argued that Carpenter Turner's narrative in the *Hampshire Review* followed the approach typified by Freeman, L'Estrange, Belloc, Williamson and others. She started by stating that 'the mediaeval Jew could lend money on interest, a financial transaction forbidden by canon law to the Christian. Thus the Jews became the great usurers and moneylenders of the early Middle Ages.' Her desire, however, was to understand the inner dynamics of the 'flourishing Jewish quarter' of Winchester: 'Though everyone in Winchester knows Jewry Street, very little has been written about the Jews who gave the street its name.'[181]

In 1962, having read H. G. Richardson's recent work on medieval Anglo-Jewry, Carpenter Turner acknowledged that the Jews 'could never have lived by money-lending alone, and there were Jewish goldsmiths, physicians,

victuallers, fishmongers and cheesemongers' (and, one might add with particular reference to Winchester, perhaps also shoemakers).[182] The emphasis
in her earlier article, however, was purely focused on the 'moneylending activities of the Winchester Jews [which] were widespread'. In this respect, its
conclusion was remarkable, with the fate of the Jews and the fate of the city
tied together inseparably. The expulsion of the Jews was a 'severe economic
blow to Winchester's prosperity' and Edward I's granting of a charter to the
city, three weeks after, was, Carpenter Turner believed, not coincidental, but
it offered inadequate compensation:

> It is not too much to suggest that the decay of the mediaeval city probably dates
> from 1290 when the Jews were expelled and their financial transactions, though
> sometimes extortionate and nearly always unpopular, came to an end. Jewish ac-
> tivity in the early mediaeval period helped to make possible long term credit and
> capital investment. It is not surprising that the part of the city which they had
> inhabited began to decline.[183]

Carpenter Turner's narrative was not totally free of the 'pathological' Jewish
usurer whose activities were 'sometimes extortionate and nearly always unpopular'. Moreover, her Jews, whilst crucial to the well-being of the city, were
not fully part of it. The expulsion brought the decline of Jewry Street for
the next five hundred years but 'The more serious effects on Wintonians of
their loss of contact with parts of wider, even if *alien world* it is not possible
to estimate' [my emphasis].[184] Yet the 'otherness' of Winchester Jewry which
loosely framed Carpenter Turner's accounts of this community was radically
undermined by her focus on individuals within it. Unlike the characteristics of the 'majority historians' outlined by Langmuir, Carpenter Turner had
read and engaged with the work of Jewish historians when it had touched
upon Winchester. She supplemented it with her own research adding the
context of the specific dynamics of this important medieval city. Rather than
the faceless and evil Jewish usurers presented by most majority historians,
Carpenter Turner presented them as people taking risks, facing persecution,
and rooted in Winchester society. Of particular note was her emphasis on
Jewish women. If 'majority historians' such as Freeman referred to Jews as individuals, it was only usually to dwell briefly on the fantastic wealth of Jewish
men such as Aaron of Lincoln.[185] They thereby conformed to the gendered
and inhuman Shylock stereotype, represented in its most evil in the form
of the (always male) Jewish ritual murderer. In contrast, Carpenter Turner's
Winchester Jews could be identified with positively. Jewish finance, she highlighted, 'was family finance, the business of lending money on interest being
handed down from one generation to the next'. In this respect, Carpenter
Turner's Winchester financiers were not dissimilar from the likeable Jews

in the hugely successful family sagas written by her contemporary novelists, Louis Golding and Naomi Jacob. If the idea of the family firm helped
to soften the image of Jewish moneylending, it was further humanised by
Carpenter Turner's gendering of such activities:

> A large proportion of the usurers were women. One of the most interesting of all
> these ladies, Chera, the wife of Ysaac the Chirographer, carried on the business
> when her husband died, and was able to pass it on in a flourishing state to her sons
> Elias, Simon, Deulebenye and Deulesant. In turn Elias' many unfinished transac-
> tions were passed on to his son Abraham and grandson Cokerell.[186]

Chera's family was thus comparable in Carpenter Turner's vision to that of
the later Huguenot Portals in Hampshire, other than that persecution and
expulsion was the unjust and unwise treatment of the former.

Chera was very much part of the local economy – she 'lent money to
Jew and Christian alike, in Hampshire and out of it'. But Carpenter Turner
was keen to show that she was not unique as a Jewish female entrepreneur.
'Another mother-and-son family business was that of Glorietta and her son
Samkin' and after Chera's death in 1244 'the best known Jewess was undoubtedly Liquoricia, who apparently came to the city after the death of her husband, the Jew David of Oxford. Like the other moneylenders, she suffered
grievously as a result of the damage done by the younger de Montfort.'[187]
Carpenter Turner further rendered her Jews human by referring to court
cases brought by one Jew against another, in her words, 'not relating to debt'.
In 1253 Liquoricia's son brought action 'against Bonamy, the son of Samarian
of Winchester, for the return of a Hebrew book worth 20s'. In a sympathetic
touch, connecting the 'everyday' of medieval Winchester Jewry to a modern
audience used to library fines, Carpenter Turner mused that it 'would be
interesting to know what excuse he was able to offer'.[188]

Although not fully free from a discourse that assumed a disproportionate (if largely positive) Jewish influence, and with a focus still almost solely
on usury, Carpenter Turner still managed to create a coherent and often
sensitive narrative of Winchester Jewry. Unlike most 'majority' historiography, she subtly utilised Anglo-Jewish scholarship that had evolved since the
1870s. Carpenter Turner thus moved beyond the idea of Jews in the medieval era as a 'problem' to be solved one way or another. Carpenter Turner's
achievement was such that her work was soon to be embraced by the world
of Anglo-Jewish history and heritage, most notably in the tercentary celebrations marking the readmission of the Jews to England in 1656.[189]

Carpenter Turner's focus on individuals such as Chera, Liquoricia and
her son, Benedict the Gildsman, enabled her to present Winchester Jewry as
a dynamic community that, while suffering persecution from those outside

the city, were far from passive victims. Yet if the focus on Benedict's civic recognition allowed mutual pride in the achievements and acceptance of a Winchester Jew from both a local and a Jewish perspective, the emphasis on very wealthy financiers, even if female, was potentially more problematic. The rest of this section will explore how questions of gender, through the representation of Jewish male and especially female capitalists, have been treated respectively in Jewish and non-Jewish historiography.

Until the 1900s, the early Anglo-Jewish historians failed to mention women in their work. There were two factors responsible for their lacuna. First, they mirrored the bias in history writing as a whole with its focus on 'great men' and added an ethno-religious element to it. Jewish scholarship was still largely the study of male contributions to the development of Judaism. Second, it reflected the poverty of readily available sources. M. D. Davis's narrative on 'Early Winchester Jews' reveals such limitations and tendencies. This prominent member of the JHSE (a society, it should be added, that has still yet to have a female president),[190] failed to mention any women and, after listing twelve prominent male Jewish financiers involved in a legal case, commented that he doubted 'if we can recall anywhere a Minyan in any town in England as recently as a century ago, while here we have a round dozen co-religionists in Winchester, anno 1225'.[191] The secularisation of Jewish studies would slowly enable the first factor to be challenged and for other areas, aside from religion, to be considered. More immediate, however, as a motor for change, was the publication of material from the Public Record Office such as J. M. Rigg's *Select Pleas, Starrs and Other Records from the Rolls of the Exchequer of the Jews* (1902)[192] and his first volume of the *Calendar of the Plea Rolls of the Exchequer of the Jews* (1905). The latter had eleven entries focusing on Licorice (i.e. Liquoricia or Licoricia) alone and many others on her family connections.[193] Joseph Jacobs, who was always more sociologically and anthropologically minded than his fellow members of the JHSE, quickly incorporated this primary evidence in his article on Winchester in *The Jewish Encyclopedia*, published in New York in 1906. Roughly one quarter of his entry was devoted to the 'Several Jewesses … lending money at Winchester, notably Chera in the twelfth century and Licorice in the thirteenth'. Jacobs focused especially on the latter, arguing that an 'elaborate list of transactions between [Licorice] and Thomas of Charlecote … shows that Jewesses of those days had the right of holding land as security for payment of debt', adding that she had also 'agreed to pay the large fine of £5,000 on succeeding to the estate of her husband, David of Oxford, in 1244'.[194] Jacobs was at least hinting that Jewish women could be historical figures in their own right. Just twelve years earlier, Jacobs had contributed an extensive overview on 'The Jews of England' to Traill's *Social England* collection without even mentioning women.[195]

Yet if material from the Pipe Rolls of the Exchequer and Plea Rolls of the Exchequer of the Jews was revealing the prominence of Jewish women such as Chera and Licorice, there was little awareness of what to do with this information other than to include it for antiquarian interest. Typical of this tendency was a short piece on 'Jewesses' published in the popular journal, *Notes and Queries*, in 1934. Its author, JHR (no doubt J. H. Round of the Pipe Roll Society), provided a chronological list of Jewish women mentioned in the printed Calendars. Winchester Jews featured prominently within his register although Round failed to understand that Licoricia of Winchester was the same person as the widow of David of Oxford and therefore understated her dynamism and overall significance.[196] While Round's account is notable for its absence of analysis, it could be argued that it acted as a stimulus for future research as well as a warning about potential pitfalls. He commented that in the 'copious records of Jews' in the thirteenth century 'there is not seldom mention of women, though definite information about them occurs rarely'.[197] The context he provided for his article is also revealing. It says little or nothing about Jewish women in medieval England but much about the author's attitude and the time in which he wrote. Round started by referring to Caesarius of Heisterbach's thirteenth-century *Dialogue on Miracles* and its stories relating to Jewesses. These stories included the familiar tropes of beautiful Jewish women marrying Christian men and converting. He concluded that 'In Caesarius it is clear that there was no racial prejudice to be overcome; once a Jew had been baptized he [*sic*] was one of the "even Christians"'.[198] Nazi Germany, and not just medieval England, was clearly on Round's mind.

In Rigg's *Calendar of the Plea Rolls* Licorice is presented within the context solely of Jewish moneylending. Rigg, not unreasonably, stated that she 'lived to make a great figure as a litigant'[199] – a much later historian suggests that Licorice's last twenty years 'were most notable for the aggression with which she pursued her Christian debtors'.[200] More generally, Rigg believed that that the causes 'which made the Jews unpopular were economic rather than religious … Feudal society could not be expected to transform itself in their interest, and as they could not disarm its hostility, their continued presence in the country could but have served to perpetuate a social sore.'[201] In Round's account, female Jewish moneylenders were initially placed within a Christian discourse and then purely in relation to finance and property. He thus followed Rigg and other turn of the twentieth-century editors of English medieval documents. It was in the increasingly distressing times of the 1930s, and working against the limited and distorting frameworks of existing scholarship, that the first major treatment of the Jewish woman in medieval England was published. What then would the Reverend Michael

Adler, President of the JHSE in 1934 and chaplain to the Jewish forces in the British Army during the First World War, make of such remarkable characters as Chera and Licorice?

Adler devoted his presidential address in November 1934 to the 'Jewish woman in medieval England'. His explanation for this choice was, superficially, on grounds of prominence within the records of pre-expulsion Anglo-Jewry. More important was what that prominence represented: 'Again and again she comes to the front in a way that proves that she occupied a position in the life of Jewry, both within and without the community, probably unequalled in those days in any other country'.[202] Ethno-religious pride in these women was clearly present in Adler's address. Their achievements were enabled, Adler claimed, through 'complete freedom within the limits of the Rabbinic Law'. The Jewish woman thus was far more liberated than her Christian counterparts in medieval England. 'The business activities of the pre-Expulsion woman', he claimed, 'show her to have been a vigorous and determined individual with marked commercial ability and enterprise; she certainly suffered from no "inferiority complex", but held her own with remarkable courage'.[203] Yet any tendency towards vaingloriousness towards these women was tempered by the parallel defensiveness of Adler's approach. It was said after his death that he devoted his whole career to creating 'Jewish-Gentile comradeship[,] ... remov[ing] Jewish-Gentile misconceptions [and] striv[ing] ... for the honour of the Jewish name'.[204] The subject of Jewish women in medieval England provided Adler with an opportunity to help further these objectives.

As with his later work on Benedict the Gildsman, Adler strove to find cases of Jewish/non-Jewish harmony. Indeed, he believed that there was 'striking evidence of the existence of amicable relations between the women of both communities', referring to examples where Jews entrusted 'their valuables to non-Jewish friends at times of disturbance'.[205] Adler had made clear from the start that 'The English Jewess shared all the persecutions suffered by her people' including imprisonment and murder.[206] By setting such a context, Adler enabled the Jewish woman to be regarded more sympathetically and their business achievements to be viewed even more positively. Adler listed fifteen prominent female moneylenders, including Belia and Chera of Winchester, before moving on to the 'Grande Dame of the pre-Expulsion community', Licoricia.[207] She was, in Adler's words, 'an outstanding personality'. He emphasised that 'Among all these women capitalists of England, none approaches the eminence of Licoricia of Winchester' with her 'direct relations with the king and the Court, her extensive and successful transactions [and] her cooperation with the principal Jewish bankers of the day'.[208]

Michael Adler had not a bad word to say for Licoricia and her financial activities. His approach in dealing with her wealth and ruthlessness as a moneylender and that of her fellow 'women capitalists' was to emphasise their sex and then to frame his narrative within a strictly religious framework. In the medieval period, claimed Adler, the 'laws of the Rabbis were loyally obeyed by the Jews of England'. He concluded that

> The study of the activities of these women throws considerable light upon the social and economic conditions of Anglo-Jewry, and in spite of their weaker sisters, as a body they lived up to the high traditions of Jewish womanhood and deserve our fullest tribute of admiration and esteem as 'women of valour'.[209]

Michael Adler was trained at Jews' College and was an orthodox rabbi in United Synagogue congregations before becoming Jewish chaplain. It is not surprising, therefore, that his portrait of medieval Anglo-Jewish women should reflect his religious background as well as the Jewish insecurity when faced with the 'devil's decade'. The final example within this section provides both a very different Jewish context – secular – and temporal location – the twenty-first century. Furthermore, it reflected a new and challenging development with regard to the subject matter of this chapter: memory work that was both local *and* Jewish.

Sue Bartlet was born into a radical Jewish East End family in 1933 and moved to Hampshire in 1960. Inspired by the discovery of the medieval Jewish cemetery in Winchester, close to her house, in the mid-1990s, she has subsequently been driven by 'the need to tell of the life of Winchester's medieval Jews'. In particular, her focus has been on the role played by Jewish women in this community and especially that of Licoricia who was murdered in Scowertenestret in 1277. Indeed, Bartlet has continued her quest, in spite of serious illness, because she 'felt that I was being nagged to keep going by the ghost of Licoricia'.[210]

Bartlet has written both an overview of medieval Anglo-Jewish women and a specific case study of 'three Jewish businesswomen' – Chera, Belia and Licoricia – in thirteenth-century Winchester.[211] Her work acts as a corrective to the approach of Michael Adler in two respects. First, Bartlet is less optimistic about the potential of the surviving medieval records, concluding 'that the history of Anglo-Jewish women has yet to be written, and may never be known in its entirety'. Second, she is far less sanguine about the relative freedoms enjoyed by Jewish women as suggested by Adler and later by Dobson.[212] It must be suggested that the absence of Adler's defensiveness enables Bartlet to present the patriarchal limitations imposed on medieval Anglo-Jewish women. Furthermore, her gender-informed analysis highlights how the records themselves provide only a partial and distorted picture of their lives. She adds that 'the modern editors of the pipe rolls have also to share the blame for obscuring medieval Jewish women. They thought fit to omit lists of debts and pledges, deeming them of little interest but depriving researchers of possible evidence of the whereabouts or even the continued existence of the male and female individuals being traced.'[213] But through painstakingly careful and detailed research, Bartlet has managed to partially re-create the careers of Chera, Belia and Licoricia, revealing 'a distinct identity for each of our three women, as well as several experiences they had in common'.[214] Do, however, such attempts to incorporate the historical presence of women bring their own problems?

In 1991, Barrie Dobson devoted his Presidential Address at the Ecclesiastical History Society annual conference to the subject of Jewish women in medieval England. He warned that 'one of the hazards facing the historian of the medieval Jewess may be the temptation to idealize her just because she is a Jewess'.[215] Dobson's subject matter and approach deserve further analysis. With regard to the former, that the Ecclesiastical History Society should devote itself to 'Christianity and Judaism' showed the progress that had been made in the area of 'majority history'. Dobson, however, has played an exceptional role in bridging the gap betwen 'majority history' and Jewish history through his earlier work on the Jews of York. Few historians of medieval England have matched his efforts and achievements in this respect.[216] As Dobson himself suggests, the growing interest and awareness of the Jewish heritage in York in the late twentieth century 'owes much less to the researches of professional historians than to the dramatic expansion of interest in medieval Jewry among Christians and Jews alike'.[217] In respect of the latter, Dobson points out the dangers of celebratory history, in this case from either a feminist or ethnic/pro-ethnic perspective. Have we moved, therefore, from a perspective in which Jewish moneylenders were represented in majority history as faceless and rapacious usurers to one in which such figures, especially women, have been put forward as iconic heroes/heroines, regardless of reality?

The risk of ethno-religious cheerleading and romanticism was exposed in Pamela Fletcher Jones's popularist history of the Jews of Britain (1990). Here Licoricia is presented as 'the most outstanding woman of her time – Jew or gentile'. Her description is accompanied by an illustration from a 1233 Exchequer document relating to Norwich Jewry which included a largely positive image of a Jewish woman. Fletcher Jones, without any evidence, suggests that 'Licoricia of Winchester, the great female financier, would probably have looked very like the woman in the drawing'.[218] Here, critical history has given way to celebratory heritage. Such tendencies are *not* present, however, in Bartlet's treatment of her three Winchester businesswomen. Gender and probable family solidarity are underlined, but the fact that they were very wealthy financiers determined 'to pursue their interests' is never forgotten.[219] Although some emphasis is placed on the non-moneylending activities of medieval Jewry, Bartlet's work is generally free of the more apologetic approach of earlier Anglo-Jewish historiography.[220] The 'success' of Chera, Belia and Licoricia is firmly placed in a context of external pressure, marginality and frequent persecution.

Colin Richmond provocatively asks 'Were these three women good Jews?' He adds,

> Certainly, the gentiles they dealt with, whether sheriffs, justices, lords, gentlemen, abbots, or bishops, were bad Christians. Almost everyone in upper-class England in the thirteenth century was on the take and on the make, none more so than Peter des Roches, the bishop of Winchester. There were no saints among the lot of them, but then while there was a patron saint for every other line of work, who is the patron saint of those who go about accumulating capital?[221]

Have we, as exemplified by Richmond, Dobson and Bartlet, reached a new maturity and the end of the division between majority and Jewish history? Is it now possible to treat Jewish moneylenders, male and female, as human beings, with all the triumphs, failings and (most of all) the ambiguities that therefore entails, rather than as evil Shylocks or Jewish saints? If Bartlet's work points in one direction in answering this question, it has also to be recognised less optimistically that the distorting legacy of 'majority history' persists. In an English Heritage pamphlet, *The Book of Winchester*, published as late as 1997, a small section is devoted to the Jewish community. It starts by asserting that 'By the middle of the thirteenth century, Jews had become a powerful force in the city.' It is true that Jews such as Licoricia and her son Benedict were clearly important both locally and nationally in matters financial. Yet what is remarkable about them is how they survived, through a mixture of skill and good fortune, so long. Even then, they were utterly exceptional within the Jewish community in terms of their wealth and the protection they (sometimes) enjoyed. To describe such individuals, let alone the community as a whole, as powerful, is to fail to understand the marginal and, at best, tolerated status of Jews in medieval England. The pathological approach of English Heritage's *The Book of Winchester* continues by referring to the growing national unpopularity of the Jews. In this context, their expulsion in 1290 seems both natural and sensible. The English Heritage account thus follows the logic, if not the crudity, of Edward Freeman's late nineteenth-century analysis. In contrast, Bartlet ends her exploration of the lives of Chera, Belia and Licoricia by stating one of the things they had in common: 'All three had sons who were executed.'[222] It is thus clear with regard to medieval Jewry, as exemplified by Winchester, that issues of power and powerlessness, of actual and historiographical marginality, of majority and Jewish history, have yet to be fully resolved. The continued tensions over ownership and belonging, as well as absence and presence, will now be explored in the final section of this chapter.

Jews, others and constructing Winchester's heritage

'This museum tells the story of Winchester'. It is surely significant that there is no mention of medieval Jewry in the narrative provided by Winchester City Museum,[223] and that absence is replicated elsewhere in the heritage world of the city. It would be wrong to suggest that there is an active denial of the former Jewish presence – as has been mentioned, the name 'Jewry Street' sometimes, but not always, prompts mention in shopping, nightlife and other informal guides to the city.[224] But when Jewry Street is not mentioned, as is the case in the most ubiquitous current guidebook to Winchester, the Jews are invisible in the history and chronology provided.[225] Had the Pavement Commissioner in 1856 voted in favour of re-naming Jewry Street, then it is possible that there would be no attention at all paid to the past presence of Winchester's Jews. It has been suggested that the medieval 'Jewish quarter of London was not allowed to re-invent itself. It disappeared and survives only as a name: the Old Jewry that today's office workers, exiting Starbucks or the Old Seattle Coffee House on Cheapside, pass by without a moment's thought.'[226] The same is true of Jewry Street in Winchester today.

This chapter has shown that, post-expulsion, Winchester Jewry has never featured prominently in the city's historiography and heritage construction. Nevertheless, there have been moments when more attention has been given to the Jews, as in the late Victorian and Edwardian era when tourism to Winchester was expanding. Even then, at key moments of historical reflection, as with the King Alfred Millenary in 1901 and the Winchester National Pageant in 1908, the extensive narratives of the city's evolution produced for these occasions made no mention of the Jews.[227] Yet, as we have seen, silence has never been totally dominant. The King Alfred Millenary, for example, prompted further memory work within which the Jews *were* included.[228] From the 1950s through to the early 1990s, the strong interest of Barbara Carpenter Turner in Winchester Jewry ensured their inclusion in popular guides and histories of the city.[229] But the almost absolute absence from the end of the twentieth century onwards is particularly noteworthy for two reasons. First, knowledge of the medieval Jewish community is now far more profound. Second, Winchester's heritage has been packaged more professionally and extensively than ever before. The remainder of this chapter will analyse the second factor and what *is* highlighted within Winchester. Before then, however, it will be necessary to review briefly what is now known about the history of Winchester Jewry.

Aside from the subtle and multi-layered work of Sue Bartlet on the elite Jewish women, the most recent major synthetic account of Winchester Jewry is within Derek Keene's monumental multi-volume *Survey of Medieval Winchester* (1985). All in all, roughly just ten pages are devoted to the Jews out of a total close to fifteen hundred.[230] Superficially, it could also be argued that the Jews are marginalised within the narrative, confined in a section on 'others' alongside aliens and women. Indeed, the section on the Jews opens by stating that 'The most distinctive of the separate communities in Winchester during the Middle Ages was that of the Jews.'[231] Nevertheless, Keene's overall treatment provides an excellent example of the integration of the Jewish experience into the wider locality, using both historical and archaeological evidence. The case of Benedict the gildsman is used not for celebratory purposes, but to show the dynamics of Winchester politics in the 1260s and 1270s. Keene reveals the complex situation in which there was 'a community of interest between the Jews and leading citizens' in relation to the financing of trade. Yet the admittance of Benedict as a gildsman in 1268 further alienated the commonalty from these leading citizens and 'seems to have crystallized the distinction between pro- and anti-Jewish factions in the city'. Keene even suggests that Roger de Dunstable's election as mayor in 1273, 'which broke Simon le Drapir's long term of seven years in the office, had perhaps taken place on a tide of anti-Jewish and communal feeling.'[232] His account is freed of the philosemitism of Carpenter Turner's narrative of Winchester, in which the economic well-being of the city depended on the Jewish presence. Nevertheless, Keene shows that the treatment of the Jews can only be understood by contextualising it within the specific (non-Jewish) power politics of the medieval city. Rather than being a marginal and unrelated issue, it was key to the governance of Winchester. Keene is thus aware of the dangers of generalising about Winchester's reputation 'of a city where there were exceptionally good relations between Christians and Jews', allowing for both popular anti-Jewish feeling, as with ritual murder accusations, and the common economic interests of some Jews and the city's leading citizens.[233]

What is equally impressive in Keene's account is the use of evidence from both the plea rolls and archaeological excavations to place the Jews firmly in the local context. A map of the medieval Jewry within the city is thus provided which 'clearly shows ... their properties were intermingled with those of the Christian population'. The Jews' connections to other towns in England, as well as to France, are made clear, but so is their rootedness to the everyday in Winchester.[234] It is worth comparing Keene's map with those produced in the early 1900s by Stokes and then Jacobs. In Stokes's vision, Winchester Jewry almost *is* the city, with synagogues in abundance. In contrast, they are almost invisible in Jacobs's equivalent. Keene's map and accompanying narrative show the Jews to have been engaged in a wide range of occupations and financial activities, even suggesting that Richard's *Cronicon* might be accepted as evidence of their involvement in shoe-making (and therefore their settlement in that particular Winchester street). There is a tendency in Keene's account to refer to 'the Jews' as a unified interest group – as with the politics of the 1260s/70s and internal conflict, whether personal or economic, is underplayed. It is doubtful whether the Jews in Winchester were any more unified than their Christian neighbours and it should not be assumed that persecution necessarily created consensus within the Jewish world. Nevertheless, Keene at least recognised that the Jewish community had 'more day-to-day economic concerns and its poorer members presumably included those who supplied its special requirements in food and other items'. A lead disc with a Hebrew inscription, which was found in an excavation in Tanner Street, is also referred to as evidence of Jewish involvement at a mundane level 'with the lesser craftsmen of the city'.[235] The map and narrative also include references to the county gaol in Jewry Street and Winchester Castle and the special role they both played in the protection and punishment of the Jews. Finally, mention is made of the Jewish cemetery, located outside the city walls and next to the castle, and its partial excavation in the 1970s.[236] Keene's *Survey of Medieval Winchester*, while acknowledging itself that it is far from a full account of the city's Jews, is free of almost all the limitations of 'majority history' or the twin tendencies of defensiveness and ethno-religious pride that shaped early Anglo-Jewish historiography as illustrated in the maps of Stokes and Jacobs. Keene, in 1985, hoped that the 'topographical comments' might help in the future study of a topic that contained so much 'fertile ground'. Within Jewish studies Sue Bartlet has taken on his challenge to explore 'the business and family connections of the Winchester Jews'. More generally, however, with regard to the heritage work associated with the topography outlined by Keene, those responsible have far from fulfilled his hopes.[237] Instead, what *is* presented within Winchester could, perhaps controversially, be labelled anti-Jewish memory work.

'Jews disappeared from England in 1290; "the Jew" did not. In wall-paintings, as at Chalgrave in Oxfordshire and in St Stephen's Chapel, Westminster, or in wall-tiles, like those at Tring ..., he could have been seen.'[238] To Colin Richmond's list one could add Winchester Cathedral within which a range of imagery of 'the Jew' (male and female) is to be found. Some of it pre-dated the expulsion, as was the case with sculpture of a woman representing the 'blinded' synagogue, literally unable to see the light of the true church. It has been described as 'One of the most precious of Winchester's treasures' and more generally as 'one of the glories of Western sculpture'.[239] It has also been suggested that in the 1190s 'the famous Chapel of the Holy Sepulchre was built, complete with wall-paintings depicting anti-semitic grotesques'.[240] The focus here will be on the Cathedral's Lady Chapel and 'the Jews' within its early sixteenth-century wall paintings.

These paintings were commissioned by Prior Silkstede of the Cathedral who, twenty years earlier, had been responsible for the creation of similar images at Eton College Chapel. All the paintings in both chapels depict miracles associated with the Virgin and several have a particular Jewish focus. One, the 'Miracle of the Jewess', depicts 'the story of a Jewess endangered in childbirth. A light appeared and a voice bade her call on the Mother of Christ, which doing she was safely delivered and became a Christian.' Another, 'The Miracle of the Jew of Bourges', also has a strong conversion theme, but it also has more diabolic undertones: 'The Jewish boy chanced to be with his Christian playfellows when they received the communion, and partook with them. His father, hearing of it, cast him into the heated oven, where he remained unhurt. On being rescued he told how a beautiful lady had stood by him and protected him with her garment. The boy became a Christian, the father was cast into the oven and perished.'[241] As Miri Rubin has illustrated in her *Gentile Tales*, the general narrative of the 'Jewish boy' was transformed into the myth of host desecration, a late medieval accusation against the Jews that proved as murderous as the parallel blood libel.[242]

Inevitably, given its size, architectural and artistic importance, as well as its ecclesiastical and historical significance, Winchester Cathedral has dominated topographical descriptions of the city and has been subject to intense local pride. According to one guide, 'Winchester Cathedral may fairly be regarded as among the three or four most interesting monuments in the north of Europe'.[243] John Hooper Harvey's 1944 description of its nave as 'one of the supreme triumphs of English Gothic' was reproduced with satisfaction in an anthology to mark its thousandth anniversary in 1970, oblivious to the dubious ideology underlying this architectural historian's work.[244]

How then has the image of the 'Jewish boy' been treated within Winchester heritage? Such Marian-inspired imagery as the Lady Chapel paintings was viewed with hostility, and often erasure, during the Reformation. Alongside the sheer antiquity of the paintings, they were, by the eighteenth century, faded almost beyond recognition. Copies were then drawn and engraved alongside the originals.[245] It is clear that the writers of early histories and guidebooks of Winchester from the late eighteenth century onwards did not know what to make of these paintings. Drawing upon Milner's history, mid-

Victorian accounts of the city described them as essentially 'other': 'Various attempts have been made to deface them; but they are still curious, from the knowledge they convey of the customs of former times.'[246] In *Winchester: the Cathedral and See* (1903) they are again described as 'curious' and 'decidedly archaic, but they are extremely interesting'. Within the delineation of the Lady Chapel wall paintings, the information provided about 'the Jewish boy' is largely descriptive and 'neutral': 'after receiving the Eucharist [he is] thrown into a furnace by his father, but delivered from the flames by the Virgin'.[247] Similarly, in the Cathedral's 'Walk Around Guide', the paintings and their subject matter were regarded as 'strange enough'.[248]

The Cathedral authorities have also celebrated these images. In a 1948 guide to *The Glories of Winchester Cathedral* they are described as 'delightful'.[249] To such neutrality or enthusiasm, however, Winchester Cathedral added another layer of offensiveness, labelling the painting not as 'The Jew of Bourge', or 'Jewish boy', but simply as 'Jew-boy'. This hostile epithet was then incorporated into Winchester guidebooks.[250] It is significant that the term had been utilised before in a Winchester context to describe the ritual murder narrative within the *Cronicon*: the index to Kitchin's 1890 historic guide to *Winchester* placed Richard of Devizes' story under the heading 'Jew boy'.[251]

The images of the Jewish mother and especially the Jewish boy are clearly problematic in the belief system they reveal. It is, for example, difficult to accept, as was argued in *The Glories of Winchester Cathedral*, that visitors to the Cathedral, when confronted with these paintings, as the stories within them were 'so plainly set forth', would 'hardly need the help of a guide to explain their significance'.[252] Yet rather than assist those trying to make sense of the 'teaching of contempt' towards the Jews that these images represent,[253] the Cathedral authorities added insult to injury by persisting with the title 'Jew-boy' until 1985. Indeed, in spite of earlier complaints from Jewish visitors, it was not until the *Jewish Chronicle* and a Labour MP drew attention to it that the Cathedral changed the caption to read 'Jewish boy'. Furthermore, the response of the Cathedral administrator, that it had 'been there for umpteen years and no one has ever noticed it before', revealed more about the insensitivity on this issue than he had intended.[254] The 'Jew' in Winchester's most iconic building is thus represented as, at best, a suitable case for conversion or, as in its remarkable medieval and later imagery of David, as proto-Christian.[255] At worst, the 'Jew', especially the male Jew, is a figure closely in league with the devil. A pathological imagery thus survives representing the attempt of medieval Christianity to define itself against what it was not – the Jewish 'other'. Richard of Devizes queried, through his 'Jewish' story, whether his fellow Christians were naturally righteous. While unable to include the

'Jew' within his moral universe of obligation, through satire he undermined in his *Cronicon* this crude self/other binary. On the everyday level, however, 'Winchester's Jewish community had close links with St Swithun's, and possibly funded the ambitious rebuilding and development programme at the cathedral.'[256] We have noted how Richard of Devizes was aware of this link in reference to a loan from a 'Lombard Jew' and how, in classic majority history mode, Kitchin, then dean of the Cathedral, suggested that this was 'probably not the first or last "accommodation" of the kind'.[257] Kitchin's successors at Winchester Cathedral have, so far, failed to re-assess how the building's rich heritage (ironically enabled in part through the local Jewish presence) represents 'the Jew'. In this respect, it is revealing how a very different narrative is presented in relation to another minority group, the Huguenots, within the monuments of the Cathedral.

If Kitchin was uneasy with the idea of Jewish moneylending in medieval Winchester, he was, as has been noted, proud of the city's alleged 'liberality' shown to Winchester Jewry. Similarly, in the case of the Huguenots and other refugees, he praised the fact that 'Throughout the eighteenth century Winchester was a kindly host to foreigners in trouble.' What differentiated his account of the later arrivals, however, was the empathy he showed towards them as well as their treatment. While foreign, there is no doubting that they had a legitimate place within the history and heritage of Winchester:

> Not a few Huguenot refugees settled in the town: one of them, thrown up by the after-wave of the persecutions of Louis XIV, lies buried in the Cathedral. This was a gentleman of a well-known southern name, Joseph de Serres, a native of Mentauban. After seven and twenty years in the galleys at Marseilles for his faith he was set free by the intervention of Queen Anne ... and mindful of her goodness in the matter, turned his steps – his own home having been long broken up by his cruel slavery – towards England, and settled in this city. Here he lived in tranquil freedom to a good old age, and died in 1754.[258]

Serres, in his years at Winchester, enjoyed friendship with Thomas Cheyney, later dean of the Cathedral.[259] It was Cheyney who was responsible for the Serres monument in the Cathedral's Epiphany Chapel. Outlining the persecution Serres had endured, the memorial highlights how 'he had fought, with indomitable mind, for the work and faith of Protestants'. It was important, in Cheyney's words,

> That the memory should not be lost completely
> From the reformed religion
> Of such exceptional merit
> Of one who endured so many burdens
> From the papal superstition.[260]

The ease with which Huguenot and Winchester history and heritage could be seamlessly joined was illustrated in 1889 when the Huguenot Society of London held its annual conference in the city. Those of Huguenot origin within Hampshire, especially William Portal, descendant of Henri de Portal, combined with the civic and ecclesiastical dignatories of Winchester to celebrate the past role of the city and wider county in welcoming these Protestant refugees. The stirring story of Serres and his brothers, as told through the monument in the cathedral, was a major focus of this pilgrimage to Winchester.[261] The Portal family itself was prominent within the Cathedral, marked later by a memorial to the military role of two of its members in Uganda in the 1890s.[262]

The Serres monument is, as a 1919 guide commented, 'in one sense unique in the Cathedral. Very few foreigners have been buried there, at any rate since the Reformation.' The story it related, however, was 'one of the most instructive and interesting memorials in the Cathedral'.[263] Entering the twenty-first century, another guide to the Cathedral comments briefly that 'it tells a gripping tale of a man who never abandoned his Protestant principles'.[264] The 1969 edition of the Cathedral's 'Walk Round Guide' devotes much of its section on the Epiphany Chapel to Serres, concluding that 'He died in 1754 mourned by English friends in whose country he had taken refuge and who had admired his indomitable spirit and faith in the Protestant religion.'[265] The compatibility of this Protestant morality tale within a leading Anglican place of worship, alongside the role of those of Huguenot descent in its later development, explain the lack of tension in incorporating the Huguenot story within Winchester Cathedral. Nevertheless, an element of caution is in order. Earlier and later versions of the 'Walk Round Guide' do not mention Serres. Furthermore, his monument is not a feature of cathedral tours. Even the 1969 'Walk Round Guide' glossed its comments on Serres by suggesting his monument would be of 'particular interest to French visitors' as if it was of less relevance and somehow alien to a British audience.[266] If Huguenots have privileged status within the memory of past immigrants and refugees in Britain, they are still subject to the marginality imposed by a nation that has yet to come fully to terms with its past diversity.[267] But medieval Winchester Jewry, as a non-Christian and persecuted group, has been far harder to incorporate. In the secular world, Winchester Castle was to play a key role in the lives of local Jewry. Does the heritage associated with the castle remains present the Jews any less problematically than the Cathedral?

Begun in the early days of the Norman invasion, Winchester castle expanded in the twelfth century and was strengthened and enlarged by Henry III in the 1240s and 1250s especially. The first reference to the Jews' tower in the castle was in 1249 and it has been assumed that it was used both as a safe refuge and a place of imprisonment for Winchester Jewry, a dual role that the county gaol played on a smaller level (as probably was the case with the ritual murder accusation in 1232). It has also been suggested that the Jews' tower might have been 'where the local archa was kept, and where local cases involving Jews were heard'.[268] The Jewish cemetery, located outside the city walls, was behind the castle, again providing some form of protection. Winchester Castle was thus an integral part of everyday Jewish life in both calmer times and periods of attack.

Winchester Castle went into decline after the thirteenth century and much of it was destroyed during the Civil War in the 1640s. Today, only the Great Hall, regarded as one of the finest surviving medieval buildings in England, survives of the Castle other than small fragments of the earlier structures. The fame of the Great Hall has been enhanced by housing the late thir-teenth-century 'Round Table', Winchester's most iconic artefact – one that has come to advertise the city in much the same way as the Royal Pavilion at Brighton or the Houses of Parliament and Tower Bridge in London. Indeed, more generally it is regarded as 'one of the world's great symbols'.[269] The Great Hall was used after the Civil War by the county authorities for the ad-ministration of justice (most notoriously by Judge Jeffreys) and was opened fully to the public as a major tourist attraction from the 1970s. In 1998, an extensive and permanent exhibition on the history of the castle and the site was opened.[270]

No mention is made of the Jews' tower or of Winchester Jewry in this sixty-five panel exhibition, although there are many sections in which they could have been incorporated (including the siege of the city by the younger Simon de Montfort in 1265 which had such disastrous results on the Jewish community).[271] The short guide to the Castle and Great Hall also includes no reference to the Jews.[272] There is, however, a sentence in the more sub-stantial Hampshire County Council guide to the site. It comes within a sec-tion devoted to the later middle ages and the royal gaol within the Castle: 'A Jew named Assher [or Asher] who was confined in it in 1287 left his name scratched on a wall.'[273] No explanation or context is given for this statement, the wider significance of which is thus totally lost.

In 1640, the philosopher, Christian Hebraist and antiquarian, John Selden, published *De Jure Naturali et Gentium Juxta Disciplinam Ebraeorum*, a study of the relationship between Jewish and natural law.[274] In the context of a dis-cussion about the ill-treatment of Jews without legal recourse, including the expulsion of 1290, Selden related that he had been told by the Royal Librarian about a Hebrew inscription carved into stone in a vault of Winchester Castle. Selden reproduced the Hebrew which stated that on a particular day in 1287 'all the Jews of this island were imprisoned', concluding that 'I, Asher, inscribed this'.[275] It seems unlikely, even if this information came to Selden second- or third-hand, that it had been made up, as no particular purpose would have been served in fabricating the inscription.

The importance of Selden's reference was not lost on early Anglo-Jewish historians. D'Blossiers Tovey incorporated the inscription in his 1738 *Anglia Judaica*, helping him to create a chronological framework for the expulsion of the Jews. The inscription was used thereafter in Anglo-Jewish historiography relating to the medieval period.[276] Moreover, the work of scholars such as Sue Bartlet mean that rather than simply a name, it is possible to speculate with little doubt who Asher might have been. Licoricia had two sons – Lumbard and Asher – who survived long enough to suffer the expulsion in 1290.[277] Asher's inscription and the existence of the Jews' tower thus provides the basis for a narrative of the castle that incorporates the Jewish presence in Winchester and the expulsion in 1290. Instead, the history presented within the Great Hall excludes consideration of the Jews and fails to engage directly with England's expropriation and expulsion of them in 1290. It is possible to argue, however, that this first such 'act of ethnic cleansing'[278] is commemorated *indirectly* within the heritage of Winchester Castle through the celebration of figures who were influential in arguing for its necessity – the mother and wife of Edward I, Eleanor of Province and Eleanor of Castile respectively.

In 1986, to mark the Domesday 900 celebrations, a thirteenth-century 'castle herber' was re-created next to the Great Hall in Winchester and opened by the Queen Mother as 'Queen Eleanor's Garden'. It was named after 'two garden-loving thirteenth-century queens who would once have walked on this spot'.[279] One of the co-designers of the garden explained that it was

> not to be a physic or kitchin garden but one in which a queen such as Eleanor of Castile might sit and play chess, perhaps using the jasper and crystal set given to her by Edward I ... It was finally decided that an overall spirit of the past could be evoked with the chivalric quality of fidelity as a central theme.[280]

This gentle royalism sits comfortably alongside the Round Table, which it has been suggested probably dates from April 1290 when Edward I 'held a tournament at Winchester ... to celebrate the arrangements made for the marriages of his children'.[281] Again, an alternative and far less comfortable reading of Queen Eleanor's Garden and the Round Table is provided by relating them to the Jewish experience.

It is clear that Eleanor of Province played a key role in the eventual expulsion of Anglo-Jewry. Robin Mundill, writing of 'Edward I and the Final Phase of Anglo-Jewry', comments that in 1275 the king visited his mother and granted her that 'no Jew shall dwell or stay in any towns which the queen mother holds in dower'. The Jews were then expelled from Marlborough, Gloucester, Worcester, Cambridge, Bath, Guildford and Andover in Hampshire (including Licoricia's grandson, Jacob Cok). As Mundill adds, 'Perhaps such actions were, as Barrie Dobson has hinted, dry runs for total expulsion'.[282] Much earlier, Stokes had argued that Eleanor of Castile 'was as deadly an enemy of Israel as the Dowager Eleanor of Provence'.[283] Ideological factors have to be considered alongside economic opposition to the Jews in the decision to expel the Jews in 1290. Both queens were integral in creating the mindset that led Edward I to take this drastic action. In *England's Jewish Solution: Experiment and Expulsion, 1262–1290* (1998), Mundill argues that while both Eleanors had earlier 'provided patronage for particular Jews and profited by them', by the 1280s 'they had openly turned against the Jews'.[284]

Colin Richmond asks, 'If by 1290 being Christian meant being anti-Jewish, did being anti-Jewish mean being English?' He answers affirmatively: that those who would have regarded themselves as English – the governing elite – were the first to 'equate Englishness with non-Jewishness'.[285] David Stocker has argued that the shrine to Little St Hugh in Lincoln Cathedral was part of a programme of 'political propaganda' by Edward I and one that was connected to the earlier Eleanor Crosses which were constructed after the death of his wife in November 1290. In their different ways both the shrine and the Eleanor Crosses intimately connected the crown to the church.[286] Richmond takes the analysis further: Edward's expulsion of the Jews, memorialised by building a shrine to the most famous 'victim' of the blood libel, was the flip side of the same coin that was, in the 1290s, constructing a sense of Englishness through a cult of the Crown and its (non-Jewish) Christianity as exemplified through the Eleanor Crosses.[287] To this example of instant heritage-glorifying Englishness, constructed out of crown and church, could be added the Winchester Round Table made 'at the height of the age of chivalry'.[288] As has been suggested, 'There is no other table which represents a large act of public propaganda in which antiquarianism, politics, and diplomacy are compounded.'[289] The choice of Winchester to hold this tournament was not accidental – it was linked to the 'city's supposed Arthurian past'.[290] The Round Table thus connected Edward's offspring with the mystical English past but, through the tournament, it also celebrated 'the culmination of King Edward I's plans for the future of his dynasty and of the English crown'.[291]

Is there a further connection between this politicised medieval memorialisation in the late thirteenth century and the creation of Queen Eleanor's Garden in the Great Hall of Winchester in 1986? The linkage is made through the figure of John Hooper Harvey, consultant and co-designer of the 1986 garden. To Harvey, the greatness of Edward I was his creation of England as a national entity. Undermining its potential unity of purpose were the Jews who Harvey regarded as an 'alien body'. Their explusion, Harvey was convinced, was thus a great act of statesmanship.[292] 'England had been given back to the English by Edward I'.[293] It was the actions of Edward I, he continued, that enabled the flowering of a true English culture in the fourteenth century, as exemplified by the literature of William Chaucer or the architectural achievements of Henry Yevele.[294] It is in this exclusionary context that the ideological impulse behind Queen Eleanor's Garden, now firmly established as a major tourist site within Winchester, has to be understood. More generally, the failure to confront the Jewish and anti-Jewish past in Winchester has enabled the celebration of heritage that is presented as harmonious, pastoral and inclusive but was, in fact, violently prejudiced and exclusionary. Such commemoration does not have the blatancy of De Montfort University in Leicester in which an extreme antisemite has been rewarded with his name attached to a place of higher education.[295] Nevertheless, it takes us back to Patrick Geary's emphasis on 'the political or intentional dimensions of both collective memory and history'. Both, he argues, have been orchestrated as strategies 'for group solidarity and mobilization through the constant processes of suppression and selection … All memory … is memory *for* something, and this political (in a broad sense) cannot be ignored'.[296]

As with Winchester Cathedral, however, not all diversity in the city's past is removed or pathologised in the Great Hall. Within the permanent exhibition, there is extended reference to the King's House, intended by Charles II as a summer residence and designed by Sir Christopher Wren in the 1680s to be built within the ruins of Winchester Castle. As with the neighbouring Great Hall, it later served many purposes, including acting as a prison for French soldiers in the 1750s. As the exhibition explains,

> In the last decade of the eighteenth century the King's House was transformed from prison to refuge when the government offered it as accommodation for up to one thousand clergy in flight from Revolutionary France. The first refugees moved in during the autumn of 1792 and some remained there until early 1796.

The narrative presented of these French refugee priests is non-threatening, in spite of their Catholicism. Their stay in Winchester is not permanent, they are on the right side politically, and they are grateful for the temporary refuge. In respect of the last factor, an inscription is reproduced in the exhibition 'which was placed in the King's House by the French exiles in gratitude for the mercy shown to them by George III in support of the royalist cause in France'.[297]

At a more popular level, the same pattern of heritage inclusion and exclusion is present within Jewry Street itself. In 1997, the pub chain J. D. Wetherspoon took over what had been, since the early 1960s, Habels furniture shop in Jewry Street. The Jewish connections to this site were both ancient and modern. With regards to the latter, the furniture shop's origins go back to 1945 when Jack Habel, a refugee from Nazism, opened a store elsewhere in Winchester.[298] In respect of the former, the site was formerly the county gaol, the extension of which in the eighteenth century temporarily led to the street name change. It was also the site of the much earlier medieval gaol. The gaol, as noted, would have been used before the Jews' tower to protect and imprison Winchester Jewry.

Wetherspoon called the former furniture store The Old Gaol House and, following their approach elsewhere, have decorated its interior with photographs and texts relating to the history of the building and its neighbourhood. A full chronology of Winchester history is provided in The Old Gaol House as well as details of the specific building itself. No reference is made to medieval Jewry, however, in spite of the street name in which the pub is located or the connection to the former gaol. There is, however, near the entrance, a tribute to religious tolerance in the English past in which another minority group coming to the locality is highlighted – again the French Protestant refugees who came to Winchester in the late seventeenth century:

> In Catholic France in 1685, the Edict of Nantes, which tolerated Huguenot Protestants, was revoked. Cruel persecutions followed and large numbers fled to England. [James II] welcomed and protected them. There was a great influx of Protestant 'asylum seekers' into Winchester and the King supported them from his own purse, and began general subscription for their relief. He also rushed through citizenship for them at no expense.[299]

French Protestant refugees, and even French Catholic refugees, have thus a place in Winchester's representation of its past while medieval Jewry, with its more soul-searching connotations, have not. But there is one final element to add to this picture of late twentieth- and early twenty-first-century heritage exclusion which changes the focus to the Jewish sphere. It relates to the tragicomedy of the medieval Jewish cemetery and its re-discovery in the last quarter of the twentieth century.

In 1974/75 and more extensively in 1995, excavations took place in what was almost certainly the Jewish cemetery in Winchester. This cemetery had a wide significance. It serviced many of the Jewish communities in the south of England and reflected the freedom of Jews to have cemeteries outside London, granted in 1177.[300] According to the director of the Survey of the Jewish Built Heritage in the United Kingdom & Ireland, 'For Jews, cemeteries are a sensitive area, given their status as sacred places in perpetuity according to Jewish law. Disturbing the dead, however long they were buried, is forbidden in Jewish law.' Aside from the risk of 'neglect, vandalism and unsympathetic development', such sites have been threatened by archaeology: 'possible sites of Medieval Jewish cemeteries have in the past been partially excavated at York and Winchester, and this has aroused opposition within the Jewish community'.[301]

The excavation in 1995 led to the investigation of the graves and remains of fifty-four infants, fifteen adolescents and three adults. A year later the Chief Rabbi, Jonathan Sacks, became aware of the excavations and demanded that any other 'Jewish' bones discovered in Winchester should be left where they were. Meanwhile, the skeletons, he wrote to Winchester City Council, 'must be returned immediately for Jewish burial'. Sacks added that '*we* would regard any further archaeological testing, further research on human bones or, indeed, any further work to be continued at the site to be a desecration of the memory of those buried there and strictly forbidden in Jewish law' [my emphasis].[302]

Sacks started his letter by stating '*I* write to express the grave concerns of the Jewish community' [my emphasis].[303] His seamless movement from singular voice to plural and his claim to speak for all Jews at all times revealed the Chief Rabbi's inability to accept the limitations of his office: non-orthodox and secular Jews do not accept his authority and this is also true of some of those to his religious 'right'. Ironically, and without his permission, very orthodox Jews took matters into their own hands and demanded that they be given the skeletons. The Head of Winchester Museums Service was 'unexpectedly visited by a group of orthodox Jews' in March 2006. In what was an understatement of the actions of what might not unfairly be called a threatening vigilante group, he later reported that 'They were fairly forceful in their request for an immediate handover of the remains'.[304] Such intimidatory behaviour led to the bones being passed on to these Jewish communal figures and they were then buried in an orthodox cemetery in north Manchester. That, however, was not the end of the matter: when these very orthodox Jews became aware that it was impossible to fully authenticate the origins of the bones, they then fenced off the burials of these medieval bones from the rest of the cemetery.[305]

Where did these remains belong? To the chairwoman of South Hampshire Reform Jewish Community, it was to the locality. The finds were 'absolutely fascinating' and they added 'to the Jewish history of the city. It will be a very special corner of Winchester which proves Jewish connections with the city are even stronger than we first thought.'[306] In contrast, Rabbi Malcolm Weisman, acting on behalf of the Chief Rabbi's office, believed that once dug up, it was 'better to have them in Manchester because there is no Jewish community to speak of in Winchester'.[307] If the local heritage world has failed to integrate the presence of the Jews, the orthodox Jewish authorities in London have equally failed to consider the possibility of a 'Jewish' Winchester. This extends to the past – guides to British and international Jewish heritage do not include this ancient city.[308] In both cases – Jewish and non-Jewish – perceptions of the 'local' are restrained and exclusionary. The bones have thus ended up in Manchester, segregated from a cemetery which largely houses those who came from eastern Europe at the end of the nineteenth century and their descendants. What might well have been 'a very special corner of Winchester' has thus become another element of the near total absence in the memory work of the city. To Sue Bartlet, as a secular Jew living on the edge of the excavation, the outcome showed 'where a conflict between modern extreme religious views and Archaeology can lead'. Nevertheless, 'science', as represented by archaeology (which can manifest its own arrogance of assumed ownership in such matters), was not totally defeated. The limited analysis of the bones suggested that rickets was 'common among the Winchester children, less so in York'.[309] If some members of the medieval Winchester Jewry were, like the family of Licoricia, extremely wealthy, others – the majority – were very poor. The divisions between these Jews must not be underplayed. It was the latter who were also more vulnerable to physical persecution, evidence of which is present in the Winchester cemetery. Excavations revealed the bones of a young man who had 'sustained two cuts to his head, probably from a sword or axe'.[310]

Winchester Jewry was a multi-layered and fast-evolving community stretching between the secular and religious worlds. The richness as well as the tragedy of its past has so far not been reflected in the memorial landscape of the city. Medieval Winchester Jewry is currently invisible. Is, however, a more inclusive heritage possible or even desirable? Barrie Dobson has suggested that

> After centuries during which the atrocities that victimised the York Jews in 1190 have been deliberately remembered as infrequently as possible, they have ... at last found a place in whatever 'English Heritage' is supposed to be.

Dobson provides an example from a 1943 guide to Clifford's Tower in which 'the events of March 1190 are mentioned but – almost perversely – without any reference to the fact that Jews were killed there'.[311] Such amnesia prompted the Anglo-Jewish poet, Jon Silkin, to write in his poem, 'Astringencies' (1961)

> Absence of Jews
> Through hatred, or indifference,
> A gap they slip through, a conscience
> That corrodes more deeply since it is
> Forgotten – that deadens York.[312]

The 1943 guide, however, contrasts to a 1995 English Heritage pamphlet which 'discusses the massacre in considerable detail but ignores the architectural history of Clifford's Tower almost completely'. Dobson, over a period of three decades, has done more than any other to integrate medieval English and Jewish history. His conclusion on the meeting of heritage and the Jewish medieval past must be taken seriously. Dobson warns that the extensive commemoration of the 1190 York massacre and such developments as a 'Jewish Heritage Walk' for visitors to follow has not necessarily led to critical engagement. 'The transformation of the complex experience of the medieval Jewry into the simplified language of English Heritage and modern mass tourism ... is not perhaps to be deplored but is equally not without its dangers'.[313] Colin Richmond is blunter: 'the embrace of English Heritage is the opposite of a Kiss of Life'. Richmond also warns that any current interest within heritage of the Jewish past is ephemeral and is 'no guarantee that Jewish History, let alone Culture, is here to stay. Besides, too often it is still missing.'[314] Elsewhere, he has pondered 'what would a Jewish history of England consist of?', asking why, for example, 'does it have to be a history of the Jews in medieval Oxford which discusses the Jews of Oxford in the Middle Ages?'[315]

This chapter has explored many of the elements that a 'Jewish history of Winchester' would consist of. It has analysed why and when Jewish and local memory work have coincided and suggested where (everywhere) Winchester Jewry is now missing from the city's heritage. More, ironically, is now known about the medieval Jews of Winchester than ever before, perhaps one strong indication that the strength of heritage and history are inversely related – more of one is less of the other. That knowledge of the medieval Jewish community makes it harder to insist on one level that Winchester was 'the Jerusalem of the Jews', as a place free of persecution. Returning to the *Cronicon*, Anthony Bale argues that

> The idea of Winchester being 'the Jerusalem of the Jews' not only teases the city's large Jewish population (and perhaps mocks the financial dealings between churchmen and the Jews) but ironises the body-text, which at this point follows Richard I's lame progress in his journey to Jerusalem. The Jerusalem of the Jews is Jerusalem, whilst Winchester was an ecclesiastical and royal centre for Christians![316]

If, however, a more pluralistic and diasporic reading of Jewish memory is employed, it is perhaps possible to re-establish Richard of Devizes' outlandish and undoubtedly ironic claim.

In *The Jewish Search for a Usable Past* (1999), David Roskies outlines his route which 'has skirted the deserts, mountains, valleys, and steppes and has taken us instead through cities and towns, some real, some imaginary. This is because, ever since the Babylonian Exile, the Jews have been city dwellers and have learned, since the Destruction of the Second Temple, to compensate the loss by building communities, which in turn sustain an impressive network of religious, social, and educational institutions.'[317] For one and a half centuries, Winchester Jewry was part of that network. Nor did the Jews disappear from the city in 1290. Aside from 'the Jew' negatively represented in the Cathedral, there were those who chose the path of conversion and thereby avoided the expulsion, including Belia's son Benedict.[318] Others were present in Winchester from the eighteenth century through to the present day.[319] In 1996, a barmitzvah took place in Winchester Guildhall. The ceremony was 'symbolically important', according to the presiding rabbi, because it 'signified the return of Jews to Winchester, where, in the Middle Ages, before their expulsion from England, there existed one of the oldest Jewish communities in the country'.[320] In reality, the Jews had never totally left Winchester.

To draw this chapter to a close: the link between past and present, and the possibility of connecting the quintessentially diasporic Jewish experience with that of the local through *inclusive* memory work, was illustrated in 1985 through the efforts of a city guide, Barbara Hall. Hall had agreed to take a group of Bournemouth Jews around Winchester, later writing up her notes and experiences of the visit:

> Our most eminent Jewish citizen, Mr Bernfeld, retired only recently from the Jeweller's business in God Begot House [one of the oldest and most loved buildings in Winchester]. One of [our party] told me they believed a doctor at the hospital could trace his descent from one of the returning Jewish doctors under Charles II. Even as I was speaking to them behind God Begot House, Mr Bernfeld and his wife went walking along St Peter Street, which seemed symbolically significant!

Influenced by Barbara Carpenter Turner, Hall concluded that aside from the 'empty space' that followed from the expulsion of the Jews, 'Winchester citizens suffered a loss they would never have dreamt of; a valuable contact with a wider more cosmopolitan world which the Jews ... had provided'.[321] Winchester Jewry, past and present, have had origins and connections with all parts of the world. They also established, when free to do so, deep local roots. Doreen Massey has concluded that

> The attempt to align 'us' and 'them' with the general concepts of 'local' and 'global' is always deeply problematical. For in the historical and geographical constructions of places, the 'other' in general terms is already within. The global is everywhere and already, in one way or another, implicated in the local.[322]

In 1985, Barbara Hall, following Barbara Carpenter Turner, had, in practice, recognised the force of Massey's theoretical intervention. The inability subsequently to incorporate Jewish memory into local memory is thus a denial of the global in Winchester's past. It represents a major failure of imagination in the 'city of memories' and the triumph of a form of localism defined by parochialism and exclusivity. With regard to medieval Winchester Jewry, it represents their second removal.

Notes

1 For its origins, see Derek Keene, *Survey of Medieval Winchester* Part 1 (Oxford: Clarendon Press, 1985), p. 385; Suzanne Bartlet, 'Three Jewish Businesswomen in Thirteenth-Century Winchester', *Jewish Culture and History* vol. 3 no. 2 (Winter 2000), p. 34.

2 Keene, *Survey of Medieval Winchester* Part 1, Chapter 9. Sue Bartlet estimates that the maximum figure of Winchester Jewry was probably around 150. Conversation with the author, 4 March 2006.

3 See Vivian Lipman, 'The Anatomy of Medieval Anglo-Jewry', *Transactions of the Jewish Historical Society of England* vol. 21 (1962–67), p. 66; Keene, *Survey of Medieval Winchester*, p. 384.

4 *Hampshire Chronicle*, 24 March 1906 for Isaac of Russia.

5 Especially Oxford, Lincoln and York.

6 Telford Varley, *Winchester* (London: Adam and Charles Black, 1910), p. 4.

7 See, for example, G. W. Kitchin, *Winchester* (London: Longmans, Green & Co, 1890) within the 'Medieval towns' series, edited by Edward Freeman and William Hunt, and W.Lloyd Woodland, *The Story of Winchester* (London: J. M. Dent, 1932). The latter included thirty-four towns, seven of which were British.

8 Kitchin, *Winchester*, p. v.

9 A. R. Bramston and A. C. Leroy, *A City of Memories* (Winchester: P. and G. Wells, London, 1893), pp. 1–2.

10 Besant in Alfred Bowker, *The King Alfred Millenary: A Record of the Proceedings of the National Commmemoration* (London: Macmillan, 1902), p. 9.

11 Ibid., p. 3.

12 Krishan Kumar, *The Making of English National Identity* (Cambridge: Cambridge University Press, 2003), p. 232.

13 A. G. MacDonell, *England, Their England* (London: Reprint Society, 1941 [1933]), pp. 286, 298.

14 Ibid., p. 299.

15 Varley, *Winchester*, p. 3.

16 S. E. Winbolt, *The Penguin Guides: Hampshire and the Isle of Wight* (Harmondsworth: Penguin, 1949), p. 60.

17 Yosef Yerushalmi, *Zakhor: Jewish History & Jewish Memory* (New York: Schocken Books, 1989), p. 5.

18 Jonathan Safran Foer, *Everything is Illuminated* (London: Penguin Books, 2003 [2002]), p. 198.

19 Yerushalmi, *Zakhor*, p. 5.

20 Jonathan Boyarin, *Storm from Paradise: The Politics of Jewish Memory* (Minneapolis: University of Minnesota Press, 1992).

21 Patrick Geary, *Phantoms of Remembrance: Memory and Oblivion at the End of the First*

Millennium (Princeton: Princeton University Press, 1994), p. 9.

22 Herbert Powell, *Lyrics of the White City* (London: Simpkin, 1896), p. 7.

23 Ibid., pp. 9–10.

24 Doreen Massey, 'Places and Their Pasts', *History Workshop Journal* no. 39 (spring 1995), p. 186.

25 Richard Sieburth, 'Benjamin the Scrivener', in Gary Smith (ed.), *Benjamin: Philosophy, History, Aesthetics* (Chicago: University of Chicago Press, 1989), p. 14.

26 Walter Benjamin, *The Arcades Project* (Cambridge, MA: Harvard University Press, 1999, translated by Howard Eiland and Kevin Mclaughlin), p. 833.

27 Raphael Samuel, *Island Stories: Unravelling Britain* vol. II *Theatres of Memory* (London: Verso, 1998), p. 354.

28 Boyarin, *Storm from Paradise*, p. 4.

29 Brian Vesey-Fitzgerald, *Winchester* (London: Phoenix House, 1953), p. 169.

30 Ibid., p. 170.

31 Ibid., p. 176.

32 WHJ letter to *Hampshire Chronicle*, 9 September 1892.

33 W. Page (ed.), *The Victoria History of the Counties of England: A History of Hampshire and the Isle of Wight* vol. 5 (London: Constable, 1912), p. 32.

34 See Henry Moody (ed.), *Hampshire Three Hundred Years Ago Transcribed from the Itinerary of John Leland Aniquary Royal* (Winchester: John Doswell, 1868), p. 7.

35 Winchester City Council, *Explore Every Winchester: Days to Treasure* (Winchester: Winchester City Council, 2005), p. 11.

36 Discover Winchester Group, *The Winchester Walk* (Winchester: Winchester City Council, 2003), p. 8.

37 Charles Bell, *An Historical Account of Winchester, With Descriptive Walks* (Winchester: James Robbins, 1818), pp. iii, 201–2.

38 Sieburth, 'Benjamin the Scrivener', pp. 14–15. See also Benjamin, *The Arcades Project*, p. 840 for a slightly varying translation.

39 Barbara Carpenter Turner, 'Winchester Jewry', *AJA Quarterly* vol. 1 no. 4 (March 1956), p. 122.

40 The reference to the name change is in British Library Manuscripts, Stowe 846, ff.6v–7, reproduced in Michael McVaugh, 'The Position of Alware Street in Medieval Winchester', *Proceedings of the Hampshire Field Club* vols 24–5 (1967–68), p. 84 note 9.

41 Bernard Bolingbroke Woodward, *A History and Description of Winchester* (Alresford, Hants: Laurence Oxley, 1974 [1860]), p. 22.

42 Barbara Carpenter Turner, 'A Distinguished House and Some of its Owners: A Brief Account of 29, Jewry Street', *Hampshire Chronicle*, 15 November 1969.

43 See, for example, A. R. Bramston and A. C. Leroy, *Historic Winchester: England's First Capital* (London: Longmans, Green & Co, 1884), pp. 364–5 and Peter Kilby, *Winchester: An Architect's View* (Southampton: WIT Press, 2002), p. 40.

44 Winchester Pavement Commissioners, minutes 23 August 1830 in Hampshire Record Office (HRO), W/J1/7.

45 Winchester City Council records, W/J1/31, HRO.

46 John Arlott, 'The Shop Facade of History', *Hampshire: The County Magazine* vol. 4 no. 11 (September 1964), p. 15.

47 Winchester Pavement Commmissioners, minutes 31 March 1856 in HRO W/J1/7.

48 Carpenter Turner, 'A Distinguished House'.

49 *Hampshire Chronicle*, 5 April 1856.

50 *Hampshire Chronicle*, 3 May 1856.

51 Thomas Warton [J. Wilkes], *A Description of Winchester* (Winchester: W.Greenville, 1774), p. 19.

52 Henry Riley (ed.), *Chronicles of the Mayors and Sheriffs of London A.D. 1188 to A.D. 1274* (London: Trubner & Co, 1863), p. 78 attributed to Alderman Fitz-Thedman which refers to 'Simon de Montfort the Younger, with other Barons and their adherants, took and plundered Winchester and destroyed the Jewry there' and similarly William Wright (ed.), *The Metrical Chronicle of Robert of Gloucester* Part II (London: HMSO, 1887), p. 760.

53 John Milner, *The History, Civil and Ecclesiastical, and Survey of the Antiquities of Winchester* vol. 1 (Winchester: Robbins, 1798), p. 259.

54 John Milner, *The History, Civil and Ecclesiastical, and Survey of the Antiquities of Winchester* vol. II (Winchester: Robbins, 1801), p. 180.

55 Using the model estimates provided by Lipman, 'The Anatomy of Medieval Anglo-Jewry', p. 65. Patricia Allin, 'Richard of Devizes and the Alleged Martyrdom of a Boy at Winchester', *Transactions of the Jewish Historical Society of England* vol. 27 (1978–80), p. 32 suggests that at the end of the twelfth century, the Jews 'numbered at most about ninety including women and children' out of a population of over 8000.

56 W. Mates, *Illustrated Handbook to Southampton* (Bournemouth: W. Mates & Son, 1900), no page.

57 Wright, *The Metrical Chronicle of Robert of Gloucester*, p. 760.

58 *The New Winchester Handbook* (Winchester: Tanner & Sons, 1868), p. 81.

59 Varley, *Winchester*, p. 97.

60 *The New Winchester Handbook*, pp. 83–4.

61 Reverend Moses Margoliouth, *The History of the Jews in Great Britain* (London: Richard Bentley, 1851), p. 294.

62 Ibid., p. 62.

63 Celia and Marion Moss, *Early Efforts: A Volume of Poems* (London: Whittaker, Portsmouth, 1839), pp. 11–19.

64 Celia Levetus, *The King's Physician, And Other Tales* (Portsmouth: T. Hinton, 1865), p. 254.

65 Ibid., pp. 127, 137.

66 Gavin Langmuir, 'The Knight's Tale of Young Hugh of Lincoln', *Speculum* vol. 47 (1972), pp. 459–60.

67 Israel Abrahams, 'Draft of Prospectus', reproduced in *Transactions of the Jewish Historical Society of England* vol. VII (1911–1914), p. 220.

68 John Appleby (ed.), *The Chronicle of Richard of Devizes of the Time of King Richard the First* (London: Thomas Nelsen, 1963), pp. xi, xv.

69 Anthony Bale, 'Richard of Devizes and Fictions of Judaism', *Jewish Culture and History* vol. 3 no. 2 (Winter 2000), pp. 56–7.

70 Ibid., p. 60.

71 Ibid., p. 66.

72 Appleby, (ed.), *The Chronicle of Richard of Devizes*, pp. 3–4.

73 Ibid., pp. 64, 67.

74 Ibid., p. 64.

75 See, for example, Sukhdev Sandhu, *London Calling: How Black and Asian Writers Imagined a City* (London: HarperCollins, 2003), p. xiv.

76 Appleby, *The Chronicle of Richard of Devizes*, p. 65.

77 Ibid., pp. xv, 66.

78 Ibid., p. 69.
79 Ibid., p. xv.
80 Richard Howlitt (ed.), *Chronicles of the Reigns of Stephen, Henry II and Richard I* vol. 3 (London: Longman & Co, 1886), p. lxxii.
81 Nancy Partner, *Serious Entertainments: The Writing of History in Twelfth-Century England* (Chicago: University of Chicago Press, 1977), pp. 177–8.
82 Bale, 'Richard of Devizes', p. 65.
83 Ibid., p. 65.
84 Ibid., pp. 68–9.
85 Charles Dellheim, *The Face of the Past: The Preservation of the Medieval Inheritance in Victorian England* (Cambridge: Cambridge University Press, 1982), p. xiii.
86 Ibid., p. 59.
87 Ibid., pp. 61–4; Kitchin, *Winchester*.
88 Ibid., p. 106.
89 Ibid., p. 106.
90 Ibid., p. 107.
91 Ibid., p. 108.
92 Dellheim, *The Face of the Past*, p. 64.
93 Ibid., p. 108.
94 Tony Kushner, 'Heritage and Ethnicity: An Introduction', in Tony Kushner (ed.), *The Jewish Heritage in British History: Englishness and Jewishness* (London: Frank Cass, 1992), p. 16.
95 James Picciotto, *Sketches of Anglo-Jewish History* (London: Trubner, 1875).
96 Nils Roemer, 'Towards a Comparative Jewish Literary History: National Literary Canons in Nineteenth-Century Germany and England', in Bryan Cheyette and Nadia Valman (eds), *The Image of the Jew in European Liberal Culture 1789–1914* (London: Vallentine Mitchell, 2004), pp. 35–6.
97 David Cesarani, 'Dual Heritage or Duel of Heritages? Englishness and Jewishness in the Heritage Industry', in Kushner, *The Jewish Heritage in British History*, p. 31.
98 *Jewish Chronicle*, 21 October 1881 quoted by Cesarani, 'Dual Heritage', p. 31.
99 Joseph Jacobs and Lucien Wolf (eds), *Bibliotheca Anglo-Judaica: A Bibliographical Guide to Anglo-Jewish History* (London: Jewish Chronicle, 1888), section on 'Pre-Expulsion Period'.
100 Joseph Jacobs, 'An English Jew Admitted to the Merchant Guild of Winchester A.D. 1268', *Jewish Chronicle*, 9 August 1889.
101 Joseph Jacobs (ed.), *The Jews of Angevin England: Documents and Records* (London: David Nutt, 1893), pp. 133–4.
102 *Jewish Chronicle*, 9 August 1889.
103 Wlliam Warren (ed.), *Winchester Illustrated* (London: Simpkin, 1903), pp. 128–33.
104 'Early Winchester Jews', reproduced in *Hampshire Chronicle*, 24 March 1906.
105 'Winchester, 1195', *Jewish World*, 28 August 1903.
106 M. Gudemann, *Geschichte des Erziehungswesens und der Cultur Der Juden in Frankreich und Deutschland* (Vienna, Alfred Holder, 1880), p. 86.
107 'Early Winchester Jews', *Hampshire Chronicle*, 24 March 1906.
108 See, for example, the close parallels in H. P. Stokes, *Studies in Anglo-Jewish History* (Edinburgh: Ballantyne, Hanson & Co, 1913), pp. 52–3, 132 and the critique of Joseph Jacobs's work. More generally, see the tribute to Stokes in *Transactions of the Jewish Historical Society of England* vol. 12 (1928–31), pp. 267–9.
109 'Early Winchester Jews'.

110 Sidney Heath, *Winchester* (London: Blockis & Son, 1910), p. 44.
111 Ibid., pp. 44–5.
112 Varley, *Winchester*, p. 2.
113 Ibid., p. 97.
114 Picciotto, *Sketches of Anglo-Jewish History*, p. 3.
115 Cesarani, 'Dual Heritage or Duel of Heritages', p. 30.
116 M. D. Davis, 'Early Winchester Jews', *Jewish Chronicle*, 16 September 1892, reproduced in *Hampshire Chronicle*, 31 December 1892.
117 Ibid. See *Papers Read at the Anglo-Jewish Historical Exhibition, Royal Albert Hall, London 1887* (London: Jewish Chronicle, 1888), p. 150 for Walter Rye's analysis of the *Cronicon*.
118 Augustus Jessopp and M. R. James, *The Life and Miracles of St William of Norwich by Thomas of Monmouth* (Cambridge: Cambridge University Press, 1896).
119 Gavin Langmuir, *Toward A Definition of Antisemitism* (Berkeley: University of California Press, 1990), p. 295.
120 James, 'Introduction', p. lxxvi.
121 W. H. Hutton, 'The Church and National Life', in H. D. Traill (ed.), *Social England* vol. 1 (London: Cassell, 1898 [1893]), p. 407.
122 James, 'Introduction', p. lxxvii; Traill, *Social England*, p. 407.
123 Colin Holmes, 'The Ritual Murder Accusation in Britain', *Ethnic and Racial Studies* vol. 4 no. 3 (July 1981), p. 280.
124 For the later accusations see Nicholas Vincent, 'Jews, Poitevins, and the Bishop of Winchester, 1231–1234', in Diana Wood (ed.), *Christianity and Judaism* (Oxford: Blackwell, 1992), pp. 128–9.
125 *The Jews' Who's Who* (London: Judaic Publishing Co, 1920), pp. 64–4.
126 See Holmes, 'The Ritual Murder Accusation', pp. 272–3.
127 Arnold Leese, *My Irrelevant Defence being Meditations Inside Gaol and Out on Jewish Ritual Murder* (London: Imperial Fascist League, 1938), p. 12.
128 Ibid., pp. 2, 15.
129 *The Fascist* no. 86 (July 1936).
130 National Archives, HO 45/24967/674960/105–9.
131 *The Independent*, 25 November 1997; *Archives* no. 99 (October 1998), p. 99.
132 John Harvey, *The Plantagenets* (London: Fontana, 1972 [1948]), pp. 119–20, 235.
133 J. Blakiston (ed.), *Winchester Cathedral: An Anthology* (Winchester: Friends of Winchester Cathedral, 1970), p. 25.
134 Winchester Preservation Trust, *Jewry Street Winchester* (Winchester: Winchester Preservation Trust, 1984), p. 1.
135 *Jewish Chronicle*, 18 October 1985.
136 'Early Winchester Jews', *Jewish Chronicle*, 16 September 1892.
137 Robert Levine, 'Why Praise Jews: Satire and History in the Middle Ages', *Journal of Medieval History* vol. 12 (1986), pp. 294–5.
138 Antonia Gransden, *Historical Writing in England c550 to c1307* (London: Routledge & Kegan Paul, 1974), p. 251.
139 Colin Richmond, 'Englishness and Medieval Anglo-Jewry', in Kushner (ed.), *The Jewish Heritage in British History*, p. 55.
140 Bale, 'Richard of Devizes', p. 65.
141 Ibid., p. 69.
142 Reverend A. G. L'Estrange, *Royal Winchester: Wanderings in and about the Ancient Capital of England* (London: Spencer Blackett & Hallam, 1889).

143 Ibid., p. 35.
144 Ibid., p. 123.
145 Ibid., pp. 123–4.
146 Bale, 'Richard of Devizes', p. 68.
147 Colin Richmond, 'Introduction: The Jews in Medieval England', *Jewish Culture and History* vol. 3 no. 2 (Winter 2000), pp. 5–6.
148 Vincent, 'Jews and Poitevins', pp. 128–9.
149 Davis, 'Early Winchester Jews'.
150 J. A. Giles, (trans and ed.), *The Chronicle of Richard Devizes* (London: James Bohn, 1841), p. 5.
151 H. G. Richardson, *The English Jewry under Angevin Kings* (London: Methuen, 1960), p. vii; A. L. Poole, *From Domesday Book to Magna Carta: 1087–1216* (Oxford: Clarendon Press, 1951), p. 353.
152 Originally published in the *Journal of the History of Ideas* and reproduced in Langmuir, *Toward a Definition of Antisemitism*.
153 Langmuir, *Toward A Definition of Antisemitism*, pp. 31, 39.
154 Richmond, 'Englishness and Medieval Anglo-Jewry', pp. 52–3; J. C. Holt, *The Northerners: A Study in the Reign of King John* (Oxford: Clarendon Press, 1961), p. 165.
155 Langmuir, *Toward A Definition of Antisemitism*, p. 39.
156 Richmond, 'Englishness and Medieval Anglo-Jewry', p. 43.
157 Langmuir, *Toward a Definition of Antisemitism*, p. 39.
158 Hugh MacDougall, *Racial Myth in English History: Trojans, Teutons and Anglo-Saxons* (Hanover: University Press of New England, 1982), p. 91.
159 Ibid., pp. 100–1.
160 David Feldman, *Englishmen and Jews: Social Relations and Political Culture 1840–1914* (London: Yale University Press, 1994), p. 92.
161 Edward Freeman, *The Reign of William Rufus* vol. 1 (Oxford: Clarendon Press, 1882), p. 160.
162 Ibid.
163 Hilaire Belloc, *The Old Road (from Canterbury to Winchester)* (London: Constable, 1948 [1904]), p. 11.
164 Ibid., pp. 56–8.
165 Ibid., p. 58.
166 Colin Holmes, *Anti-Semitism in British Society 1876–1939* (London: Arnold, 1979), pp. 76–7.
167 Belloc, *The Old Road*, p. 118.
168 See Robert Skidelsky, *Oswald Mosley* (London: Papermacs, 1981 [1975]), pp. 350, 439.
169 Hugh Ross Williamson, *The Ancient Capital* (London: Frederick Muller, 1953), p. 34.
170 Ibid., p. 35.
171 Ibid., pp. 35–7.
172 Holt, *The Northerners*, p. 166.
173 S. Ward-Evans, 'The Jews in Ancient Winchester', *Hampshire Chronicle*, 28 September 1935.
174 Ibid.
175 *Hampshire Review* no. 18 (Winter 1953/54), p. 67.
176 See the obituaries in *Hampshire Chronicle*, 24 January 1997; *Winchester Cathedral Record* no. 66 (1997), pp. 2–4; *Winchester Preservation Trust Newsletter*, Spring 1997 and *Hampshire Archives Trust Newsletter*, Spring 1997.

177 Barbara Carpenter Turner, 'The Winchester Jewry', *Hampshire Review* no. 21 (Winter 1954/55), pp. 17–21.

178 Michael Adler, 'Benedict the Gildsman of Winchester', *Miscellanies of the Jewish Historical Society of England* Part IV (London: JHSE, 1942), p. 8.

179 Barbara Carpenter Turner, *A History of Hampshire* (London: Darwen Finlayson, 1963), pp. 6, 68.

180 Barbara Carpenter Turner, 'The Jewish Community in Mediaeval Winchester', *Hampshire Chronicle*, 27 January 1962.

181 Carpenter Turner, 'The Winchester Jewry', p. 17.

182 *Hampshire Chronicle*, 27 January 1962.

183 Carpenter Turner, 'The Winchester Jewry', pp. 19, 21.

184 *Hampshire Chronicle*, 27 January 1962.

185 Freeman, *The Reign of William Rufus*, p. 160, note 2.

186 Carpenter Turner, 'The Winchester Jewry', p. 19.

187 Ibid., pp. 19–20.

188 Ibid., p. 20.

189 Carpenter Turner, 'Winchester Jewry', *AJA Quarterly*, pp. 120–5.

190 Davis was a member of the JHSE's council from its inception. For an appreciation of his work see Lucien Wolf, 'Origin of the Jewish Historical Society of England', *Transactions of the JHSE* vol. VII (1911–14), pp. 207–10.

191 *Jewish Chronicle*, 16 September 1892.

192 J. M. Rigg (ed.), *Select Pleas, Starrs and Other Records from the Rolls of the Exchequer of the Jews A.D. 1220–1284* (London: Selden Society, 1902), pp. 19–27.

193 See the index of J. M. Rigg (ed.), *Calendar of the Plea Rolls of the Exchequer of the Jews* vol. 1 (London: Macmillan, 1905), esp. p. 365.

194 *The Jewish Encyclopedia* vol. 12 (New York: Funk & Waynall, 1906), p. 531.

195 In Traill, (ed.), *Social England*, pp. 471–82.

196 JHR, 'Notes on Jews in XIII Century England: i. Jewesses', *Notes and Queries*, 13 October 1934.

197 Ibid., p. 255.

198 Ibid.

199 Rigg, *Calendar of the Plea Rolls*, p. xvi.

200 Barrie Dobson, 'The Role of Jewish Women in Medieval England', in Wood, *Christianity and Judaism*, p. 162.

201 Rigg, *Select Pleas*, p. xliii.

202 Michael Adler, 'The Jewish Woman in Medieval England', in Michael Adler, *Jews of Medieval England* (London: JHSE, 1939), p. 17.

203 Ibid., pp. 18, 37.

204 Tribute to Adler by Arthur Barnett in *Transactions of the JHSE* vol. XV (1939–45), pp. 192, 194.

205 Adler, 'The Jewish Woman', p. 28.

206 Ibid., p. 19.

207 Ibid., pp. 37, 42.

208 Ibid., p. 39.

209 Ibid., pp. 23, 42.

210 John Docherty, 'Revealed – the lost world of Licoricia and a city's Jews', *Hampshire Chronicle*, 7 September 2001.

211 Suzanne Bartlet, 'Women in the Medieval Anglo-Jewish Community', in Patricia Skinner

(ed.), *Jews in Medieval Britain* (Woodbridge: Boydell, 2003), pp. 113–27 and Suzanne Bartlet, 'Three Jewish Businesswomen in Thirteenth-Century Winchester', *Jewish Culture and History* vol. 3 no. 2, pp. 31–54.

212 Bartlet, 'Women in the Medieval Anglo-Jewish Community', pp. 119, 126.

213 Ibid., p. 116.

214 Bartlet, 'Three Jewish Businesswomen', p. 50.

215 Dobson, 'Jewish Women in Medieval England', p. 146.

216 R. B. Dobson, *The Jews of Medieval York and the Massacre of March 1190* (York: Borthwick Papers no. 45, 1974).

217 Barrie Dobson, 'The Medieval York Jewry Reconsidered', in Skinner, (ed.), *The Jews in Medieval Britain*, p. 145.

218 Pamela Fletcher Jones, *The Jews of Britain: A Thousand Years of History* (Moreton-in-Marsh: Windrush Press, 1990), p. 57.

219 Bartlet, 'Three Jewish Businesswomen', p. 50.

220 Ibid., p. 32 and Bartlet, 'Women in the Medieval Anglo-Jewish Community', p. 113.

221 Richmond, 'Introduction: The Jews of Medieval England', p. 4.

222 Tom James, *Book of Winchester* (London: B. T. Batsford/English Heritage, 1997), p. 70; Bartlet, 'Three Jewish Businesswomen', p. 51.

223 Permanent exhibition of Winchester City Museum, visited 4 March 2006. The Museum was re-designed in the late 1990s and re-opened in 2000.

224 See *Days to Treasure* or *The Winchester Walk*. See also Lonely Planet, *England* (London: Lonely Planet, 2005), p. 207 which states that Jewry Street was 'once part of the city's Jewish quarter – today it is where you'll find a chunk of the town's nightlife'.

225 Vivien Brett, *Winchester* (Norwich: Pitkin City Guides, 2002).

226 Colin Richmond, 'Jews and the Medieval Origins of the English State', unpublished paper delivered at the University of Princeton, December 2005.

227 Bowker, *The King Alfred Millenary; Winchester National Pageant: The Book of the Words and Music* (Winchester: Warren & Son, 1908).

228 See Warren, *Winchester Illustrated*, pp. 128–33.

229 See, for example, Barbara Carpenter Turner, *City of Winchester: The Ancient Capital of England* (London: Pitkin Pictorials, 1974), pp. 9–10; *Winchester* (Southampton: Paul Cave, 1980), pp. 34–6; and *A History of Winchester* (Chichester: Phillimore, 1992), pp. 28–31.

230 Keene, *Survey of Medieval Winchester*, Part 1, pp. 76–9, 324–5, 384–7; Parts II and III, pp. 1034–5.

231 Keene, *Survey of Medieval Wincester* Part 1, p. 384.

232 Ibid., pp. 76–7.

233 Ibid., p. 387.

234 Ibid., pp. 384–5.

235 Ibid., p. 386.

236 Ibid., p. 386 and *Survey of Medieval Winchester*, Part II and III, p. 1034.

237 Keene, *Survey of Medieval Winchester*, Part 1, p. 384.

238 Richmond, 'Englishness and Medieval Anglo-Jewry', p. 56.

239 Raymond Birt, *The Glories of Winchester Cathedral* (London: Winchester Publications, 1948), p. 113.

240 Bale, 'Richard of Devizes', p. 65.

241 M. R. James and E. W. Tristram, 'The Wall Paintings in Eton College Chapel and in the Lady Chapel of Winchester Cathedral', *Walpole Society* vol. 17 (1929), pp. 22–3, 31.

242 Miri Rubin, *Gentile Tales: The Narrative Assault on Late Medieval Jews* (New Haven: Yale

University Press, 1999), chapter 2 and p. 18 for the Lady Chapel where the images are described in error as stained-glass.

243 John Vaughan, *Winchester Cathedral: Its Monuments and Memorials* (London: Selwyn & Blount, 1919), p. 1.

244 Blakiston, (ed.), *Winchester Cathedral: An Anthology*, p. 26 from John Harvey, *Henry Yevele* (London: Batsford, 1944), pp. 69–70.

245 Frederick Bussby, *Winchester Cathedral 1079–1979* (Southampton: Paul Cave, 1979), p. 58 and James and Tristram, 'The Wall Paintings', pp. 4–8, 14–15.

246 *Historical and Descriptive Guide to Winchester* (Winchester: Nutt & Wells, 1864), p. 34.

247 Gleeson White and Edward Strange (eds), *Winchester: The Cathedral and See* (London: George Bell, 1903), pp. 87–8.

248 *A Walk Around Guide to the Cathedral Church of Winchester* (Winchester: Warren & Sons, 1934), p. 7 and in later versions of this guide until the early 1960s.

249 Birt, *The Glories of Winchester Cathedral*, p. 26.

250 William Warren, *Illustrated Guide to Winchester* (London: Simpkin, 1907), p. 86.

251 Kitchin, *Winchester*, p. 222.

252 Birt, *The Glories of Winchester Cathedral*, p. 26.

253 Jules Isaac, *The Teaching of Contempt: Christian Roots of Anti-Semitism* (New York: Holt, Rinehalt & Winston, 1964).

254 '"Jew-boy" Removed', *Jewish Chronicle*, 25 October 1985. See also letter from David Spector to the same paper, 1 November 1985, in which he claims an earlier protest had failed to be acted upon.

255 Julie Adams, 'Images of David', *Winchester Cathedral Record* no. 74 (2005), pp. 28–32.

256 Bale, 'Richard of Devizes', p. 65.

257 Kitchin, *Winchester*, p. 106.

258 Ibid., p. 212.

259 'The Monument of Jean Serres, Huguenot', *Winchester Cathedral Record* no. 9 (1940), p. 12.

260 My thanks to Dr Sarah Pearce for her translation of the Latin inscription on the Serres memorial.

261 See *Hampshire Chronicle*, 27 July 1889.

262 Vaughan, *Winchester Cathedral*, p. 300 on the Portal Memorial.

263 Ibid., pp. 261–2.

264 John Crook, *Winchester Cathedral* (Andover: Pitkin Unichrome, 2001), p. 70.

265 Winchester Cathedral, *A Walk Round Guide: The Cathedral Church of Winchester* (Winchester: Winchester Cathedral, 1969), p. 11.

266 Ibid.

267 See Tony Kushner, *Remembering Refugees: Then and Now* (Manchester: Manchester University Press, 2006).

268 Zefira Rokeah, (ed.), *Medieval English Jews and Royal Officials: Entries of Jewish Interest in the English Memoranda Rolls, 1266–1293* (Jerusalem: Magnes Press, 2000), pp. 77–8.

269 Martin Biddle, 'Problem and Context', in Martin Biddle (ed.), *King Arthur's Round Table* (Woodbridge: Boydell, 2000), p. 3.

270 See Martin Biddle and Beatrice Clayre, *The Winchester Castle Great Hall & Round Table* (Winchester: Hampshire County Council, 2000), pp. 28–36.

271 Permanent exhibition at the Great Hall, panel 14, visited 4 March 2006.

272 John McIlwain, *Winchester Castle and the Great Hall* (Norwich: Jarrold Publishing, 2003 [1994]).

273 Biddle and Clayre, *The Winchester Castle*, p. 15.

274 On this work, see Reid Barbour, *John Selden: Measures of the Holy Commonwealth in Seventeenth-Century England* (Toronto: University of Toronto Press, 2003), pp. 214–33.

275 John Selden, *De Jure Naturali et Gentium Juxta Disciplinam Ebraeorum* (London: Richard Bishop, 1640), p. 195. My thanks to Dr Chris Woolgar for his help with this text.

276 D'Blossiers Tovey, *Anglia Judaica or the History and Aniquities of the Jews in England* (Oxford: James Fletcher, 1738), p. 150.

277 Bartlet, 'Jewish Businesswomen in Winchester', p. 51.

278 Jason Burke, 'England Accused of Ethnic Cleansing … 700 Years ago', *Observer*, 1 October 2000.

279 Biddle and Clayre, *The Winchester Castle*, p. 48 quoting one of the co-designers of the gardens.

280 Sylvia Landsberg, *The Medieval Garden* (London: British Museum Press, 1996), p. 121.

281 Biddle and Clayre, *The Winchester Castle*, p. 44.

282 Robin Mundill, 'Edward I and the Final Phase of Anglo-Jewry', in Skinner (ed.), *Jews in Medieval Britain*, pp. 57–8.

283 H. P. Stokes, *A Short History of the Jews in England* (London: Central Board of Missions, 1921), p. 6.

284 Robin Mundill, *England's Jewish Solution: Experiment and Expulsion, 1262–1290* (Cambridge: Cambridge University Press, 1998), pp. 62, 267–8.

285 Richmond, 'Englishness and Medieval Anglo-Jewry', pp. 44–5, 56.

286 David Stocker, 'The Shrine of Little St Hugh', *The British Archaeological Association Conference Transactions for the Year 1982* (Leeds: British Archaeological Association, 1986), pp. 115–16.

287 Richmond, 'Englishness and Medieval Anglo-Jewry', pp. 44–5.

288 Biddle and Clayre, *The Winchester Castle*, p. 44.

289 Simon Jervis, 'The Round Table as Furniture', in Biddle (ed.), *King Arthur's Round Table*, p. 57.

290 Martin Biddle, 'The Making of the Round Table', in Biddle (ed.), *King Arthur's Round Table*, p. 374.

291 Martin Biddle, 'Symbol and Epilogue', in Biddle (ed.), *King Arthur's Round Table*, p. 475.

292 Harvey, *The Plantagenets*, p. 119.

293 John Harvey, *Gothic England: A Survey of National Culture* (London: Batsford, 1947), p. 15.

294 Harvey, *Henry Yevele*, p. 77.

295 See *The Times*, 17 January 2001 for the controversy this created.

296 Geary, *Phantoms of Remembrance*, p. 12.

297 Permanent exhibition, Winchester Great Hall, panel 41.

298 See *Hampshire Chronicle*, 23 August 1996.

299 'The Old Gaol House', visited 8 December 2005.

300 See Sue Bartlet, 'Wooden Pegs – A Comparison of Two Thirteenth Century Jewish Cemeteries', (unpublished MA essay, University of Southampton, 1999), p. 1. I am grateful to Sue Bartlet for her discussions on the Winchester excavations and for allowing me to cite this essay. See also *Hampshire Chronicle*, 18 June 1995 for a report on the early stages of the excavation.

301 Memorandum by the director, Dr Sharman Kadish, in www.parliament.the-stationery-of-fice.co.uk/pa/cm200001/cmenvtra/9, accessed 10 February 2006.

302 Jonathan Sacks, letter to Winchester City Council, 14 March 1996, in private papers of Sue

Bartlet.

303 Ibid.

304 Letter from the head of Winchester Museums Service to Councillor Davies, 20 June 1996, in the private possession of Sue Bartlet.

305 See David Rose, 'Jewish Bones of Contention Laid to Rest', *Observer*, 16 June 1996.

306 Quoted in *Hampshire Chronicle*, 18 June 1995.

307 Rose, 'Jewish Bones of Contention'.

308 See, for example, Toni Kamins, *The Complete Jewish Guide to Britain and Ireland* (New York: St Martin's Griffin, 2001) and Michael Zaidner (ed.), *Jewish Travel Guide 2000* (London: Vallentine, Mitchell, 2000).

309 Bartlet, 'Wooden Pegs', pp. 4–5.

310 Ibid.

311 Dobson, 'The Medieval York Jewry Reconsidered', pp. 145–6.

312 Quoted in Peter Lawson, *Anglo-Jewish Poetry from Isaac Rosenberg to Elaine Feinstein* (London: Vallentine Mitchell, 2006), p. 127.

313 Dobson, 'The Medieval York Jewry Reconsidered', pp. 145–6.

314 Richmond, 'Introduction: The Jews in Medieval England', p. 3.

315 Richmond, 'Englishness and Medieval Anglo-Jewry', p. 43.

316 Bale, 'Richard of Devizes', p. 62.

317 David Roskies, *The Jewish Search for a Usable Past* (Bloomington: Indiana University Press, 1999), pp. 172–3.

318 Adler, *Jews of Medieval England*, p. 309 and Bartlet, 'Jewish Businesswomen', p. 51.

319 See Roth, *A History of the Jews in England*, p. 230.

320 *Hampshire Chronicle*, 19 January 1996.

321 Barbara Hall, 'The Story of the Jews in Medieval Winchester', December 1985 in Hampshire Record Office, 120 M94W/f23/3.

322 Doreen Massey, 'Double Articulation: A Place in the World', in A. Bammer (ed.), *Displacements: Cultural Identities in Question* (Bloomington: Indiana University Press, 1994), p. 120.

4

Point of contestation: Jews in Portsmouth during the long eighteenth century

Introduction

Reference has already been made to Bill Williams's portrayal of Manchester Jewry from the late 1820s as 'two communities ... the one increasingly anxious to live down the reputation of the other'. Williams eloquently explores the divide:

> On one side, there was a settled community of shopkeepers, overseas merchants, share brokers, and professional men, anglicised in speech and custom, comfortably off (or reasonably so), generous to local causes, the providers of essential goods and services to the middle classes; on the other, a flotsam of pedlars and petty criminals, some of the unsuccessful residuum of eighteenth-century Jewry, other pauper immigrants of the post-war years, illiterate in English, incoherent in speech, uncouth in appearance, often associated with the criminal underworld, most frequently as the receivers of stolen jewellery and plate.

What made the tension between them even greater was that the former often had the same origins as the latter. Therefore, the 'further the early members moved from their itinerant origins, the more they were plagued by the memory of them'. Acceptance of the settled community and its good local reputation was at risk through 'evidence of Jews in crime, or in occupations such as hawking or slop selling, which were no longer economically viable or socially reputable'.[1]

While the nineteenth century was to witness the Jews of Manchester emerging as a far larger and important provincial settlement, Portsmouth Jewry's roots were deeper. Indeed, some members of the early Manchester and other provincial Jewish communities originated from Portsmouth.[2] Post-readmission of the Jews to England during the 1650s, Portsmouth was the oldest and initially the most substantial Jewish settlement outside London,[3] and there is 'sufficient evidence to indicate a community of Jews in Portsmouth prior to the 1740s'.[4] Even as late as the 1850s, with a Jewish population of some 300, it was still the fourth largest provincial community in the country behind the industrial cities of Liverpool (with around 2500 Jews), Manchester (approximately 2000) and Birmingham (750–1000).[5]

With its earlier origins than Manchester, it is not surprising that the types of tensions and divisions identified by Williams occurred within Portsmouth Jewry well *before* the nineteenth century. Thus the complex organisational structure devised by the Jewish elite in mid-Victorian Manchester to deal with poor immigrants was modelled on earlier bodies set up in Liverpool, London and Portsmouth.[6] Yet situated in what was one of the most notorious seaports in the western world, it is also clear that it was much harder – both inside and outside the Jewish community – to construct who were the 'respectable' and 'unrespectable' Jews of Portsmouth. It was a problem of identification that was intensified by the transitory nature of the Jewish community, one that mirrored that of Portsmouth as a whole. In turn, such population flux reflected the unusual social relationships created through the naval domination of the town. If Manchester, Liverpool and Birmingham Jewry all had their roots in the settling of formerly itinerant pedlars, those of the naval ports reflected a different style of trading: 'Why should they peddle their wares about the country when a more or less captive customer was to be found in the men-of-war lying at Portsmouth, Plymouth, Chatham and Sheerness?'[7] In the long term, because of the volatility of naval trading, Jewish naval-related communities experienced intense periods of growth and decline. In contrast, those in the new industrial centres expanded exponentially during the nineteenth century. Only Portsmouth, of the four major Jewish naval communities that emerged in the long eighteenth century, was to experience renewed growth thereafter. Of particular relevance here, however, is that the early naval port Jewish communities had a specific ethos; their collective identities were shaped by the particular dynamics of the local context.

As Gillian Rose suggests, 'although senses of place may be very personal, they are not entirely the result of one individual's feelings and meanings; rather, such feelings and meanings are shaped in large part by the social, cultural and economic circumstances in which individuals find themselves'.[8] Her fellow social geographer, Richard Meegan, puts it bluntly: 'Social relations make places, make local worlds', adding the complicating factor that 'not all the social relations helping to shape [a specific] place are confined to it. Some stretch beyond it … It is this stretching of social relations across space that connects places and the people who live in them with other places and other people.'[9] Behind such social relations are the issues of power and powerlessness, the complex dynamics of which will be explored in the following analysis of Portsmouth, its Jews and collective memory.

This chapter will analyse the nature of an intriguing, if sometimes troubled, community of Port Jews, and its complex and multi-layered image inside and outside of Portsmouth. Ultimately it will explore why *particular* memories of Portsmouth Jewry – as both a part of and apart from the town's dangerous 'sailortown' community – were so persistent in the nineteenth century and beyond. As was the case with the Jews of medieval Winchester, the representation of Portsmouth Jewry had, through the workings of place identity, a wider significance beyond the locality in question. Returning to the work of social geography, it has been suggested that 'place is a negotiated reality, a social construction by a purposeful set of actors. But the relationship is mutual, for places in turn develop and reinforce the identity of the social group that claims them'.[10] Just as the memory of early Winchester as capital of Wessex was utilised in the (racial) construction of Englishness and the British Empire, so the later history of Portsmouth, as home of the navy, was employed for a wider purpose. As Ken Lunn and Ann Day have argued, although neglected in academic literature, 'maritime identities have been painstakingly constructed and reinvented over the centuries as part of that complex creature that is "Britishness"'. Within such 'island stories' of the 'island race', 'Jack Tar', the sailor stereotype, especially in the Victorian era, 'came to embody national virtues and dependable strength'.[11] A study of *The British Tar in Fact and Fiction* (1911) referred to the 'particular genius of the English race for maritime adventure'. Such inherent nautical greatness was matched, the author believed, by a parallel tradition of documenting it in literary and artistic form from the story of Beowulf onwards.[12] Central within later racial constructions of maritime myths were the French Revolutionary Wars and Napoleonic Wars, and most notably the role of the *Victory* in the Battle of Trafalgar and the ensuing cult of Nelson.[13] It ensured that Portsmouth, as a focal point of naval activity and reflected triumph, has had and continues to play a special role in the construction of national identity, especially at times of subsequent military conflict and celebrations of past victories.

The origins and nature of Portsmouth Jewry

Push and pull factors explain the origins of the Portsmouth Jewish community. According to Lucien Wolf, the desire of the Corporation of London, and the elite Sephardi Jews of the late seventeenth century, to keep out poor Jews of Ashkenazi origin 'gave an impulse to the formation of provincial communities, especially in Portsmouth and Hull'.[14] The growth of Portsmouth as a whole – roughly doubling in population during the eighteenth century to 16,000 – and especially the increasing naval presence attracted further

Jews to the town: 'the thousands of sailors who tramped in and out of it constituted an enormous market for dealers in slops [second hand clothing etc] and trinkets'. The origins of Portsmouth Jewry were thus largely with itinerant pedlars and a smaller number of craftsmen who had struggled to make a living in London. Economic opportunities, or their absence, ensured that many of these Jews would continue their geographical mobility beyond Portsmouth within and beyond Britain. Some, however, settled permanently in the Hampshire town.[15]

Portsmouth and Portsmouth Jewry had their own unique characteristics. In her analysis of violence against and between Jews in Portsmouth, to which we will return shortly, Jessica Warner reminds us that it was 'easily one of the roughest towns in eighteenth-century England'. If the Jews of Portsmouth were relatively law-abiding, this was in the context of a town in which crime was at an extremely high level. Typical of everyday disorder was an attack in 1777 on Jacob Isaac, a pedlar, and his wife Rachel, who were attacked within their home by five men who, having forced the door open, struck both of them down 'without the least cause', leaving them 'much hurt and bruised'.[16] Jews, however, were not simply the victims of violence in this disorderly town. Indeed, cases of Jewish criminality, including violence aimed at both fellow Jews and non-Jews, suggests a strong level of social integration, albeit not one welcomed by those trying to present the community in a positive light.[17] In many respects, the Jews of Portsmouth reflected the town as a whole – 'rough' and 'respectable', settled and transient. 'Eighteenth century Portsmouth', local historian, James Thomas, reminds us, 'was marked by contrasts'. Beyond the surface glamour brought by royal visits and naval triumphs 'lay a bewildering mass of seething tensions, tensions which frequently erupted in open conflict'.[18] What partially differentiated the Jews of Portsmouth from those in the rest of the town was the desire of the Jewish communal gatekeepers, or ethnic brokers, to police their less 'polite' brethren. It proved a difficult task and one further exacerbated by divisions amongst the Jewish elite.

Until the work of Bill Williams, Jewish (including British Jewish) historiography largely emphasised homogeneity and consensus. The possibility of conflict and fundamental clashes of interest *within* Jewish communities was downplayed in most history writing and heritage representation. Narratives of Portsmouth Jewry have reflected the consensual approach. There has been acknowledgement of the diverse geographical origins of the community which included German, Dutch, and 'other parts of the Continent' – the earliest name-lists, it was suggested, 'read like a gazetteer of central Europe' – as well as English.[19] Nevertheless, it has been emphasised from the earliest historiography of Portsmouth Jewry that 'members of the congregation were agreed and united in their attachment to the Synagogue, and to every-thing conducive to its interests'.[20] The obvious dangers, however, of treating Portsmouth Jews as a unified and acquiescent minority were revealed at a religious level through the three schisms that divided the community in the eighteenth and nineteenth centuries. This chapter will deal only with the first which occurred in 1766 when a secessionist group broke away from the synagogue and set up its own congregation, leaving the future divisions to later parts of this study. The fracture in 1766, however, was by far the longest, lasting twenty-three years.

Cecil Roth, following the work of Lucien Wolf,[21] regarded the first Portsmouth schism as a provincial version of the contemporaneous battle between the two leading Ashkenazi London synagogues which, in turn, re-flected a struggle to impose overall rabbinic control of British Jewry. To Roth, the later significance of the secessionists' return was not local but national and international – in essence, recognition of the Chief Rabbi's authority within the whole British Empire. Yet rather than simply representing the 'repurcussions' of a metropolitan power struggle,[22] or what a later historian of Portsmouth Jewry claimed was a 'bitter dispute ... the cause of which was entirely external',[23] the schism also reflected the tensions between centre and periphery, as well as the growing self-confidence of (and divisions within) Britain's largest Jewish provincial community.

British Jewish historiography when referring to Portsmouth has tended to treat it in isolation or only in relationship to London. A more realistic if complicated picture emerges if Portsmouth Jewry is situated as part of a rich and complex diasporic network and one, it will be argued here, that helps explain the nature and intensity of the 1766 schism. Looking beyond Britain, for example, it is clear that Jewish immigrants to Portsmouth main-tained links to and affections towards their places of immediate origin. Thus Moses Mordechai, a goldsmith and bookplate designer who settled first in Portsmouth before moving in 1788 to Exeter, bequeathed in his will of 1808 'ten guineas to the synagogue at Maintz so that his soul might be commemo-rated there on Festivals, as well as numerous legacies to his family who lived in that locality'.[24] Indeed, the diasporic connections of Portsmouth Jews went beyond Europe and to the 'new world'. The 'humble Portsea parents' of Lewis Aria were two amongst many Portsmouth Jews who emigrated to the West Indies. Aria made his fortune as a Jamaican merchant and left part of his wealth in the 1870s to set up a rabbinical college in Portsmouth to train Hampshire Jews. Its students took up posts in South Africa, Australia and many other places in the British Empire. Equally reflecting its international role, synagogues in St Thomas, New York and Barbados were architectur-ally-based on the Portsmouth model,[25] and, in 1816, Jews from Portsmouth founded the Cincinnati Jewish community in Ohio.[26]

At a national level, the deep roots and relatively large size of Portsmouth Jewry ensured that it played a very significant role within Anglo-Jewry. There were, for example, strong trading, family and religious links to other naval ports, especially Plymouth. Many of the Plymouth Jewry originated from Portsmouth and, beyond the bonds of such family connections, for the Jews of south-west England, Portsmouth was the nearest 'large' Jewish community.[27] It is significant in the religious sphere that the leader of the secessionists, Reb Leib, exemplified the regional power basis of Portsmouth Jewry. As the communal *mohel* he travelled with other local Jews to carry out circumcisions across Hampshire, the Isle of Wight, Dorset, Somerset and Essex. At a local level, the first Portsmouth schism could be dismissed as 'parochial' reflecting animosity over misappropriated funding (in which Reb Leib was implicated). The schism was, however, much more than a personal squabble. It reflected the desire amongst half the Portsmouth community to maintain a strong degree of independence from London and to carry on its function as the head of a regional Jewish centre covering much of southern England.[28] From a London perspective, the 1766–89 secession was a battle between the capital and provinces over communal authority. Finally, at an international level it reflected the intricacies of transnational networks and the preference inside the London and Portsmouth Jewish communities for different geographically located continental rabbinic traditions.[29] Portsmouth Jewry, if only briefly, became a hub in diasporic movements, a role that increased its importance but also led, at times, to internal and external tension within the Jewish world. It was also dynamic – the fact that the original seventeen secessionists were soon joined by fifteen new members suggests that the old congregation was seen as exclusive to newcomers to the town.[30] It suggests that alongside religious controversy, class, status, nationality and notions of respectability were continually contested within Portsmouth Jewry.

Conflict amongst the Jews of Portsmouth could be at a basic personal level. Analysing the town's session papers, Jessica Warner comments that by the late 1730s, 'Jews in Portsmouth were getting into fights with each other, which in and of itself speaks to a certain critical mass'.[31] It would be wrong to limit the relevance of this violence to individual conflict. James Thomas notes that the growth of the Jewish community in mid-eighteenth-century Portsmouth 'was accompanied by a feeling of resentment against some of the Jews, and of antipathy by some of their own kind towards them'.[32] In 1757 a fight so intense took place inside the synagogue that it required outside intervention to bring it to a halt.[33] On its own, this violent incident does not negate Geoffrey Green's suggestion that, in contrast to its rough neighbourhood, 'in the Portsmouth Synagogue all was exemplary – decorum reigned supreme. No one was allowed to talk, or to leave his seat, and the children sat under the charge of their Hebrew teacher'.[34] What *does* seriously bring Green's analysis into question is the labyrinth of constantly updated laws on behaviour imposed by synagogue leaders and the constant imposition of fines for their breakage. In 1834, for example, the elders of the congregation called a special meeting 'in order to secure due and proper decorum in our Synagogue, *upon all* and *every* occasion, and not to allow any *talking* or *irregularity* of behaviour' [original emphasis].[35]

The attempt at such social control extended into the secular realm. Law 7 of the community insisted that 'Should a dispute arise between our members, they must not dare to go to the non-Jewish tribunal, but it is to be settled by our congregation.'[36] It is clear that the leaders of the community were concerned about the reactions and responses of their non-Jewish Portsmouth neighbours. The existence of violent antisemitism, physical and verbal, even in the context of a particularly rough town, provided ample evidence of Jewish vulnerability. It led to the elders' desire to show a respectable face to the outside world. One local historian has suggested that as early as the 1740s 'Evidence suggests that a growing mood of anti-semitism pervaded the foetid air of Georgian Portsmouth. During the years 1742–1755 twelve incidents took place involving Jews. All were assaults of one form or another and, save for one incident, Jews were always victims.'[37] Todd Endelman, writing of the Jews of Georgian England, suggests that 'There were many more instances of small-scale anti-Jewish hooliganism than have previously been recognised'. Endelman, however, concludes that 'it is impossible to find any political content in these beatings and pranks'.[38] Whether Endelman's dismissal of the political intent of violent antisemitism is correct or not, its impact on Jewish individuals themselves should not be dismissed. In April 1810, a series of incidents occurred in the first of which Rosa Nathan, the wife of a Jewish slopseller, was physically assaulted in her home by a naval officer and two others who called her a 'bloody Jew bitch'. Her husband, Asher, was then assaulted and the following night further threats were levelled and several men beaten up, mistaken for Jewish shopkeepers.[39] As will emerge in the next section, these attacks occurred at a particularly difficult time – linked to war tension – for the Jews of Portsmouth. Yet as Warner has acknowledged, it 'seems unlikely that incidents such as these did not also occur in the eighteenth century'. She is at a loss, however, to explain why 'the town's early Jewish settlers suffer[ed] in silence' and rarely reported such violence.[40] Some Jews may have responded in kind, but the fear and reality of physical antisemitism was undoubtedly part of the everyday world of Portsmouth Jewry, especially given its relatively small size.

More generally, Warner is unwilling to acknowledge the marginality of

Portsmouth's Jews (and hence their reluctance to report attacks), or the impact of local animosity, concluding that 'ordinary gentiles were fairly tolerant in their dealings with Jews'. Her belief that antipathy towards the Jews in British culture and society was peripheral is part of a larger historiographical tendency. Indeed, it fits within the wider argument that the absence of 'native' antisemitism separates Britain from the rest of Europe – that is the belief in 'British exceptionalism'. But the confusion created by assumptions of overriding tolerance on the one hand, and evidence to the contrary on the other, leads to Warner's remarkable assertion that Jews in Portsmouth 'were likelier to be attacked because they were Jews, but only some, and perhaps a minority, of these attacks were anti-Semitic in nature'.[41] It is also hard to justify her comment that 'None of the assaults among Jews was especially violent'.[42] In February 1764, for example, an elderly Jew, Hyam Solomon, was attacked by a mob of angry men crying out 'Five Pounds for a Jew's Head'. Solomon was 'struck … a violent blow on the head' with a 'great stick' and hit further on the ground leaving him 'almost dead'. His surgeon believed that he had 'been in great danger of his Life'.[43] In contrast to Warner's analysis, by reflecting on the representation of Portsmouth Jewry and especially the linkage made between it and the town's most infamous place, 'The Point', the reticence of its members to report assaults, as well as the desire to keep communal tension within the private realm, is made more comprehensible.

Jews and 'The Point'

'The Point' was notorious in depictions of 'sailortown' Portsmouth. A narrow strip through the harbour mouth and the Sally Port, with a street in the middle, it has been immortalised in words, drawings and music. Stephen Martin-Leake, a clerk in the Navy Pay Office, famously described 'The Point' in a series of letters in 1728/29 as

> the Wapping of Portsmouth. Here the Johns carouse, not being confined to hours, and spend their money for the good of the public, which makes alehouses and shops thrive mightily upon this spot. Some have compared it to the Point at Jamaica that was swallowed by an earthquake, and think, if that was Sodom this is Gomorrah; but it is by no means so bad as some would make it, though bad enough.[44]

The general district of 'The Point', the 'nightly scene of Bacchanalian orgies and tumults', was known also as '"Spice Island", either because of the bad odours through lack of sanitation or its spice-laden atmosphere as ships from the Indies discharged their cargoes there'.[45] With these references to such evocative times and spaces – from Biblical to colonial – no better example could be found of Doreen Massey's argument that the 'local uniqueness' of places 'is always already a product of wider contacts [at the global level] where global in this context refers not necessarily to the planetary scale, but to the geographical beyond, the world beyond the place itself'.[46] The previous chapter focusing on Winchester Jewry has already utilised her argument that in 'the construction of places, the "other" in general terms is already within'.[47] The racialisation of 'The Point' further illustrates the validity of her analysis.

Around 1800, Thomas Rowlandson executed 'one of the most popular of [his] drawings', *Portsmouth Point* which was engraved in 1814 and successfully marketed thereafter.[48] Its vivid and lewd imagery presented 'lustful carousing amid mercantile ships, a tavern, and a lender's bank ... a drunken, peg-leg street fiddler narrowly avoid[ing] trodding on a mongrel hound ... [while] an older couple quarrels in the foreground, the robust female clearly winning ... [with] sailors and prostitutes cavort[ing] freely'. It inspired, over a century later, William Walton to compose his overture of the same title. Walton, from small-town Lancashire, likened the liveliness, dislocation and 'confused bustle' that he experienced in 1920s London to Rowlandson's imagined Portsmouth of the 1800s.[49] At the end of the street and next to the harbour in Rowlandson's etching is the shop of 'Moses Levy', proclaiming 'Money Lent'.[50] Geoffrey Green comments that although there never was a 'Moses Levy on the point ... the artist obviously knew of the Jewish presence'.[51] What is of greater significance than the 'reality' of Moses Levy, or otherwise, is that Rowlandson, as a commercial artist, created a representation of this disreputable place that his audience expected. It is thus significant that there is no reference to a Jewish moneylender in an earlier sketch of 'The Point' by Rowlandson drawn in 1784, but not intended for the public realm. Instead there is a more neutrally labelled 'Slop Shop' with not even an implicit Jewish reference.[52]

It is, of course, possible that the Jewish presence was more visible when Rowlandson visited 'The Point' again, ten years later, but it is more likely that Rowlandson was adding an ingredient which would add to the commercial potential of his work. Even Bill Rubinstein, at the historiographical forefront of the 'British exceptionalism' school of thought, acknowledges that 'contemporary prints and caricatures of life in ... Portsmouth ... depict the stereotyped Jewish money-lender or hawker as a matter of course'.[53] What that Jewishness explicitly might mean to Rowlandson's clientele was made clear in a contemporaneous guide to *The History of Portsmouth* (including its 'present state'), published by J. C. Mottley in 1801.[54]

In this seminal local guide, 'The Point' is evoked as 'a place equally known and celebrated for its eccentricities in all parts of the world'. Separated from the rest of the port, 'This street is filled with one of the most heterogeneous assemblages of traffic and conviviality that is, perhaps, to be found in … any one part of the world'. The justification for this claim was made in the following sentence. It was one that was to be much reproduced in general histories of Portsmouth and specific studies of Portsmouth Jewry, as well as writing about Hampshire more generally, thereafter:

> Liquor-shops, contrast taverns; Jew slopmen, taylors, and drapers; jostle Christian pawnbrokers, watch jobbers, and trinket merchants, cook shops, eating houses, and ordinaries, vie each other to entertain all classes, from the guests of the cabin to those of the forecastle … [55]

Taken on its own, the description is not hostile and, alongside Rowlandson's etching, suggests that the Jews were an integral part of this cosmopolitan and exciting local scene. They may be linked to the dangers of 'sailortown' but these Jews still belong to Portsmouth, or at least Portsmouth's place of 'otherness' ('other' that is to the lighted, paved and improved sections that made Portsmouth 'a regular handsome borough town').[56] There was, however, further comment in this history which isolated 'the Jew' and problematised 'his' presence, even in 'The Point'.

Mottley's *History of Portsmouth* is, for the most part, sober in its description, and the vivid portrayal of 'The Point' is out of character with the book as a whole. As with Rowlandson's etching, the book's description of 'The Point' meets the expectation of the reader, but at the same time it provides the opportunity for social commentary. The description is biting in its satire concerning the 'honest Jack' who is allowed to squander his money on the pleasures and vices of 'The Point'. It is in the context of the temptations put before these 'noble defenders of [their] country' that a note is added that makes clear not only the separation of the Jews from those who are 'perpetually risking their lives to preserve [freedom]', but also what differentiates the Jews from other traders in Portsmouth:

> The Jews having considerable privileges in this town, have so far availed themselves of such a favourable opportunity as to occupy houses and shops in the first style of mercantile consequence in the … trades [listed above], whilst Christian artizans, who are not so wealthy, are obliged to content themselves with sheds, bulks, or any other similar place, which can afford them a chance of supporting themselves by a traffic limited in proportion to the small extent of their little capitals.[57]

In short, although the Jewish traders had established themselves firmly in terms of property ownership in Portsmouth, and more so than their Christian counterparts, it was a permanence of presence that had been achieved through unfair and unclear means. Similarly, the synagogue in

Portsea reflected what was perceived as the alien presence of the Jews. Portsea was 'the great resort of traders and dealers' which was 'peopled, like London, with an inundation of exotic inhabitants'.[58]

As the nineteenth century progressed, descriptions of Portsmouth, while normalising the place of the synagogue within the town, maintained the orientalised narrative of the Jewish trading community. In Henry Slight's *A Looking Glass for Portsmouth and Its Environs* (1843), a detailed account is given of the 'Jewish Synagogue, founded originally in [1742] by subscription of the then small congregation' and its present state after re-building in 1780. Whilst some emphasis is placed on the expense entailed and ostentation created in the re-building of the synagogue, otherwise, as an example of contemporary anthropological writing, it is not overly-essentialised in its representation of the Jews. Reference to the 'king's arms', the origins of which will be explored shortly, in front of the ladies' gallery, highlighted patriotism, and the presence of a Jewish burial ground 'eastward of the town' emphasised, alongside the brief history provided, rootedness in Portsmouth's past and present. Yet outside the religious sphere, the perceived alien otherness of the Jews remained intact. Without explanation, the section of Slight's account devoted to Portsea began with a poem:

> In line with [Queen Street, its principal thoroughfare] is found the busy hive
> Where Israel's sons their various traffic drive,
> And many a gazing passenger is caught
> With treasures rich as those from Egypt brought.[59]

However hard the leaders of Portsmouth Jewry attempted to emphasise the respectability of themselves and of their synagogue, the image of the exotic descendants of the Bible, and, as we will see, Shakespeare's Shylock, came bouncing back to haunt this port community.

The idea of Portsmouth Jewry as alien itinerants, racially prone to exploiting sailors and other seafarers, inevitably failed to do justice to this complex and constantly evolving minority group. While the size of the Jewish community did change – rising, for example, when economic opportunities arose as was the case in the French Revolutionary Wars and early years of the Napoleonic Wars – such flux was part of the wider nature of Portsmouth's demographic profile. Even so, of the 120 Jews who appeared before Portsmouth's justices of the peace between 1718 and 1781, only seven, according to Warner, 'never settled in the town'. Even in areas of Jewish concentration, Jews and non-Jews were neighbours in the same streets, and there is evidence of business cooperation even in the eighteenth century.[60] Similarly, while there clearly was tension between the Jewish traders and the seamen which could break out into violence, it was also noted that it was 'one of the many odd traits which make up Jack [Tar's] odd character, that though his dislike of Moses exceeds all the bounds of *decorum*, it is to *him* he confides all his grievances and by *his* advice most of his actions are governed'.[61]

After the Napoleonic Wars, it is clear that a wealthier, settled group of middle-class Jewish shopowners and professionals had emerged in Portsmouth. Before then, there were individual examples of Jewish surgeons, sailors and painters and other professions. Nevertheless, the majority of Portsmouth's Jews were in occupations ranging from pedlars, pawnbrokers and slop dealers to 'engravers, goldsmiths, silversmiths and jewelers'.[62] The activities of this majority, to a greater or lesser extent, inter-related and were subject to rapid upward and downward mobility. Such social and economic fluidity made it hard to differentiate the 'respectable' from the 'unrespectable' Jew. Yet the essentialised and limited representation of Portsmouth Jewry made little account of the complex layers and dynamism of the community. In 1812, just before Rowlandson's typically scurrilous *Portsmouth Point* was to be marketed, Judith Montefiore, wife of the future famous Jewish philanthropist and diplomat, Moses, wrote her honeymoon diary. On 20 September 1812 the couple arrived in Portsmouth. The next day they insisted upon visiting the docks and were thrilled to be shown the workings of the naval academy and its role in the future defence of the realm. After this tour the Montefiores returned to their inn and

> passed our time with reading till dinner-time, for which we had a roast duck, boiled salmon and vegetables. We then finished our book, took a pleasant walk, returned back to tea. Read our prayers and retired at eleven o'clock, grateful for having passed a very happy day.[63]

Here was bourgeois respectability and patriotism personified. But, as the next section will illustrate, Judith Montefiore's 1812 diary provided a very different vision of Jewishness from that otherwise presented in wartime Portsmouth.

(Local) Patriotism and the Jews

For the Jews, the issue of patriotism and loyalty – both local and national – mattered particularly in relation to Portsmouth because of the wider significance of and meanings attached to the town with its Royal Navy domination. The leaders of Portsmouth Jewry were determined that they should belong to the virtues – patriotism and self-sacrifice in action – rather than the vices – mutiny, greed and disorder – associated with this special place. Their desire to express loyalty was manifested acutely in June 1773 when George III paid an official visit to Portsmouth.

The tone of this royal visit was set by the Mayor and Corporation in their address to the King:

> We ... humbly beg leave to pay our duty to your Majesty upon your arrival in this town; nothing can give us greater joy and satisfaction than to see your Majesty shewing so much attention, and doing so much to honour to the glory and bulwark of these Kingdoms. We desire to express the warmest affection for your Majesty's person and government, and to offer our earnest prayers, that the fleet may prove victorious under the auspices of your Majesty ... and redound to the glory of the Sovereign of the British Empire.[64]

Subsequently, the five days of the royal stay have featured prominently in the 'annals of Portsmouth'.[65] Forgotten, however, has been the Jewish input into the visit which was recorded by the *Hampshire Chronicle*:

> Tuesday evening the Jews Syna[go]gue was illuminated and ornamented within with flowers and when the Jews all assembled, and prayed for His Majesty and the Royal Family, and sung several psalms and an acoustic Ode on his Majesty wrote on the occasion, accompanied with musical instruments, till 10 o'clock, when they went in procession from the Synagogue towards the Dock, each with a wax taper, singing *God Save the King*, accompanied with musical instruments.

These prayers, the local paper added, 'continued every evening during his Majesty's stay'.[66]

Bryan Cheyette has powerfully argued that '"the Jew", like all "doubles", is inherently ambivalent and can represent both the "best" and the "worst" of selves'. In contrast to 'colonial subjects', who were 'for the most part, confined racially to the "colonies" in the late nineteenth century, Jews were simultaneously at the centre of European metropolitan society and, at the same time, banished from its privileged sphere by a semitic discourse'.[67] In the late eighteenth century, however, the elite of Portsmouth Jewry were still struggling to present the 'respectable' face of the community and to claim their place at the centre of local society. Criminality and alienness, rather than loyalty, were, in spite of the best efforts of the communal leaders, the words associated with the Jews of Portsmouth. It was in a general context in which, as Roxann Wheeler argues,

> A large proportion of English subjects seemed to find most other people, both inside and outside their borders, contemptuous. This suspicion arose mainly from political and religious matters, and it could assume physical or cultural terms. Even those who resembled the English most closely, such as the French or Irish, were targets of verbal and even physical abuse in the streets of eighteenth-century Britain.

Jews, as has been noted throughout this chapter, could be added to Wheeler's list, perceived as being of uncertain religious and moral status within the

Enlightenment's 'elastic conception of race'.[68]

In the first Lady Magnus Memorial Lecture, delivered to the Jewish Historical Society of England (JHSE) in 1935, Cecil Roth commented on the royal arms, facing the Ten Commandments, in the Portsmouth synagogue. These were, he suggested, 'presumably set up in honour of some member of George III's prolific brood who was associated with Portsmouth, and perhaps even visited the synagogue'. Roth relegated to a footnote of the published lecture the more likely explanation that 'this coat-of-arms was affixed in order to vindicate Jewish loyalty at the time of the [French Revolutionary Wars and] Napoleonic Wars, when the Portsmouth community appears to have suffered from a certain degree of discrimination'.[69] It is much more likely that the royal arms were added at the time of the 1773 visit, reflecting this earlier local manifestation of minority patriotism. What is not in doubt, however, is the crisis of Portsmouth Jewry in the last decade of the eighteenth century and first decade of the nineteenth century which Roth so quietly alluded to within his footnote.

As was to be the case in later wars during the nineteenth and twentieth centuries, British Jewry in the war years from 1793 to 1815 was to face the burden of two inter-related accusations. First, it was alleged, through their diasporic connections, that Jewish loyalty rested elsewhere. Two popular caricatures from 1803 illustrate that this was an issue of national concern, albeit one that was being contested. The first, by George Cruickshank, *Easier to Say than Do*, 'showed Napoleon scraping England off the map with the assistance of a Dutchman, a Spaniard and a Jew'. Jews joined this 'unholy alliance' because it was suspected that they supported Napoleon as he had 'freed' European Jewry from their medieval restrictions.[70] The second, *The Loyal Jew*, consisted of a 'bearded Ashkenazi stand[ing] bayonet to bayonet against a French infantryman who has challenged him to surrender, exclaiming in broken English: "Vut Shurender Jean Bools property – never while I am a Shew – I'll let you know Mounsheer, dat I fight for King Sheorge, and de Shynagogue!!"'[71] The latter image at least allowed for Jewish patriotism – indeed it parodied its exaggerated nature – while still confirming, through comic speech, the foreignness of the Jew. As was the case with the 1753 Jew Bill controversy some fifty years earlier, the question of whether Jews could be considered part of the nation emerged strongly again at this moment of national tension. The increasing link made between Jews and Napoleon from the early 1800s further highlighted their alleged lack of loyalty and the danger they therefore were perceived to pose to the safety of Britain. It is no coincidence that earlier intensified assaults on Portsmouth Jews had corresponded to other points of international stress, namely 'the three major wars that occurred between 1718 and 1781 [that is] the War of

Austrian Succession (1740–1748), the Seven Years' War (1756–1763) and the American Revolutionary War (1775–1783)'.[72]

The second, linked, allegation levelled at the Jews was that they were physically cowardly, and not only failed to contribute to the military defence of the country but also benefited financially from the opportunities brought by war. The dominant trend within British Jewish historiography has been to suggest that Jewish military efforts in the army and navy during the French Revolutionary Wars and Napoleonic Wars helped to break down such accusations of war-shirking and cowardice. Frank Felsenstein, in his study of antisemitic stereotypes in English popular culture from 1660 through to 1830 believes that when, 'as late as 1810, George Crabbe wrote, "Nor war nor wisdom yields our Jews delight./ They will not study, and they dare not fight," he was obdurately refusing to lay to rest a prejudice that had far less currency than it might have had only fifty years before'.[73] Even more dramatic claims have been made by Geoffrey Green in the conclusion to his evocative study of the Royal Navy and Anglo-Jewry:

> By 1820 a tradition of Jewish service in, and trading with, the Royal Navy had been established. One important result was that a small number of relatively poor Jews had come into direct and continuous contact with the wider indigenous population. A small contribution had been made by the Jews in their connections with the Royal Navy towards the wider aspirations of the Anglo-Jewish community. *The beginning of the quest for emancipation of British Jewry was not far away.*[74] [My emphasis.]

Similarly, in 1940, at another deeply troubled moment for British Jewry, Cecil Roth in his presidential address to the JHSE, pointed out that 'When Jewish emancipation was being discussed in Parliament in 1833, the Duke of Wellington admitted that fifteen Jewish officers had fought with him at Waterloo', adding evidence of those who had served under Nelson and fought at Trafalgar.[75] A different reading of Jewish emancipation and its local input and ramifications will be left to Chapter 5. Here, a more critical perspective of the impact of the Napoleonic era on 'semitic discourse' is necessary. It will be provided with specific reference to the Jews of Portsmouth and their contributions to the war effort.

In 1798, five years after the start of the French Revolutionary Wars, Jacob Levi, a grocer and pawnbroker from Portsea, wrote to the Secretary of War, 'on behalf of myself and Bretheren the Congregation of Jews residing within the Borough of Portsmouth'. It was in response to the 'notice you gave to the Public, directing all good subjects to train themselves to arms, and thereby become enabled to stand forward in the Defence of their King & Country'. Levi wrote after the offer of local Jews to enter the Portsmouth Volunteers had been turned down. Portsmouth Jewry was 'greatly hurt by such refusal' and Levi was anxious to assure that 'there exists not within His Majesty's Realms a more Loyal People than the Jews'. The image and reputation of the Jews was to the forefront of Levi's concerns – he concluded that even if the rejection be continued, 'we beg … you make it known to the Public that we wish to do our Duty as good Citizens, and that we have used our best endeavours to obtain leave so to do'.[76] Levi was clearly anxious about the well-being of the Jewish community if the Jews continued to be refused entry into the local volunteer companies: 'should we become proscribed', he wrote, not only would it 'great hurt our feelings', it would also 'perhaps endanger our personal safety'.[77] The violence against Jews in Portsmouth in the years that followed suggest that Levi's fears were not totally imaginary.

A response to Levi's plea came from the Portsmouth Garrison Commander, Sir William Pitt, who wrote to the Secretary of War explaining his earlier refusal and outlining clearly the bifurcated image of the local Jews:

> some months ago, upon application being made … relative to the propriety of enroling Jews into [the Volunteer Companies] I discouraged, it on account of there being a great number of suspicious itinerent Jews, at that time in the Town of Portsmouth, all of whom have since been found out & removed from hence by the activity & vigilence of the Magistrates. There still remains however a considerable number of that sect who I find have been long residents of this Town, & of Portsea, many of them very respectable Tradesmen, & are considered as Loyal good subjects …

Pitt wanted to enrol these 'good' Jews into a separate company 'entirely of their own sect', but this was turned down by the Jewish leaders. Reluctantly Pitt agreed to distribute the Jewish volunteers more generally within local companies.[78]

The magistrates in Portsmouth, and elsewhere in England, had used the Aliens Act of 1793 to deport the 'undesirable' and 'dangerous' itinerant Jews referred to in Pitt's letter.[79] The attempt to divide the respectable from the unrespectable was, however, also carried out at this time within the Portsmouth Jewish community. The first sustained history of Portsmouth Jewry was delivered to the JHSE in 1907 by the Reverend I. S. Meisels, then minister of the community. Meisels was struck, reading through the minutes from a hundred years earlier, by the obvious desire 'to preserve the name of the Jew pure and unsullied' and the insistence that its members lived 'in strict accordance with Jewish law'. In the war years from 1793 to 1815 especially, fines were imposed for trading with navy ships on the Sabbath, bringing together the need to combine local civic respectability with maintaining Jewish religious observance. Meisels was keen to emphasise the charitable activities in 'helping its own poor', but, as elsewhere, these were only the ones deemed to be deserving.[80] Of even greater significance in terms of giving during the Napoleonic Wars was the decision in 1812 to impose a substantial tax on synagogue seat holders in order to present the mayor of Portsmouth with a lump sum 'for the benefit of the widows and orphans of the men lost in the wreck of the three men-of-war – *St George, Defence*, and *Hero*'. A year earlier another collection was made for the relief of British prisoners in France.[81] All efforts, therefore, were made by the religious and civic leaders of Portsmouth Jewry during the war era to present the community as loyal, manly, patriotic, generous and unselfish. Yet as even Felsenstein concedes, the memory of that contribution was distorted and the branding of Jews as 'natural cowards' remained 'a recurrent charge in later periods'.[82] Felsenstein is partly at a loss to explain the continuity of the pusillanimous image given the evidence to the contrary. Naval related material from the 1830s and 1840s, previously neglected in Jewish literary studies, provide strong evidence of its continuity. They also give insights into the functions of this particular, place-related semitic discourse and why it was so persistent.

Losing the point: fictionalising Portsmouth Jewry

Portsmouth Jewry, in the years following the Napoleonic wars, was a much changed community. Membership of the synagogue, reflecting only a proportion of its total size (roughly 20–25 per cent), had increased from 49 in 1790 to 85 in 1810 before falling back to 52 in 1820 and 35 in 1830.[83] It has been noted by Aubrey Weinberg that towards the end of the Napoleonic wars, 'there were 41 Jewish naval agents registered in the town, clustered around the dockside area and constituting a significant element in the supplying of warships and their crews'.[84] After 1815, the town went into major economic decline and many of the more recent Jewish arrivals left for other parts of England, America or the British Empire. Though smaller, there was now a more settled community of shopkeepers and professionals, some of whom had been able to consolidate their businesses during the war and to maintain their status afterwards. Other Jews continued to move to the port after the war.

At a local level, there was recognition of the growing respectable reputation of Portsmouth Jewry, as was the case in 1815 when the *Hampshire Telegraph* reported a synagogue service which was attended by many 'distinguished visitors' including Sir George and Lady Grey and Sir George and Lady Bingham.[85] Never far away, however, was the figure of the subversive and alien Jew, one that had haunted the community before and during the wars. The same report in the local newspaper, the detail and positive nature of which suggest that it may well have been scripted by leaders of Portsmouth Jewry themselves, emphasised that the 'beauties' of the service were exemplified by 'the Prayer for the Royal Family and the Nation'.[86] Within Portsmouth, the Jewish image was bifurcated into 'good' and 'bad'. But outside the town and in the literary realm, it was *only* 'The Point' Jew that was drawn. Indeed, the further one moved from the war and the decline of the actual Jewish presence in the Portsmouth docks, the stronger became the semitic discourse of dislocated 'otherness' associated with 'The Point'.

David Cesarani has argued that in the twentieth century, 'ports became associated with squalor, social chaos, criminality, miscegenation, irresponsible unrestricted commerce, rootedlessness, and all those who were alien'. He adds that it was 'no coincidence that when T. S. Eliot selected the images for the deracination, corruption, decay and degeneracy that he associated with modernity he selected Jews and ports: in fact, port Jews'.[87] It might be added to Cesarani's analysis that Eliot's 'Mr Bleistein' in 'Burbank with a Baedecker' (1920) makes explicit, through sense of place, the connection to Shakespeare's Shylock and the Rialto of Venice. Such references to *The Merchant of Venice* will be apparent also in nineteenth-century maritime discourse. Yet the persistent, if largely unrecognised, literary-cultural trope of the dangerous 'port Jew' – in works from Shakespeare through to Eliot and beyond – should not disguise the 'tremendous dynamic in the role, function and cultural meanings' associated with it.[88] The literary 'port Jew' of the early Victorian decades has to be contextualised in time as well as place.

In what is the only sustained modern study of maritime fiction, John Peck has analysed the rise of the naval novel in England during the 1830s. Led by Captain Marryat, and followed by his contemporaries, Captain Glascock and Captain Chamier, Peck concludes that, in a decade of political and social unrest, their novels were 'overwhelmingly conservative in their thinking'.[89] All three and their impersonators were veterans of the Napoleonic Wars, and their novels focused largely on that period of naval triumph. 'They imply that the peace and national prestige enjoyed by their first readers in the 1830s and 1840s are founded upon valiant deeds that comprise the glory of British history.'[90] While little was written of this experience immediately after the wars,[91] several decades later there clearly was a large and growing market for it. As John Sutherland suggests with regard to Captain Marryat, 'though the critics might give him a "confounded licking", contemporary readers and their descendants loved his easy-going novels. He is among the most reprinted of Victorian novelists.'[92]

Patrick Brantlinger argues that 'The maritime tales of the 1830s, of which Marryat's are only the best known, portray the adventures of boy-heroes – usually midshipman, usually during the Napoleonic Wars – providing a nostalgic, swashbuckling, but also conservative contrast to the literature of social reform which explored slums and workhouses and criticized corn laws and game laws.'[93] Peck has criticised Brantlinger for homogenising this genre, and has revealed the variation and flux within it, including in the work of its leading figure, Marryat. Even so, Peck still acknowledges its overarching conservative agenda.[94] It has been noted that British Jewish literary studies have failed to incorporate maritime fiction. Equally, Brantlinger, Peck and their predecessor, Robinson, who *have* studied this genre, have failed to acknowledge the presence of 'the Jew' within it. Yet an anthology of 'The British Navy in Fiction', neatly entitled, for the purposes of this study, *Portsmouth Point*, makes clear how frequent the 'Jewish' presence was within it.[95]

Space does not permit a full study of this maritime fiction and 'the Jew'. Not surprisingly, given the focus on the Napoleonic Wars in these books, Portsmouth features prominently as the place of naval embarkation and return. Here, the focus will be on the figure of the Jew in the town, one that was recurrent in the genre and came to represent the alleged traits of all Jews in Britain and beyond. Several dominant trends in the representation of the Jews can be noted. The repetition and sameness observed by Bratlinger is certainly evident with regard to the Jews of Portsmouth within this literature, as well as in related naval ballads and visual imagery. The Jews are almost exclusively male and they are presented as dishonest, alien traders and occasionally as crimpers (those who trick returning sailors through charging them extortionate rates of interest and then sell them onto other vessels). There is no sense of a settled, everyday, Jewish community or of its intricate and complex dynamics as illustrated in the long-lasting synagogue schism. Indeed, collectively the Jews in this discourse combine only to conspire against 'Jack Tar'. The implications of such fiendish deception are severe given the setting of Portsmouth at a critical time in the country's military fortunes and when the possibility of a French invasion was a constant fear.[96] Utterly selfish and cowardly, each Jew is interchangeable. The lack of individuality associated with these Jews is made clear in a passage from *Ben Brace, the last of Nelson's Agamemnons* (1836), one of the classic nautical novels of Captain Frederick Chamier:

> So I left [the ship] and away I steered to Moses [who lives on 'The Point']. He was at home, or some one so cursedly like him, that I should not have known one from the other; but all Jews are alike. The shark knew me, for many's the time I had taken a jacket from his kit when he came on board …[97]

The 'racial' characteristics of the Jew which manifest themselves in the form of cheating and money obsession, and stereotyped physical appearance, dress and accent, are tediously reproduced in this literature. Yet there *are* variations in who wins out in the battle between the scheming foreign Jew of 'The Point' and the honest English 'Jack Tar'. In turn, the outcome correlates with the different social function of the novels. In *Rattlin, the Reefer* (1836), by Edward Howard, the exploitation of sailor's wages and prize money, concomitant with the abuse of alcohol, is a constant theme. Howard concluded that 'By all this demoralization and this great expense, nobody ever benefits, but the Jews and the keepers of public-houses'. He added bitterly

> The pawnbroker, the publican, and the Jew, share the spoils between them. During the late war many a vast fortune has been picked up in this shabby manner. It is a pity some means cannot be devised to make Jack almost as prudent as he is brave. More liberty on shore would, perhaps, teach him to make better use of it.[98]

Such Jewish trickery was presented conspiratorally in the popular ballad, *The Sailor's Garland*, in which Shylock/the devil calls a 'Sanhedrim' [*sic*] or Jewish court to set a trap to make sure 'the heedless seamen enter'.[99]

Howard's *Rattlin, the Reefer*, however, is exceptional within the naval literature of the 1830s and 1840s. Howard, as Peck recognises, is willing to challenge an unfair system. His novel is caught between accepting abuses at sea – which are part of the system – and those on land – which need reforming.[100] His criticism of the way sailors were paid, and the attack on the Jews, is part of Howard's domestic critique. Marryat's *Peter Simple* (1834) presents a more ambivalent situation: 'At one moment a Jew was upset, and all his hamper of clothes tossed into the hold; at another, a sailor was seen hunting everywhere for a Jew who had cheated him'.[101] This mixed picture reflects the difficulty of fixing Marryat more generally in his racial and social attitudes. Elsewhere, however, while the semitic discourse is equally negative and damning, if not more so, it is significant that ultimately 'Jack Tar' gets the better of 'the Jew' or, if not, is rescued by the workings of English justice. The sailor's world is rough, but it represents the natural order of things. Indeed, even in the paranoid anti-Jewish world of *The Sailor's Garland*, the ballad concluded

> But these their plots we know our liege will all to nothing bring;
> Then sailors may throw up their caps and cry, 'God save the King'.[102]

The maritime fiction of the 1830s and 1840s is notable for 'a sadistic delight in presenting scenes that feature abuse of the body'.[103] Such pleasure in depicting cruelty is prominent in this literature when 'Jack Tar', in contrast to *Rattlin, the Reefer*, is ultimately triumphant over the Jewish trader from 'The Point'. It is especially evident in the work of Captain Chamier and in the work of 'The Old Sailor' (M. H. Barker), as well as in William Robinson's *Jack Nastyface: Memoirs of an English Seaman* (1836). Thus in Chamier's

The Arethusa (1837), a sailor 'shaved off the beard' of a Jew and stuck it on the trader's coat, 'remarking that bear-skin collars were coming back into fashion; he then lashed him up in a hammock, took him into the cable-tier, stowed him in the heart of it; and then told him he ought to be very happy, as he resembled his namesake [Moses] whilst living and whilst dead; in the one instance, because he was always in pursuit of the promised land; and in the other, "because no man knew of his burying-place even unto this day"'.[104] More comically, in *Jack Nastyface* the sailors docked in Portsmouth harbour turned 'their thoughts to the Jew pedlars' with their 'precious' goods of gold, jewellery and watches 'with which many an honest tar has been taken in'. The Jew goes on board and suits of clothes are obtained from him by trickery:

> Mortified to think he should be done, he swore by Moses and the Prophets he would find the villain; became exasperated, and left the ship, amidst the grins and jeers of the whole crew, who were much diverted and pleased to think that any of their shipmates had tact enough to retaliate nicely on a Jew.[105]

It is within Barker's *Jem Bunt* (1841), however, that the sadism and humiliation aimed at the Jews is most pronounced. Several chapters of the book are devoted to the Jewish traders of Portsmouth, all containing grotesque figures, some accompanied by vicious stereotyped illustrations by Cruickshank. Barker's description of Portsmouth Point brings the Jews together as a collectivity, and repeats the image of their conspiratorial deception presented in *The Sailor's Garland*:

> The Point was also famous for the dwellings of those *kind-hearted* children of Israel, who supplied the wants of the seamen at the *moderate* interest of about 500 per cent. Talk of your London Jews – keen as they are – a Point Jew would have cheated a dozen of them in an hour. The sea-line of this neck of land was prepared as a fortification, and its semi-circular arches used to remind me of an enormous mouse-trap.[106] [Original emphasis.]

Early in the story, Jews are introduced, all of whom speak lisping, broken English. They eagerly await their spoils with the return of a ship to Portsmouth. On its arrival, they attempt to board it through shore-boats, providing the opportunity for 'comic' persecution and exposure of their naturally cowardly nature. One Jew, over-eager to be the first on board, is left suspended on ropes off the ship as the sailors enjoy their sport: '"Oh blesshed Abrahams, look down upon a poor Chew", cried the half-drowned wretch; "shave me, an I'll give a gold candleshtick to de shinagogue"'. The Jew is caught between fear of his own life – 'I shall be drownded' – and the loss of his possessions – 'oh me boxsh, me boxsh'. This rough treatment turns out to be much deserved as the Jewish trader had tricked one of the sailors on an earlier visit. While eventually 'rescued' by his tormentors, he is made to pay for his earlier exploitation.[107] Pusillanimous and effeminate, money-obsessed and selfish, these port Jews of Portsmouth Point are, at this stage in the novel, merely figures of fun who deserve what they get.[108]

At the end of *Jem Bunt*, however, the Jewish presence turns truly nasty. One of its concluding chapters is headed by a quote from *The Merchant of Venice*: 'You called me Jew, And spat upon my Jewish gaberdine' and from then on *Jem Bunt* is a story of (attempted) Jewish revenge. Barker introduces Nathan, 'a Jew crimp, going down to look after "bishness" amongst the Indiamen' at Spithead.[109] Nathan attempts to cheat the sailors of their prize money, but again they are too clever to be tricked. In 'fun', a knuckle of ham is smuggled into Nathan's pocket without him realising it. Here, Barker, within the literary realm, was repeating an actual assault on Jews carried out in Portsmouth during 1781: 'Israel Abraham and his wife were eating dinner when Henry Fisher opened the door to their house and threw in a dead pig, causing Abraham's wife, who was pregnant at the time, to be "greatly terrified"'.[110] On finding this 'joke', Nathan is transformed into a monster of Shylock proportions – Barker clearly has no empathy for the religious sensitivity of the Jews and he assumes a similar absence of respect from his readers; pork has long been associated with antisemitism, manifested either in physical abuse or literary attack. Nathan is determined to get his own back for this humiliation, not merely financially, but also by implicating the sailors in mass desertion. Ultimately, his plot fails and it is Nathan who is arrested.

The 'Point Jews' in this maritime fiction are thus not merely comic figures. They inflict harm and would do so more if not combated by the resourcefulness of 'Jack Tar' and the decency of British justice. Their presence in Portsmouth is parasitic and alien. Technically they may live in the town but they are foreigners to it, as confirmed by their presence in Portsmouth's place of otherness, 'The Point'. Ultimately the Jews presented are contrasted to the honest Englishness of the sailors. The sailors are rooted in England through blood and loyalty whereas the Jews have no proper place within it, especially at a time of military conflict. As Barker concluded in *Jem Bunt*, 'The English are a brave and intelligent people when dealing with an open enemy; but they suffer themselves to be too easily gulled and deluded by pretended friends amongst themselves, and who only use them as tools and instruments to secure their own aggrandizement.'[111]

Conclusion

What, if anything, is the significance of this Portsmouth-focused maritime fiction? While undoubtedly popular and much reprinted (just a small sample has been presented here), did it have any bearing on or relevance to the 'real' Jews of Portsmouth and their history or British Jewry more generally? Timing is critical. Much of this literature coincided with the debates about Jewish emancipation in Britain. While, in 1858, after a struggle taking the best part of three decades, Jews were freed from almost all legal restraints, it remains that the gaining of emancipation, as David Feldman argues, 'did not bring the problem of Jewish integration to a close'. Feldman particularly identifies the problem that 'support for the Jews' equality did not require a positive view of the Jewish minority and this ... contributed to the instability of emancipation'.[112] These popular maritime novels, ballads and illustrations of the first half of the nineteenth century were part of a wider discourse which morally situated the Jews as operating outside the nation. While the connection has not been made before, the influence of this maritime discourse can be seen at its most profound level through the diabolical figure of Fagin in Dickens's *Oliver Twist* (1838). Dickens's biographer, Peter Ackroyd acknowledges that while 'Of course he is the novelist of the city, the novelist of the huddling tenements and the crowded streets; nevertheless, it is hard to think of one of Dickens's novels that does not take place within earshot of the rivers or of the tides.'[113] It is within the twilight world of the Thames in which Fagin operates. Dickens's childhood, through his father's work for the navy, was based in Portsmouth, Chatham and Sheerness – all of which had developed strong port Jewish communities in the Napoleonic Wars and were later represented in maritime fiction. Furthermore, Dickens was also deeply influenced by the work of Captain Marryat. Fagin may live in London, but he would not have been out of place in Portsmouth Point. If British Jewry in the early Victorian era was becoming ever more bourgeois and respectable, its image in popular culture, in which maritime literature is just one of many neglected sources, lagged far behind. If the Duke of Wellington had, in the 1830s, to be reminded of his former Jewish officers at Waterloo, this was at a point when the naval authors of that decade were reviving the term 'sham-Abrahams', those who cowardly attempted to avoid service by malingering.[114]

Returning to the 'local', some recent historians of Portsmouth Jewry have suggested that the maritime discourse examined above had a basis in reality. Thus Warner suggests that the treatment of the Jewish pedlars in Robinson's *Jack Nastyface* was simply part of the rough and tumble of 'daily life in early modern England',[115] and Green tries to identify the Jews in Chamier's *Ben Brace* as 'the well-known Jewish slopsellers Abraham and Lewis Moses of Broad Street, Portsmouth'.[116] Yet while it is no doubt the case that Barker's Nathan, in *Jem Bunt*, is modelled on the 'real' crimp, Henry Nathan, the fictional version is simply a monster, a Shylock without any of the human complexity of Shakespeare's character. It is significant that while Warner accepts that Portsmouth Jews spoke with a strong foreign accent and in broken English, the letters of Henry Nathan reveal his linguistic fluency and clarity.[117] Ultimately, these maritime novels reflect the construction of a certain kind of Englishness in the 1830s and 1840s and cannot be treated as unproblematic sources for the re-creation of local Jewish history. They represent the dominant memory work on the role of the navy before and during the French Revolutionary Wars and Napoleonic Wars in which the Jews are presented as parasitic and unmanly.

Studies of antisemitism have not fully recognised the pleasure in humiliation that has often accompanied both the persecution of the Jews and literary and historical accounts of it. While the maritime novels relish the sadistic, they are part of a longer tradition of enjoying the discomfort of the cringing Jew. In this sense, there is particular insensitivity within Barker's *Jem Bunt* in the portrayal of the Jewish pedlar who is left dangling at the side of a navy ship and at huge risk of drowning. In 1758 a boat carrying Jewish traders, who were returning from HMS *Lancaster* at Spithead, capsized. Eleven Jews drowned, literally decimating the local Jewish community. Roth believed there was only one survivor from the boat, although this has been disputed.[118] Even if more survived, the impact on Portsmouth Jewry was profound and longlasting. Green has researched the log for HMS *Lancaster* and notes that what it 'did not record was a major loss to the small Jewish community of Portsmouth'.[119] The Jewish tragedy was, however, reported at the time in the *Gentleman's Magazine* but in a way that would undermine sympathy for the victims. The wealth of the Jewish traders was highlighted as was their desire to make a profit. Having been thwarted, the failure of the Jews to get back to shore was explained by their poor nautical skills.[120] The Jews, again, neither belong on land or water – they are 'other' to both Portsmouth and Spithead. Through a tombstone inscription in the Jewish cemetery and in special prayers in the synagogue, this loss was remembered *within* Portsmouth Jewry for generations.[121] It was not, however, recalled beyond this community other than to confirm Jewish cowardice and unmanliness at sea. It was left to Cecil Roth, in 1935, to suggest another explanation for the return of these Jewish traders in spite of the high winds – they wished to get back 'in time for the Sabbath'.[122]

In 1808, a Jewish trader was shot dead trying to board HMS *Mars* at Spithead. Five years later at the same place a marine shouted at those on a wherry: 'You Jew-looking buggers if you don't keep the boat off I'll blow your brains out' and then shot (a non-Jewish) slopseller.[123] Trading on the ships was thus a dangerous occupation. While serving a critical function, and both appreciated and resented by the sailors, this Jewish role was subsequently pathologised in dominant memory work. Indeed, the assumption, as with the shooting of a non-Jew at Spithead in 1808 and the attacks on two non-Jews two years later in Portsmouth itself, was that all maritime traders were Jews. Yet as Geoffrey Green has estimated, by the end of the Napoleonic wars, only roughly one-third of navy agents were Jewish.[124] It was extremely rare, however, for this to be acknowledged in maritime fiction, as was the case in the anonymous *Saucy Jack* (1840) where the ship anchoring at Spithead is soon surrounded by traders: 'Jew jostled Christian, and Christian jostled Jew'.[125] Moreover, in such literature and elsewhere, outside the sphere of Jewish family memory, there was near total amnesia of the Jews who fought at Trafalgar and elsewhere.[126] Rather than Jewish bravery in the fighting forces and integration into the everyday life of Portsmouth, it was the 'alien' Jew as coward and exploiter of 'Jack Tar' that was subsequently recalled. The losses on the *Lancaster* and *Mars* were left to be memorialised in the private Jewish realm while the activities that led to them were viciously parodied, as in *Jem Bunt*. In Barker's book, when the first lieutenant is told that there is a man overboard, he is reassured that 'it's ounly a Jew, Sir'.[127]

In 1900, a lavishly illustrated *History of Portsmouth* was published by the local newspaper chain to mark its centenary. As will be explored further in the next chapter, a section of this history was devoted to the Jews of the town, emphasising their civic contribution and loyalty. Yet within the same book, another chapter provided 'The Story of Point'. Reproduced within this story, alongside Rowlandson's etching and poems referring to the 'gay shops of Israel's seed', was Barker's description of the 'Point Jew' in *Jem Bunt*. There was no editorial intervention and Barker's account was presented as part of the factual basis of Portsmouth's history.[128] These alternative narratives of respectability and contamination ran parallel within the text without one querying the accuracy of the other. A similar tension will be apparent in the story of Jewish emancipation, the local dynamics and memory of which will be the focus of Chapter 5.

Notes

1 Bill Williams, *The Making of Manchester Jewry 1740–1875* (Manchester: Manchester University Press, 1975), p. 57.

2 Ibid., p. 36.

3 See I. Meisels, 'The Jewish Congregation of Portsmouth (1766–1842)', *Transactions of the Jewish Historical Society of England* vol. 6 (1908–10), pp. 111–27; Cecil Roth, 'The Portsmouth Community and Its Historical Background', *Transactions of the Jewish Historical Society of England* vol. 13 (1932–35), pp. 157–87; and Aubrey Weinberg, 'Portsmouth Jewry' in *Portsmouth Papers* no. 41 (1985), pp. 1–20.

4 Weinberg, 'Portsmouth Jewry', p. 3.

5 From the religious census figures as analysed by Vivian Lipman, 'A Survey of Anglo-Jewry in 1851', *Transactions of the Jewish Historical Society of England* vol. 17 (1951–52), pp. 179, 181, 183, 188.

6 Williams, *The Making of Manchester Jewry*, p. 280 and *Jewish Chronicle*, 11 March 1853.

7 Geoffrey Green, 'Anglo-Jewish Trading Connections with Officers and Seamen of the Royal Navy, 1740–1820', *Transactions of the Jewish Historical Society of England* vol. 29 (1982–86), p. 97.

8 Gillian Rose, 'Place and Identity: A Sense of Place', in Doreen Massey and Pat Jess (eds), *A Place in the World?* (Oxford: Oxford University Press, 1995), p. 89.

9 Richard Meegan, 'Local Worlds', in John Allen and Doreen Massey (eds), *Geographical Worlds* (Oxford: Oxford University Press, 1995), p. 55.

10 David Ley, 'Behavioral Geography and the Philosophies of Meaning', in Kevin Cox and Reginald Golledge (eds), *Behavioral Problems in Geography Revisited* (London: Methuen, 1981), p. 219 summarising the view of geographic humanism.

11 Ken Lunn and Ann Day, 'Britain as Island: National Identity and the Sea', in Helen Brocklehurst and Robert Phillips (eds), *History, Nationhood and the Question of Britain* (Basingstoke: Palgrave Macmillan, 2004), pp. 126–7.

12 Charles Robinson, *The British Tar in Fact and Fiction* (London: Harper and Brothers, 1911), p. 161.

13 Jeannine Surel, 'John Bull', in Raphael Samuel (ed.), *Patriotism* vol. III *National Fictions* (London: Routledge, 1989), p. 11.

14 Cecil Roth (ed.), *Essays in Jewish History by Lucien Wolf* (London: Jewish Historical Society of England, 1934), pp. 123–4, based on *Jewish Chronicle* articles first published in August 1903.

15 Jessica Warner, 'Violence Against and Amongst Jews in an Early Modern Town: Tolerance and its Limits in Portsmouth, 1718–1781', *Albion* vol. 35 (Fall 2003), p. 432.

16 Portsmouth City Record Office (PCRO), S3/177/17.

17 Warner, 'Violence Against and Amongst Jews', pp. 438, 448.

18 James Thomas, 'Tension and Conflict in Eighteenth Century Portsmouth', *Portsmouth Archive Review* vol. 5 (1981), pp. 17,19.

19 Meisels, 'The Jewish Congregation', p. 121; Roth, 'The Portsmouth Community', p. 167.

20 Meisels, 'The Jewish Congregation', p. 121.

21 Lucien Wolf, 'A Peep into the Portsmouth Pinkes', *Jewish Chronicle*, 15 August 1890.

22 Roth, 'The Portsmouth Community', pp. 167–75.

23 Eugene Newman, 'Some New Facts About the Portsmouth Jewish Community', *Transactions of the Jewish Historical Society of England* vol. 17 (1951–52), p. 256.

24 Bernard Susser, *The Jews of South-West England* (Exeter: University of Exeter Press, 1993), p. 40.

25 William Gates, *Illustrated History of Portsmouth* (Portsmouth: Carpenter & Co, 1900), p. 366.

26 Susser, *The Jews of South-West England*, p. 58 and 'The Jews of Ohio', *The Occident and American Jewish Advocate*, February 1844.

27 Susser, *The Jews of South-West England*, p. 126.

28 Newman, 'Some New Facts', pp. 262–3 summarises the geographical scope of Reb Leib's work; Roth, 'The Portsmouth Community', p. 175 dismisses the local aspect as 'parochial'.

29 Roth, 'The Portsmouth Community', pp. 168–9 provides details of the rabbinic division.

30 Weinberg, 'Portsmouth Jewry', p. 15.

31 Warner, 'Violence Against and Amongst Jews', p. 433.

32 Thomas, 'Tension and Conflict', p. 26.

33 Newman, 'Some New Facts', pp. 253–4.

34 Geoffrey Green, *The Royal Navy & Anglo-Jewry 1740–1820* (London: Geoffrey Green, 1989), p. 116.

35 Minute book of Portsmouth Hebrew Congregation, September 1834, quoted by Meisels, 'The Jewish Congregation', p. 114.

36 Ibid., p. 114.

37 Thomas, 'Tension and Conflict', p. 35.

38 Todd Endelman, *The Jews of Georgian England 1714–1830: Tradition and Change in a Liberal Society* (Philadelphia: Jewish Publication Society of America, 1979), p. 47.

39 Green, *The Royal Navy*, pp. 152–3.

40 Warner, 'Violence Against and Amongst Jews', p. 439.

41 Ibid., pp. 442, 448.

42 Ibid., p. 444.

43 PCRO, 11A/16/748.

44 'Portsmouth – As others have seen it: Part I 1540–1790', *Portsmouth Papers* no. 15 (1972), p. 14.

45 William Gates, *The Portsmouth That Has Passed* (Portsmouth: Portsmouth & Sunderland Newspapers, 1946), p. 202.

46 Doreen Massey, 'Places and Their Pasts', *History Workshop Journal* no. 39 (spring 1995), p. 183.

47 Doreen Massey, 'Double Articulation: A Place in the World', in A. Bammer (ed.), *Displacements: Cultural Identities in Question* (Bloomington: Indiana University Press, 1994), p. 120.

48 Joan Grigsby, 'Portsmouth Point by Thomas Rowlandson', *Hampshire* vol. 3 no. 12 (October 1963), p. 19.

49 Gary Cannon's notes on Walton's *Portsmouth Point* which was completed in 1925 and first performed a year later. See www.williamwalton.net/works/orchestral/portsmouth_point. html, accessed 10 July 2006.

50 The image is reproduced in Gates, *The Portsmouth that Has Passed*, p. 202.

51 Green, *The Royal Navy*, p. 114.

52 Robert Wark (ed.), *Rowlandson's Drawings for a Tour in a Post Chaise* (San Marino, California: Huntington Library, 1963), plate 65. See also the Rowlandson sketches held by Portsmouth Museum and Record Office.

53 W. Rubinstein, *A History of the Jews in the English-Speaking World: Great Britain* (Basingstoke: Macmillan, 1996), p. 65.

54 *The History of Portsmouth* (Portsmouth: J. C. Mottley, 1801).

55 Ibid., pp. 7–8. For its subsequent use, see, for example, Roth, 'The Portsmouth Community', p. 163 who misquotes it as does R. B. Wade, 'Portsmouth in the 18th Century', *Hampshire* vol. 11 no. 8 (June 1971), p. 29. See also S. E. Barrington, 'Portsmouth from High Street to Spice Island', *Hampshire Review* no. 19 (Spring 1954), p. 38.

56 *The History of Portsmouth*, p. 5.

57 Ibid., p. 8.

58 Ibid., pp. 79, 83.

59 Henry Slight, *A Looking Glass for Portsmouth and Its Environs* (Portsmouth: Henry Slight, 1843), pp. 2, 9.

60 Warner, 'Violence Against and Amongst Jews', pp. 433–5.

61 Anon [William Glascock], *A Naval Sketch Book* vol. 2 (London: Whittaker, 1834 [second

series]), p. 38, note 2. Glascock had just commented (pp. 37–8) that 'Jack's … Israelite friends' were 'a fraternity … in sea-port towns, more cognoscent, touching the ultimate destinies of vessels of war, than any other authority, private or public'.

62 Warner, 'Violence Against and Amongst Jews', pp. 435–6.

63 Diary entry, 21 September 1812 reproduced in Roth (ed.), *Essays in Jewish History*, pp. 251–2.

64 *Hampshire Chronicle*, 28 June 1773.

65 W. H. Saunders, *Annals of Portsmouth* (London: Hamilton, Adams, 1880), pp. 65–7.

66 *Hampshire Chronicle*, 28 June 1773.

67 Bryan Cheyette, *Constructions of 'the Jew' in English Literature and Society: Racial Representations, 1875–1945* (Cambridge: Cambridge University Press, 1993), p. 12.

68 Roxann Wheeler, *The Complexion of Race: Categories of Difference in Eighteenth-Century British Culture* (Philadelphia: University of Pennysylvania Press, 2000), pp. 300–1.

69 Roth, 'The Portsmouth Community', p. 178 note 63.

70 Weinberg, 'Portsmouth Jewry', p. 12.

71 Frank Felsenstein, *Anti-Semitic Stereotypes: A Paridigm of Otherness in English Popular Culture, 1660–1830* (Baltimore: Johns Hopkins University Press, 1995), pp. 231–2.

72 Warner, 'Violence Against and Amongst Jews', p. 442.

73 Ibid., p. 231.

74 Green, *The Royal Navy*, p. 182.

75 Cecil Roth, *The Jews in the Defence of Britain* (London: JHSE, 1940), pp. 13, 22.

76 Levi to Secretary of War, 4 May 1798 in National Archives (NA), HO 50/43, reproduced, as is the response, with minor inaccuracies in Green, *The Royal Navy*, pp. 62–4.

77 Levi letter of 4 May 1798 in HO 50/53, NA.

78 Pitt to Henry Dundas, 1 June 1798, in HO 50/43, NA.

79 Endelman, *The Jews of Georgian England 1714–1830*, pp. 275–6. On the wider context of the Aliens Act of 1793 see Clive Emsley, *British Society and the French Wars 1793–1815* (London: Macmillan, 1979), pp. 15, 20–1.

80 Meisels, 'The Jewish Congregation', pp. 112, 117.

81 Ibid., pp. 117–18.

82 Felsenstein, *Anti-Semitic Stereotypes*, p. 231.

83 Henry Roche, 'The Jews of Portsmouth', *Shemot* vol. 2 no. 1 (1995), p. 28.

84 Weinberg, 'Portsmouth Jewry', p. 15.

85 *Hampshire Telegraph*, 13 March 1815.

86 Ibid.

87 David Cesarani, 'The Forgotten Port Jews of London', in David Cesarani (ed.), *Port Jews* (London: Frank Cass, 2002), p. 122.

88 Ibid., pp. 122–3.

89 John Peck, *Maritime Fiction: Sailors and the Sea in British and American Novels, 1719–1917* (Basingstoke: Palgrave, 2001), Chapter 3, especially pp. 54, 68.

90 Patrick Brantlinger, *Rule of Darkness: British Literature and Imperialism, 1830–1914* (Ithaca: Cornell University Press, 1988), p. 48.

91 See C. Northcote Parkinson, *Portsmouth Point: The British Navy in Fiction 1793–1815* (Cambridge, MA: Harvard University Press, 1949), pp. 12–13.

92 John Sutherland, *The Longman Companion to Victorian Fiction* (Harlow: Longman, 1988), p. 414.

93 Brantlinger, *Rule of Darkness*, p. 49.

94 Peck, *Maritime Fiction*, pp. 54, 68.

95 C. Northcote Parkinson, *Portsmouth Point: The British Navy in Fiction 1793–1815* (Cambridge, MA: Harvard University Press, 1949).
96 See Linda Colley, *Britons: Forging the Nation 1707–1837* (London: Pimlico, 1992), p. 286.
97 Captain Chamier, *Ben Brace* vol. 2 (London: Richard Bentley, 1836), p. 219.
98 Edward Howard, *Rattlin, the Reefer* vol. 2 (London: Richard Bentley, 1836), p. 198.
99 C. Firth (ed.), *Naval Songs and Ballads* (London: Naval Records Society, 1907), pp. 231–2.
100 Peck, *Maritime Fiction*, pp. 67–8.
101 Captain Marryat, *Peter Simple* (London: Macmillan, 1895 [1834]), p. 68.
102 Firth (ed.), *Naval Songs*, p. 232.
103 Peck, *Maritime Fiction*, p. 68.
104 Captain Chamier, *The Arethusa* vol. 2 (London: Richard Bentley, 1837), p. 181.
105 William Robinson, *Jack Nastyface* (London: Chatham Publishing, 2002 [1836]), pp. 96, 99–100.
106 The Old Sailor, *Jem Bunt* (London: How & Parsons, 1841), p. 54.
107 Ibid., Chapter 2, esp. pp. 27–8.
108 Ibid., p. 27.
109 Ibid., pp. 289–90.
110 Warner, 'Violence Against and Amongst Jews', p. 439.
111 Ibid., p. 363.
112 David Feldman, *Englishmen and Jews: Social Relations and Political Culture 1840–1914* (New Haven: Yale University Press, 1994), p. 75.
113 Peter Ackroyd, *Dickens* (London: Sinclair-Stevenson, 1990), p. 25.
114 Parkinson, *Portsmouth Point*, p. 31.
115 Warner, 'Violence Against and Amongst Jews', pp. 428–9.
116 Green, *The Royal Navy*, pp. 134–5.
117 Warner, 'Violence Against and Amongst Jews', pp. 429–50; Green, *The Royal Navy*, pp. 69–73.
118 Roth, 'The Portsmouth Community', pp. 164–5; Weinberg, *Portsmouth Jewry*, p. 6.
119 Green, *The Royal Navy*, p. 28.
120 *Gentleman's Magazine* vol. 28 (February 1758), p. 91.
121 Roth, 'The Portsmouth Community', pp. 164–5.
122 Ibid., p. 164.
123 Green, *The Royal Navy*, pp. 153–5.
124 Ibid., p. 146.
125 A Blue Jacket, *The Saucy Jack* (London: Richard Bentley, 1840), quoted by Parkinson, *Portsmouth Point*, p. 103.
126 Geoffrey Green, 'Jews in the Royal Navy from Trafalgar onwards', *Shemot* vol. 14 (March 2006), pp. 3–7 deals with family memory.
127 The Old Sailor, *Jem Bunt*, p. 27.
128 Gates, *Illustrated History of Portsmouth*, pp. 212–17, 364–8.

5

Jewish emancipation and after: locality, brotherhood and the nature of tolerance

Introduction

David Katz has argued that the 'gifted amateurs' who dominated the writing of Anglo-Jewish history [until the late twentieth century] were motivated by a 'dual wish to praise their people and their country'. He adds that 'Almost any subject that was liable to place the Jewish community in a negative light was self-censored, and any twist of interpretation which might spark gentile anger was banished and buried.' The result, he concludes, was that

> Anglo-Jewish historiography has always been patriotic, conservative and Whig, that is, ends-oriented, written with one eye on the final destination of the history train, the End of Anglo-Jewish History – 'Emancipation', that minor alteration in the oath of office which allowed Baron de Rothschild to take his seat in the House of Commons on 26 July 1858 and never utter a word thereafter.[1]

The memory work associated with the two largest Jewish communities in Hampshire during the nineteenth century – Portsmouth and Southampton – largely conforms to the storyline of progress and achievement. Indeed, this progressive model of resettlement and eventual toleration is replicated within both the Jewish and non-Jewish spheres, adding, in both cases, a strong element of local patriotism. The particular focus has been on several prominent Jewish individuals/families and their gaining of civic office in these two neighbouring port towns.

The short-lived Portsmouth paper, *Pinks' Pictorial*, devoted a feature in April 1909 to the history of the local Jewish community which now numbered up to one thousand. Written at a point when the synagogue was being extensively enlarged to accommodate growth in the Jewish community, the article provided an opportunity to outline the improving treatment of the Jews in England. 'This country,' it admitted, 'is by no means free from the stigma of persecuting this downtrodden, malignantly harried race'. But Cromwell's readmission of the 'aristocracy of the Jewish race', and the 'large proportion of well-educated individuals who made this country their home', had enabled 'so many [to] have attained high position and honour in municipal, political and commercial circles'. Within Portsmouth, these Jewish holders of office included what was perceived as the same Emanuel family:

> Alderman Emanuel Emanuel, from 1841 to the time of his death in 1888, did yeoman service to the town, in fact it is doubtful if any other man ever took part, or was instrumental, in obtaining for the town so many advantages and improvements. Several other members of this family have also taken part in the public life of the town, notably the late Alderman A. L. Emanuel, who died during the alterations to the Synagogue, the cost of which he was defraying.[2]

In fact, the neatness of this account of local family benefaction was misleading – the two aldermen were unrelated.[3]

A similarly positive narrative was constructed in William Gates's *Illustrated History of Portsmouth* (1900) which opened its chapter on the Jews by suggesting that for 'nearly two hundred years Portsmouth has been the abiding place of a numerous Jewish colony, which has ever maintained the most friendly relations with the other townspeople and cheerfully borne its share of local burdens and responsibilities'.[4] As with *Pinks' Pictorial*, emphasis was placed on the Emanuel family, especially Emanuel Emanuel, and his civic achievements: 'His activity was something abounding and wonderful. He was the first Jew elected to the Corporation, and he proved to be one of the most persistent and successful reformers the town has ever known.' Indeed, the *Illustrated History* acted as a eulogy to Emanuel Emanuel: he was the 'perfect citizen' and Portsmouth would do 'well to remember with deep gratitude how many of the great improvements of the last half century are the outcome of his reforming zeal'.[5] After the end of the First World War, the local Education Committee sponsored *The Story of Portsmouth*, aimed at schoolchildren. It included a succinct and relentlessly Whiggish account of the Jewish experience: 'The Jews ... after much persecution at various times, are now free to worship in their own way ... This once cruelly treated race has won the distinction in the civic life of the town. One of their number, Mr Emanuel, was mayor in 1866, and for many years did valuable work on the Town Council.'[6]

In these popular accounts, Jewish achievement and contribution were presented as the just recompense for the local 'spirit of toleration'.[7] The *Illustrated History* thus argued that 'To the fact that Portsmouth has always been found on the side of civil and religious liberty must be attributed the early entry of the Jews into municipal life.'[8] The 'old disability days' had forced the Jews of Portsmouth to 'live a life apart', but with 'full political liberty', brought about partly through local townsmen standing by their principles, 'they at once displayed all the qualities that make for good citizenship ... and Portsmouth gladly bears testimony to the loyalty, the zeal, and the camaraderie of the entire community'.[9] Such mutual congratulation was to be replicated within Jewish historiography. In 1935, in a lecture in memory of the Jewish historian and daughter of Emanuel Emanuel, Lady Magnus, Cecil Roth paid tribute to the 'notable share which the congregation played in the nineteenth century in civic life and in the movement for Jewish emancipation'.[10] Fifty years later, Aubrey Weinberg's more ambitious overview of Portsmouth Jewry from the eighteenth through to the late twentieth century highlighted how 'responding to the liberality of the civic structure, the Jewish contribution to Portsmouth has been undeniable'. Weinberg added that the antisemitism which had 'riven other urban entities ... has always remained marginal to the life of Portsmouth's communities'. Local tolerance was at least partly attributable 'to the nonconformist civic leadership which has been a protective force against ongoing anti-semitism' and was especially responsible for the early representation and subsequent prominent role of Jews in the town's governance.[11]

In 1951, Rabbi Eugene Newman of the Portsmouth congregation extended, along the Hampshire coast, the geographical scope of his community's civic and religious virtues during the nineteenth century. He focused on the 'other' Emanuel family 'which produced Mayors and Wardens of Southampton and Portsmouth':

> Michael Emanuel (1767–1838) was a leading figure in the Portsmouth Community for over three decades. He had several sons of whom Samuel Michael Emanuel (1802–1894) was Sheriff of Southampton in 1865 and Mayor in 1866 and 1867, and Jacob Isaac Emanuel (1804–1846) was the founder of the Southampton Hebrew Congregation.[12]

Unsurprisingly, Portsmouth's rival town developed its own mythology of local tolerance. On 1 November 1838 in Southampton, pre-dating Emanuel Emanuel's election by three years, Abraham Abraham became Britain's first Jewish councillor. Abraham risked prosecution by refusing to take the Christian oath (a regulation that would remain in force until 1845 and the passing of 'An Act for the Relief of Persons of the Jewish Religion Elected to Municipal Offices'). Fortunately for Abraham, in the words of Southampton's mayor, no one 'had the bad taste to do so'.[13] When Samuel Emanuel was successfully nominated as Sheriff in 1864, the *Southampton Times* took the opportunity of reflecting on the liberality revealed by the town in electing his Jewish predecessor to the same office over twenty years earlier:

> In the appointment of sheriffs Southampton has evidently shown its attachment to the great principles of civil and religious liberty. We believe it was the first

corporation in the United Kingdom to admit a member of the Hebrew persuasion. That gentleman was afterwards sheriff, and now we have had two successive appointments of the same character. Mr Emanuel will no doubt carry out the duties of his office in an honourable and dignified manner, and we hope that the great political principle involved in his election will be more truly and extensively appreciated.[14]

More generally within British Jewish historiography, post-1815 the Jews of Portsmouth and Southampton only merit a mention because of their path-breaking role in being elected to municipal office and the progress in the treatment of Jews thereby revealed.[15] This chapter will explore, through the experiences of and responses to the two Emanuel families and the Abraham family, the nature of liberal tolerance towards the Jews within Victorian politics. Were these leading Jews accepted locally, and if so, on what terms?

Emanuel Emanuel: the making of an elder statesman

Before rising again from the mid-nineteenth century onwards, membership of the Portsmouth synagogue peaked in 1812. Its growth during the French Revolutionary Wars and Napoleonic Wars was, indeed, spectacular, increasing by roughly three-quarters.[16] Yet the subsequent decline in the Jewish community after 1815 was equally dramatic. *Pinks' Pictorial* in 1909 claimed that at 'the beginning of the last century Portsmouth was the home of many of the best and highest-class Jews, but on the cessation of the war, when business deserted the town, numbers of them went to various parts'.[17] Post-1815, the diasporic movement of Jews from Portsmouth was notable in several respects. First, it was truly global, reflecting the energy of these Jews, a dynamism marked also by subsequent commercial success. Second, their stay in Portsmouth clearly mattered to them – whether reflected in the communities across the world that they helped create or develop further, or in maintaining links with their former Hampshire home. Portsmouth, in spite of the antipathy that the Jews were to experience, was also for many a place of inspiration. In turn, the Jewish traders and others had contributed to the town's development before and during the war. The port setting, as elsewhere in the world, was not necessarily more tolerant, but it was, nevertheless, energising and stimulating.[18] The foundation in 1804 of the Hebrew Benevolent Institution to provide relief for the Jewish 'resident poor' was an indication that not all shared the prosperity of the war years.[19] Yet its existence, alongside donations to local and national non-Jewish charitable causes, indicated the emergence of an elite who were able to administer and fund such activities. This dispensation also reflected the desire to show respectability and civic duty in a town whose previous reputation for violence was made potentially more threatening by war-time xenophobia. While dimished in numbers, the Jews in post-1815 Portsmouth revealed similar tendencies to their predecessors, manifested by a mixture of public prominence and risk-taking as well as behaviour marked by defensiveness and insecurity.

In 1907 the *Jewish Year Book* claimed that in Portsmouth 'After the peace of 1815, the Jewish inhabitants dimished to such an extent that the newly-erected Synagogue was transferred to a dry-store dealer'.[20] Portsmouth, however, was not the worst-affected of the naval-dominated Jewish port communities. As with Plymouth and Chatham, its deeper roots ensured post-war continuity, whereas as Sheerness, which was 'virtually a creation of the war ... declined rapidly when peace returned'.[21] Sheerness struggled on with a handful of Jewish families before the synagogue finally closed in the 1880s. Falmouth's demise was slightly earlier, especially with the loss, to Southampton, of the mail packet services during the 1840s. Elsewhere in Cornwall, Penzance struggled on to the early twentieth century.[22]

In contrast, while many left Portsmouth after 1815, others were attracted to the port for the economic opportunities it still offered. Moses Emanuel, born in Bavaria, settled in Portsmouth after the war, having been based in London. His son, Ezekiel, ran a shop on the Hard, Portsea, 'trading as a silversmith, jeweller, and watchmaker'. The London connection, especially in trade in precious metals, was important in the success of this enterprise, providing the foundation for Ezekiel's brother, Emanuel, to build his subsequent career in local politics. Emanuel became a prominent jeweller in Portsmouth with a sister business in London. His prominence and respectability, contrasting to his Jewish trading predecessors in the port, was reflected in his status as silversmith to Queen Victoria and to the Royal Navy.[23]

Emanuel Emanuel was born in London's West End in 1807 and, aged eleven, he moved with his father and brother to Portsmouth. His death in 1888 was marked by obituaries in the local and Jewish press, the *Hampshire Telegraph* highlighting how 'all through his long life, [he had] been intimately, actively and honourably identified with the Borough of Portsmouth, both as a public man and one representing the highest commercial interests of the place'.[24] The *Jewish Chronicle* added in an editorial that Emanuel's death

> recalls once more to the present generation the memory of the pre-Emancipation struggles. He was enabled to make friends far and wide for the Jewish cause by the profound respect for Jews with which he embued all those who came within the circle of his good influence. For upwards of half a century he worked, not for personal aggrandisement, but for the glory of God's name and his people's renown.

The editorial concluded that 'There was a modesty and unostentation about the worthy Alderman's piety, charity and public spirit that had a great charm for men accustomed to ambitions of a less ennobling character.'[25]

The representation of Emanuel Emanuel as an elder statesman within both Portsmouth society and Anglo-Jewry is not surprising given the length and impact of his public service and the genuine affection with which he was held. Nevertheless, a deftness was required in both newspapers in passing over what had been deeply controversial and divisive issues in the career of Emanuel across the Jewish and non-Jewish spheres. Indeed, Emanuel Emanuel's public persona had a notorious debut. Six years after his arrival in Portsmouth, aged just seventeen, he was charged at the Quarter Sessions for an assault against Lewis Lazarus, 'a respectable pawnbroker' who was also a Licensed Navy Agent [and] an elder of the Portsmouth Hebrew congregation'.[26] Such behaviour was reminiscent of the intra-communal violence within the Jewish community during the eighteenth century. Then such open lawlessness deeply disturbed the Jewish elite and its search for public approbation. The fears of being labelled unrespectable still haunted Portsmouth Jewry's leaders after 1815. Thus the week after the assault was reported in the *Hampshire Telegraph*, Michael Emanuel, head of what was now the longest-established Jewish family in Portsmouth, wrote to the newspaper 'quick to disclaim any connection with Emanuel Emanuel'.[27] Michael Emanuel, a leading figure in the synagogue, was anxious to distinguish his family from that of the newcomers to the town who shared his surname.

In both the local and Jewish obituaries of Emanuel Emanuel the dismissal of the need for him to recite a Christian oath when he became a councillor in 1841 was treated lightly. Technically, as the *Hampshire Telegraph* noted, Emanuel was liable to a fine of £500 if he voted in the council, but it was 'hardly surprising to know that the penalty was never enforced'.[28] In fact, six years earlier Emanuel had gracefully declined to stand as councillor, having been nominated to do so, because of 'doubt as to my eligibility'.[29] Two years later in 1837, David Levy, similarly invited to represent a ward refused to do so for fear of the operation of the 'religious test'.[30] Moreover, it has been suggested that 'First elected to the Council in 1841, Emanuel was forced to resign when a local radical drew attention to the fact that as a Jew he was unable to swear the necessary oaths'.[31] While no evidence has been found to corroborate this claim, it is clear that in 1843 Emanuel and a fellow Liberal, Henry Slight, lost their seats through the intervention of radicals.[32] Their election defeat followed a heated debate in the Council over the recognition of non-Anglicans in the town. A vote arguing for equality in treatment was won only very narrowly exposing Emanuel's marginality.[33]

In relation to Emanuel's civic impact, the obituarists similarly smoothed over what had been divisive issues within local society. In 1847 he was largely responsible for abolishing the ancient Free Mart Fair which the *Hampshire*

Telegraph described as an 'unnecessary nuisance', the *Jewish Chronicle* adding that it was the source of 'immorality and lawlessness'.[34] For the growing number of the 'respectable' bourgeoisie in Portsmouth, this fair encouraged the dangerous mingling of classes in an annual event characterised by the destabilising presence of vulgar cosmopolitan showpeople and stallholders, drunkenness, petty crime, rowdiness and prostitution.[35] It was a world made up of figures such as 'dextrous Lane', characterised in a poem of 1801,

> who rivals old Nick,
> In a cut or a shuffle, or clean shifting trick;
> And, to your surprise, he'll certainly show,
> How a Christian may baffle a Turk, or a Jew.[36]

Indeed, the fair was perhaps too close to his roots for Emanuel Emanuel to appreciate. It still attracted the Jewish pedlars who had been the basis of the Portsmouth community in the previous century, including '"Old Sammy", an aged Jew, [who] walked seventy-two miles from London to Free Market fair in Portsmouth, and was said to have walked this route once a year for fifty years. When he arrived he always stood in the same place [while] Cheap Jack mentioned quite casually that he himself walked from Birmingham to Portsea.'[37]

If subsequently the Free Mart Fair was remembered affectionately, but as 'a thing of the past [which had] served its time',[38] at the time Emanuel's championing of its abolition helped focus radical opinion against him. In 1848, when attempts to revive the fair were quashed, anger was specifically aimed at Emanuel and his house was attacked.[39] Such antipathy was intensified by his growing relationship with the unpopular aristocrat and entrepreneur, Lord Frederick Fitzclarence. In 1849, when Emanuel tried to have Southsea Common renamed Clarence Park, the *Hampshire Telegraph* called him an 'officious little Jew'.[40] While in the 1850s and 1860s, Emanuel's public career took off, with a civic banquet in his honour in 1857 and the mayorship in 1866, the controversy that had accompanied his early career never disappeared. Indeed, in 1874 it reached a climax with the so-called 'Battle of Southsea'.

Emanuel Emanuel was the most influential director of a company that was determined to make Southsea Pier exclusively for the use of 'Ladies and Gentlemen'. Its directors decided 'to put a stop to the promiscuous mingling of the classes around its premises' by erecting a barrier between the Pier and the surrounding area. Crowds of up to five thousand gathered to open up access which, after much public disorder, was eventually granted, if only partially.[41] To radicals, Emanuel typified the forces of class oppression in the town and his Jewishness provided a convenient peg to hang public animosity.

In a popular ballad, 'The Glorious Battle at Southsea', the imagery associated with Jewish traders in maritime discourse a generation earlier was now re-produced to attack Emanuel. He was accused of 'slyly scheming' and, with the other directors, lining his 'greedy pockets'. In language reminiscent of *Jem Bunt*, the 'little Jew' Emanuel was portrayed as unmanly, running 'home in a fright' from the ordinary Portsmouth folk who win the local 'battle'. Again echoing Barker's virulent novel, reference to pork and humiliation came in the ballad's conclusion: 'May a pig's foot stick in the little Jew's gills/ May the Directors suffer humanity's ills'.[42]

Emanuel Emanuel is the only Jew in Hampshire to be memorialised through a public monument – a fountain in his memory was donated by his son and daughter to the people of Portsmouth, located in Southsea, the area which he had done so much to 'improve'.[43] Within the historiography of Portsmouth Jewry, and Portsmouth itself through the popular narratives of William Gates, Emanuel's successful public career has been utilised as an example of the progressive and tolerant nature of local politics and society. There were, undoubtedly, within Portsmouth, those who as early as 1835 wanted to promote the '*local* emancipation [of the Jews] by nominating an Israelite as one of the Town councillors for this Borough' and Emanuel was the first of many Jews who were elected to the municipality.[44] Others in the town, however, including the MP, were opposed to Jewish emancipation and the radical opposition to Emanuel, and the antisemitic discourse associated with it, revealing the dangers of generalising in isolation about local traditions of tolerance. In reality, Emanuel was part of an energetic group of reform-ing entrepreneurs who linked municipal improvement with profit-making and who desired a clear separation, moral and physical, of the classes. They re-modelled and re-packaged Portsmouth, attempting to remove its earlier 'sailortown' reputation. Emanuel was fortunate to be (largely) on the win-ning side. Nevertheless, a celebratory reading of Emanuel's career that omits the antisemitism he encountered is ultimately misleading. It ignores the re-ality that legal emancipation was hard fought and that his fight against prej-udice and for social acceptance was a separate and ongoing battle. Emanuel's career was thus often brave, if foolhardy, in which his own political/class bias was manifest throughout. The ambivalence Emanuel faced was replicated in a different context in the aborted political career of Abraham Abraham in Southampton. Indeed, the success of one and the (relative) failure of the other revealed that good luck, as well as intense self-belief and a thick skin, had played a sizeable role in the political fortunes of Emanuel Emanuel.

Abraham Abraham: from pioneer to obscurity

In the medieval period few English Jews settled in port towns. Winchester Jews had strong business interests in Southampton and owned property within it but there was no organised community within this international hub. In the thirteenth century Jews were formally banned from Southampton and it was a port of expulsion in 1290. Nevertheless, this 'ethnic cleansing' did not totally remove the Jewish presence from England and English memory. A tenement near West Quay in 1340 was described as being next to the 'Jew's House'. Within later Southampton Jewish folklore, it was seen as evidence of a building for converted Jews, following the example in London. It was more likely to have been a property formerly owned by a Winchester-based Jew, still locally remembered as such in the fourteenth century.[45] Similarly, while Wilks's claim in 1861 that Masse Salman, sheriff of Southampton in 1489, was Jewish may be put down to antiquarian naivety,[46] it is undoubted that there were Marrano traders operating in the port in the period between expulsion and readmission. Amongst these 'secret' Jews of Spanish and Portuguese origin was Christopher Fernandes. In the 1540s Fernandes was 'in the service of Diogo Mendes in London, and employed by him to intercept the Portuguese spice ships touching at Southampton and Plymouth [warning] the Marranos on board if any danger awaited them at Antwerp'. The 'House of Mendes' was of great financial significance in sixteenth century England, so much so that Diogo gained the protection of Henry VIII when prosecuted for practising Judaism in 1532.[47]

In contrast to the medieval period, almost all of the early Jewish readmission settlements in England were located in ports. Cecil Roth identified roughly twenty provincial communities by 1800. The number had doubled by 1840. Although inland settlements had increased, half in the early Victorian era were still located in sea-ports. By 1833, Southampton had joined their number when a room was rented for prayers, acting as a temporary synagogue 'in the Orthodox tradition' catering for roughly a dozen families.[48] There were Jews in the town in the eighteenth century, including Mordecai Moses, a watchmaker. Yet while Southampton's fortunes were reviving from the late eighteenth century as a spa town, it could not rival neighbouring Portsmouth for the economic opportunities it offered. For the rare Jewish individuals operating in Southampton, Portsmouth, through the services of Reb Leib Aleph, provided for their religious needs. Only after the Napoleonic Wars, with the decline of Portsmouth and fewer alternatives elsewhere, as well as the slow progress in re-establishing the port of Southampton on an international scale, did the town become more attractive for Jewish settlement. By 1817, while stating that 'there was no congregated body of Israelites there', Moses Sailman, who was teaching Hebrew in Southampton, was in communication with a co-religionist in the town concerning the activities of a Christian conversionist. Their correspondence suggests that there was the beginnings of a small Jewish network in Southampton.[49]

The key figures within Southampton Jewry as it formalised itself during the mid-decades of the nineteenth century were sons of Jewish entrepreneurs who had established themselves in other provincial settings. The first to be analysed is Abraham Abraham. In 1906 the eugenicist Francis Galton published *Noteworthy Families*. Based on family trees provided by members of the Royal Society, it was designed to prove that 'Success is, statistically speaking, a magnified, but otherwise trustworthy, sign of Ability'. Included within it was Raphael Meldola, a professor of chemistry whose grandfather had been rabbi of the Spanish and Portuguese synagogue in London. Amongst the 'proof' of the family's genetic propensity for success was Meldola's uncle, Joseph Abraham, who 'founded a large and successful firm in Bristol; took a prominent part in municipal affairs, and became the first Jewish mayor of Bristol'. In turn, Joseph's nephew, Harry [Henry] Abraham, was 'a man of business, and councillor and Mayor of Southampton'.[50]

In the light of the narrative to follow, it was perhaps appropriate, if regrettable, that Abraham Abraham, brother of Joseph and father of Henry, should be missing from this list of family achievers related to Meldola. Abraham Abraham, too, was a successful businessman and also a prominent local politician. His absence from Galton's list partly reflected the obscurity of his later life – indeed, he disappears from the historical record in time and place. The amnesia about him also perhaps was connected to the nature and brevity of his political career. Celebrated both at the time and subsequently as the first Jewish councillor in Britain, just four years later, when his progress was at its height, Abraham Abraham became linked to a political scandal which destroyed his public ambitions.

Before discussing his rise and fall, however, brief discussion of the wider implications of the Abraham's family's prominence is required. Galton's eugenicist model of success, underpinned as it was by raciology, provided a simplistic and misleading explanation. Circumstance, location and opportunity provide more insight into why this family, or sections of it, achieved what they did – in essence, in the case of Abraham and Joseph's father, the need to survive and to make a living. It meant that geographical mobility was particularly intense. Moses Abraham was born in London during the early 1770s. He had moved to Frome, Somerset, and raised a family there, practising as an optician, Moses thus presumably avoiding the economic competition of the capital and providing for the needs of the growing bourgeoisie in a developing market town. In turn, two of his sons left for the larger commercial opportunities of Bristol, some twenty miles to the north-west, where they ran a wine business. The historian of Bristol Jewry omits the existence of Moses' eldest son, Abraham, who left Frome in 1826, aged twenty-eight with his wife, two-year-old son, Henry, and two of his sisters. They moved close to fifty miles south-east to Southampton.[51]

Abraham Abraham set up a jewellery, pawnbroking and silversmith shop in the High Street, Southampton, which he passed on to his son, Henry, in 1847.[52] The shop, also Abraham's home, was at the heart of the most prestigious commercial area of the town and suggests that he came with significant capital. In his *Picture of Southampton* (1847), Philip Brannon wrote of High Street that 'Few towns can boast of a much finer main street than Southampton possesses',[53] and an earlier guide suggested that its 'inhabitants vie with each other in fitting up their houses in the best and most genteel manner to accommodate the company; and the shop-keepers are equally strenuous to excel in the elegance of their shops and display of their goods'.[54] Aside from developing a successful business, Abraham developed strong links with other entrepreneurs in a town that was starting to expand quickly with the arrival of the railways and the re-development of the docks. The historian of Southampton, Temple Patterson, argued that the town was transformed in the 1830s not so much by the extension of the franchise but by the arrival of a 'different kind' of person, especially the

> emergence of a new and frequently nonconformist type of business man, often not born in the town but coming into it because of the new opportunities it now offered, enterprising, sceptical and impatient of old ways.

He added that while these men were 'sometimes self-made and selfish but also sometimes imbued with Christian zeal and humanitarian ideals'.[55] Abraham, who became a leading Conservative in Southampton, certainly fits Temple Patterson's model – aside from his faith – and his Jewishness, initially, provided no immediate obstacle to progress. In February 1842, shortly before his fall from grace, *The Voice of Jacob* proclaimed Abraham's unanimous election as Sheriff for Southampton following the position he held as Returning Officer for the town in 1841. From the moment of his election in 1838 onwards, the Jewish newspaper commented, 'On no occasion has he made any other Declaration than is consistent with his creed as a Jew.'[56] Although defeated in an earlier election in the mid-1830s, Abraham Abraham remarked in 1842 that he had subsequently 'the honour of being returned twice by a large majority'.[57] It is significant that he was elected as a councillor in 1838 alongside another newcomer to Southampton, Joseph Stebbing, also the son of an optician. Nevertheless, their careers would soon take very different paths.[58]

Alongside his burgeoning political career in the local Conservative group-
ing, Abraham Abraham was a leading member of the Southampton Hebrew
Congregation. In 1842 he was its President, the year his sister Sarah married
the spiritual leader of the Jewish community, the Reverend J. A. Goldman.[59]
Abraham was then at the pinnacle of his public career and it was the norm,
other than in exceptional circumstances, for the Sheriff of Southampton, the
following year, to become the town's mayor. The reason why this failed to ma-
terialise was not the result of explicit antisemitism. Nevertheless, Abraham's
Jewishness was far from irrelevant in his political and social downfall.

This is not the place to discuss at length electoral scandal in early Victorian
Britain and the various cases of local abuse and corruption, especially the
buying of votes, that were investigated in various parliamentary proceedings relating to the 1841 election.[60] One of the most blatant cases was in
Southampton where it was claimed at least £7000 had been spent in 1841
on less than 1,500 voters. In the first proceedings in May 1842, Abraham
Abraham was mentioned only once and without any particular significance being attached to his role in alleged 'treating' of voters.[61] Wrongdoing
was especially attached to John Wren, a local dyer, who, angered by the
Conservatives making him the scapegoat – they claimed he had operated on
his own initiative – turned against them. His particular animus was directed
towards Abraham Abraham who Wren clearly thought was vulnerable to accusations of financial malpractice. In the further House of Commons Select
Committee inquiry held in June and July 1842, Wren and Abraham were the
main focus: the case rested on which of them was telling the truth about the
buying of votes.[62]

The report concluded that that there was 'no reasonable doubt' that bribery had taken place, but it remained unclear whether it was systematic and
organised. Between one and three hundred voters had been 'treated' – that
is entertained, given food and drink and tickets – and there was 'ample evidence' of payment for voting or promises to that effect.[63] Asked why he had
not mentioned Abraham's role in the earlier proceedings, Wren responded
that 'knowing Mr Abrahams [sic] was the returning officer, I did not wish
to implicate him'.[64] Much was made in the inquiry about specific places and
their local meanings. Abraham's shop and house was opposite the 'Dolphin'
in High Street, described by Colonel Peter Hawker in 1827 as the 'flash hotel
of Southampton, and the only place there where I ever tasted real comfort'.[65]
It was there and in Abraham's shop that Wren argued that the conspiracy
of vote buying and treating had been organised and taken place. Quizzed
whether the shop was not 'perfectly open – one of the most public places
in Southampton' to carry out such devious and secret activities, Wren argued that Abraham's premises were used for 'various purposes'. Much of the

questioning concerned the physical layout of the shop and the way in which business was conducted within this space, public and private. It especially focused on what happened within a 'hidden' back parlour, separated by a 'slight partition'.[66] What was simply a property that was used by Abraham and his sister, Mrs Levi, for a variety of commercial purposes, as well as a home, was presented as something unnatural and underhand. The blurring of the space between commercial and domestic, intensified by repeated questioning of the role, place and presence of his sister, added a further dimension to the suspicion that was aroused during the proceedings. Both the premises and Abraham himself were in the process of being racialised and the gendering of the premises undermined the masculinity (and therefore the trustworthiness) of this Jewish politician.

The first reference to Abraham Abraham's 'racial' roots came in the context of his activities as a discounter of bills. Abraham had acted in this respect for Wren, charging just over ten per cent for one such transaction. It prompted one of the Select Committee to ask whether 'Mr Abrahams [*sic*] is of the Jewish persuasion?'[67] The issue was raised again in relation to the questioning of a witness, Thomas Trew, general manager of the Hampshire Banking Company, who provided sympathetic evidence concerning Abraham Abraham and whether he was a 'a man of character'. Trew's response was positive – Abraham kept a 'most respectable shop, and is a respectable man'. The examination of Trew dwelt on Abraham's Jewishness, revealing a complex set of attitudes as well as the nature of his integration in local society:

> Q. He is of the Jewish persuasion, I believe?
> A. Yes, he is a Jew; I have always understood so.
> Q. I believe he is almost a singular instance in the kingdom of a Jew being a member of a municipal corporation?
> A. I do not know that.
> Q. He goes to church? Yes, he goes to church occasionally.[68]

Ultimately the proceedings returned to the detail of whether a signature on a document making clear electoral bribery was that of Abraham Abraham or a forgery. His integrity as an individual was thus critical to the case and, as part of the process, his Jewishness was raised throughout almost arbitrarily. Another witness, a Radical councillor and nonconformist, Joseph Lankester,[69] raised this issue himself positively. In spite of their different political perspectives, Lankester had proposed Abraham as sheriff. Asked whether he 'thought him a fit person for office', Lankester replied that he 'did upon the ground that he was a Jew; I thought it necessary we should show the town-council we would break down that line of distinction, and show that a Jew is as eligible for the situation as any other denomination.'[70] Lankester, a beneficiary of municipal reform that let him, as a Congregationalist, take part in local politics, was keen for religious toleration to be extended further. There was a wider significance to this discussion beyond the question of electoral mispractice. Was Abraham, Lankester was asked, 'a respectable Jew'?' He responded positively, but adding 'for aught I know'.[71] By his actions and character, Abraham was deserving of municipal office, but the questioning of Lankester and his responses to it bifurcated the Jews into types, acceptable and otherwise. It mirrored and in many ways anticipated the national debate on Jewish emancipation, revealing an unexplored and important provincial dimension. Those such as Abraham Abraham were treated as test cases revealing whether Jews were morally fit for public office – promoted by their friends and viewed with suspicion by their opponents.

Other local businessmen and public figures spoke positively about Abraham's public esteem and respectability. In the case of Mr Joseph Ball, however, a Conservative party agent who claimed to have known him 'longer than any man in Southampton',[72] a different perspective was provided whereby Abraham's Jewishness was used, backhandedly, to 'prove' his innocence. Ball denied that the handwriting in Wren's book proving corruption was that of Abraham and suggested that 'Mr Abrahams [sic] was the last man in Southampton to commit an act of this sort'. The reason he was the 'least likely' was that 'being of the Jewish persuasion we give them credit for being a little bit more alive than Christians in these matters'. Ball was also asked whether Abraham went 'to church sometimes' to which he responded 'I have seen him at church', but with the corporation. Again matters were not left to rest there and Ball was pressed by Sir John Hamner of the Select Committee: 'Is he a Jew by religion?' to which he replied 'I believe he is'.[73]

Strictly irrelevant to the details of the case, members of the Select Committee were clearly concerned about the implications of Abraham Abraham's Jewishness. Local witnesses such as Lankester were happy to defend Abraham on grounds of religious freedom as well as his character, whereas others utilised semitic discourse to deny the allegations against him. To Joseph Ball, Abraham, as a Jew, would have been too financially astute to implicate himself so blatantly in corruption. In relation to his integration in Southampton society, references to Abraham Abraham's church attendance – part of what the Jewish councillor thought was required of his civic duties and public profile – rather than gaining support for his moral character, cast doubt about who he really was, just as the business role played by his sister undermined his masculinity. The alleged slipperiness of defining his gender, 'race' and religion thus raised questions about Abraham's overall integrity to the Select Committee. The case against Abraham was unproven. Wren's evidence was far from convincing as he had clearly been happy to accept money from all sides. Yet if Wren had felt spurned after the first proceedings, it was Abraham Abraham's turn after the second. Many in the Conservative group turned away from him and in 1843 he was defeated, despite all local traditions, on the vote for the mayorship.[74]

Within Jewish and non-Jewish memory work, only the civic tolerance towards Abraham Abraham in the period from 1838 to 1842 has been recalled. In 1964 the Chief Rabbi, when a new Southampton synagogue was being consecrated, paid tribute 'to the attitude of understanding, tolerance and respect of the town' towards the Jews, as was illustrated in the case of Abraham Abraham. It was 'typical of the relationship which had existed in Southampton' throughout the existence of its Jewish community.[75] Similarly for Temple Patterson, writing a few years later, when in February 1841 the town council passed a resolution in favour of the Jews' Disabilities Bill, 'Mr Abraham's civic prominence and the respect for him were no doubt partly responsible for the Council's support of this measure'.[76]

It was left within the confines of a local liberal journal, nearly forty years after the rise of Abraham Abraham to the shrievalty, to hint at a less edifying part of his biography. Profiling Captain Henry Abraham, it briefly outlined his connection to his father, strongly hinting at the family hurt caused by the 1843 rejection:

[Abraham Abraham] ought to have been Mayor, but the Conservative party, to which he was attached, thought they must draw the line at the office of Sheriff, and declined to confer upon him an honour to which he was fully entitled on the score of his public service. It is by no means improbable that the slight thus put upon him by his Tory friends may have had some influence on the mind of his son … who has been throughout his life a true and consistent Liberal.[77]

Four years after his mayoral defeat, Abraham transferred his business to Henry and by 1851 the former Sheriff of Southampton had left Britain and was resident in Brussels.[78] He thereafter disappears without trace. Henry did indeed obtain the honour of mayor that was denied to his father. Yet Henry, although involved with the synagogue at some point, was married in a church and his children were baptised.[79] Whereas Joseph Stebbing was to play 'a pioneering part in almost all aspects of the town's commercial and civic progress',[80] his Jewish contemporary, Abraham Abraham, ended up exiled from the place of his adoption. His Jewishness had been no barrier to his initial success, and it may indeed have helped his progress in a wave of local self-conscious tolerance. That Abraham was Jewish, however, helped the process of his isolation within his own party, leading to his ultimate political decline. Abraham was certainly no more guilty of bribery than any other local politician in 1841, but he ended up paying a heavy price as scapegoat for the political fallout of the 1842 inquiry. No such bad luck was to affect our final example in this chapter, Samuel Michael Emanuel.

Jewishness, 'race' and brotherhood

Michael Emanuel's distancing from his namesake in 1825, thereby protecting the reputation of his (male) children, has been noted. In fact, two years earlier, two of his sons, Samuel and Jacob, had left Portsmouth for Southampton. The two were to play a major role in the organised Jewish community in Southampton – Jacob was the first President of its Hebrew congregation and a major force in its establishment in 1833. Jacob died in 1846 and thereafter Samuel became a key figure in the Southampton Hebrew Congregation's development.[81] Unlike Abraham Abraham, the business set up by the two brothers in Southampton was in a far less salubrious district – a jewellers and pawnbrokers at the corner of Back-of-the-Walls. It was a notorious area that will feature in Chapter 8. Yet if its beginnings were humble, the business soon moved to more prominent and desirable premises on the High Street.[82]

Samuel Emanuel was a 'staunch Conservative'.[83] A key figure within the local party, and through masonic involvement, the local business community, he rose further than his Jewish predecessor, Abraham Abraham. In 1864, as has been noted, he was elected sheriff of Southampton and mayor for the two years after. In relation to the shrievalty, the *Southampton Times*, a Liberal newspaper, remarked that 'Mr Emanuel will no doubt carry out the duties of his office in an honourable and dignified manner, and we hope that the great political principle involved in his election will be truly and extensively appreciated.'[84] With respect to questions of religious liberty, it is significant that Emanuel was proposed as sheriff by Joseph Stebbing, the contemporary of Abraham Abraham. Stebbing stressed that electing Emanuel

> would show to the country a striking example of the liberality of sentiment and public estimation accorded to the services of members of the Hebrew persuasion … He had known Mr Emanuel for many years; they were in fact fellow-townsmen [from Portsmouth], and had grown up together from childhood, and it was a great fact to say of him, as of other members of the same persuasion, that they were among the most honourable men in the community.[85]

Emanuel was re-elected as mayor in 1866. Whether his two years in this role could be described as 'honourable and dignified' divided Southampton opinion. Indeed, his actions prompted a huge rift in the world of British politics and culture more generally. '[D]uring both years of office', as the *Southampton Times* cryptically noted on Emanuel's death in 1894, 'there was no doubt about his determination that the reputation of the town for hospitality should not suffer at his hands'.[86] In fact, the entertainment he offered as mayor was lavish and excessive, most notoriously, as we will see, in welcoming back ex-Governor Eyre from Jamaica in 1866.

Samuel Emanuel was a 'colourful' character,[87] his public persona clear from a trade advertisement from the early 1850s. By then he had extended his business to include a tailoring and outfitting establishment, also on High Street, with a similar desire to attract both a local and international market. 'The Proprietor', the advert emphasised, had spared no expense 'in rendering this establishment a desideratum so long required for the County'. Both quality and pricing would match those in London: 'a single visit from those who have not yet derived benefit from making purchases at this Establishment will prove, that, for cheapness of article, fashion in appearance, and durability of wear, none can surpass, very few equal it'. Reflecting Southampton's growing maritime strength, it concluded that 'In the Hosiery and Outfitting Department will be found every article calculated for any part of the Globe [as were] Regulation Uniforms for the Peninsular and Oriental and West India Navigation Companies, as well as for Her Majesty's Royal Navy'.[88] Even allowing for the hyperbole within the genre of mid-Victorian advertisements, Samuel Emanuel was no shrinking violet. He was a larger than life character, avuncular but also not adverse to suing his opponents.[89] His generosity, as well as his stridency, were exposed when ex-Governor Eyre returned to England in August 1866.

Eyre's brutal repression of the Jamaican uprising of 1865, in which over four hundred black men, women and children were executed, 'became the touchstone of ultimate political convictions'. Abuse abroad and political reform at home became intimately connected. The wider question of who was fit for 'self-government' underpinned much of the debate. There were those tempted to forgive any error of judgement on Eyre's behalf because it 'involve[d] only negro blood'. Indeed, Bernard Semmel, the major historian of the controversy, concluded that 'Race prejudice ... was the principle underlying the acceptance of the deeds of Governor Eyre'.[90] Radicals and Liberals, such as John Bright and John Stuart Mill, wanted Eyre prosecuted for murder whereas his defenders, including Charles Kingsley, Thomas Carlyle and John Ruskin, saw him as a hero who had protected the lives of the 13,000-strong white population of Jamaica from widespread slaughter. A particular concern of the pro-Eyre camp was the threat of rape against white women which the ex-Governor was deemed to have thwarted.[91]

Southampton opinion, too, was polarised and local tension surrounding Eyre's return was heightened by national activists coming to the town. His ship arrived in Southampton on 12 August 1866. Eyre was persuaded by the mayor and his allies to stay in the town until 21 August in order to arrange a banquet in the ex-governor's honour. An address on behalf of the 'citizens of the town' was drawn up and presented to Eyre, concluding that 'We rejoice to be the first to welcome you with this testimony of public opinion'. It was countered by Liberals, Radicals and working men in Southampton who proclaimed that the dinner for Eyre was a 'feast of blood' and a 'banquet of death'. They not only condemned 'the wholesale hanging, shooting, and flogging that followed the suppression of the outbreak in Jamaica', but also protested 'against the ill-advised attempts of a few persons in this town to connect the people of Southampton with a demonstration in favour of ex-Governor Eyre'.[92]

The atmosphere in Southampton on the night of the banquet was close to riotous and the public demonstration against it was reported as the largest in the town's history.[93] Roughly one hundred 'gentlemen' attended the banquet, accompanied by their wives, representing aristocrats, Jamaican landholders, national campaigners including Kingsley, as well as prominent local Conservatives. Samuel Emanuel had assembled what he described as 'the most influential residents of this county and the neighbourhood', including the Earl of Hardwicke. Other noblemen from outside Hampshire such as the Earls of Shrewsbury and Cardigan also attended.[94] Emanuel's identification with this elite, and his construction of Englishness based on 'race' and gender, were made clear in his speech on behalf of Eyre:

> in alluding to a cartoon from *Punch* placed at the end of the hall, [the mayor] said it was all very well to talk of the negro being a man and a brother, but would these people have him for a brother-in-law? (laughter) – would they be willing to have their beautiful and elegant sisters allied to the negro – debased and despised as he was? ... [I]f Ex-Governor Eyre had not stamped out this rebellion, many beautiful and elegant ladies ... present that evening would have been debased and disgraced and in sackcloth, desponding and mourning (cheers) and [he] regretted that a gentleman who was entitled to the honour and praise of the country had to a certain extent received its censure.[95]

Two years later *The Times* referred to the banquet as 'the absurd demonstration in honour of Mr Eyre at Southampton', but, as Semmel notes, at the time, this paper 'like the bulk of the English middle-classes ... maintained a discreet, sympathetic silence, if not a wholly approving one'.[96] Nevertheless, Emanuel, in celebrating Eyre's return so ostentatiously, was taking a tremendous political gamble. He was also, through his Jewishness, risking personal attack. Emanuel's strategy was to identify with Eyre's muscular protection of Englishness and to object to what he called the 'unmanly' local and national opposition to the ex-Governor.[97] The local Jewish politician was allying himself not only with the aristocracy and monied elite, but also to concepts of Englishness defined by masculinity, 'race' and class. He was operating in a frenzied atmosphere in which local opposition to the banquet could be dismissed on racial and other hierarchical grounds. 'There are a good many negroes in Southampton,' argued the *Daily Telegraph*, 'who have the taste of their tribe for any disturbance that appears safe, and who are probably imbued with the conviction that it is a proper thing to hoot and yell at a number of gentlemen going to a dinner party'. These 'negroes', as Douglas Lorimer points out, 'were in fact the very English and very white Southampton mob'.[98]

For Carlyle and Kingsley, the racial and gendered defence of Englishness necessitated the promotion of 'muscular Christianity'. In the works of both, but especially Carlyle, an opposition was drawn 'between Jewishness and toughness': Jews, with their unwillingness to engage in manual labour, were, by nature, unmanly.[99] In Disraeli's fiction, an attempt was made, through raciology, in Nadia Valman's words, 'to remasculinise the Jewish body'.[100] In the Eyre controversy, Emanuel made no reference to his Jewishness. It was only good fortune that most of the Radical opposition focused on Charles Kingsley rather than the mayor of Southampton. 'The Radicals sensed betrayal in Kingsley's participation in the Southampton events. He who in days past had defended the workingman had deserted'.[101] Locally, after the banquet, animosity was largely aimed at 'the Earl of Hardwicke and other peers in entertaining ... Eyre'. Again Emanuel avoided direct attack.[102]

Catherine Hall has drawn attention to Carlyle and Mill's 'critical part in reformulating ideas about manliness and about English identity in the 1860s'. Institutionally it was reflected in the opposing Jamaica and Eyre Defence Committees. 'In the course of exchanges over Jamaica two different identities ... were being offered to English middle-class men. Both identities depended for their articulation on a sense of difference, not only from black men but also from black and white women.'[103] Emanuel, as a founder member of the Eyre Defence and Aid Fund,[104] placed himself strongly in the Carlyle camp. Yet the question of whether Samuel Emanuel himself would have been fully welcomed as 'a brother-in-law' by the elite company he was keeping was far from certain. In reality, Emanuel was tolerated because he had provided, through the privilege of his civic office, a public forum for the celebration of Eyre's return to England. The fortunes of his son, who also became mayor of Southampton, indicates that acceptance of Jews in late Victorian England remained both incomplete and conditional.

Michael Emanuel was, following his father, a leading Conservative in Southampton, and similarly a senior figure in the local Masonic movement. A leading member of the local Volunteers and a major force in local government, especially as chairman of the Watch Committee, and then mayor in 1895, Michael Emanuel's career suggests full integration.[105] Yet his position as a jeweller and silversmith, incorporating the role of pawnbroker, was always close to the surface of local memory. In an official visit to the Electric Light Works, visitors were warned to take off their watches due to the danger of magnetisation. Emanuel was deemed to be the best person to take care of these watches for which the distinguished guests received a 'ticket' from him in exchange. Playing the part of pawnbroker fully, he 'provoked a general laugh by saying "I wonder if I have 'taken care' of any of these before"'. On another occasion, the question of Emanuel's masculinity was raised in relation to his admittance to the local masonic lodge. On completion Emanuel responded 'Now you can call me "brother" – I may have been "Uncle" to some of you before!'[106] Although rising to the level of major in the local infantry battalion and with a reputation for 'hardihood',[107] the 'unmanliness' of his business profession, and the racialisation that was associated with it, never escaped him or his father. In 1880, a thinly disguised attack on the Emanuels appeared in a local Liberal journal. The emphasis was on their pawnbroking activities and hinting at corruption at election time (reminiscent of the scandal associated with Abraham Abraham). It also connected those 'who live[d] where hangs three golden balls' with their appeal to 'elderly females in the local Israel'.[108] A link was thus maintained with the 'effeminate' Jews of the eighteenth- and early nineteenth-century port towns and their trading activities. Yet just four months earlier the same journal had praised the local Liberal, Lord Mount-Temple, for his work in obtaining Jewish emancipation and the ending of religious tests in the universities.[109] Such was the ambivalence faced by the Abrahams and the Emanuels of Victorian England in which they were eventually granted full political rights but who were never quite regarded as 'one of us'.

Conclusion

Many other examples could have been chosen from the twin towns of Portsmouth and Southampton to illustrate the civic role of Jews as councillors, sheriffs and mayors, one that was totally disproportionate to the overall size of these Jewish communities. The energy of these Jews, often as newcomers to these towns as they developed in the nineteenth century, was partly responsible for their prominence. In this respect, the two Emanuel families and the Abraham family were part of networks that produced mayors and councillors in a variety of Victorian port settings.[110] A sense of place was thus important in stimulating the economic, social and political ambitions of these port Jews. It is also clear that some in Portsmouth and Southampton, especially but not exclusively nonconformists, took pride in promoting Jews to civic office ahead of other localities. In the 1840s and 1850s, the councils in both towns passed resolutions urging the full political emancipation of the Jews. This local input into the emancipation debate has been largely ignored, but the examples of Abraham Abraham and Emanuel Emanuel were an important part of the slow progress that was made in the status of Jews in Victorian Britain. In 1843, David Salomons, a leading national Jewish campaigner, used the examples of Southampton and Portsmouth prominently in 'an impressive list' or the 'facts of the case', as he referred to them, to show to the Prime Minister 'evidence of favourable public opinion'.[111] Yet equally, an opponent of emancipation could have used these two cases to show local opposition to the Jews, leading in one case to the ending of a political career and, in the other, a hesitant start and brief removal from office.

In a history of the 'Battle of Southsea', Emanuel Emanuel is described as a 'powerful' local figure.[112] The mentality and actions of his namesake in Southampton at the time of the Governor Eyre controversy could similarly be described as being part of the world of authority and influence. If such Jews were far from marginal in some respects, they were still risk-takers who could, as in the case of Abraham Abraham, easily fall from grace. Moreover, the stridency of both Emanuel Emanuel and Samuel Emanuel, as well as the military toughness of Michael Emanuel, suggest a degree of over-compensation and a desire to appear manly in a context in which Jews were still portrayed as effeminate, untrustworthy and unEnglish. By concentrating on local politics, this chapter has inevitably focused on the careers of Jewish men. In this respect, it is important to return to the Moss sisters, featured in Chapter 3. Brought up in Portsmouth, and the first Victorian Jewish women writers, their books, including *The Romance of Jewish History* (1840), and *Tales of Jewish History* (1843), 'tended to associate Jewish women with heroic national liberation … historicizing the suffering Jewess'. These female figures were portrayed in a manner designed to gain sympathy from non-Jewish readers.[113] With the Moss sisters an apologetic approach was employed in relation to Jewishness, masculinity and Englishness. Their fiction was a counterpart to the more dangerous strategy employed by Disraeli in his novels (and the Emanuels of Portsmouth and Southampton in politics and society) when dealing with the image of the male Jew as cowardly, racially unfit and usurious. As Michael Galchinsky suggests, 'A middle-class reformer and emancipationist – he is the Mosses' ideal of the early Victorian Jewish man.'[114] In such light, their fellow Portsmouth Jew, Emanuel Emanuel, may well have been a model for some of their fiction. The battle for inclusion was thus as much about gender as about 'race' and religion.

On the one hand, the Jewish politicians of Portsmouth and Southampton, pre- and post-emancipation, benefited from the desire of their non-Jewish contemporaries to show their tolerance. Such acceptance was fictionalised by Israel Zangwill in his short story, 'Anglicization' (1907): 'S. Cohn was indeed a personage in the seaport of Sudminster, and his name had been printed on voting papers, and what is more, he had at last become a Town Councillor. Really, the citizens liked his staunch adherance to his ancient faith'.[115] On the other, the Abrahams and Emanuels were subject to antisemitism that cut across the political spectrum. As late as 1888, A. L. Emanuel, a direct descendant of Reb Leib from mid-eighteenth-century Portsmouth, stood as a local councillor with his opponent warning the electors 'that he was a Jew and should on that account be rejected'.[116] It is for these reasons that Zangwill's character abbreviates his name from Solomon to S. Cohn, proclaiming 'When we are in England, we are in England'.[117] Such anglicising tendencies parodied by Zangwill bring to mind the real example of Abraham Abraham and his attendance at church in Southampton in order to garner civic respect. Given the conflicting pressures under which they operated, the civic and other achievements of these Jewish pioneers of local office were all the more remarkable. Slowly, however, they have been forgotten or memories of them have become de-racinated. For fifty years after his death, Emanuel Emanuel was recalled as a major political figure within Victorian Portsmouth and local acceptance of his Jewishness was remembered with pride. Yet subsequently Emanuel does not feature in narratives of the town and his memorial in Southsea makes no reference to his Jewishness. In Southampton there is now only a whisper of memory work within the public sphere of the 'other' Emanuel family who, through the Victorian era, played such a prominent role in the economy and governance of the town.[118]

In 1914, the *Southampton and District Pictorial* devoted a feature to the 'watchmaking marvels' of Emanuel's jewellers in High Street. It remarked that

> Though it is in a sense a local institution – two members of the firm have been Mayors of the town – the business recognises no such limitation as a geographical line, for a very considerable export trade is carried on, especially with the new lands overseas.[119]

With its strong links to South America and South Africa, Emanuel's was now truly a global business, echoing the success of Jewish merchants from Portsmouth in the post-Napoleonic era. The Jewishness of the firm, however, remained unmentioned in the article.

Emanuel's became a major landmark in inter-war Southampton until it was blitzed in 1940.[120] By then it had become totally assimilated into the Southampton landscape: the destruction of this business was not perceived more widely, as it was within Southampton Jewry, as the symbolic end of the Jewish presence in the High Street.[121] The Emanuel family's neighbours in the High Street, the Abrahams, have similarly been forgotten, in spite of Abraham Abraham's status as the first Jewish councillor in Britain. The amnesia relating to this singular local Jewish political connection was neatly illustrated in Elsie Sandell's popular history of Southampton published in the aftermath of the Second World War. In what was an evocative and poignant book of memories and a eulogy to the built heritage lost during the war, both family businesses were juxtaposed without any awareness shown of the minority history which they so neatly encapsulated:

> In late Victorian times, Abraham, the jeweller, had a clock controlled by Greenwich … At Emanuel's … a large clock projected high up across the pavement and was very helpful to passers-by.[122]

In a section ironically devoted by Sandell to timekeeping and loss, the process of forgetting itself was inadvertently revealed. As Jonathan Boyarin suggests, 'Memory – the free-association counterpart of forgetting – has become associated prominently in our era not only with time, but with space as well.' This study, in relation to Winchester Jewry in Chapter 3, has already noted Boyarin's further comments on the process of forgetting and how it is 'sometimes a technique of the dominated, used to enable memory'.[123] Sandell was anxious to show the collective loss to Southampton inflicted through the blitz and there was thus no room for ethnic particularity in this crucial part of her narrative. This absence is particularly revealing as Sandell, as will emerge later in *Anglo-Jewry since 1066*, was generally sensitive and perceptive when representing the past diversity of Southampton.

In 2003, Parvin Damani, a Ugandan Asian refugee, became the first Muslim mayor of Southampton. A large portrait of her now hangs in the mayoral parlour, with Parvin overlooking the historic medieval walls of Southampton.[124] It announces boldly that she is part of, and not apart from, Southampton's history. Yet sadly in its celebration of contemporary diversity and tolerance marked by Parvin Damani's gaining of office and the affection with which she is held in Southampton, the city's collective memory, as is the case in Portsmouth, no longer encompasses (other than in the faintest of traces), the triumphs, trials and tribulations of its Victorian Jewish civic leaders. Often controversial figures, they helped shape Portsmouth and Southampton into modern port towns. These men employed different political strategies to confront (successfully or otherwise) issues of gender, class, religion and ethnicity not only to further their own careers, but also to develop the local Jewish communities and the towns of their birth or adoption. The Abraham and Emanuel families represented a new generation of port Jews, one step removed from the sea, but still intimately connected to the international maritime links of these Hampshire towns. Typical in this respect was Michael Emanuel who, while later becoming a dedicated member of the Hampshire Battalion, earlier in his manhood 'went out to Australia to try his luck at the "gold diggings" in Ballarat'.[125] As will be illustrated in Chapter 6, from the 1850s to 1914 the relationships between the local and the global, and settlement and movement, continued to remain central to the dynamics of Hampshire's old and new Jewish communities.

Notes

1 David Katz, 'The Marginalization of Early Modern Anglo-Jewish History', in Tony Kushner (ed.), *The Jewish Heritage in British History* (London: Frank Cass, 1992), p. 61.

2 'The History of the Jews in Portsmouth', *Pinks' Pictorial*, April 1909.

3 Aubrey Weinberg, 'Portsmouth Jewry', *Portsmouth Papers* no. 41 (1985), p. 15.

4 William Gates, *Illustrated History of Portsmouth* (Portsmouth: Evening News/Hampshire Telegraph, 1900), p. 364.

5 Ibid., p. 367.

6 Henry Sparks, *The Story of Portsmouth* (Portsmouth: Portsmouth Education Committee, 1921), p. 288.

7 Ibid., p. 287.

8 Gates, *Illustrated History*, p. 366.

9 Ibid., p. 364.

10 Cecil Roth, 'The Portsmouth Community and Its Historical Background', *Transactions of the Jewish Historical Society of England* vol. 13 (1932–35), p. 179.

11 Weinberg, 'Portsmouth Jewry', pp. 13–15, 18.

12 Eugene Newman, 'Some New Facts About the Portsmouth Jewish Community', *Transactions of the Jewish Historical Society of England* vol. 17 (1951–52), p. 261.

13 A. Temple Patterson (ed.), *A Selection from the Southampton Corporation Journals, 1815–35 and Borough Council Minutes, 1835–47* (Southampton: Southampton University Press, 1965), pp. 94, 105 entries relating to 1 November 1838 and 9 November 1840.

14 Editorial, 'The Shrievalty', *Southampton Times*, 12 November 1864.

15 See, for example, Todd Endelman, *The Jews of Britain 1656–2000* (Berkeley: University of California Press, 2002), p. 103.

16 Henry Roche, 'The Jews of Portsmouth', *Shemot* vol. 2 no. 1 (1995), p. 28.

17 'The History of the Jews in Portsmouth', *Pinks' Pictorial*, April 1909.

18 See David Cesarani (ed.), *Port Jews* (London: Frank Cass, 2002) and David Cesarani and Gemma Romain (eds), *Jews and Port Cities, 1590–1990* (London: Vallentine Mitchell, 2005).

19 See the entry on Portsmouth in Aubrey Newman (ed.), 'Provincial Jewry in Victorian Britain' (unpublished papers, Jewish Historical Society, 1975).

20 *The Jewish Year Book 5668–9* (London: Greenberg & Co, 1907), p. 194.

21 Harold Pollins, *Economic History of the Jews in England* (London: Associated University Presses, 1982), p. 83.

22 Ibid., p. 83; Keith Pearce and Helen Fry (eds), *The Lost Jews of Cornwall* (Bristol: Redcliffe Press, 2000).

23 Geoffrey Green, *The Royal Navy & Anglo-Jewry 1740–1820* (London: Geoffrey Green, 1989), pp. 170–1; obituary in *Hampshire Telegraph*, 4 January 1889; Weinberg, 'Portsmouth Jewry', pp. 13–14. For an example of his 'elegant design and exquisite workmanship'

– a candelabra testimonial presented to the Lieutenant-Governor of Portsmouth – see *Illustrated London News*, 16 January 1847.

24 *Hampshire Telegraph*, 5 January 1889.

25 *Jewish Chronicle*, 4 January 1889.

26 Green, *The Royal Navy*, p. 171 and *Hampshire Telegraph*, 24 October 1825.

27 Green, *The Royal Navy*, p. 171 and *Hampshire Telegraph*, 31 October 1825.

28 *Hampshire Telegraph*, 5 January 1889.

29 Emanuel leaflet 'To the Burgesses of the Ward of St. Thomas', 17 December 1835, in Saunders collection, item 17, Portsmouth Library Local History collection (PLLH).

30 Gates, *Illustrated History*, p. 366.

31 J. Field, 'The Battle of Southsea', *Portsmouth Papers* no. 34 (1981), p. 10.

32 *Hampshire Telegraph*, 28 August 1843.

33 Portsmouth Council minutes, 21 August 1843 in Portsmouth City Record Office, CM1/2.

34 *Hampshire Telegraph*, 5 January 1889; *Jewish Chronicle*, 4 January 1889.

35 See John Webb, 'Portsmouth Free Mart Fair: The Last Phase 1800–1847', *Portsmouth Papers* no. 35 (1982).

36 Ibid., p. 20 which reproduces the anonymous poem from *Hampshire Telegraph*, 20 July 1801.

37 Betty Nagler, *Jewish Pedlars and Hawkers 1740–1940* (Camberley, Surrey: Porhyrogenitus, 1992), p. 22.

38 W. H. Saunders, *Annals of Portsmouth* (London: Hamilton, Adams, 1880), pp. 203, 206.

39 *Hampshire Telegraph*, 15 July 1848.

40 *Hampshire Telegraph*, 23 June 1849 cited by Field, 'The Battle of Southsea', pp. 10–11.

41 Field, 'The Battle of Southsea', pp. 11, 12.

42 Saunders collection, item 171, PLLH, and reproduced in Field, 'The Battle of Southsea', p. 17.

43 See www.memorials.inportsmouth.co.uk, accessed 27 August 2006.

44 Letter from 'Tolerator' in *Hampshire Telegraph*, 7 December 1835.

45 John Davies, *A History of Southampton* (Southampton: Gilbert, 1883), p. 456. Ivor Weintraub, 'The Jews of Southampton' (unpublished ms), argues that this 'seems to be evidence of a Domus Conversorum'. In Southampton Hebrew Congregation archives (hereafter SHCA).

46 Theodore Wilks, *A General History of Hampshire* vol. 2 (London: Virtue, 1841), p. 262 under the heading 'Jewish officers'.

47 Lucien Wolf, 'Jews in Tudor England' in Cecil Roth (ed.), *Essays in Jewish History by Lucien Wolf* (London: Jewish Historical Society of England, 1934), pp. 75–8.

48 Cecil Roth, *The Rise of Provincial Jewry* (London: Jewish Monthly, 1950), pp. 24, 100; Weintraub, 'The Jews of Southampton'; *Jewish Chronicle*, 1 June 1934.

49 Moses Sailman, *The Mystery Unfolded* (Southampton: Sailman, 1817), pp. 58–9.

50 Francis Galton and Edgar Schuster, *Noteworthy Families* (London: John Murray, 1906), pp. xxvi, 47–8.

51 Judith Samuel, *Jews in Bristol* (Bristol: Redcliffe Press, 1997), p. 143; 'Captain Abraham', *Southern Reformer* no. 13 (21 August 1880), pp. 1–2 and notes of Sidney Weintraub, SHCA.

52 Sidney Weintroub notes, SHCA.

53 Philip Brannon, *Picture of Southampton* (Southampton: Brannon, 1847), p. 5.

54 *The Southampton Guide* (Southampton: E.Skelton, 1818), p. 51.

55 A. Temple Patterson, *A History of Southampton 1700–1914* vol. 2 (Southampton:

Southampton University Press, 1971), p. 1.

56 *The Voice of Jacob*, 18 February 1842.

57 *Report from the Select Committee on the Southampton Town Election Inquiry; with the minutes of evidence* (London: House of Commons, 18 July 1842), p. 151.

58 A. Temple Patterson, *Southampton: A Biography* (London: Macmillan, 1970), p. 222 and Temple Patterson, *A History of Southampton*, p. 52.

59 Sidney Weintraub notes, SHCA.

60 See Norman Gash, *Politics in the Age of Peel* (London: Longmans, 1953), pp. 258–9; Philip Salmon, *Electoral Reform at Work* (Woodbridge: Boydell, 2002), p. 101.

61 *Minutes of Proceedings and Evidence Taken before the Select Committee on the Southampton Town Election Petition* (London: House of Commons, 9 May 1842), p. 26.

62 *Report from the Select Committee*, passim.

63 Ibid., pp. iv–vi.

64 Ibid., p. 12.

65 R. Payne-Gallwey (ed.), *The Diary of Colonel Peter Hawker 1802–1853* (London: Greenhill Books, 1988), p. 323.

66 *Report from the Select Committee*, pp. 44, 115.

67 Ibid., p. 53.

68 Ibid., pp. 60–1.

69 Temple Patterson, *A History of Southampton*, p. 24.

70 *Report from the Select Committee*, p. 74.

71 Ibid., p. 74.

72 Ibid., p. 277.

73 Ibid.

74 Temple Patterson, *A History of Southampton*, p. 41.

75 *Southern Evening Echo*, 11 May 1964.

76 Temple Patterson, *A Selection From the Southampton Corporation Journals*, p. 107.

77 'Captain Abraham', *The Southern Reformer*.

78 See the lease of a Southampton property for his Belgian connection in SC 4/3/1737, Southampton City Record Office (SCRO), 8 March 1851.

79 See PR1/1/17 for his wedding certificate and index of baptisms in SCRO.

80 Temple Patterson, *A History of Southampton*, p. 52.

81 Sidney Weintroub notes, SHCA.

82 *Southampton Times*, 16 June 1894.

83 *Jewish Chronicle*, 15 June 1894.

84 *Southampton Times*, 12 November 1864.

85 *Jewish Chronicle*, 18 November 1864.

86 *Southampton Times*, 16 June 1894.

87 The description is by Ivor Weintraub, 'The Jews of Southampton', SHCA.

88 *The Post Office Directory of the Borough of Southampton* (Southampton: Forbes and Knibb, 1851), p. 79.

89 *Southampton Times*, 16 June 1894.

90 Bernard Semmel, *The Governor Eyre Controversy* (London: Macgibbon & Kee, 1962), pp. 13, 171, 178–9.

91 For the wider intellectual debate and its relationship to 'race' and national identity, see Ian Baucom, *Out of Place: Englishness, Empire, and the Locations of Identity* (Princeton: Princeton University Press, 1999), chapter 1.

92 Semmel, *The Governor Eyre Controversy*, pp. 88–9. See also Gwen Oliver, 'Southampton

and the Governor Eyre Controversy' (unpublished BA History dissertation, University of Southampton, 2000) and *Hampshire Advertiser*, 18 and 25 August 1866 for local placards against Eyre.

93 *Hampshire Independent*, 25 August 1866 quoted by Oliver, 'Southampton', p. 13.

94 *Southampton Times*, 25 August 1866.

95 Ibid.

96 Semmel, *The Governor Eyre Controversy*, pp. 95–6.

97 *Southampton Times*, 25 August 1866.

98 *Daily Telegraph*, 21 August 1866 quoted by Douglas Lorimer, *Colour, Class and the Victorians* (Leicester: Leicester University Press, 1978), p. 195.

99 Nadia Valman, 'Manly Jews: Disraeli, Jewishness and Gender', in Todd Endelman and Tony Kushner (eds), *Disraeli's Jewishness* (London: Vallentine Mitchell, 2002), pp. 83–4.

100 Ibid., p. 92.

101 Semmel, *The Governor Eyre Controversy*, p. 99.

102 *Southampton Times*, 1 September 1866.

103 Catherine Hall, *White, Male and Middle Class* (Cambridge: Polity, 1992), pp. 264, 277.

104 *Hampshire Advertiser*, 1 September 1866.

105 See the obituaries in *Jewish Chronicle*, 10 February 1911 and *Southampton Times*, 4 February 1911.

106 *Southampton Times*, 11 February 1911.

107 *Southampton Times*, 4 February 1911.

108 *Southern Reformer* no. 30 (23 December 1880).

109 *Southern Reformer* no. 12 (14 August 1880).

110 Such prominence in local governance was also apparent beyond Britain. See, for example, Robert Liberles, 'Conflicts over Reforms: The Case of Congregation Beth Elohim, Charleston, South Carolina', in Jack Wertheimer (ed.), *The American Synagogue: A Sanctuary Transformed* (Cambridge: Cambridge University Press, 1987), p. 280.

111 M. C. N. Salbstein, *The Emancipation of the Jews in Britain* (London: Associated University Presses, 1982), p. 131.

112 Field, 'The Battle of Southsea', p. 10.

113 Bryan Cheyette, 'Introduction', in Bryan Cheyette (ed.), *Contemporary Jewish Writing in Britain and Ireland: An Anthology* (Lincoln, NE: University of Nebraska Press, 1998), pp. xiv–xvi.

114 Michael Galchinsky, *The Origin of the Modern Jewish Woman Writer: Romance and Reform in Victorian England* (Detroit: Wayne State University Press, 1996), p. 124.

115 In Israel Zangwill, *Ghetto Comedies* (London: William Heinemann, 1907), p. 50.

116 *Jewish Chronicle*, 12–26 November 1888.

117 Ibid., p. 49.

118 Emanuel Emanuel bequeathed to the town of Southampton in 1894 a silver candelabra and paintings of himself and his wife which had been presented to him at the close of his two years as mayor in 1867. These gifts were in recognition of the duties 'he faithfully, zealously and ably discharged'. The silver candelabra is still on show in the mayor's parlour, although its inscription is very faded and there is no awareness of its history in the mayoral office. While there are paintings of former mayors within the civic centre, the portrait of Emanuel is not displayed and it has been loaned elsewhere by Southampton City Art Gallery. Site visit to Southampton Civic Centre and Art Gallery, 22 August 2006.

119 *Southampton & District Pictorial*, 4 February 1914.

120 Jim Barnes, *Southampton Reflections* (Southampton: Southampton City Council,

1989), p. 31; Elsie Sandell, *Southampton Panorama* (Southampton: G. F. Wilson, 1958), p. 18.

121 See Sidney Weintroub's various unpublished histories of Southampton Jewry in SHCA.

122 Elsie Sandell, *Southampton Cavalcade* (Southampton: G.F.Wilson, 1953), p. 80.

123 Jonathan Boyarin, *Storm from Paradise: The Politics of Jewish Memory* (Minneapolis: University of Minnesota Press, 1992), pp. 1, 4.

124 Site visit to the mayoral office, 22 August 2006.

125 *Hampshire Advertiser*, 4 February 1911.

Settlement and migration from the 1850s to 1914

Introduction

From the mid-nineteenth century through to the First World War, the Jewish world was re-shaped by mass migration resulting from a combination of factors – demographic and economic as well as the impact of persecution and discrimination. It was a part of a wider global shift in population from south to north and east to west that reflected the (uneven) impact of a new economic age and the forces of modernity that accompanied it.

It is, however, especially the movement of Jews that has attracted the greatest attention and subsequent reflection. Not surprisingly, as so much emotion and experience has been at stake, the memory work associated with Jewish migration has been affected by powerful mythologies. These mythologies, in turn, have led to hierarchies of attention and neglect. Within the copious historiography, museum displays, literature, autobiographical practice, films, art and other cultural expressions relating to the emigration of Jews are silences, absences and distortions in representation and perception. Chronologically, the period from 1881 to 1914 has overshadowed earlier migration which had already begun to transform the Jewish landscape. In relation to geography, America has often been assumed to be the *only* favoured destination and even then the focus has been on New York and the Lower East Side, largely ignoring other places of settlement within the United States. As Hasia Diner suggests, 'The story of the Lower East Side has become almost universally understood to be synonymous with the story of Jewish life in America … It emerged, and still serves, as the point of reference for all other American Jewish stories in its singularity'.[1] As she adds, the mythic status of the Lower East Side hides the reality 'that Jews from eastern Europe went to all sorts of places, not just to America'. Indeed, at an even more fundamental level, 'The power of the "America" idea in … memory culture jars with the fact that most Jews did not leave eastern Europe'.[2]

Britain, in spite of the large numbers settling there, has not featured prominently in Jewish historiography. The assumption, within the country, that it has not, until recently, had a tradition of immigration, has further marginalised recognition of Britain's key role in earlier migratory movements. And similar to the American model, if on a smaller scale, when consideration *has* been given to Jewish migration to Britain it has been on London to the exclusion of the provinces and especially smaller communities.

Within the capital itself the focus has been largely on the East End at the expense of communities that developed in the West End and south of the river. There have been other biases: on settlement rather than transience, including return migration to eastern Europe; on the persecutory causes of emigration rather than economics and chain migration; on the lives of men as against women; on the era of mass migration at the expense of the experiences of the second and third generations; on the Jewish elite's responses to immigrants and not on immigrant life stories; on ethno-religious consensus within the Jewish world, downplaying class and other internal conflicts; on immigrant economic progress and entrepreneurship, thereby understating the continuity of poverty and the possibility of downward mobility; and on conformity and homogeneity rather than acknowledging the existence of 'deviance', whether in the form of sexuality, criminality, religion or politics.

This chapter cannot address all these silences and marginalities which have emerged in previous Jewish historiography and other forms of memory work. Nevertheless, the aim is to provide alternative and critical narratives, thereby challenging those who limit Jewish migration to particular times and places. The dynamics of Jews on the move between and within countries and continents are far too multi-layered and intensive to be encapsulated in one story, even if as epic as the Lower East Side. It is only by incorporating the impact of Jewish migration where and when it is, perhaps, least expected that its full complexity and scope can be appreciated.

The mid-nineteenth century: growth and tension

Bill Williams notes that by 1875 'over half of Manchester's Jewish population was of Russian or Polish origin', adding that a 'significant movement of Eastern European immigration is itself older than has been supposed – dating back, perhaps, to the mid-1840s, or even earlier'.[3] While the absolute numbers could not match the spectacular rise of Manchester Jewry in the mid-nineteenth century, percentage-wise, the communities of Portsmouth and Southampton still expanded impressively. In Portsmouth, for example, membership of the synagogue increased sixty per cent from 1840 to 1866.[4]

In the 1850s a Jewish trading community was formed in Aldershot, linked to the new barracks. Aldershot, excluding soldiers, soon had a Jewish population of over fifty.[5]

Jews of central, and especially eastern European origin were responsible for these growths and new communities, confirming Williams's analysis concerning the importance of pre-1881 immigration. While in the case of the new army barracks town of Aldershot, it 'was economic necessity and not the attraction of the Hampshire countryside which persuaded the Jewish tradesmen to set up their businesses',[6] Portsmouth and Southampton, with their long histories and modern commercial districts, were more attractive propositions. Yet the growth and re-growth of these two Jewish communities in the mid-nineteenth century led to their own tensions: Southampton, from the early 1840s through to 1851, and Portsmouth, from 1855 to 1860, both experienced schisms.

It has been estimated that in 1850 Southampton had a Jewish population of seventy-five, one-quarter of Portsmouth's total.[7] On the surface, the ability of these neighbouring port communities to split in half, almost amoeba-like, is intriguing. Given their size (they represented around one per cent of the population in Portsmouth and one-fifth of one per cent in Southampton), that they had the energy required for formal separation seems remarkable. In both cases, however, while superficially the divisions concerned personal disputes between prominent personalities, wider principles were at issue, following the example of the earlier eighteenth-century schism in Portsmouth.

Evidence that would have provided fuller details of the Southampton schism has now been lost to posterity. In August 1851, the newly-installed Chief Rabbi, Nathan Adler, came to Southampton 'advocating peace and unity' within the Jewish community, a mission that was apparently successful.[8] The division was over the activities of Revd Joseph Goldman,[9] who had been the shochet and spiritual leader of the community since its formal inception in 1833. It has been noted that

> Shechita and kashrut have always been areas of conflict in Jewish life not because anyone felt that they should be dispensed with but because they often formed the communal exchequer. Shechita and kashrut were the principal means of financing religious institutions and where belief impinges on the purse, as it so often does, a certain amount of friction is inevitable.[10]

In the early twentieth century, as will emerge, the 'illegal' activities of a later reverend/shochet led to his dismissal in Southampton. It is possible that financial 'irregularity' may have played a role in the controversy concerning Goldman. Yet the splitting of this new and small community indicate that there were wider questions about the direction the Southampton Hebrew Congregation was taking. It is clear that Samuel Emanuel was at the head of the anti-Goldman faction and, as in his later prominent civic role, he stood no opposition. On the other side, Goldman was married to the sister of Abraham Abraham. None of the protagonists had been born in Southampton. Nevertheless, the Emanuel family had stronger roots in Hampshire, dating back to the mid-eighteenth century, and may thus have regarded Goldman and the Abraham family as relative newcomers. Ultimately Emanuel turned to London and the office of the Chief Rabbi to assert his authority. It is significant that Adler was critical of the facilities in the rented synagogue in Southampton.[11] Soon after, Emanuel led the appeal for funds to enable the building of 'a fitting place of worship, where all may assemble with comfort and devotionally participate in the blessful influence the synagogue is calcu-lated to affect'.[12] Emanuel wanted a building that would match his desire for civic recognition and respectability in Southampton.

Albeit from a small basis, the fast growth of the Southampton Hebrew Congregation led to internal friction. The schism reflected rival desires for status as well as concern over the image of the Jewish community within wider local society. For Emanuel, who was ultimately to emerge as the pow-erhouse in the Jewish community after the schism, the synagogue, which he used as a focal point during his period of sheriff and mayor of the town, was to confirm he had a place of prestige within it. The spiritual leader was to be under Emanuel's command and was to be a figure of probity – financial and otherwise.

The rift in Portsmouth was more overtly political. Aubrey Weinberg dates the start of the controversy to 1853 when, for two years, 'there was severe disagreement over who should be appointed to represent Portsmouth' on the London Board of Jewish Deputies, the body that assumed responsibil-ity for British Jews at a political and legal level.[13] Again, Adler tried to sort out differences on the south coast by visiting the riven community. This time, however, he failed. It was reported locally in January 1855 that the 'Hebrew congregation of this borough is divided into strongly opposed par-ties'. Indeed, 'the politics of the synagogue, aggravated by external influences of the most malignant character [had] reached so violent a head, that the noble [Portsmouth Hebrew] Benevolent Institution ... seemed destined to become a wreck'.[14] A breakaway group was formed in Portsmouth soon after. Styling itself the 'Hebrew New Congregation', it employed its own minister/shochet and had its own meeting room and burial ground.[15]

It has been noted that some of the secessionists were 'leading figures in Portsmouth's civic and political activities'.[16] One notable absentee, in this respect, was Emanuel Emanuel. In contrast, the rival Portsmouth Emanuel family were highly prominent in the list of secessionists. The distancing of the older Emanuel family from the newcomers in 1825 at the time of the assault case concerning Emanuel Emanuel has been noted in Chapter 5. The animosity appears to have been mutual. In the Portsmouth trade directory for 1865, the entry for Emanuel Emanuel and his brother's shop contained the firm reminder 'N.B – This house … is unconnected with any of the same name'. The Emanuels, as has been suggested, 'must have been interesting characters'.[17] The feud between the two families was about status, economic rivalry, rootedness in Portsmouth, and politics (Conservative versus Liberal – the *Portsmouth Times* alluded to 'very warm manifestations of party feeling' in the emerging schism).[18] Within the specific Jewish sphere there was conflict over the leadership and direction of the long-standing Hebrew Congregation. Recovering from the immediate post-1815 decline, the arrival of new immigrants to the town intensified internal disputes and rivalries. Yet increased size also enabled the (temporary) viability of two rival congregations within Portsmouth.

The bitter dispute over representation on the Board of Deputies suggests that the relationship between the provinces and London remained an important issue, as was the case in the eighteenth century schism, albeit now being more concerned with secular governance. Ultimately, in both Southampton and Portsmouth the secessionists re-joined the established Hebrew congregations. Nevertheless, the pressure of adjusting to growth through immigrant arrival within the context of two rapidly modernising towns, and the desire to retain respectability within them, ensured that tensions would continue. It explains why both communities were at the forefront of movements to discourage the settling of the casual Jewish poor.

Seaports and the control of mendicity

By the end of the nineteenth century, British Jewry had set in place an impressive set of welfare organisations, designed particularly to manage the large influx of east European immigrants to Britain.[19] It was, however, initiatives within the seaport communities from earlier in that century which provided the model for nationally-based organisations such as the Jewish Board of Guardians (1859). We have already noted the Portsmouth Hebrew Benevolent Institution, formed in 1804, whose remit was limited to 'relieving Hebrew residents residing in Portsmouth' as opposed to newcomers to the town.[20] But it was the Liverpool Hebrew Mendicity Society, founded in 1846, which was the 'first serious attempt within Anglo-Jewry to deal in a systematic manner with itinerant poverty and its attendant problems'.[21] It endeavoured 'by the careful distribution of its funds, to relieve the necessitous wants of the Jewish casual poor, who visited that great commercial seaport, without permitting them to adopt the pernicious system of soliciting alms from the residents'. Seven years later, the Society had ceased to function and attempts were thus made to revive it as since 'that time the itinerant poor have had recourse to the *old* system of "soliciting alms", much to the annoyance of the inhabitants'.[22]

With mass migration facilitated by cheaper and faster ships increasing from the 1840s onwards, the Jewish seaport communities were at the frontline of new influxes. In 1860, Portsmouth followed Liverpool and formed its own Hebrew Mendicity Society.[23] Revealing a classic Victorian commitment to self-help and the necessity of helping only the 'deserving' poor, its ideology and *modus operandi* were made clear in the Society's fourth annual report:

> The intelligent giver, before he gives, must first enquire whether the recipient is worthy of relief, and how far his condition is capable of improvement. If satisfied on these points, he must discover what are the pressing wants, and next what means may be adopted to conduce to permanent benefit. Perhaps a loan may be more useful than a gift; perhaps employment only is needed; ... perhaps removal to another town is expedient.

The report concluded with a strong moral warning. The 'intelligent giver' must discover the best way of ensuring 'lasting advantage', recognising that 'it is occasionally a duty to withhold rather than to give'. Any doubts about the harshness of imposing scientifically-based charity could be removed because 'The most importune beggars are frequently imposters', and a gift to them would be a 'robbery of the [genuine] poor'. The goal in dealing with the 'deserving poor' was to give them 'their greatest riches, self-respect'.[24]

The leaders of the old and new Jewish port communities shared the philosophy and praxis of these 'Hebrew Mendicity' societies. Nevertheless, the exponential rise in migration and the emergence of transmigrancy in the second half of the nineteenth century both extenuated the scale of the problem and created tensions *between* the port communities. Conflict was particularly pronounced with regard to the 'moving on' of the casual poor from one town to another.

In the treatment of transient Jews, the Southampton Hebrew Congregation emerged as one of the least sympathetic when dealing with those transferred from other towns. In 1888, for example, Nathan Levy, its President, wrote to the *Jewish Chronicle* complaining that a Jewish man prosecuted for begging in Portsmouth was discharged on condition he was given the train fare, through the synagogue, to move to Southampton. Levy pointed out that 'The number of members and seatholders at Portsmouth exceeds four times our numbers, added to which while the funds of the Portsmouth C[h]evra, or Relief Fund, amount to ... £1,200. Our funds *in hand* are only £7.'[25] Seven years later, Southampton's Reverend Fyne moaned about the energy and resources taken up within his community in 'the relief of casual poor, which being a seaport, we get comers [from the four corners of the earth]'.[26] But both Portsmouth and Southampton Jewry, alongside other port communities such as Cardiff, also benefited financially from one notorious aspect of mass migration – the 'white slave' traffic. In Southampton especially, the local Jewish congregation was paid by the Jewish Association for the Protection of Women and Children (JAPWC) to ensure that no females disembarking from ships would fall under the evil influence of those who would trick them into a life of prostitution. Until the 1930s, maintaining the local branch of the JAPWC remained an important income source for the minister of the Southampton Hebrew Congregation.[27] The wider issue of Jewish transmigrancy will be left to Chapter 7. Yet, in the last decades of the nineteenth century, in spite of the gentle, and not so gentle, encouragement given to the 'casual poor' to move on in Portsmouth and Southampton, both communities continued to grow through the settlement of east European Jews. Furthermore, early in the twentieth century a further two Jewish communities, almost exclusively of east European origin, were to be formed in Hampshire.

The era of mass migration

It has been estimated that between the 1870s and 1914 some half a million east European Jews spent at least two years in Britain.[28] An even greater number, well over a million, passed through the country en route to the New World including North and South America, South Africa and Palestine. Numerically, therefore, those that settled on a more permanent basis – around 150,000 – were a small minority of those that had set foot in Britain more fleetingly. The experiences, treatment and representation of transient Jews will feature heavily later in this study. Here attention will focus on those who at least temporarily made their homes in specific locations within Hampshire. Even then, there is no escaping the impact of flux and mobility which was so central to the Jewish experience in these years.

It was reported in Portsmouth in 1902 'that the number of families had doubled since 1873'.[29] By the 1900s, the synagogue was unable to cope with the size of the community which had risen to two hundred families, and it was re-built to cater for a community that now totalled around one thousand.

The growth rate of the Southampton Hebrew Congregation was a little less rapid. It was still impressive, rising from less than 100 in the 1870s to perhaps 150 by 1914, most of this occurring close to the First World War. In both cases, as had been the case half a century earlier, the arrival of newcomers to the respective Hebrew congregations increased internal division. From 1891 to 1897 Portsmouth suffered its third and final major schism and in the years preceeding the First World War Southampton came very close to suffering its second. Although the start of the Portsmouth schism predated the climax to the problems within Southampton by two decades, the causes were similar and tension in the latter community had been simmering since the 1890s.

In July 1891 the *Jewish Chronicle* reported the consecration of the synagogue of the 'Portsmouth New Hebrew Congregation'.[30] For six years a bitter feud continued within Portsmouth Jewry. At its most desperate it included the refusal to allow the dissidents burial rites – that relating to their shochet's granddaughter led to the acrimony being aired in public through a legal trial.[31] Underneath the personal rancour, however, was the issue of seat rentals in the synagogue and the elitism it represented within the Portsmouth Hebrew Congregation. Many Jewish newcomers to Portsmouth were, effectively, being excluded from either membership or prominence in the synagogue by the high fees and limited seat-holdings that were available. In 1893 reconciliation failed with the insistence of the 'old' synagogue that 'no changes to the existing rules of the congregration were to be made for at least two years'. Four years later the dissidents were allowed to rejoin.[32] Although they had not, in the short term, altered the rules, they had, if traumatically, opened up the synagogue to the possibility of a more democratic and egalitarian future, further enhanced when the building was expanded in the 1900s.

In Southampton an even more hierarchical situation had developed. At the top were members of the Jewish 'aristocracy', Lady Eliot Yorke (a Rothschild daughter), Samuel Montagu (later Lord Swaythling) and Claude Montefiore, each owning large houses and estates in the area. All three were prominent in national Jewish welfare organisations dealing with poor immigrants including the JAPWC (Yorke was co-founder with her sister, Constance Battersea, and Montefiore was a prominent member of its national committee), and Montagu founded the Jewish Working Men's Club and Federation of Synagogues in the East End. Their attendance at the synagogue was rare, prompting the minister in 1895 to waspishly comment that they could 'hardly be called Southamptonians'.[33] In fact Yorke, Montagu and Montefiore were heavily involved with civic life and improvements in the town, even if socially they lived in a different world, typified by their sporting and hunting activities. At Townhill Park, home of the Swaything family, 'cricket matches were played against other country houses ... Edmund de

Rothschild of Exbury remembers long summer afternoons of fielding and batting at the house, with delicious teas spread out on trestle tables under the veranda'.[34] Despite the social gulf between them and the ordinary members of the Southampton Hebrew Congregation, Yorke, Montagu and Montefiore were elite seat-holders in and trustees of the synagogue. At times of financial and internal crisis they were called upon for support and arbitration.

On the next level of stratification was the Emanuel family, members of which were presidents of the Southampton Hebrew Congregation from the 1850s through to 1914. While, as we have seen, Michael continued the family business as a silversmiths/clockmaker/pawnbroker, other members of this family had moved into the respectable professions. The social distance between the Emanuels and the rest of the congregation was revealed in 1912. Charles Emanuel, the President, threatened to resign if his members continued to 'misbehave'. He particularly objected to those discontented within the community visiting him at work: 'My office is for the conduct of my own professional business [he was a lawyer] and I cannot waste my time over questions which have no interest for the Congregation or with which they have nothing whatever to do'.[35] In fact, his pompous dismissal of such delegations disguised the deep anxiety within the community at a point where internal pressure threatened to blow it apart. While Charles Emanuel was attempting to keep aloof from the tension, there was, at that point, almost open warfare between other members of the synagogue council and some of their constituents over the running of the Southampton Hebrew Congregation.

As was the case in Portsmouth, the rules and exclusivities of the synagogue, and especially the high cost of seat rentals, were key issues in Southampton. In 1894 new rules were incorporated but seat rental remained expensive and membership depended, amongst other conditions, on having been a seat holder for two years.[36] The small traders and artisans of east European origin felt marginalised by those who were more established in the town. In a small community, honour and recognition mattered greatly, and the newcomers were largely excluded from playing a part in the running of the community and in gaining the respect they coveted within the synagogue. As more immigrants settled in Southampton, tension intensified and it came to a head over the appointment of a new minister in 1908, Reverend J. Bogdanski. Bogdanski replaced the Reverend Holdinsky who had left Southampton to try his luck as a rabbi in San Antonio, Texas. While not at the bottom of desirable posts in Britain (there were twenty-four applications, mostly from those already ministers of even smaller British communities),[37] the New World appeared to offer more attractions. An earlier minister, Abraham Boas, had left for Adelaide in 1869 after just two years at Southampton.[38] While Boas made a solid career for himself in Australia, sadly, and reflecting the mythology of Jewish economic advancement, Holdinsky's life in America was far more troubled. His wife died shortly after arrival in Texas and Holdinsky's four-year-old daughter was placed in a Jewish Orphans' Home in New Orleans.[39]

Shortly after his appointment in Southampton, Bogdanski changed his name to Morrison, but this attempt to disguise his east European origins ultimately failed to bring him credibility amongst the more anglicised members of the community. For an annual salary of £100, the minister was expected to carry out 'all duties connected with the offices of Reader and Shochet and to teach at the Sabbath School'.[40] The high expectations and low remuneration put intense pressure on the minister and three years after his appointment, relations between Morrison and the synagogue commit-tee had reached breaking point. He was accused especially of the 'grave ne-glect of his proper duties in preference to acting as "kosher meat" merchant'. Rather than dealing with the local butcher who officially sold kosher meat in Southampton, Morrison was 'trading' illegally, an activity that was 'common knowledge'.[41] Given a final warning, Morrison continued to 'trade' and was eventually forced to resign.[42]

Rather than simply a rogue minister of dubious honesty, the Morrison affair revealed much about the nature of Jewish migration at the turn of the twentieth century. Small communities and congregations depended on ministers from eastern Europe to provide basic religious functions includ-ing shochet, mohel and educator as well as a leader of services.[43] An anec-dote told about the Reverend Cohen, who served at both Portsmouth and Bournemouth Hebrew Congregations, neatly encapsulates the many roles expected of the minister: 'In the middle of a cheder lesson ... a little boy was misbehaving ... Reverend Cohen was reaching the end of his tether and in a raised voice said he had killed 100 chickens that day and one little boy would not make a difference'.[44] Many of those recruited lacked the level of respectability required of them by the status-driven leaders of these Jewish communities. Before 1914, dissatisfaction on both sides led to a rapid turno-ver of ministers.

What is significant in the case of Morrison is that despite the blatant-ness of his offences, a sizeable minority within the Southampton Hebrew Congregation committee wanted to revoke acceptance of his resigna-tion.[45] If Morrison was trading illegally, it revealed that some Jews in the Southampton community were buying kosher meat from him at a cheaper rate than through the approved butcher. It is no coincidence that those who supported Morrison were also disatisfied with the running of the Hebrew Congregation as a whole. In 1911 Charles Emanuel acknowledged that 'some of the laws required altering, especially [concerning] the price of member-ship and seat-holders'.[46] There were also moves to bring in new trustees who were 'members of the Congregation and reside[d] in the town', reflecting an animosity against the Jewish aristocrats still at the apex of the community.[47] Yet in spite of the loosening of the rules and restrictions on membership, throughout 1911 and 1912 internal division continued, focusing on the running and location of the Hebrew school. Although schism was avoided, two differing visions of the Hebrew Congregation were being contested. On the one hand, those who were longer established envisioned it as a small-scale, respectable, relatively exclusive and anglicised community. On the other hand, there were the more recent newcomers from eastern Europe who wanted it to be expanding, accessible and closer religiously and culturally to the world they had left behind. Slowly, the more humble traders and artisans found their way onto the committee and, with their larger families, started to numerically dominate Southampon Jewry. Yet while a distinguished visitor in 1913 could claim that 'he rarely had come among a community where peace and harmony reigned as in Southampton', in reality the internal tension had continued to build up.[48]

Early in 1914, Morrison's replacement, Reverend Brown, was sacked for financial misappropriation. As with Morrison, in spite of his dishonesty, there were still those that were willing to defend Brown. These included Samuel Silverman who did so on the 'grounds of fraternalism and solidarity' relating to their common Polish birth. It was argued that Brown 'appealed to a great many members as [a] Brother and as from the same country and as foreigners of the same blood'.[49] At the same point, Charles Emanuel resigned as President and refused to have anything more to do with the Southampton Hebrew Congregation.[50] Through the First World War the power struggle continued. But what Emanuel referred to as 'petty jealousies' were, in fact, the manifestation of the slow and painful shift to a new type of community which reflected the desires of the new Jewish immigrants to Southampton.[51] It is no accident that Brown's successor, Reverend Gordon, who was born in Poland, became the longest serving minister in the Hebrew Congregation's history, appointed in 1914 and continuing until his death in 1949. The empathy between Gordon and his co-religionists was shown shortly after his appointment when he was applauded at a meeting he had set up to institute a Polish Jewish Relief Fund.[52] Increased membership and better relations with his community brought higher wages and, with the bitter departure of Emanuel and his supporters, there was a greater sense of harmony and common purpose. In 1919 it was decided to amalgamate the management of the synagogue and religion school, the battleground of the rival camps which had come close during the preceeding decade to becoming two separate communities.[53]

The Abraham and Emanuel families had dominated the communal leadership of the Southampton Hebrew Congregation until the First World

War and had played a major role within the civic governance of the town. Symbolic of the change in the sociological makeup of the community was the family of Samuel Silverman. Born in the small town of Suwolski in Polish Russia in 1850, Samuel emigrated to England and settled in Liverpool, the home town of his wife Rachel. Their first two children were born in Liverpool and the family moved to Portsmouth, adding a third daughter. A further two children, a girl and a boy (Joseph) were born when they moved to Southampton where Samuel's occupation in the 1891 census was listed as a house furnisher. By the time of the 1901 census, Joseph, aged sixteen, had moved to Bournemouth and was an upholsterer's assistant. Such internal migration was typical of the immigrant experience and in this particular case showed the continuing importance of ports and coastal settlements within the Jewish experience.[54]

When, in 1914, Samuel Silverman had defended his fellow Pole, the erring Reverend Brown, he was told very firmly 'to mind his own business and not interfere here' by a more established member of the community. Samuel was, at the same time, denied the right to be a seat-holder in the synagogue and it appears that he played no further role in the congregation.[55] In contrast, his son Joseph, returning to Southampton from Bournemouth, became a councillor during the war and in 1925 he was the fifth Jewish mayor of Southampton following the tradition set by Samuel Emanuel (twice), Henry Abraham and Michael Emanuel. The older leadership of the Hebrew Congregation had patronisingly dismissed Samuel Silverman just before the war by stating that 'we would be quite able to manage our affairs without his help'.[56] By 1919, however, the older east European members, now in control of its committee, were happy to accept that Samuel's son Joseph 'represents us on the Council'.[57] Similarly in Portsmouth, it was recalled how 'the leadership of the ... Hebrew Congregation was in the hands of a few long-settled families, until, in the 1920s, some of the bolder spirits among the newer settlers began to rebel against the oligarchy and gain some authority of their own'.[58]

Elsewhere in Hampshire new Jewish communities, made up almost exclusively of those of east European origin, were formed – Basingstoke in 1904 and Bournemouth the year following. Basingstoke soon claimed to have a Jewish population of fifty-two and a synagogue furnished in rented accommodation.[59] Bournemouth's growth was more remarkable. Within a year of being formed 'there were 130–140 Jewish souls' in the town and by 1911 enough funds had been found to complete the building of a large synagogue. At that point the Bournemouth Hebrew Congregation consisted of fifty families, a total size of around 250, and expansion continued thereafter.[60] By the end of the Second World War, Bournemouth had become the largest Jewish community in Hampshire.[61] Those coming to the town were 'in trade' – tailors, furniture-makers and small shopkeepers.[62] Typical in this respect was Harris Shoerats who came to London from the Ukraine in 1898 as a sixteen-year-old. The early death of his wife necessitated that he make a living beyond the intense competition of the capital. Harris moved to Bournemouth to 'set up business as a craftsman leatherworker' and, surviving well beyond his hundredth birthday, became the longest serving member of its Hebrew Congregation.[63]

The rapid growth of Bournemouth's Jewish community was no accident. It has been noted that in the eighteenth century 'there was no such place as Bournemouth' and by 1851 its population was still less than 700.[64] In fact, its development into a modern town coincided with the period of mass Jewish immigration. In 1881 Bournemouth's population was just under 17,000 but this had increased to over 78,000 by 1911.[65] The transformation from a set of small rural villages to a large commercial centre meant that there were far more economic opportunities for newcomers in Bournemouth than in neighbouring Southampton where there was already a strongly-established class of artisans and shopkeepers serving the port. The family story of Louis Herrman illustrates this point neatly.

Louis Herrman was born in Southampton in 1883. His parents were Russian-born Jews and his father had a business as a draper in Southampton.[66] His father died when Louis was three years old and his mother moved to Portsmouth where she made her living as a saleswoman in house furniture.[67] In order to make a living Louis' brother emigrated to Canada working on a farm which bred racehorses: 'he corresponded with us regularly for a year or two, then his letters became less and less frequent until [contact] was finally lost'.[68] Louis became a schoolteacher in Portsmouth before emigrating to Cape Town in 1907 where he became a leading academic in literary, anthropological and historical spheres.[69]

The final chapter will explore the desperation that pushed a new influx of Jews into Southampton after the First World War, but before 1914 it was Bournemouth and Portsmouth that saw the greatest increase in their Jewish populations. With regards to the latter, growth came through the unique circumstances of naval expansion in the 1900s resulting from Anglo-German military rivalry. Portsmouth was to become a magnet to east European Jews looking to make ends meet in the clothing workshops linked to the dockyards, a story that will be explored shortly. Through the 1911 census, it can be estimated that roughly half the east European Jewish newcomers were in the clothing trades (including footwear and headwear), with a further 10 per cent in furniture manufacture.[70] The vast majority of these workers were employed in small workshops. Jewish marriage records for Portsmouth at the same point suggest a similar percentage were working in tailoring – the classic immigrant occupation – mainly in small-scale enterprises.[71]

On a general level, the growth of the old two communities and the creation of a further three (Basingstoke, Aldershot and Bournemouth, the last two in what were effectively new towns) from the 1850s through to the 1900s reflected the impact of Jewish migration across Britain as a whole. In its review of the Jewish year just past, the *Jewish Chronicle* in 1904 commented that 'the formation of congregations in such places as Darlington and Basingstoke illustrates at once the increasing dispersion of Anglo-Jewry, and the steady maintenance of the religious activity of provincial Jews'.[72] Although the Basingstoke Hebrew Congregation did not survive long into the inter-war period, its existence, alongside four others in Hampshire, showed that many places in the British Isles – ninety-six in total, according to the *Jewish Year Book* for 1907 – now possessed a Jewish community. Each one had its own dynamics, reflecting past histories, scale and patterns of migration. As they developed, internal conflict was, as has been explored, as common as consensus. The complexity and diversity of these communities were further intensified by the thousands of individual stories that remain hidden underneath the statistics of mass movement and settlement. The next section focuses on two families in what remained, before 1914, the largest Jewish settlement in Hampshire – Portsmouth. On their own, they cannot be used to show the full range of Jewish experiences. They will, however, reveal the difficulties in generalising about the rich and multi-layered (if far from trouble-free) lives made by Jews in Britain from the mid-nineteenth century through to the First World War. Yet again they will reveal the importance of place in constructing and reconstructing Jewish identities.

Testimony and the making of local identities

Having outlined the overall shape and direction of Jewish migration and settlement in Hampshire from the 1850s through to the First World War, the remainder of this chapter will focus on the memory work that has subsequently been devoted to this movement and expansion. As was the case with many other examples in this book, absence and obscurity are perhaps the dominant themes, leading to an invisibility within the public realm of the former Jewish presence. There are, for example, no traces of the former Basingstoke Hebrew Congregation and only the Jewish cemetery in Aldershot stands in the way of similar oblivion. Even in the case of Portsmouth, which grew rapidly with east European immigration, especially at the start of the twentieth century, few traces of this movement have been left either in the world of heritage or history. In the public sphere there are only two autobiographical/biographical accounts relating to those of east European Jewish origin who settled in Portsmouth. Both relate to individuals who became nationally famous – Hertha Ayrton in the world of science and Ian Mikardo in the world of politics. Ayrton and Mikardo were thus untypical of 'ordinary Jews' with respect to the prominence and recognition they achieved in their careers. Yet in reflecting the interplay of movement and settlement, the family background of both, as well as the local Jewish milieu in which they grew up, were far from unusual.

Hertha Ayrton was born Sarah Marks in Portsea, in 1854. In 1899 she became the first female member elected to the Institution of Electrical Engineers and 1904 the first to read her own paper to the Royal Society, winning its Hughes Medal in 1906 'for her experimental investigations on the electric arc'.[73] Not surprisingly, from the late twentieth century onwards, Ayrton has been the subject of much interest for those rediscovering the historic role of women in British science.[74] Such rescue work of the female contribution balances the dismissal of Ayrton's research by some of her contemporaries simply because of her sex. As a married woman Ayrton was refused membership of the Royal Society in 1902 and an obituary in *Nature* patronisingly concluded that 'she was a good woman, despite of ... being tinged with the scientific afflatus'.[75]

Ayrton's whole life was marked by examples of female solidarity. Her father died in 1861 when she was six and thereafter she helped her mother look after her siblings, including a younger and sickly sister. A female benefactor helped her to go to Girton College, Cambridge, where she was befriended by George Eliot. Not surprisingly with this background and the battle she had to fight to gain credibility as a female scientist, Ayrton became a strong supporter of the suffragette movement.[76] It is equally unsurprising that Ayrton's life story would be attractive to contemporary feminist historiography within which most of her rediscovery has taken place. But with the focus on gender, little attention in recent scholarship has been given to Ayrton's Jewish background.[77] If referred to at all, it has been relegated to a sentence or two. A thorough account of her life as 'a persistent experimenter', published in the *Journal of Women's History* in 1995 described Ayrton's family origins as such: 'Her father, the son of an innkeeper, fled Poland to escape the Jewish persecutions during the Tsarist regime'.[78] It is a summary that is taken directly from the memoir of Ayrton written in 1926 by her close friend, Evelyn Sharp.[79] In contrast, Sharp's account, based on close reading of Ayrton's papers and intimate knowledge of her life story, emphasises the scientist's Jewishness throughout. Indeed, Sharp started her memoir by insisting that 'To understand the various elements that went to the making of Hertha Ayrton it is essential to know something about her family.'[80] To Sharp, as we will see shortly, both Ayrton's mother's and her father's Jewish backgrounds were important in forming her subject matter. Ayrton married out of her faith and changed her first name in honour of the poet Swinburne's Hellenistic hero. Nevertheless, Sharp was insistent that Hertha 'did not renounce her Judaism when its religious observances ceased to have any meaning for her [and] she never lost an opportunity of expressing pride in her Jewish descent'.[81]

It is significant that later scholars and others have focused solely on one specific sentence in Sharp's memoir relating to her Jewish background – that which explains why Ayrton's father came to England. His persecution in Poland was used by Sharp to explain his subsequent life and death: 'His health, probably undermined by these useful experiences, was never good; he died early, and he cannot be said to have made a success of life, as success is generally understood'. This lack of success, however, was not due to 'lack of natural ability'. Instead, it could be explained by the 'confusion of massacre and revolt' and its impact on a 'clever, if somewhat unworldly, political refugee'.[82]

It is clear that, from the 1840s, the incorporation of Jews in Russian Poland into the Tsarist system made life increasingly difficult. Nevertheless, rather than the image of physical persecution constructed by Sharp, it was economic pressure, especially through massive population growth and the concentration of Jews into the Pale of Settlement (the area of permitted Jewish residence within the Russian empire) that caused the greatest problems. It was these more general factors, alongside the opening up of the rail network on the continent, that led to the increase in Jewish migration from the 1840s of which Levi Marks, Hertha's father, was a part. Mass violence against Jews in the form of pogroms did not occur until the last two decades of the nineteenth century and even then the area which Marks came from was not especially affected.[83] Yet by portraying Levi as a refugee – indeed as a political refugee – Sharp was both eliciting sympathy and explaining his business problems in England that left his family impoverished. Within Hertha's family tradition, the narrative of escape from eastern Europe was powerful and played an important function in coming to terms with ongoing problems. It was a storyline that Sharp, as a devoted admirer of Hertha, was happy to polish and embellish and one that later scholars have been willing to accept uncritically – especially as it conforms to the narrative expectations of Jewish refugee movement. In fact, Levi Marks's fortunes were typical of many in the mid-nineteenth century and again act as a corrective to the myth of upward Jewish mobility.

Levi Marks settled in Portsmouth, marrying Alice Moss in the synagogue in 1851. Marks ran a watchmaking business and, reflecting the economic competition he would have faced in Portsmouth, transferred his business to the small Sussex town of Petworth. Before Hertha's birth, he moved back to Portsmouth but by 1860 was forced to become a pedlar, hawking his watches and clocks across the Hampshire countryside.[84] The economic fluidity that had typified the experiences of Portsmouth Jewry in the eighteenth century thus continued as late as the 1860s. For every Emanuel Emanuel, silversmith to the Queen, there were probably five times as many Levi Marks who struggled and eventually failed to make a living.

Sharp was equally concerned to outline the influence of Hertha's mother, Alice Moss, and her family. Alice's father, Joseph Moss, a glass merchant, 'was a well-known and respected tradesman in Portsea'.[85] In spite of the pressures of bringing up twelve children, Alice was brought up in a comfortable and cultured home, reflecting the status of the respectable, shopowning class of Jews in early Victorian Portsmouth. Indeed, it was claimed within family tradition that her great-great-grandfather was one of the founders of Portsmouth Jewry and her great-grandmother, Sarah Davids, 'was the first Jewish child born in Portsmouth'.[86] What was exceptional about the Moss family, and especially the women, was their artistic talent – Celia and Marion, as has been noted, became prominent writers on Jewish themes. The description of the Moss sisters as 'the unacknowledged Mendelssohns of England' may be going too far,[87] but their importance as pioneers, on a world stage, as Jewish women writers and educators should not be underestimated. Indeed, Marion Moss, aged just sixteen, opened a school for girls in Portsea.[88] It was an indication not only of her commitment to education but also a reflection that some young females within Portsmouth Jewry, especially from its burgeoning middle classes, had the space and opportunity to develop their intellectual potential but had also to earn a living.

While Alice's talents were not literary like her sisters, Celia and Marion, she, too, was a forceful figure who brought up her family on her own and was known for her support of others in the town, Jewish or otherwise. In spite of the patriarchy inside and outside Portsmouth Jewry, Hertha learned through family example of the possibility of female independence. Celia and Marion also provided a cultural and pedagogical model for those in the Portsmouth Hebrew Congregation. 'In 1850 there was founded a Literary Society which met weekly in the Synagogue Hall … There was [also] a weekly lecture which once a month dealt with subjects of Jewish history or literature'.[89] Out of this context, Lady Katie Magnus, daughter of Emanuel Emanuel, emerged, on both sides of the Atlantic, as a prominent and successful populiser of Jewish history later in the nineteenth century.[90] The vibrancy of Portsmouth Jewry, enriched as it was by constant migration and the dynamism of the town as a whole, enabled the space for such female talents as the Moss sisters, Hertha Ayrton and Lady

Magnus to flower.

It was suggested at the time that George Eliot's character, 'Mirah', in *Daniel Deronda* (1876) was modelled on Hertha Ayrton. There is little doubt that Eliot's friendship with Hertha made an impact on her, although the author's interest in matters Jewish predated their connection. Hertha's own response to the book, in a letter to her benefactor, is revealing not only in endorsing the authenticity of Eliot's fictional account, but in confirming the importance of Portsmouth to the scientist, a place she returned to regularly. It is worth quoting at length also because of the world that Hertha Ayrton evokes. Although romanticised, it shows that a distinctly Jewish sub-culture, with a strong east European flavour, existed in Portsmouth several decades before mass immigration at the turn of the century:

> The description of the family of Ezra Cohen is absolutely true. Mrs Lewes [George Eliot] *must* have seen and known some Jews of that class; she could not possibly describe them so truly otherwise. One thing she forgot, and that was to make a strong smell of boiling oil (fish frying) round the shop when Daniel first went into it … How often, when I was at Portsmouth, I have wished that Mrs Lewes would see and describe exactly the life there, little thinking that she really would do it one day. The small Adelaide Rebekak, with her monumental features and her crinoline, is such a well-known child to me; I could name at least half-a-dozen of them among my own acquaintance![91]

The intensity of this Jewish milieu was to be reinforced but also to be transformed by the arrival of east European Jews to Portsmouth at the start of the twentieth century. Born into it, Ian Mikardo was, in his autobiography, to reflect on Portsmouth with far greater ambivalence than was the case with Hertha Ayrton. Both, however, were clearly shaped by their early years in the port town. The place of birth mattered to them and Ayrton and Mikardo were deeply influenced by the everyday Jewish and non-Jewish life they encountered in Portsmouth.

Ian Mikardo's *Back-Bencher* (1988) is an intriguing piece of autobiographical practice. It includes details of his personal life as well as of his years in parliament as a prominent socialist within the Labour party. Without a personal archive to draw upon, Mikardo emphasised from the start that his autobiography consisted 'only of those flashbacks which have stuck in my memory'. Mikardo was also aware that 'memory is an impressionist painting, not a photograph: it is inescapably selective, and it's often impossible to know to what extent any particular story has grown in the telling or any particular recollection is coloured by hindsight or wishful thinking or vanity – or just colouring'. But such awareness of the importance of subjectivity in constructing a life story was then qualified by Mikardo in his statement that 'I've tried hard to tell it as it was.'[92]

Back-Bencher is typified by a tension between the author's self-reflexivity and his desire for objectivity, one intensified by the politicised nature of Mikardo's narrative. This tension is typified by Mikardo's confrontation with his Jewish background. A sense of Jewishness within the autobiography, especially with regard to place, is shaped by two forces. On the one hand, *Back-Bencher* reveals a determined political commitment that sometimes debunks Jewish mythology. On the other, elements of nostalgia towards a lost and idealised world counteract its grim realism.

On the surface, it appears that Mikardo's affection for Portsmouth and his family background matched that of Ayrton. Before he was born in 1905, his parents moved from London to Portsmouth and 'that's how I came to be a Hampshire hog instead of a cockney … and a fanatical supporter of "Pompey" … These childhood loyalties get into one's blood and stay there'.[93] So strong was this bond that Mikardo always thought he was 'in a sort of exiles' *lantzmanshaft* whenever … attend[ing] a get-together of the London Section of the Portsmouth Football Supporters' Club'.[94] But as a late teenager Mikardo was to leave Portsmouth for London. Thereafter, whenever he returned, 'it was always as a visitor and not any more as a settled member of the family'. Mikardo saw himself 'living in two conflicting, clashing cultures at the same time'. At the heart of his existential turmoil was the nature of his Jewishness and its relationship to Portsmouth.[95]

Mikardo was brought up in Portsea which, with its naval dockyard and barracks, was the 'natural centre of the trades of naval tailoring and outfitting'. It was here that Mikardo's parents, and most of the east European Jews who came at the start of the century, were to settle:

> The spine running through Portsea is Queen Street, and it was there, and in the smaller streets on the south side of it, that the Jewish quarter developed, with its synagogue, its community centre and its *kosher* butcher and poulterer and fishmonger.[96]

Mikardo, in this description, presented the topography of Portsmouth Jewry as something new, ignoring the Jewish presence in Portsea that stretched back to the eighteenth century. While Mikardo provides a sketch map of Portsmouth's maritime history going back to Henry VIII and the *Mary Rose*, Jews are not mentioned within it and there is only the smallest acknowledgement that Jews had a longer history in the town. Mikardo briefly refers to the existence of a deeper-rooted Jewish elite within Portsmouth but only to indicate his (class) alienation from it.[97] The sense of Jewish Portsea being out of place and alien to the town was further reinforced by it being perceived by Mikardo as simply a feeble imitation of the East End: 'The ghetto-like huddling-together of the immigrants in Queen Street and its environs was almost a carbon copy of that same phenomenon in the Commercial Street area of Spitalfields in East London, though in much smaller numbers and more thinly spread.'[98]

Hasia Diner has explored how, within a history of Jewish settlement in Hartford, Connecticut, there are repeated parallels drawn between its immigrant area and that of New York. By making such linkages, she argues, the authors 'unintentionally seemed to legitimize their more provincial subjects'. Diner adds that 'Rather than allowing the story of Hartford to speak for itself, as well it could, they validated the ordeal of that city's Jews and their transition to America in Lower East Side terms'.[99] In the case of Mikardo, however, a different version of centre-periphery is constructed. The East End of London is referenced as the authentic, or more authentic, Jewish experience and one that Portsmouth could not match up to. Jewish Portsea becomes simply a lesser version of Spitalfields. Indeed, Chaim Raphael, reviewing *Back-Bencher* in the *Jewish Chronicle*, continued the bias of Mikardo's geographical preferences, as well as the wider British Jewish tendency to marginalise the provinces, when he mistakenly claimed that the autobiography began with 'both the poverty and loyalties of his life as a child in London's East End'.[100]

In *Back-Bencher*, Mikardo allows for the uniqueness of place, but only through the proximity of the naval presence and the culture that accompanied it. Jewishly, in Mikardo's mind, Portsea became insignificant once he had discovered London. Frustrated as a scholar in Aria College where he was trying to fulfil his mother's dream of him becoming a rabbi, Mikardo was liberated by 'lighting upon another brave new world, one teeming with fresh and exciting and challenging perceptions. It was the world of the Jewish East End, which I discovered, and was drawn into, some twenty years after my father discovered it and became part of it'. In recalling earlier trips made with his mother to the East End, Mikardo made explicit his disappointment with Portsmouth. He was

> fascinated by the sharp contrast between its colourful liveliness and the grey conformity of my home town. I delighted to hear Yiddish spoken in the streets, I enjoyed reading the Yiddish posters on the hoardings, and I loved the noisy, babbling Jewish eating-houses and their Yiddish-speaking waiters.[101]

Mikardo's autobiography provides an absorbing case study in which a hierarchy of Jewish, or more precisely, east European Jewish, authenticity is constructed. Within Mikardo's concept of Jewishness, Yiddish language and culture, especially when manifested through radical politics, was at the apex. Mikardo did not romanticise Jewish life in eastern Europe and he had little time for the 'religious fundamentalism' within it. Nevertheless, once translated through migration it became the catalyst for a progressive Jewish sub-culture which had within it, he believed, the potential to change the world and act as an example to end injustice.[102] Yet if Jewish Portsea represented to Mikardo a diluted version of the 'real thing' in comparison to the East End, the latter too was a poor imitation of the Lower East Side.

David Cesarani has noted how in many autobiographies of those whose families came from eastern Europe to Britain, a mythology developed that they thought that they had arrived in America.[103] The frequency of this story points to the idea of America as the *goldene medinah* to which Britain was a poor alternative. Ian Mikardo's family possessed an extreme version of this legend, relating to his father, Morris. In the Mikardo case it was so absurd as to point to its factual falseness, but it was a fiction that the son reinforced rather than queried: 'Morris was in London four months before he discovered that he wasn't in New York. That sounds incredible, but it happened, not only to my father but to quite a number of other immigrants I got to know'.[104]

In fact, in the cases of his father (born near Lodz) and mother (from the Ukraine), both had siblings who had settled in London. It was thus family connections as well as the possibilities of work that attracted them to England, which was cheaper to reach than America. Yet alongside the Jewish mythology bought into by Mikardo, the socialist analysis that runs through *Back-Bencher* cut through some of its assumptions. He adds that a short time after having arrived in London 'Morris decided to go to New York to see what he had missed (a few pounds paid for a passage in steerage), but he found the sweatshops were worse than in London, and so he came back'.[105] Mikardo's acknowledgement of the economic misery facing many immigrants on both sides of the Atlantic pointed to the fluidity of migration and the reality that, for many, America did not fulfil its promise as the land of opportunity and success.

Back-Bencher differs from many other life stories relating to the migration of east European Jews in accepting that 'The poverty and bleakness of life within the Pale was one of the potent incentives to emigration'.[106] Mikardo mentions fleeing antisemitism and pogroms, but not as the major cause of movement. In contrast, many Jewish autobiographies highlight persecution in order to legitimise migration to Britain when it was questioned by those hostile to it, a campaign that culminated in the 1905 Aliens Act.[107] Highlighting pogroms was also a tactic employed to distance the authors from more recent arrivals who have been widely regarded within British society and politics as undeserving and 'bogus'.[108]

Mikardo, however, was eager to connect the Jewish immigrant experience to those who, after 1945, came from the New Commonwealth and elsewhere. Making this linkage reflected the conscious anti-racist and multi-cultural politics pursued by Mikardo, especially when he was an MP in the East End of London. *Back-Bencher* is also unusual within the genre of east European origin autobiography in referring to other immigrants who came to Britain at the same time – in this case the Maltese men who largely worked in the dockyard and whose children were at school with Mikardo.[109] Yet it was perhaps his empathy with the new immigrants, alongside a socialist belief in progress, that was responsible for Mikardo accepting uncritically the idea of the newcomers' upward economic mobility. He wrote proudly of a generation of Jewish immigrants who overcame the 'handicap' of poverty and strangeness and 'created a stable and honourable place in society for themselves and their children. How they did it, how they succeeded against the odds, is a story of no mean achievement.'[110] Mikardo did not quite meet the heroic family narrative of his fellow Portsmouth Jew, the actor Wolfe Morris, whose grandfather, a Russian Jew, allegedly 'carried his son … on his shoulders across Europe to start a new life in Britain'.[111] Nevertheless, *Back-Bencher* triumphantly charts his parents' progress in Portsmouth from hired hands through to shopkeepers repairing and selling naval uniforms. Even if inadvertently, Mikardo confirmed the dominant upwardly mobile narrative of east European immigrants provided within much Jewish historiography and other memory work. In what has become the standard history of the Jews of the town, and probably inspired by Mikardo himself, it is noted that 'In Portsmouth, as elsewhere, many an eventual entrepreneur commenced commercial activity in this country sleeping under the counter in the local tailor shop.'[112] Yet throughout the early chapters of *Back-Bencher* there are descriptions of Jewish life in Portsmouth and the East End which focus on the rat and bug-infested slums, the misery of the sweatshops, the cultural dislocation experienced by the older generation of immigrants and what Mikardo somewhat callously labelled 'the world's natural losers' within the east European community.[113] Indeed, Mikardo's description of how his parents, and many other hundreds of east European Jews, ended up in Portsmouth in the 1900s is a classic example of class-conscious writing:

> Some master tailors would travel up from Portsmouth to a sort of open-air job-centre … on a stretch of pavement on the north side of Aldgate High Street … Immigrants looking for work would gather there, and the master would look them over and would take his pick. Sometimes, following the practice of the slavemasters of ancient times, he would take his newly acquired 'hand' back to Portsmouth with him and put the man to work immediately, leaving him to sleep his first few nights under the cutting table until he could find bed and board.[114]

The memory work by and about Ian Mikardo and Hertha Ayrton reveals the complexity of growing up Jewish in Portsmouth. Ayrton's family background and life story reflect the importance and long-standing nature of migration and add the neglected area of women's experiences and identities inside and outside the Jewish community. Mikardo's socialist-inspired account of Portsmouth Jewry, while revealing the divisions within the community, led him to dismiss those in the community who had longer roots in the town such as the maternal family of Hertha Ayrton. It also meant there was a failure of imagination in recognising that Jewish migration and poverty had occurred before the influx at the start of the twentieth century. In this respect there is a certain irony and serendipity in comparing the life stories of Hertha Ayrton and Ian Mikardo – both became fervent supporters of the Labour movement and when the latter was first elected as a Labour MP, the party was chaired by the former's daughter, Barbara Gould. Taken together and read critically and closely, the auto/biographical practices relating to Ayrton and Mikardo reveal the intricate and complicated lives made by east European Jews in Portsmouth from the 1840s through to the outbreak of the First World War. How and why these remarkable stories, and others relating to the other four Jewish settlements of east European Jews in Hampshire, have been lost and forgotten within the public sphere will now be teased out in the final section of this chapter.

Privatising memory

The start of the First World War brought an abrupt halt to Jewish migration. The 1905 Aliens Act had been important on a symbolic level, signalling that Britain was no longer a country of free entry. In practice, it had many loopholes and its implementation varied between laxness and severity in the years up to 1914 depending on the wider public and political mood. The Aliens Restriction Act of 1914, in contrast, was a draconian measure essentially curtailing immigration into Britain and making it much easier for the Home Secretary to deport individuals when he deemed it necessary for the public good. Thereafter, Jewish migration from eastern Europe to Britain was negligible. For much of the 1920s, for example, more Jews were deported from Britain than were allowed entry.[115] As will be explored in Chapters 7 and 8, the issue of Jewish transmigrancy had still to be addressed from a legislative perspective, and movement within Britain of Jews of east European origin continued after 1914. In effect, however, August 1914 brought to a halt almost a century of escalating east European Jewish migration to Britain.

The fluidity of Jewish movement, alongside the failure until recently to validate immigration within national and local memory work, largely explain the failure, outside the capital, to recognise the pre-1914 presence of east European Jews. Often, the only surviving evidence of Jewish settlement has been in the form of cemeteries. Nevertheless, the importance of flux was such in the east European experience that not all those who settled in towns such as Southampton would do so permanently. Hence, in this particular case, those buried in the cemetery reflect only a fragment of what was a dynamic community. The creation of a Jewish cemetery was important from a practical perspective to an emerging Jewish community. In Southampton, for example, the necessity of taking bodies to Portsmouth caused major logistic and financial problems for its Jewish minority during the second quarter of the nineteenth century. In 1850, Samuel Emanuel asked 'for justice to be done' to the Jews as ratepayers of Southampton and to give them a section of the new municipal cemetery. At present they were 'twenty miles distant from any place of Jewish burial, and the charges made at that ground were very extravagent and enormous'. Soon after, the council agreed to put into action what it had promised the Jewish community some years earlier. A small section of the cemetery was set aside and an *ohel* (burial prayer room) was constructed nearby.[116]

Beyond such practical, everyday matters, the existence of a Jewish cemetery was also significant in relation to a sense of belonging and place in the locality, implying that Jews were now a permanent part of the landscape. Guide books for both Portsmouth and Southampton during the nineteenth century included descriptions of the Jewish cemeteries which were matter-of-fact and accepting of the 'considerable community' which they represented.[117] It is no accident, therefore, that Jewish cemeteries have been especially singled out for attack by antisemitic hooligans – by destroying and defacing gravestones those responsible have also been attempting to obliterate evidence of the local Jewish presence. Since the 1990s, within Hampshire, serious damage has been caused to the Jewish cemeteries in Southampton (1993 and several times thereafter) and Aldershot (2004 and 2005), leaving behind irreparable gravestones and antisemitic graffiti.[118]

Yet the neglect of cemeteries within the Jewish community, especially when they are no longer used for interments or, as in the case of medieval Winchester, the removal of remains to outside the region, has been equally if not more damaging than deliberate and malevolent violence. Usually for reasons of security, Jewish cemeteries have become fenced off and are thus outside the public gaze. The absence of Jews in public memorial work can remain unchallenged if their presence in the past, as represented through cemeteries, is obscured by walls or by destruction, malicious or otherwise. Thus some of the tombstones of the Southampton Jews featured in this chapter are broken or simply indecipherable today. Such invisibility is particularly unfortunate as memorials to the dead, especially those that lost their lives in conflict, are central to the construction of memory at both a national and local level. The final case study from this chapter will focus on Southampton and the First World War to show the processes by which Jewishness has been concealed from considerations of the past. It will explore the interplay between private Jewish spaces, exemplified by the synagogue and cemetery, and the public sphere, manifest through the Cenotaph to the local war dead, which was unveiled in November 1920.

Three Southampton Jews lost their lives fighting for Britain between 1914 and 1918. Two – Mendel Levene (or Levine) and Reuben Jeski – were of families of recent east European migration. Reuben's parents, for example, Jacob and Sarah, were born in Poland and initially moved to St George's in the East, the largely non-Jewish and poverty-stricken dock area of the East End. They moved with their young son to Southampton in the early 1900s where Jacob continued to earn his living as a tailor.[119] The third, Charles Emanuel, was the son of Michael Emanuel and a member of the Royal Army Medical Corps. He was the only one of the three to be remembered on Southampton's Cenotaph. As we will see, the inclusion and exclusion on the Cenotaph reveals much about the workings of class and ethnicity in the construction of local memory and how it was that the Jews of east European origin could be so easily forgotten.

The first to die 'whilst in the service of his country' was Charles Emanuel. Charles had been sent to Netley Military Hospital, a few miles down the coast from Southampton, to recuperate but he had not recovered and died in January 1917. Charles's death in the locality enabled him to be buried in the Jewish cemetery in Southampton and he was honoured with a public memorial service.[120] Three months later Mendel Levene, aged nineteen and a seaman, died when his hospital ship, the *Salta*, was sunk by a mine and finally, just three weeks before the end of the war, Reuben Jeski was killed in action in France.[121]

Levene and Jeski are remembered by plaques within the synagogue, a privilege that would have been given to Charles Emanuel had his family remained members of the Southampton Hebrew Congregation.[122] It was expected, however, that all three would be recognised in the memorial that was being planned for the war dead in Southampton. Early in January 1919, the Jewish community raised substantial funds towards the mayor's memorial fund. Joseph Silverman, representing the council, assured the Hebrew Congregation that the 'money collected should be sent to the Mayor without any condition attached as the memorial would not be of a religious nature as it would represent [the] Population of Southampton as a Body in General'.[123]

Such a non-denominational, universal approach would have met the vision of Edward Lutyens and it was manifested in the neutrality of his

Whitehall Cenotaph with its open inscription to 'The Glorious Dead' and the absence of any particular religious symbolism.[124] Nevertheless, in the case of Southampton, which Lutyens designed as a precursor to the national memorial, the church intervened and the monument is dominated by a huge cross which did not feature in Lutyens' plans.[125] The Christianisation of the Southampton Cenotaph was further emphasised when it was officially dedicated by the Bishop of Winchester 'in lasting memory of those of this Town, who have offered their lives for World Freedom and for International Righteousness, in the name of the Father and of the Son and of the Holy Ghost'.[126] Not surprisingly, the relatives of Mendel Levene and Reuben Jeski were unwilling to add the names of their lost ones to the Southampton Cenotaph. Its inscription to 'Our Glorious Dead' is thus exclusive, or rather, as was the case with Charles Emanuel, inclusion had its price – there was acknowledgement of his loss, but only within a fundamentally Christian memorial.

Bill Williams has written how the Jews of late Victorian Manchester 'were validated not on the grounds of their Jewish identity, but on the basis of their conformity to the values and manners of bourgeois English society'.[127] The Emanuel family had come to personify such values and manners within Hampshire over three centuries. Yet when it came to the final sacrifice, Charles Emanuel's Jewishness was ignored and his life, in the public sphere, framed within a Christian discourse. As Williams adds, conditional acceptance remains 'the quintessential means by which British society accommodates ethnic minorities'.[128] Charles Emanuel could thus be remembered within the private and public realm in Southampton whereas Mendel Levene and Reuben Jeski were relegated to small memorials purely within the synagogue.

The effective exclusion of Levene and Jeski from the Southampton Cenotaph is of wider significance given the central place it played and continues to play in the city's memorial topography and culture. There was no possibility, then, for their relatives to emulate those of Southampton-born poet, Martin Bell, whose uncle Cyril 'copped it' in the First World War:

> My mother showed him to me,
> Neat letters high up on the cenotaph
> That wedding-caked it up above the park ...[129]

In its official description, it was noted that on the Southampton Cenotaph 'is placed a recumbant effigy of a fighting man. In that the effigy is placed high up, the face is not to be seen, so that in imagination it represents to every mother her son'.[130] In this respect, the failure to provide space within this epicentre of local memory work in which the Jews, as Jews, could be incorporated revealed an insensitivity and inflexibility on behalf of the civic and religious authorities of Southampton. More generally, the absence of Levene and Jeski on the Cenotaph is illustrative of the wider marginalising of memory relating to the pre-1914 settlement of east European Jews in Hampshire. It is an amnesia that is even more profound in the case of the tens of thousands who came through the county as transmigrants and to whom we shall now turn.

Notes

1 Hasia Diner, *Lower East Side Memories: A Jewish Place in America* (Princeton: Princeton University Press, 2000), p. 13.

2 Ibid., p. 23.

3 Bill Williams, *The Making of Manchester Jewry 1740–1875* (Manchester: Manchester University Press, 1976), p. vii.

4 In 1840 there were 30 members and 48 in 1866. See Henry Roche, 'The Jews of Portsmouth', *Shemot* vol. 2 no. 1 (1995), p. 28; *Jewish Chronicle*, 11 January 1907.

5 See Malcolm Slowe, 'The Foundation of Aldershot Synagogue', in Aubrey Newman (ed.), 'Provincial Jewry in Victorian Britain' (unpublished papers, Jewish Historical Society of England, 1975).

6 Ibid.

7 V. D. Lipman, 'A Survey of Anglo-Jewry in 1851', *Transactions of the Jewish Historical Society of England* vol. 17 (1951–52), pp. 179, 188.

8 *Jewish Chronicle*, 8 August 1851.

9 See letter of V. D. Lipman to Sidney Weintroub, 6 December 1979 in Southampton Hebrew Congregation archives (SHCA).

10 Editorial, 'Boards, Commissions and Kashrut', *Jewish Chronicle*, 6 August 1965.

11 *Jewish Chronicle*, 8 August 1851.

12 *Jewish Chronicle* appeal reproduced in Ivan Weintroub, 'Jews of Southampton', unpublished ms, SHCA.

13 Aubrey Weinberg, 'Portsmouth Jewry', *Portsmouth Papers* no. 41 (1985), p. 8.

14 *Portsmouth Times*, 29 January 1855.

15 Weinberg, 'Portsmouth Jewry', p. 8.

16 Ibid., p. 19 (note 35).

17 Letter of Divisional Librarian, Portsmouth Local Librarian, 22 March 1985, in Portsmouth City Library Local History Collection, LP 921 EMA.

18 *Portsmouth Times*, 9 February 1855.

19 Eugene Black, *The Social Politics of Anglo-Jewry, 1880–1920* (Oxford: Blackwell, 1988).

20 See *Hampshire Telegraph*, 26 March 1904 for an account of its centenary celebrations.

21 Williams, *The Making of Manchester Jewry*, p. 144.

22 *Jewish Chronicle*, 11 March 1853.

23 *Jewish Chronicle*, 2 March 1860.

24 *Jewish Chronicle*, 5 February 1864.

25 *Jewish Chronicle*, 8 June 1886.

26 Fyne to Hirsh, 3 January 1896, Central Zionist Archives, Jerusalem (CZA), A2/78.

27 Minutes of Jewish Association, 21 June 1896, 15 October 1899, 19 November 1899 and 4 October 1900 in University of Southampton archives, MS 173/2/2/5; Southampton

Hebrew Congregation minutes, 6 November 1912. More generally, see Edward Bristow, *Prostitution and Prejudice: The Jewish Fight Against White Slavery, 1870–1939* (Oxford: Oxford University Press, 1982); Lloyd Gartner, 'Anglo-Jewry and the Jewish International Traffic in Prostitution 1885–1914', *Association for Jewish Studies Review* vol. 7 (1982), pp. 129–78; and Susan Tananbaum, '"Morally Depraved and Abnormally Criminal": Jews and Crime in London and New York, 1880–1940', in Michael Berkowitz, Susan Tananbaum and Sam Bloom (eds), *Forging Modern Jewish Identities: Public Faces and Private Struggles* (London: Vallentine Mitchell, 2003), pp. 130–3.

28 Lloyd Gartner, 'Notes on the Statistics of Jewish Immigration to England, 1870–1914', *Jewish Social Studies* vol. 22 no. 2 (1960), pp. 97–102.

29 Weinberg, 'Portsmouth Jewry', p. 15.

30 *Jewish Chronicle*, 22 July 1891.

31 Weinberg, 'Portsmouth Jewry', pp. 9–11.

32 Ibid.

33 S. Fyne to Dr Hirsch, 31 January 1895, CZA, A2/78.

34 Rosaleen Wilkinson, *Townhill Park – The Life and Times of a Gertrude Jekyll Garden* (Southampton: Rosaleen Wilkinson, 2004), p. 55.

35 Minutes of Southampton Hebrew Congregation (SHC), 11 November 1912.

36 SHC minutes, 5 July 1894.

37 SHC minutes, 3 June 1908.

38 Louise Rosenberg, 'Rev.Abraham Tobias Boas', *Journal of the Australian Jewish Historical Society* vol. 7 no. 2 (1972), p. 90.

39 Letter of Isidore Holden, 15 September 1967 to Sidney Weintroub, SHC archives.

40 SHC minutes, July and 13 December 1908.

41 SHC minutes, 24 September 1911.

42 SHC minutes, 25 October 1911.

43 Harold Gastwirt, *Fraud, Corruption, and Holiness: The Controversy Over the Supervision of Jewish Dietary Practice in New York City 1881–1940* (Port Washington: Kennikat Press, 1974), Chapter 2 deals with the religious and financial conflicts that emerged over *shehitah* within the Jewish community, ones that intensified with increased migration from the early modern period onwards.

44 In *Bournemouth Hebrew Congregation Centenary 1905–2005: A Celebration* (Cheltenham: Zethics, 2005), p. 90.

45 SHC minutes, 26 November 1911.

46 SHC minutes, 5 March 1911.

47 SHC minutes, 24 September 1911.

48 *Jewish World*, 7 September 1913.

49 SHC minutes, 1 August 1914.

50 SHC minutes, 10 February 1914 and 18 August 1915.

51 SHC minutes, 18 August 1915.

52 SHC minutes 17 October 1915.

53 SHC minutes, 30 March 1919.

54 Information from the 1891 census for Southampton, Southampton City Library Local Studies and 1901 Census, www.1901CensusOnline.com, accessed 2 January 2007.

55 SHC minutes, 5 and 10 February 1914.

56 SHC minutes, 10 February 1914.

57 SHC minutes, 19 January 1919.

58 Ian Mikardo, *Back-Bencher* (London: Weidenfeld & Nicolson, 1988), p. 16.

59 *Jewish Year Book 5668–9* (London: Greenberg, 1907), p. 149 and *Jewish Chronicle*, 9 September 1904.

60 *Bournemouth Hebrew Congregation Centenary*, pp. 17,48.

61 *Jewish Year Book 1945–6* (London: Jewish Chronicle, 1945), pp. 151, 189.

62 Ibid., pp. 94–5.

63 Anne Ruffell, 'Bournemouth's Hebrew Heritage', *Hampshire* vol. 21 no. 1 (November 1980), p. 42.

64 Elizabeth Edwards, *A History of Bournemouth* (Chichester: Phillimore, 1981), pp. 24, 35.

65 David Young, *The Story of Bournemouth* (London: Robert Hale, 1957), p. 247.

66 Information from 1881 census and *Southampton Street Directory* (Southampton: Stevens, 1887), p. 141.

67 Information from 1901 census.

68 Louis Herrman, 'I Became a Cape Colonist' (unpublished ms), Herrman papers, University of Cape Town archive, A3/1.

69 Ibid.

70 Harold Pollins, *Economic History of the Jews in England* (East Brunswick: Associated University Presses, 1982), p. 144.

71 Weinberg, 'Portsmouth Jewry', p. 17.

72 *Jewish Chronicle*, 2 September 1904.

73 Larry Riddle, 'Hertha Marks Ayrton', in 'Biographies of Women Mathematicians', www.agnesscott.edu/lriddle/women/ayrton.htm, accessed 18 April 2006.

74 See, for example, James Tattersall and Shawnee McMurran, 'Hertha Ayrton: A Persistent Experimenter', *Journal of Women's History* vol. 7 no. 2 (summer 1995), pp. 86–112.

75 Henry Armstrong, 'Hertha Ayrton', *Nature* no. 2822 (1 December 1923), p. 801.

76 Evelyn Sharp, *Hertha Ayrton: 1854–1923 A Memoir* (London: Arnold, 1926), passim.

77 See, for example, Riddle, 'Hertha Marks Ayrton'.

78 Tattersall and McMurran, 'Hertha Ayrton', p. 86.

79 Sharp, *Hertha Ayrton*, p. 1.

80 Ibid.

81 Ibid., pp. 25–6.

82 Ibid., pp. 1–2.

83 See Michael Stanislawski, *Tsar Nicholas 1 and the Jews: The Transformation of Jewish Society in Russia 1825–1855* (Philadephia: Jewish Publication Society of America, 1983) and John Klier and Shlomo Lambroza (eds), *Pogroms* (Cambridge: Cambridge University Press, 1992).

84 Sharp, *Hertha Ayrton*, pp. 6, 9.

85 Ibid., p. 3.

86 *Jewish Chronicle*, 1 November 1907.

87 Michael Galchinsky, *The Origin of the Modern Jewish Woman Writer* (Detroit: Wayne State University Press, 1996), p. 133.

88 See her obituary in *Jewish Chronicle*, 1 November 1907.

89 Anonymous entry on Portsmouth in Aubrey Newman (ed.), 'Provincial Jewry in Victorian Britain' (unpublished papers, JHSE, 1975).

90 See, for example, her *Outlines of Jewish History* (London: Longman, 1886).

91 Sharp, *Hertha Ayrton*, p. 30 quoting a letter to Madame Bodichon (1876/7?).

92 Mikardo, *Back-Bencher*, p. 5.

93 Ibid., p. 20.

94 Ibid., p. 8.

95 Ibid., p. 37.

96 Ibid., p. 21.

97 Ibid., pp. 16, 25–6.

98 Ibid., p. 21.

99 Diner, *Lower East Side Memories*, p. 37.

100 *Jewish Chronicle*, 4 November 1988.

101 Mikardo, *Back-Bencher*, pp. 37–8.

102 Ibid., p. 10.

103 David Cesarani, 'The Myth of Origins: Ethnic Memory and the Experience of Migration', in Aubrey Newman and Stephen Massils (eds), *Patterns of Migration, 1850–1914* (London: Jewish Historical Society of England, 1996), pp. 251–2.

104 Mikardo, *Back-Bencher*, p. 17.

105 Ibid., p. 17.

106 Ibid., p. 10.

107 Cesarani, 'The Myth of Origins', pp. 248–51.

108 Tony Kushner, *Remembering Refugees: Then and Now* (Manchester: Manchester University Press, 2006).

109 Mikardo, *Back-Bencher*, pp. 24–5.

110 Ibid., p. 11.

111 Obituary in *The Times*, 13 August 1996.

112 Weinberg, 'Portsmouth Jewry', p. 17 and more generally Andrew Godley, *Jewish Immigrant Entrepreneurship in New York and London 1880–1914* (Basingstoke: Palgrave, 2001).

113 Mikardo, *Back-Bencher*, p. 38.

114 Ibid., p. 20.

115 Tony Kushner and Katharine Knox, *Refugees in an Age of Genocide* (London: Frank Cass, 1999), chapters 1–3.

116 *Report of the Preliminary Enquiry … into the Sanitary Conditions of Southampton, 1850* (Southampton: Hampshire Independent, 1850), pp. 123–4.

117 *The New Portsmouth Guide* (Portsmouth: Charpentier, 1843), p. 85; Philip Brannon, *The Stranger's Guide to Southampton* (Southampton: Sharland, 1868), p. 72 and *John Heywood's Illustrated Guide to Southampton* (Manchester: Deansgate and Ridgefield, 1895), p. 26.

118 *Southern Evening Echo*, 3 August 1993; *Guardian*, 21 January 2005.

119 1901 Census, www.1901CensusOnline.com, accessed 12 May 2007.

120 SHC minutes 20 January 1917 and headstone in Southampton Jewish cemetery.

121 See the plaques in Southampton synagogue and Michael Adler (ed.), *British Jewry Book of Honour* (London: Caxton, 1922), pp. 4, 99.

122 SHC minutes, 22 April 1917 and 24 November 1918.

123 SHC minutes, 19 January 1919.

124 See Mary Lutyens, *Edwin Lutyens* (London: John Murray, 1980), p. 165.

125 See Southampton City Record Office, SC2/4/11/1 and Sidney Kimber, *Thirty Eight Years of Public Life in Southampton 1910–1948* (Southampton: no publisher, 1949), opposite p. 49.

126 Ibid.

127 Bill Williams, 'The Anti-Semitism of Tolerance: Middle-Class Manchester and the Jews', in A. J. Kidd and K. W. Roberts (eds), *City, Class and Culture* (Manchester: Manchester University Press, 1985), p. 94.

128 Ibid.

129 Martin Bell, 'Reasons for Refusal', in Peter Porter (ed.), *Martin Bell: Complete Poems*

(Newcastle: Bloodaxe Books, 1988), p. 54.

130 Southampton City Record Office, SC2/4/11/1.

7

Historicising the invisible: transmigrancy, memory and local identities

Introduction

By the First World War, Southampton was beginning to rival Liverpool as Britain's leading transmigrant port.[1] It provided routes to north and south Atlantic destinations, especially, from the 1890s, to eastern (and, to a lesser extent, southern and northern) European migrants who had broken their journey in England. Transmigrancy was big business. It has been estimated that 'The alien passenger, and in particular the transmigrant flows through Britain' totalled one-third of all the passenger trade of British shipping companies.[2] The scale of this movement was immense. In less than a five-month period in 1905, for example, 37,285 transmigrants were inspected by the American consular officials in Southampton, of whom half were Russians.[3] From the 1830s through to 1914, roughly six million aliens left Britain, and more than half of these were transmigrants.[4] 'Great Britain', as a contemporary Jewish activist and pro-alien campaigner argued, 'owing to its geographical position and plenitude of coast-line, [was] a kind of international Clapham Junction and clearing-house for the reception and distribution of passengers … to and from all parts of the world'.[5] What this represented in human terms and beyond the statistics was revealed in 1886 by the secretary of the Southampton Hebrew Congregation, Nathan Levy:

> A large number of poor co-religionists pass through this town, and often have to remain here without any means from two to seven days, whilst awaiting the departure of the vessel which [is] to take them to America … On the night of [2 November], a family consisting of nine souls (mother and eight children) arrived here from Hull, their entire riches consisting of sixpence. Late though it was (11pm) the railway officials considerately made up a large fire in one of the waiting rooms at the station, where the strangers passed the night. The porters, with equal kindness, collected among themselves a few coppers, wherewith they provided the poor family with bread and butter and coffee.[6]

A visitor to Southampton in the early twentieth century commented how 'In the streets near the docks a rare medley of peoples, races, and languages are to be met with. Lascars, Norwegians, Japanese and many others jostle one another, and pass unnoticed – too familiar a sight here to excite remark.'[7] Similarly, modern Southampton prides itself on its multi-culturalism and immigrant contribution: 'Since the early days of the trading docks Southampton has a long history of welcoming people from all parts of the world. Today is no different – and the city thrives on its rich and vibrant diversity, with many communities living side by side.'[8] Yet in spite of this self-affirming and inclusive mythology about past and present, there is no public space that acknowledges Southampton's integral role as a vital hub in world population movements. It is a local manifestation of the forgetting of transmigrancy that has occurred at a global level. Jonathan Boyarin has argued that it is 'only by having an inkling of at least the *possible* scope of memory that we can sense the "quantity" of forgetting'. The process of forgetting, adds Boyarin, is as complex as that of remembering and its intensity is often 'localized'.[9] This chapter, by examining particularly the memory work associated with the world's most famous ship, the *Titanic*, and Britain's most beloved airplane, the Spitfire – both with intimate connections to Southampton – will analyse the amnesia surrounding transmigrancy, and the ideological and cultural factors behind it.

Titanic years

Most of the transmigrants in Southampton at the turn of the century were sent to the town (some in sealed train carriages) from other ports in England – particularly London and Hull. They were then temporarily housed in hostels and cheap hotels near the docks.[10] From there, after a matter of days (as transmigrants they were meant to stay in Britain for a maximum of two weeks), they re-commenced their journeys to North and South America, South Africa and other parts of the globe. The main hostel for migrants and especially transmigrants in Southampton was the Emigrants' Home. It was soon re-named Atlantic Hotel, which, in spite of its promising appellation, was basic in its facilities. Rather than having steerage transmigrants lingering in what was deemed an insanitary hostel in Blackwall, in the docks of East London, it was agreed that it was essential that they be sent to Southampton direct while waiting for their transatlantic passage.[11]

The opening of the Emigrants' Home revealed the various forces calling for such an institution. Aside from the mayor and representatives of Southampton council, there were representatives from the American

Shipping Line, who dominated the proceedings, and the American consul in the town.[12] The records of the American consul make clear that the American authorities had major concerns about the health risks posed to emigrants through the poor conditions and lack of medical inspection at Blackwall.[13] In 1891 the first permanent infrastructure to control immigration had been implemented in the United States, increasing inspection, especially the medical examination, of aliens. In 1892 semi-hysteria against emigrants on health grounds developed in Germany and America as a result of the cholera epidemic in Hamburg and the typhus epidemic in New York, both of which were blamed on Russian Jews. Although in the USA a more powerful immigration bill failed in 1893, a Quarantine Act was enforced in that year.[14] At a local level, the opening of Atlantic Hotel was an obvious answer to concerns – sympathetic or otherwise – about aliens wandering aimlessly around the dock area. The transmigrants, while concentrated in specific parts of Southampton, typified the town's fluidity of movement. As a contemporary noted in the early twentieth century Southampton, 'in comparison with its size has a very large floating population'.[15] On a global level, the coming into existence of Atlantic Hotel was part of an international concern about the 'fitness' of emigrants and transmigrants. It reflected a wider moral panic in which the US authorities played a leading role.

The important American involvement in creating Atlantic Hotel should not disguise the local and national initiatives in the growing medical inspection of aliens during the 1890s. Indeed, in 1892 the Southampton Port Authority employed the town's medical officer to write a detailed report on the precautions needed to avoid the importation of cholera. One particular fear was that those rejected at New York 'might be transhipped back to Europe and prove a source of danger to ourselves'. At its own expense, the municipal authorities hired a floating port sanatorium. Any passengers examined on board suspected of carrying infectious diseases were quarantined on it.[16] It was clear that such action was not simply to protect the local population. At the annual meeting of the Association of Port Sanitary Authorities held in Southampton in 1902, Alderman Walton, who was hosting the event, emphasised the 'vast responsibility [that] rested upon the ports of this country not only to keep a clean bill of health for themselves, but also the whole country of which they were the front doors'.[17]

Aside from local initiatives, central government, well before the implementation of formal alien restriction through the Aliens Act, 1905, had implemented a system of medical inspection. It was limited to those travelling steerage – an indication of the class as well as racial prejudices behind such measures. Colonel Swalm, the American Consul in Southampton, and described as a 'virile Anglo-Saxon' had, as one contemporary put it, 'decidedly strong views on the "Alien"', having 'no use for the pauper immigrant'. In several detailed reports to the Assistant Secretary of State, Swalm described the medical inspection procedures at Southampton, the thoroughness of which he totally approved. Each emigrant was doubly examined by a ship's surgeon and then by a surgeon representing the Board of Trade. With the one exception of trachoma, the virulence of which he linked to Russian Jews from the East End of London, Swalm felt that 'all is being done that rational sanitary care and science can suggest'.[18]

Swalm could only witness the medical inspections in the port. Outside it, however, the American authorities – the shipping companies alongside the consul – continued to monitor closely and examine the transmigrants housed in Southampton hostels where they had assumed control as well as those in American-owned vessels in which the consul provided its own surgeon.[19] The Aliens Act, 1905, formalised much of the medical inspection although it changed little of what was already taking place in Southampton – one of the designated immigration ports. While the restriction of pauper aliens was controversial, few disputed the need either before or after the act to keep out those deemed to be physically or mentally diseased.[20] Meanwhile, the number of aliens passing through Southampton continued at a high level in spite of the new restrictive legislation. In 1907 those from the continent alone totalled some 36,435.[21]

It is significant that the racialised discourse of Colonel Swalm, especially his fears about the health of Russians of 'the Jewish type', was not fully shared within the world of port health inspection. Indeed, it has been suggested that generally 'Medical Officers of Health [were] favourably disposed towards Jewish immigrants'.[22] On a very practical level, it was not aliens but British sailors and returning soldiers who posed the most pressing problems for Southampton's health authorities.[23] Even so, the medical inspection of aliens had now been formally instituted. Although the initial impact was relatively minor, a precedent had been set and a link had been made between aliens, infectious diseases, inspection and immigration control procedures.

To an extent isolated from the rest of the port, few in the town would have had everyday contact with Atlantic Hotel. An exception was Albert Gibbs who was at school with two sons of the owners of the enterprise, the Dolings. His testimony, recorded in the 1980s, provides an evocative portrait of Southampton as a hub for national and international migration. It highlights the 'otherness' and confusion caused to a young boy confronting the smells and sights of Atlantic Hotel and its residents. For Gibbs, its impact still resonated three-quarters of a century later:

Now the Immigrants' Home was a home that used to accommodate the people that were coming from Middle Europe as immigrants to go to a new life in America. Accommodation was very poor, they used to go to sleep on concrete floors with just the coats they came in. They always looked grubby and poor and normally the men had huge beards, I think there was a very big proportion of Jews among them, because they were mostly the people that were exported from Europe, even in those days ... [T]hey were sleeping in the basement usually and I used to go down below with the Doling brothers and stand looking at them and ... as a boy I didn't know what to think about it.[24]

What is especially intriguing about Gibb's powerful testimony is its subsequent incorporation into local memory work. Rather than being used to highlight the importance of transmigrancy in the economy of a late Victorian and Edwardian port, this element of Gibbs's life story has simply been added to the Southampton memory store of the hegemonic *Titanic*. Mrs Doling was on board the *Titanic*, and survived, yet her journey was not for pleasure but to develop her family's transatlantic transmigrancy business further.[25] Similarly, in Manchester, Kovno-born Jacob Farber had established a successful travel business in 1887 with agents in Liverpool, Manchester and Southampton providing access to the major transatlantic liners such as the *Mauretania* and the *Lusitania*. As part of this enterprise, the agency sold tickets on the *Titanic*'s maiden voyage to eastern European Jews who had first settled in Britain and were now hoping to try their luck in America.[26] Included in this category was Joseph Abraham Hyman, one of the fortunate few of those travelling steerage who survived. He returned to Manchester and set up a still flourishing Jewish delicatessen and catering business, named (in perverse gratitude as well as recognition of the moniker given to him by the local press) 'Titanics'.[27]

It is telling that there is no place for the Hyman family story in Southampton's heritage and history world. Instead, it has been told elsewhere through the testimony of Joseph Hyman's great-grandson, Richard, proprietor of a delicatessen in Cheetham Hill, Manchester, that still bears the ship's name. Richard's family history features amongst a bank of video testimony that greets the visitor at the start of Manchester's controversial museum of urban living, Urbis. Alongside it are the brief life stories of a gay couple who have settled in the city, a young Afghan refugee whose family live in its Moss Side district, and the trials and tribulations of a Manchester tattoo artist. For all its limitations, Urbis, using Manchester as its major template, at least has relished and emphasised the plurality of voices and diversity, as well as the shock of arrival and importance of migration and immigration, that make up the modern city experience.[28]

In contrast, with regard to Atlantic Hotel and Southampton, those developing the site as 'luxury' accommodation and re-naming it 'Atlantic Mansions' – after the First World War it became offices before falling into dereliction in the 1990s – have highlighted specific aspects of the *Titanic* connection. The letting agency responsible for its apartments have been eager to point out that Atlantic Hotel had been used by second-class passengers prior to departure on the *Titanic* and photographs inside its vestibule reinforce this connection. The grim description offered by Albert Gibbs has no place in selling twenty-one units which would 'Ideally suit [a] professional person or couple' in contrast to the (contrived) association with a ship now associated with the glamour and romance of James Cameron's film stars, Leonardo DiCaprio and Kate Winslet.[29] It is sad but revealing that one of the rare public acknowledgements of Southampton's role in transmigrancy, the foundation stone for the 'Emigrants' Home' unveiled in November 1893 by Mrs Eliot Yorke (as noted in the previous chapter, a locally-based member of the Rothschild family), is now totally hidden from view by industrial-size rubbish bins, fenced in to further reduce access and visibility. The imaginative journey from a re-remembered Atlantic Hotel, catering for *Titanic* passengers, to the upmarket Atlantic Mansions is not long. That from the grim Emigrants' Home to city-living professionals is figuratively huge. Physically, from the Emigrants' Home to Atlantic Mansions is literally no distance at all. But as Jonathan Boyarin writes, 'The fact that conventional delimitations of space entail collective representations implies a measure of identification among those who live within or whose ancestors have lived within a given space. The degree to which this identification fails to ground active empathy is [a] litmus test for the presence of forgetting.'[30]

In the local Southampton heritage industry, through the contribution of its oral history unit, the transmigrant function of Atlantic Hotel has not been totally obliterated and the connections between the town and this trade *have* been made. While it is true that Arthur Gibbs's testimony has been instrumentalised primarily in relation to the *Titanic*, it has, nevertheless, been given prominence, helping to emphasise that 'Many of the third class passengers were emigrants bound for Ellis Island in the United States' and to mention Southampton's 'link with this trade'.[31] Elsewhere another fragment of surviving memory connected to the building has appeared in a series of local publications – a postcard of Atlantic Hotel sent by a man to his mother in London the day after the First World War started. It was presumably on the eve of his (intended) departure. John Doling had these postcards made for publicity and advertising, attempting to establish his business as a truly international landmark. Teasing out the significance of the subsequent labelling of this much-reproduced postcard is itself revealing. Who the emigrants were staying at Atlantic Hotel is never referred to. The reproduction of the message on the back of the postcard – 'This is a photo of where we are living. I have 3 suits, 15 ties, 2 dozen collars, 3 hats, 1 pair of boots, 5 shirts and sundry other articles – and don't forget the bicycle ... Complete we are!' – suggests British rather than foreign composition. This wonderfully ordinary and 'English' list has been juxtaposed with comments on the adjoining property, that of Eli Loftus, who, from 1902, traded there as a money changer and outfitter. References are made to this shop's 'polyglot notices' and how 'It is interesting that the signwriting ... is in a language other than English'.[32] The 'exotic' nature of Loftus's shop places it 'other' to the Southampton experience. In fact, its proprietor, Russian-born Eli Loftus, was a member of the town's Jewish community. His business provided evidence of how important transmigrancy was to the local economy.[33]

In *A Defence of the Alien Immigrant* (1904), the London Committee of the Deputies of the British Jews suggested that transmigrants spent £1 million a year when passing through Britain.[34] As early as 1893 a local newspaper remarked with reference to emigrants and transmigrants, that although 'tradesmen in the centre of the town ... do not reap any apparent benefit from the American Line, such cannot be said of those immediately around the dock'.[35] Early in 1906, the London-based *Standard*, which had campaigned strongly in support of the Aliens Act, claimed that Southampton was 'heartily in sympathy with the Act, for it has suffered badly at the hands of penniless foreigners, who frequently drift to the local workhouses or infirmary, and become a permanent charge on the rates'.[36] While such local irritations and fears (especially health-related) were not totally the invention of the *Standard*, they were certainly exaggerated. For both ideological and pragmatic (largely economic) reasons the dominant mood in the town was against the necessity of legislation to control alien immigration.[37]

Returning to the *Titanic*, its subsequent memory has been strongly contested.[38] For example, at a local level, the huge loss of life of the Southampton-based crew has been highlighted against the fate of the rich and famous who have captured the wider imagination – it has been estimated that of the 900 crew members, 699 were from Southampton and only 170 survived.[39] Nevertheless, the place of transmigrants on board, who, alongside the crew, suffered the highest death rate, has been marginalised, as has, until recently, that of the Southampton connection.

In the academic sphere, Steven Biel's *Down With the Old Canoe: A Cultural History of the Titanic Disaster* (1996), the leading study, makes no mention of the town whatsoever. Biel's statement that 'No matter how many books I read, I can't keep track of who was where when' explains his unfortunate oversight.[40] The positive critical reception of this book – in spite of, or perhaps even because of this local lacuna – is indicative of the failings of cultural studies, especially when it dwells on representation and shows no interest in or knowledge of the history of the event itself. Nevertheless, Biel is aware of the racialisation of the disaster both at the time and subsequently. He highlights how the bravery of the 'Anglo-Saxon' first-class passengers, obeying the moral code of 'women and children first' was contrasted in contemporary reporting and later representation with the stories of panic and selfishness attributed to the 'racially inferior' types travelling steerage.[41] The alleged last command of Captain Smith, 'Be British!',[42] soon used as the lyrics of a charity record sold locally for widows and orphans of the crew,[43] fitted comfortably into such race discourse.

To his credit, Biel has examined the American, Finnish, Czech, Irish, Italian and Jewish newspapers and does not ignore the impact of the disaster on immigrant and minority communities. By reproducing headlines such as 'Finnish Passengers on the Titanic'; 'Irish Victims on the Titanic', and 'Many Jews were Passengers on Ill-Fated S.S. Titanic', Biel recognises that the 'ethnic press constituted its readers as communities of mourning and gave identity and dignity to the nameless "foreigners" in the conventional narrative'.[44] Yet not going further and failing, as have other 'readings' of the *Titanic*, to recover and analyse the memories and life stories of those transmigrants travelling steerage on the ship, is to continue their unsavoury image and discriminatory treatment in 1912. The *Titanic* memory and heritage industry, whether focusing on specific British places, such as Southampton or Belfast, has forgotten or marginalised those immigrants (and especially those who were transmigrants) in steerage. When the focus has been international, the attention has been on the rich and famous, and those travelling steerage are only significant as being represented as 'other' to the first-class passengers, rather than as individuals with lives of equal worth and interest. The cultural anthropologist, Liisa Malkki, has suggested that refugees are 'liminal in the categorical order of nation-states', leading them to be represented by academics, policy makers and the media as 'matter out of place'.[45] Much the same could be said of transmigrants in the early twentieth century and their subsequent invisibility – in spite of their huge numbers.

The power of exclusive narratives, both then and now, and the subsequent effort required to humanise those in the lower decks is neatly illustrated through the career of Southampton-born artist, Sam Smith. Smith was born in 1908 and it has been suggested that 'Childhood experiences of the City were to have a lasting influence on his work', especially 'watching liners and their impressive funnels drawing in and out of the docks':

> Ours was a seaport town. Funnels of great ships dominated the town; and the first drawings I remember attempting were of liners, with rows of wavy decks … I was

a bit of a funnel snob – believing that the bigger they were and the more of them, the greater the distinction that must fall, by some means of associated magic, on those who sailed with them. I loved looking at boats, and picked up all manner of cliches about them. Terms like 'Atlantic Greyhound', 'Blue Riband' and 'Britannia's Bulwark' were with me before I ever got onto 'God Save the King'. The sight of Cunarders and their sisters filled me with pride, which must have spawned from the rather heady patriotism rampant at the time.

The young Smith, however, was also alienated by confronting, even at a distance, such evidence of wealth. He remembers feeling that 'such beauties were above my station'. In a work entitled 'Bathers in Southampton Water' (1979), Smith re-visited his earlier understanding of the liners, making linkages that had earlier eluded him.[46]

The work is labelled 'July 27 1908 [the birth date of the artist]: BATHERS in Southampton Water disturbed by Wash of passing STEAMER, bound for AMERICA, with First Class, Second Class, Third Class and STEERAGE PEOPLE'. In his notes on the work Smith wrote that 'The interior of the liner illustrates the class-system afloat, where money bought space, unlimited helpings and better-sprung bunks. Down in the steerage are the real people'. Two years earlier Smith had drawn a set of sketches, 'Immigrant Studies', reflecting his desire to make visible and humanise those located in the depths of the liners. These studies were partly inspired by Smith's increasing interest and recognition in the USA and, in particular, visits to Ellis Island. On the top decks of 'Southampton Water' colourful couples in first class are shown dancing and dining in luxury. Just below the waterline and just visible in their darkened and overcrowded hold are those travelling steerage, drawn largely in shadow. Smith labels them with Emma Lazarus's words from the Statue of Liberty as the 'huddled masses yearning to breathe free'. In his sensitivity to the reality of the immigrant experience it is perhaps not surprising that Sam Smith 'obtained a substantial and dedicated following in America but recognition in his own country came more slowly'. Smith said of his own work that it was

> about situations between, or about, people. An idea can present a theme which I will work on until I can do no more. All my pieces have a strong story line. The pieces are made to be looked into and not looked at.[47]

It has taken the artistic imagination of Sam Smith, or, in literature, Antony Sher, in *Middlepost* (1988), with its east European Jewish character 'Smous' who travels from Lithuania to Cape Town, to re-connect Southampton to its intimate relationship with transmigrancy in the late Victorian and Edwardian eras.[48] Sher's novel provides a rich evocation of Jewish emigration to South Africa from eastern Europe. When 'Smous' enters Cape Town, he waits to see whether he will receive the stripping, showering and medical inspection he received at Libau or the sulky help he had received from the 'overworked Jewish Immigration people at Southampton who had arranged ... transportation to the hostel'.[49]

There are thus fragments of memory work that avoid the surface bedazzlement of the *Titanic* to reveal fluidity as central to the Southampton experience in the years before the First World War. Rather than being marginal to the town, transmigrants were present in huge numbers – if rarely seen or heard. Move beyond 1918, however, and the transmigrant becomes even more obscure within Southampton's collective memory. Ironically, however, the town, or rather its rural hinterland, was at the heart of international developments in immigration policy. Atlantic Park, situated four miles south of its docks, became a symbol, and perhaps the largest physical manifestation on a global scale, of the restriction of movement faced by immigrants and refugees after the First World War.

The last of the few: Atlantic Park vs. the Spitfire

The Aliens Act, 1905 did not apply to transmigrants and was limited to those travelling steerage. In contrast, the 1919 Aliens Restriction Act and subsequent aliens orders imposed almost total control with even greater emphasis on medical inspection. Nine pages of detailed instructions were provided for the medical inspectors in the ports, including, for the first time, clear responsibilities with regards to transmigrants. The shipping companies were now liable for any expenses incurred in keeping and returning transmigrants who were medically rejected.[50] The shipping companies, hoping for a return to the lucrative pre-war trade in international passenger movement, inadvertently found themselves victims of worldwide alien restrictionism, especially that implemented in the USA through the 1921 and 1924 Quota Laws.[51] The net result, locally, was the creation of a huge transmigrant camp, a thirty-acre site with a capacity of up to 5000 utilising the buildings of a former United States naval airbase constructed during the First World War.[52] Atlantic Park was intended not only as a money-making enterprise where the aliens could wait for their ships but also as a place of detailed medical inspection by the British and American authorities. Indeed, the British government became worried about disease spreading through the 'use of undesirable and insanitary lodging houses and so-called hostels' housing the increasing number of stranded transmigrants, which they thought would lead to another epidemic.[53]

Hostels such as Atlantic Hotel were no longer enough to deal with the racial hygiene problem allegedly posed by the alien presence. The medical function of Atlantic Park came very much to the fore, employing bathing, de-lousing and detailed medical examinations. As the American consul, John Savage, emphasised in a detailed report (in which, significantly, the section on quarantine came first), on arrival at Atlantic Park each emigrant would be 'registered, cleansed and their baggage disinfected ... irrespective'.[54] Its commercial aims, however, were undermined as the shipping companies found themselves responsible for a group of over one thousand Ukrainians, mainly Jews but also some Menonites, who had been turned back from Ellis Island, caught in the web of the American quota system and British immigration control. These stranded Jews, in the words of Home Secretary William Joynson-Hicks, were the 'class of people ... we do not want, and America does not want them either'.[55]

John Savage described the medical inspection routine at Atlantic Park:

> Each passenger will be provided with a dressing room in which to disrobe, the clothing being immediately removed and placed in a canvas bag and treated in a disinfector while the emigrant is being bathed ... Numerous shower baths and a few bath tubs for special cases are provided, and after the bath has been taken the emigrant is then examined by the resident surgeon or one of his assistants to ascertain if the passenger is free of nits and lice. If found clean they will then be allowed to proceed to a second dressing room where the clothing which has been disinfected will be returned. In this section there is also a special room for the treatment of hair. If passengers are not found clean in every respect they will be detained in the quarantine section and the operation repeated as often as is found necessary.[56]

It is not surprising that the few fragmentary autobiographical accounts of Atlantic Park that have survived emphasise the impact of the medical inspections, especially the naked bathing examinations. Often so great was the traumatic memory that it was passed on to later generations. Cyril Orolowitz's mother, Liza Shleimowitz, then a thirteen-year-old orphan with her four sisters and young brother, having escaped civil war and pogroms in the Ukraine, was 'interned' at the camp. Cyril recalls his mother relating the misery caused by having her hair shaved and being sprayed with disinfecting water: the 'four sisters form[ed] a circle to protect their baby brother, Izzy, while they were being hosed down'. The children were to spend several years in the camp.[57] Similarly, Jacob Klassen, a Menonite, left Russia in 1926 and had an extended and unintended stay in Atlantic Park. His memoirs, from the point of departure from Russia, are dominated by medical inspection. At Riga he remembered the 'laundry, bathing, combing, disinfecting and most important, the eye examinations'. Arriving at the 'famous Atlantic Park', 'another examination was requested, [h]opefully the last'. It proved to be anything but – concern about possible trachoma, periods of quarantine, hospitalisation, and endless re-examinations extended Klassen and his family's stay at Atlantic Park, leading to massive disorientation. Eventually Jacob had to leave for Canada without his wife and youngest child.[58]

Experiences of people such as Liza Shleimowitz and Jacob Klassen have not got the attention they merit in studies of migration – it is significant that, to a longsuffering transmigrant like Jacob Klassen, Atlantic Park was 'famous' but that it has subsequently been subject to historical and popular amnesia. Studies of emigration have often been limited to official responses or crude statistics and, as a result, the humanity of those in transit has been sidelined or ignored. Historians and others would do well to recall the words of Mary Antin, who suffered the distress of medical inspections en route from Polotzk to Boston: 'The plight of the bewildered emigrant on the way to foreign parts is always pitiful enough, but for us who came from plague-ridden Russia the terrors of the way were doubled'.[59] Never properly explained and crudely executed, medical examinations and procedures were particularly frightening to the already dislocated transmigrants.

Atlantic Park came into existence in 1922 and finally closed down as a transmigrant camp in 1931. It was run by a consortium of the major shipping companies operating through Southampton, including Cunard, Canadian Pacific and the White Star Line with an initial investment of $650,000. Through the Aliens Restriction Act of 1919, Britain had introduced immigration policies that were both earlier and even more restrictionist than those in the USA. In a world of increasing nationalism and racism, western countries such as France that maintained a commitment to refugee asylum and a (partial) welcome to newcomers were the exception rather than the norm. As a result, Atlantic Park became a holding station for transmigrants with no place left to go. The lucrative enterprise hoped for by the shipping companies failed to materialise and it became a drain on their resources.[60]

Scale, and the link to international politics – several major conferences were held near the site to discuss the plight of transmigrants in the 1920s – make it surprising that public manifestations of Atlantic Park's memory have been so minimal. Indeed, the ease of amnesia in this case requires thorough explanation. The most obvious point is that the site was, similar to its earlier and much smaller counterpart, Atlantic Hotel, away from the public eye – although it was next to the London to Southampton railway line it was a mile from the nearest town, Eastleigh. In terms of immediate contact, it is significant that the few traces of local autobiographical writing referring to the camp have come from a schoolteacher who worked with the children of the camp and from a man whose first job was delivering vegetables to the kitchens.[61] A third example came from Geoffrey Harrison who was brought up on a farm that neighboured the camp. To him, the inhabitants of Atlantic Park were strange and exotic and therefore 'a particular magnet' to a young boy.[62]

Yet the physical obscurity of the camp as the explanation for its subsequent absence within national/local collective memory is not fully convincing. The case of the schoolteacher points to the fact that the children were (highly successfully) integrated into Eastleigh schools: 'The children were lively and intelligent and very quickly learnt to express themselves in English. I remember that the teenagers, having little else to do, used to write extremely long essays as homework, making many hours of marking for their teachers!'.[63] Youngsters from the Eastleigh district would have come across these transmigrant children through their education. Sporting teams from Atlantic Park also played in local leagues. Further pointing towards local knowledge and integration, in the mid-1920s, a float created by the residents of Atlantic Park won second prize at the Eastleigh Carnival. In many respects anticipating the work of Sam Smith, the transmigrants' entry was a ship dominated not by its physical size but by its passengers. Yet unlike Smith's later 'Southampton Water', it is the immigrants who are on the top deck, representing the myriad nationalities that had made up, and, they hoped, would continue to make up, the American population.[64]

A surviving photograph of the Atlantic Park float shows the transmigrants dressed up in various 'authentic' ethnic outfits.[65] Playing on stereotypes, the ship 'Atlantic Park' was both a parody of ethnicity as well as of the racial essentialism that had excluded them from the USA.[66] There was also a great subtlety at work using comedy to undermine the prevailing beliefs in national-racial certainties. In its quiet way, by presenting themselves, the victims of what at the end of their century would be referred to as 'ethnic cleansing', and part of what would be the world's largest refugee crisis until the Second World War, as clichéd immigrants, the float challenged the humour of their competitors, past and present, who freely indulged in 'blacking up'. Such crude representations had long roots in local culture. Specifically relating to the transmigrants, E. Temple Thurston's play, *The Wandering Jew*, was staged at Eastleigh's Variety Theatre in 1924. Based on the early modern image of the Jew who endures perpetual exile through his refusal to accept Jesus, the play starts with the message: 'To each his destiny – to each his Fate. We are wanderers in a foreign land between the furrow and the stars.'[67] The transmigrants on the Atlantic Park float were at one level pandering to local prejudices but at another turning round assumptions of them as eternal and damned nomads or as itinerant and dubious traders.

While the good ship Atlantic Park is being steered westwards across the Atlantic, America, its integration of immigrants is not presented as unproblematic. Two figures dominate the top deck. One is a kindly and jovial captain – perhaps a tribute to the sensitivity shown to the transmigrants by the multi-lingual and culturally adept superintendant of Atlantic Park, Colonel Barbor. The other is a well-drawn impersonation of Charlie Chaplin in his comedy, *The Immigrant* (1917), a film highlighting the limitations, loss and pathos of arriving in the 'promised land' as well as the hardship and dislocation of the journey itself.[68] The multi-layered meanings revealed in this float show the sophistication and knowledge of the transmigrants and the complex political messages that can underpin apparently straightforward local activities as manifested in this case by carnival. The rival Eastleigh Carnival floats presented by large capital in the area may have engaged in satire but they were hardly subversive. That of Atlantic Park temporarily brought the camp from the margins – as the world's 'unwanted' – into the heart of local society and put their plight of statelessness into the public domain. It also challenged the anodyne description of the site by the Cunard company as 'a fascinating township … the gateway of new hopes' and its frankly misleading suggestion that Atlantic Park was simply 'a big hotel'.[69]

As has been noted, the United States was not alone in imposing racist restrictionism in the 1920s. The British government refused to give permission for those stranded at Atlantic Park to settle as had been requested by several more progressive Anglo-Jewish organisations.[70] Nevertheless, the transmigrants exempted their temporary host government from overt criticism. The transmigrants on the carnival ship represented themselves as a microcosm of the League of Nations with a plethora of flags displayed (but, significantly, without the Stars and Stripes). Yet amidst this internationalism of flag bearing, by far the most prominent and numerous was the Union Jack which festooned the ship and was worn with apparent pride by the various ethnicities on board. Such a manifestation of patriotism could be dismissed as a necessary gesture away from cosmopolitanism. It could curry favour in the carnival competition by emphasising local loyalty and thereby counter prejudice against the transmigrants as utterly alien. There is, however, no evidence of any animosity shown by the transmigrants towards the British state or British culture as a whole throughout Atlantic Park's existence.

In January 1925 there was a hunger strike against the monotonous food in the camp, which was surely one of the shortest but most effective fasts in the twentieth century. It ended at tea when peckishness overcame principle. Remarkably, in spite of only missing breakfast and lunch, the transmigrants managed to get their grievances aired across the world's media. As Colonel Barbor, ever sympathetic, suggested, the hunger strike was not, at root cause, 'a question of fish and eggs. To my mind it is much more a matter of psychology. These unfortunate people, for whom I have a very real sympathy, have been here over a year, and naturally despairing of ever reaching their goal – the United States'.[71]

As manifested in the carnival float and the hunger strike, it was America and not Britain that was the major source of the transmigrants' anger and it was hoped that the latter would force the former into accepting their entry. In June 1924 an international delegation visited Atlantic Park and were met by 'two humorously-garbed transmigrants ... with placards on their backs announcing themselves as "Lord and Lady Ellis Island"'.[72] In contrast to their dismay at America – many had been turned back on reaching Ellis Island – there seems to have been genuine affection for Barbor and, more generally, for Britain and British culture as a whole amongst the transmigrants. Proving that the game has no natural boundaries, Barbor, a Dubliner, successfully introduced cricket to the Ukrainian Jews, Menonites and other nationalities and minorities that made up Atlantic Park.[73]

The surviving schoolbooks from Atlantic Park of Liza Shleimowitz, then a thirteen-year-old orphan of Ukrainian pogroms, include the lovingly copied words of Wordsworth's poem 'Lucy'.[74] Liza's engagement with the English education she experienced at Atlantic Park clearly mattered to her – indeed, she kept her school notebooks for the rest of her life. It has been suggested that at Atlantic Park the transmigrants 'adopted a British way of life', amongst other things visiting the shops [and] going to the pictures'.[75] This is certainly true, although it needs to be set alongside other layers of identity made manifest through the transmigrants' strong interest in, amongst others, Russian, Jewish and American cultures.

It is clear from their Carnival Float, hunger strikes and protests to international delegates that the transmigrants were far from passive victims, no matter how tedious their years in the camp. They did their best to make the most of their time in Atlantic Park and took with them positive memories of the place alongside the frustrations they undoubtedly experienced. Births, marriages and deaths took place in the camp and bonds were formed that lasted beyond Britain. When the camp was officially closed in 1931 it was reported that 'After reaching the States, the immigrants formed the Atlantic Park Club of New York, where they held periodical reunions'.[76] It is ironic that the memory of the camp should have been concentrated in the country that had attempted to exclude the transmigrants rather than the country that had provided them with a home for the better part of a decade. Subsequently, its memory has rested in piecemeal form through the individual detective work of the diasporic descendants of Atlantic Park who managed to find refuge in countries such as Canada and South Africa.[77] In Britain, whether locally or nationally, there has been almost total silence, reflecting a resistance to fit the history of Atlantic Park within wider narratives. A further irony is provided in Atlantic Park's labelling both at the time and subsequently as the 'British Ellis Island' or 'An "Ellis Island" in Hampshire'.[78] Accurate in its way, such naming has *not* been to expose immigration control and restriction in Britain during the 1920s but to highlight that of the USA. Within its dominant narrative, Britain is not a country of immigrants, but, because of its self (and external) image as fair and decent, it is also imagined as a nation without discriminatory controls of entry, thus confirming the 'myths we live by'.[79]

When reference has been made to Atlantic Park in 'official' local memory, the inaccuracies in detail have been revealing. Two more prominent examples will be analysed to reveal how they have been geographically accurate but chronologically out of time. The first is through the autobiography of Sir Sidney Kimber, a figure who dominated the political life of inter-war Southampton and, more than anyone, shaped its landscape and direction before the town was wrecked by the blitz. Published in 1949, Kimber devoted one chapter of his work to the development of the municipal airport during the 1930s. In what was a chronological and apparently factual narrative, Kimber stated that

> In 1931, the Corporation was offered the 30 acres adjoining the Aerodrome Land, known as Atlantic Park Hostel, which had been used by the Cunard and White Star and other shipping companies as a transmigrant station during the war, and was complete with hangars and other buildings.[80]

The second example comes half a century later, when Eastleigh Borough Council's Highways and Works Committee agreed to call a small street in a new housing estate close to the airport 'Atlantic Park'. In explaining the naming, the Council explained that 'Southampton International Airport was originally known as Atlantic Park during the war when Spitfires were actually constructed there and it was thought appropriate that as the airfield could be seen from the estate, that name should be used.'[81]

Maurice Halbwachs, when exploring 'Localization' within his seminal *On Collective Memory*, argued that

> What makes recent memories hang together is not that they are continuous in time: it is rather that they are part of a totality of thoughts common to a group, the group of people with whom we have a relation at the moment ... To recall them it is hence sufficient that we place ourselves in the perspective of this group, that we adopt its interests and follow the slant of its reflections.

As Halbwachs adds, 'Exactly the same process occurs when we attempt to localize older memories'.[82] Atlantic Park has a place in local collective memory, but it is not because of its internationally significant role as a transmigrant camp. Instead, the site of the camp is referred to as part of the history of the airport, and more specifically its importance relates to the relationship to the Spitfire fighter plane which was first flown from what was still known as Atlantic Park in 1936. For Kimber, placing the transmigrant camp in the First World War removed any need to see it as part of the 'normal' peacetime world of Southampton in which he made such an impact. For those responsible in the ever-controversial task of local street naming, it was easier to subsume Atlantic Park into the overwhelming narrative of the Second World War and the pivotal role of the Spitfire within it. In both processes, the need for chronological cohesion within local memory work has been at the expense of the actual history and significance of Atlantic Park.

What is particularly fascinating in the case of the street naming is how two icons of local memory became interwoven and confused and how other possible readings of local history and memory were not considered. The goal of the local West End Parish Council was to have names that recognised 'the proximity of the Airport' or to have 'a West End and seafaring connection'. The naming was thus divided into two. First, 'ATLANTIC PARK was the original name of the Airport and MITCHELL, SPITFIRE, MERLIN and BROWNING are in recognition of the Spitfire which was built there.' Second, 'West End has a seafaring connection with the Titanic disaster. The captain of the CARPATHIA the ship which rescued many of the survivors, Captain ROSTON, is bured in West End. Captain SHAW was in command of the Titanic.'[83] That Atlantic Park had an intimate 'seafaring connection' was lost on the local council. Such active processes of forgetting take us back to the testimony of Allen Robinson, the grocer's delivery boy of the 1920s. Robinson also remembers the child refugees from the Spanish Civil War who in 1937 were settled in a camp a short walk from Atlantic Park. At the end of his brief memoir, he concludes that 'There is so much history in the Eastleigh and Bishopstoke districts and we older people like to look back on it all. The Russian and Basque refugees are just part of that history.'[84] Alas, when Atlantic Park's origins are forced into the Second World War, its history and local memories, such as that of Allen Robinson, are denied. Even the international diplomatic connections of Atlantic Park have been lost sight of. As noted in Chapter 6, the Townhill Park estate had been bought by Lord Swaythling, Liberal politician and prominent member of British Jewry, in the late nineteenth century. In 1924, the second international conference on post-war migration was hosted by the Swaythlings at Townhill Park, which included a visit to Atlantic Park. A year later, the second Lord Swaythling's wife wrote an open letter to the American President protesting about the continued refusal to let the transmigrants of Atlantic Park into his country. The transmigrants responded to this gesture in deep gratitude and pathos: 'you were the first to call upon the conscience of the people who inconsiderately caused us so much pain and grief and made us spend a considerable portion of our lives in great agony and despair'.[85]

The street naming in 1990 reflected the last opportunity to represent the history of Atlantic Park and the presence and activities of the Swaythling family as it was 'the final area on [the] Townhill Farm Estate [that was] now under construction'.[86] But the very idea of connecting up, through the common theme of refugee movements and transmigrancy, the story of the *Titanic* with that of Atlantic Park was (and continues to be) too alien to have been considered, let alone accepted. The memory work directly associated with Southampton International Airport confirms such processes of inclusion and exclusion.

In 1994 the new airport building in Southampton was officially opened. The old hangars which had housed first the American airforce, then the transmigrants and finally the Municipal Airport, were demolished. All traces of the transmigrant camp were thus destroyed although there was brief mention of its existence in an exhibition area created in the new airport building and located in the viewers' gallery:

> 1921: The buildings were acquired by a shipping consortium, renamed Atlantic Park Hostel, and used by European migrants bound for the USA.

> By the late 1920s national interest in municipal airports was growing. Southampton City Corporation purchased 100 acres of land adjacent to the Hostel and officially opened the Airport in 1932.

The majority of the display, however, was devoted to the development of the Spitfire in the 1930s.[87] The brainchild of Reginald Mitchell, chief engineer of the Southampton company, Supermarine, its test flight took place in Atlantic Park in 1936. A year later Mitchell, who had been seriously ill when the Spitfire was first flown, died of cancer. After his death, the Spitfire was constructed at the Supermarine works in the suburb of Woolston, overlooking Southampton's outer docks.

Since the late 1990s, the historical display at Southampton International Airport has been withdrawn and replaced by memorials and original documentation relating only to the Spitfire. In autumn 2003 a replica Spitfire was unveiled just outside the airport on a roundabout on its approach road, Mitchell Way. The replica attested to the plane's dominance in local memory and the literal wiping out of any rival histories of the site that might have complicated the narrative of the Spitfire.[88] In proposals to develop the airport site in the late 1980s, the slogan 'Pride in the Past, Confidence in the Future' was coined – the 'past' being illustrated by a Spitfire.[89] The powerful status of Spitfire memory more generally in Southampton was confirmed in 2000 with the sixtieth anniversary commemorations of the Battle of Britain.

Southampton pronounced itself as 'Proud Home of the Spitfire: Famous throughout the world as the "Port of Ocean Queens", the City ... is also rightly proud of being the home of the nation-saving Vickers-Supermarine Spitfire'.[90] In June 2000, 'Sea Wings', the climax of local commemorations of the Battle of Britain, was attended by over one hundred thousand visitors with an estimated quarter of a million people seeing the display. The central feature was the presence of thirteen Spitfires which had taken off from their spiritual home in the airport, the display concluding with a solitary fly past accompanied by a requiem.[91]

Southampton's identification with the Spitfire and R. J. Mitchell is not surprising: in the words of the first semi-official account of its history, written by John Taylor and Maurice Allward, and published in 1946: 'This is the story of the most famous aeroplane the world has ever known'. But as they added, 'It is also the story of the achievement of a great people walking together in the greatest of all causes – the cause of freedom and justice'.[92] As with the *Titanic*, the local impact of the Spitfire has been highlighted in memorialisation in Southampton and its region. This memory work has been partly made through the recognition of the devastating air raid on the Supermarine factory in September 1940 that left over one hundred of its workers dead. It has mainly been manifest, however, through the Mitchell connection. The Southampton Hall of Aviation was originally titled the R. J. Mitchell Museum and the memorial function to Mitchell is still dominant within it. Mitchell moved to Southampton during the First World War and spent the rest of his life there. He died and was buried in the town. In spite of his Potteries roots, as the local newspaper has stated, 'He has good claim to being the greatest ever Sotonian'.[93]

The Mitchell story and that of the Spitfire generally have intense mythical power and resonance. It was recognised in the war itself in the film *The First of the Few* (1942), directed by and starring Leslie Howard as the hero, R. J. Mitchell. Mitchell's self-sacrifice and gentle patriotism was the main focus of the film. Indeed, in *The First of the Few* he becomes symbolic of the later Battle of Britain – physically weak, he is mentally strong and 'always fighting' and ultimately victorious, even in death. The film also included explicit references to Southampton – no town, as the local newspaper emphasised 'has a more intimate interest'.[94]

Spitfire narratives have often incorporated a spiritual and often explicitly Christian discourse: 'The Spitfire Funds were like altars at which the man, woman and child in the back lines could light a candle for the men fighting in the nation's fight in the front line'.[95] Mitchell has been portrayed as Christ-like in his self-sacrifice, dying to make the world a better place and as an example to others: 'He has the finest memorial any man could wish for, he lives in the minds of those among whom and for whom he lived'.[96] In Bernard Knowles's *Southampton: The English Gateway* (1951), locally commissioned by the council to commemorate the town's efforts during the Second World War, the Spitfire's role is both God-given and described as being part of a seamless garment of quintessential Britishness. In the dark days of 1940

> as every Englishman realized, the time had now come when that particular responsibility must be borne in part by the little Southampton-built fighter-plane. Because of this, the *Spitfire*, like the Navy, touched 'mystic chords in the English breast that went deeper than reason'. Like the sight of a rolling Jack Tar or of a grey battleship at sea, the spectacle of a *Spitfire* in flight had for the Britisher 'the power of a trumpet call'.[97]

Knowles's national-religious framing of the Spitfire went alongside an equally powerful evocation of an essential nautical reading of the British past, adding another layer of mythology to the plane.

It has been noted in Chapter 4 of this study that maritime identities have been 'constructed and reinvented over the centuries as part of that complex creature that is "Britishness"'.[98] The Spitfire, with its roots in Mitchell's earlier design work in developing the sea plane, could be incorporated into an older mythology as well as bringing its own unique history into play. The complexity of melding sea, land and air was achieved by instrumentalising the historic maritime place identities of Southampton's recent and distant past:

> The waters from Southampton down to the Solent, which had seen so much historic progress – from the oak ships of Buckler's Hard [where Henry VIII's fleet was built] to the liners of the thirties – were now to cradle the finest and fastest flying machine ever built by man.[99]

So far, however, there has been no space within the narrative of this legend – internationally, nationally or locally – to include either the close pre-history of Atlantic Park in which it was first flown, and thereby a direct link to the transmigrants of inter-war Southampton, or the dubious anti-alien origins of Supermarine through the figure of its founder, Noel Pemberton-Billing, described in the local heritage world as 'eccentric'[100] but more accurately labelled by Philip Hoare as a 'proto-fascist'.[101] Ultimately, the myth of the Spitfire concerns an intense battle over memory and identity. Knowles used the example of Southampton's Spitfire to show that 'personal, even mystic, sense of duty which is part of the Englishman's heritage', highlighting his theme further through utilising Wordsworth:

> It is not to be thought of that the Flood
> Of British freedom, which, to the open sea

Of the world's praise, from dark antiquity
Hath flow'd, 'with pomp of waters, unwithstood'
[...]
We must be free or die, who speak the tongue
That Shakespeare spake; the faith and morals hold
Which Milton held.[102]

Through Atlantic Park, however, and the schoolbooks of a young girl, Liza Shleimowitz (who had witnessed the massacre of her parents, and the harshness of a post-war world in which there was no place for the dispossessed), we have seen how Wordsworth's poetry could reach an audience and to have a resonance that Knowles's insular vision of Englishness simply could not imagine.

Conclusion

On one level, Southampton's collective forgetting of migration and transmigrancy within its past simply mirrors that on a national level. Yet, at another, the very richness and, indeed, in the case of Atlantic Park, the uniqueness of this past points towards a particularly local process of amnesia. It might be suggested that Southampton, which experienced fast growth from the nineteenth century but lacked the internal capital to develop a strong civic culture and historical infrastructure, has not had the self-confidence to embrace past heterogenity. Instead, it has embraced and instrumentalised the memory of the iconic *Titanic* and Spitfire narrowly and exclusively as its principal blocks of memory building. In turn, the absence of physical reminders of migrancy and transmigrancy has hindered more inclusive memory work. As a black British artist, Lubaina Himid has stated with regard to her attempts to commemorate slavery at a national and local level:

> I was trying to find a way to talk of a thing that is not there, sort of *Inside the Invisible* if you like. I am interested in the politics of representation, how when something is there you can talk about it, write about it, paint about it, but when something isn't there what can you say, how can you make something of it, how can it not have been in vain, if you like. [My] idea for memorialising came from trying to visualize the invisible.[103]

Philip Hoare has become the most sophisticated interpreter of local memory in the Southampton region, especially through his work *Spike Island* (2001) on the Royal Victoria Military Hospital at Netley. In none of his works has he referred to Atlantic Park, highlighting again its obscurity and confirming Himid's fears concerning amnesia of the invisible. Significantly, however, the memory of the *American* Ellis Island *is* called upon throughout

Spike Island. At one point Hoare makes a direct comparison between the Royal Military Hospital and Ellis Island:

> The great brick hospital on the shore had become an imperial processing plant, its raw material – its patients – arriving by sea to be admitted into its interior, like the red-brick buildings of Ellis Island in New York Harbour, to which it bore both stylistic and functional similarities. Both were insular buildings invested with hope and fear, fraught with medical and bureaucratic decisions on human destinies; individuals catalogued and assessed as they arrived from foreign lands.[104]

Hoare's inability to make a more straightforward comparison between a site of memory in Hampshire and Ellis Island – that of Atlantic Park – reflects not individual failure: *Spike Island* is a work of some genius. Instead, it exposes the exclusionary power of national mythologies and the absence of a sociology and anthropology of knowledge that could bring Atlantic Park alongside Royal Victoria Military Hospital or its near neighbour, Netley Abbey, into shared landscapes of memory. Hoare's remarkable local memory work reveals the use and abuse of medical science when confronted with the trauma of war and dislocation. In this respect a further connection is made with Atlantic Park.

The medical historian Paul Weindling, referring to de-lousing in the mid-twentieth century, writes that it has

> a prehistory in the more generalised medical screening of transmigrants from the East, as they made their way via such ports as Bremen and Hamburg, Antwerp and Liverpool to Ellis Island: here we find a sequence of routines imposed under different state regulatory systems on suspect ethnic carriers of 'Asiatic' epidemics like cholera, trachoma and typhus.[105]

His list of ports is selective but could easily, as revealed in this chapter, have included Southampton. We need to add to the imaginative work of Antony Sher and the detailed research of Paul Weindling the knowledge that ports such as Southampton in Britain were part of a racial hygiene process that had, by the 1920s, through its local and national contributions, become truly internationalised and cross-pollinating. Hamburg, Bremen, Libau, Antwerp, New York but also Southampton were thus at the forefront of the inspection of alien Jews which moved from tentative steps to extreme and harrowing medical intervention, and adding to the misery of increasing numbers of stateless people. The worldwide port medical inspection of transmigrants thus needs to be added to the overall story of Port Jews such as those of Portsmouth and Southampton. Indeed, in many respects such medical intervention provided a perverse mirror image of the Port Jew: a mutually reinforcing global network of modernised expertise to stop the free flow of people.

This chapter has been equally if not more concerned about the processes of amnesia as those of remembering. 'Forgetting', to repeat Jonathan
Boyarin's observation again, can be 'a technique of the dominated, used to
enable memory'.[106] Boyarin suggests that 'more has been forgotten in and
about the Jewish Lower East Side than virtually any other place or time in
America'.[107] Southampton was never the East End of London, let alone the
Lower East Side of New York, yet it still has played a crucial role in the history of world migration and, increasingly, attempts to halt such movements.
The analysis of local memory work in relation to transmigrancy reveals how
it is not so much the past that is exposed as a foreign country. It is more that
foreignness itself has been perceived as alien to the past.

In relation to the places featured so far in *Anglo-Jewry since 1066*, transmigrancy in the late nineteenth century became increasingly focused on the
port of Southampton. By the 1920s, and the closing of the west, Atlantic
Park was a unique symbol in Britain and beyond of the ending of transmigrancy. How did the Jews of Southampton respond to its Jewish neighbours in the camp? As part of its general strategy to gain local acceptance,
the established Jewish community in the late Victorian era had done its best
to dissuade Jews without means from settling in the area. But the growth
of transmigrancy, and Southampton's increasing importance in the trade,
made this objective increasingly hard to achieve. In 1905 the secretary of the
Hebrew Congregation, Nathan Levy, wrote to the *Jewish Chronicle* to revoke
a charge that had been made in the *Empire Review* by a leading anti-alienist,
C. Kinloch Cooke. Cooke had stated that he remembered

> a batch of Jewish immigrants being sent back from the United States and landing
> at Southampton. These aliens were taken to the workhouse, as they had no money
> to support themselves, and neither their co-religionists nor fellow countrymen
> would come to their aid.[108]

Levy responded that, in fact, the Southampton Hebrew Congregation 'had always made it a special duty to see after poor Jewish emigrants or immigrants'.
Levy gave an example of ten poor Russian Jews arriving from America on
board the *St Louis*. 'We provided for their immediate needs and on Monday
paid their railway fare to their destination'. Significantly, Levy argued that
anyone still believing this 'libel on the Jews of Southampton' should seek
the truth from the chairman of the Southampton Board of Guardians, the
master of the workhouse or the Chief Constable of the town. Jewish transmigrants slipping through the net were, it is clear, in the mind of local government, the responsibility of the local Jewish community. The task of the
Jewish community was to send them onwards as humanely but as quickly as
possible. As Levy put it: 'We have the greatest difficulty in providing means

for these poor men, who are hunted from pillar to post, and who appeal to us so strongly for sympathy and help.'[109]

In respect of its place identity, the leaders of the Southampton Hebrew Congregation behaved, with good reason, as if its acceptance was dependent on keeping the required distance from the floating Jews who were largely out of sight. For a small community they did their best to ensure that on a temporary basis the transmigrants' immediate needs were met, but on condition that they did not settle permanently. This strategy largely worked. In 1905, at the height of the aliens debate, it was remarked that those of longstanding connections to Southampton, which typified many of the senior officers within the Hebrew Congregation, 'were very desirable citizens'.[110]

As has been illustrated in Chapter 6, during and after the First World War a sea-change occurred in the Hebrew Congregation which was now dominated by east European Jews and their descendants. A much more sympathetic response from the Jewish community was forthcoming to the stranded Ukrainians of Atlantic Park than had been afforded to transmigrants before 1914. Help was provided, through the creation of a synagogue Transmigration Committee, for life-cycle events, including marriages in the camp and burials in the local Jewish cemetery.[111] Yet in spite of Jewish efforts locally and nationally, the government refused to let these victims of oppression and restrictionism settle in Britain. Atlantic Park was thus a symbol of how east European Jewish immigration, and transmigrancy with it, had come to an end. The inter-war period, however, was to witness the continued movement of those of east European origin *within* Britain, and the coastal towns of Hampshire were to be part of that population flux. Having outlined here the forgotten history of transmigrancy, the final chapter of this study will explore the equally neglected story of first- and second-generation east European Jews and their search, within inter-war Britain, for a place called home.

Notes

1 See A. Temple Patterson, *A History of Southampton 1700–1914* vol. 3 (Southampton: University of Southampton Press, 1975), Chapter 9.
2 Nicholas Evans, 'Aliens *En Route*: European Transmigration Through Britain, 1836–1914' (unpublished Ph.D. thesis, University of Hull, 2006), pp. 82, 259.
3 Despatch from US Consul in Southampton, 27 November 1905, microfilm, University of Southampton library.
4 Evans, 'Aliens *en route*', p. 108.
5 M. J. Landa, *The Alien Problem and Its Remedy* (London: P. S. King, 1911), pp. 54–5.
6 *Jewish Chronicle*, 26 November 1886.
7 Telford Varley, *Hampshire* (London: Adam and Charles Black, 1909), p. 256.
8 *Southampton City View* no. 38 (August/September 2006), p. 10.

9 Jonathan Boyarin, *Storm from Paradise: The Politics of Jewish Memory* (Minneapolis, 1992), pp. 1, 2.

10 Especially through the Wilson Line. See the research of Nicholas Evans reported in *Jewish Chronicle*, 13 July 2001.

11 *Southampton Times*, 11 November 1893.

12 Ibid.

13 United States Diplomatic Records: Despatches from the US Consul in Southampton 1790–196 (T239) vol. 8, minutes and correspondence, March–April 1893.

14 John Higham, *Strangers in the Land: Patterns of American Natavism 1860–1925* (New York: Atheneum, 1978), pp. 99–100; Howard Markel, *Quarantine! East European Jewish Immigrants and the City Epidemics of 1892* (Baltimore: Johns Hopkins University Press, 1997); Richard Evans, *Death in Hamburg: Society and Politics in the Cholera Years, 1830–1910* (Oxford: Clarendon Press, 1987), Chapter 4.

15 Annual Report for the Port of Southampton, 1910, in Southampton Record Office (SRO), SC/HI/32a.

16 A. Wellesley Harris, 'A Detailed Report on the Precautions Adopted by the Southampton Port Sanitary Authority Against the Importation of Cholera' (1892) in SRO, SC/H/1/16. More generally, see Krista Maglen, '"The First Line of Defence": British Quarantine and the Port Sanitary Authorities in the Nineteenth Century', *Social History of Medicine* vol. 15 no. 3 (2002), pp. 413–28.

17 Minutes of the Association of Port Sanitary Authorities, 19 August 1902, in SRO SC/H/24/9/1.

18 See the *Annual Reports of the Port of Southampton* from 1893–1905 and United States Diplomatic Records, Despatches from US Consuls in Southampton 1790–1906, reports from Albert Swalm, 9 August 1904 and 27 November 1905 and the description of Swalm in *The Syren and Shipping*, 15 March 1905. On the concern about trachoma in America, see Howard Markel, '"The Eyes Have It": Trachoma, the Perception of Disease, the United States Public Health Service, and the American Jewish Immigration Experience, 1897–1924', *Bulletin of the History of Medicine* vol. 74 (2000), pp. 525–60.

19 Swalm report, 8 December 1905 in US Consul Records.

20 *Aliens Act, 1905* (11 August 1905, 5 EDW.7). More generally see Bernard Gainer, *The Alien Invasion: The Origins of the Aliens Act of 1905* (London: Heinemann, 1972) and Bernard Harris, 'Anti-Alienism, Health and Social Reform in Late Victorian and Edwardian Britain', *Patterns of Prejudice* vol. 31 no. 4 (1997), pp. 3–34.

21 *Annual Report on the Port of Southampton for the Year 1907* in SRO SC/H/1/16.

22 Bernard Harris, 'Pro-alienism, Anti-alienism and the Medical Profession in Late-Victorian and Edwardian Britain', in Waltraud Ernst and Bernard Harris (eds), *Race, Science and Medicine, 1700–1960* (London: Routledge, 1999), p. 209. For a local study, see Kenneth Collins, *Be Well! Jewish Immigrant Health and Welfare in Glasgow, 1860–1914* (East Linton: Tuckwell Press, 2001), Chapters 4 and 5.

23 See the annual reports on the port of Southampton for the 1890s and 1900s.

24 Testimony in Southampton City Heritage, Oral History collection and reproduced in Donald Hyslop, Alastair Forsyth and Sheila Jemima, *Titanic Voices* (Southampton: Southampton City Council, 1994), p. 175.

25 Hyslop et al., *Titanic Voices*, p. 175.

26 See the testimonies of the Farber family, Manchester Jewish Museum, J82 and J201.

27 Clarissa Hyman, *The Jewish Kitchen* (London: Conran Octopus, 2003), p. 152.

28 On its opening and objectives see *Manchester Metropolitan News*, 12 April 2002; *Guardian*,

18 June and 1 July 2002; Urbis Museum, Manchester, viewed by the author in 2002.

29 Telephone conversation with Enfields Residential letting service, 22 September 2000; adverts for Atlantic Mansions in *Southern Property Advertiser*, 21 September 2000 and 25 July 2002 and www.southampton-property.com/let_oceanvillage.html, accessed 29 July 2002.

30 Boyarin, *Storm from Paradise*, p. 5.

31 Donald Hyslop and Sheila Jemima, 'The "Titanic" and Southampton: The Oral Evidence', *Oral History* vol. 19 no. 1 (spring 1991), p. 41.

32 'Home Fit for the "New Life" Seekers', *Southern Evening Echo*, 24 February 1989; Alan Leonard and Rodney Baker, *A Maritime History of Southampton in Picture Postcards* (Southampton: Endsign Publications, 1989), p. 38; Peter and Jan Boyd-Smith, *Southampton in Focus* (Southampton: Steamship Publications, 1996), p. 27.

33 See his entry in Southampton Hebrew Congregation, Ledger, 1927.

34 *A Defence of the Alien Immigrant* (London: London Committee of the Deputies of British Jews, 1904), p. 9.

35 *Southern Echo*, 22 April 1893.

36 *Standard*, 2 January 1906. I am grateful to Greg Smart, a doctoral student at Southampton, for this reference.

37 *Southampton Times*, 22 April 1905.

38 James Guimond, 'The *Titanic* and the Commodification of Catastrophe', in Peter Gray and Kendrick Oliver (eds), *The Memory of Catastrophe* (Manchester: Manchester University Press, 2004), p. 79.

39 See Hyslop et al., *Titanic Voices*; Hyslop and Jemima, 'The "Titanic"', pp. 37–43, esp. p. 37; Anne Massey and Mike Hammond, '"It was True! How Can You Laugh?": History and Memory in the Reception of *Titanic* in Britain and Southampton', in Kevin Sandler and Gaylyn Studlar (eds), *Titanic: Anatomy of a Blockbuster* (New Brunswick, NJ: Rutgers University Press, 1999), pp. 239–64; and Michael Hammond, '"My Poor Brave Men" – Time, Space and Gender in Southampton's Memory of the Titanic', in Tim Bergfelder and Sarah Street (eds), *The Titanic in Myth and Memory: Representations in Visual and Literary Culture* (London: I. B. Tauris, 2004), pp. 25–36.

40 Steven Biel, *Down With the Old Canoe: A Cultural History of the Titanic Disaster* (New York: Norton, 1996), p. 6.

41 Ibid., pp. 46–53.

42 John Wilson Foster, *The Titanic Complex: A Cultural Manifest* (Vancouver: Belcouver Press, 1997), p. 34.

43 Hyslop and Jemima, 'The "Titanic"', p. 37.

44 Biel, *Down With the Old Canoe*, p. 124.

45 Liisa Malkki, 'National Geographic: The Rooting of Peoples and the Territorialization of National Identity among Scholars and Refugees', *Cultural Anthropology* vol. 7 no. 1 (February 1992), p. 34.

46 'Sam Smith: "Southampton Water" and Other Objects Made by Sam', Southampton City Art Gallery leaflet, no date.

47 Ibid.

48 Antony Sher, *Middlepost* (London: Chatto & Windus, 1988), p. 21.

49 Ibid., p. 21. Sher's origins were similar to that of the principal character. See his autobiography, *Beside Myself* (London: Arrow Books, 2001). A powerful testimony of a Lithuanian Jewish immigrant who contracted trachoma in the port of Libau and had to spend six months in a hostel recovering, before being detained for the same reason in London, is provided in Bernard Sachs, *Mist of Memory* (London: Vallentine Mitchell, 1973), pp. 46–9.

50 'The Aliens Order, 1920, Instructions to Medical Inspectors' in SRO SC/H 24/9.

51 Higham, *Strangers in the Land*, Chapter 11.

52 For its full history, see Tony Kushner and Katharine Knox, *Refugees in an Age of Genocide: Global, National and Local Perspectives during the Twentieth Century* (London: Frank Cass, 1999), Chapter 3.

53 Jews' Temporary Shelter, *Thirty-Third Report for the Year Ending October 31st, 1922* (London: Chas.Knight and Co., 1923), p. 8.

54 Report of John M. Savage, 27 January 1922 in Department of State, National Archives, Washington, DC (NA), 841.56/15.

55 Joynson-Hicks in *Hansard* (HC) vol. 180 cols. 313–14 (11 February 1925).

56 Savage report, 27 January 1922.

57 Cyril Orolowitz, interview with the author, Southampton, 1 June 1994.

58 Jacob Klassen, 'A Historical Autobiographical Sketch', translated by his great-granddaughter, Barbara Bradshaw, in the possession of the author.

59 Mary Antin, *The Promised Land* (Princeton: Princeton University Press, 1969 [orig.1912]), pp. 174–5.

60 Kushner and Knox, *Refugees in an Age of Genocide*, Chapter 3.

61 *Hampshire: The County Magazine* vol. 11 no. 8 (June 1971), p. 34, letter from Winifred Dominy who relates how she 'began my teaching career with the emigrant children who spoke very little English'. Allan Robinson was a teenager who delivered groceries to Atlantic Park. See his 'Refugees at Atlantic Park, 1920, and North Stoneham, 1937', *Eastleigh & District Local History Society* Special Paper no. 20 (1991) and also letter to Katharine Knox, 1 May 1995 in author's possession.

62 Geoffrey Harrison, *To Be a Farmer's Boy* (Southampton: G.Harrison, 1997), pp. 80–1.

63 Winifred Dominy in *Hampshire: the County Magazine* vol. 11 no. 8 (June 1971), p. 34.

64 It is reproduced in John Edgar Mann, *The Book of the Stonehams* (Tiveton, Devon: Halsgrave, 2002), p. 29.

65 Ibid.

66 Walter Mills, '100 Years of Carnival', *Eastleigh & District Local History Society* Occasional Paper no. 22 (1987).

67 See the advert for the play in *Eastleigh Weekly News*, 28 December 1923 and for a summary of its plot, Joseph Gaer, *The Legend of The Wandering Jew* (New York: Mentor Books, 1961), pp. 140–1.

68 For the film's origins, see Charles Chaplin, *My Autobiography* (London: Bodley Head, 1964), p. 225.

69 *Cunard Magazine* vol. 12 no. 3 (March 1924), p. 88.

70 Kushner and Knox, *Refugees in an Age of Genocide*, pp. 83, 89–90.

71 *Jewish Chronicle*, 9 January and 6 February 1925; *Daily Herald*, 7 and 8 January 1925 for coverage of the hunger strike.

72 *Southern Daily Echo*, 4 June 1924.

73 Kushner and Knox, *Refugees in an Age of Genocide*, p. 94.

74 In the possession of her son, Cyril Orolowitz, Cape Town.

75 Peter New, 'Atlantic Park', *Hampshire: The County Magazine* vol. 11 no. 6 (April 1971), p. 26.

76 *Eastleigh Weekly News*, 2 October 1931.

77 I have been contacted by relatives of those at Atlantic Park from a variety of countries, all trying to piece together their fragmented and dislocated family histories.

78 See, for example, the headline of *Daily News*, 7 January 1925: 'Hunger Strike By 700 Jews:

Complaints at British Ellis Island'; *Southern Daily Echo*, 21 February 2003 and Mann, *The Book of the Stonehams*, p. 27.

79 Raphael Samuel and Paul Thompson (eds), *The Myths We Live By* (London: Routledge, 1990).

80 Sir Sidney Kimber, *Thirty-Eight Years of Public Life in Southampton 1910–1948* (Southampton: no publisher, 1949), p. 169.

81 Eastleigh Borough Council Highway and Works Committee, 22 January 1990 'Naming of Streets Townhill Farm Estate'; Carolyn Dwyer, Principal Engineer, letter to the author, 18 June 1996.

82 Maurice Halbwachs, *On Collective Memory*, edited and translated by Lewis Coser (Chicago: University of Chicago Press, 1992), p. 52.

83 Eastleigh Borough Council, Highway and Works Committee, 22 January 1990.

84 Robinson, 'Refugees at Atlantic Park', p. 5.

85 *Southern Daily Echo*, 4 and 14 June 1924; *Eastleigh Weekly News*, 13 February 1925.

86 Eastleigh Borough Council Highway and Works Committee, 22 January 1990.

87 Author site visits to Southampton International Airport through the 1990s and early 2000s.

88 The near full-sized replica was designed and created by a local artist, Alan Manning, and it was unveiled in September 2003 as part of the programme of events 'History, Heritage and the Hamble Valley' sponsored by Eastleigh Borough Council and the Heritage Lottery Fund. See the *Festival Programme* (Eastleigh: no publisher, 2003).

89 'The Development of Eastleigh Airport', leaflet in Cope Library, University of Southampton Hartley Library.

90 *Spitfire: A 60th Anniversary Tribute by the City of Southampton* (Southampton, 2000).

91 *Southern Daily Echo*, 5 June 2000.

92 John W.R. Taylor and Maurice Allward, *Spitfire* (Leicester: Harborough Publishing Co., 1946), p. 7.

93 *Southern Daily Echo*, 10 July 2004.

94 *Southern Daily Echo*, 20 and 22 August 1942.

95 Gordon Beckles, *Birth of a Spitfire* (London: Collins, 1941), pp. 108, 130.

96 Ibid., p. 15.

97 Bernard Knowles, *Southampton: The English Gateway* (London: Hutchinson, 1951), p. 144.

98 Ken Lunn and Ann Day, 'Britain as Island: National Identity and the Sea', in Helen Brocklehurst and Robert Phillips (eds), *History, Nationhood and the Question of Britain* (Basingstoke, 2004), p. 126.

99 Beckles, *Birth of a Spitfire*, p. 74.

100 For the eccentric tag, see the Southampton Hall of Aviation and *Spitfire: A 60th Anniversary Tribute*.

101 *Observer*, 4 June 2000 in a review of Douglas Murray's biography of Lord Alfred Douglas.

102 Knowles, *Southampton: The English Gateway*, pp. 132–3.

103 Alan Rice, 'Exploring Inside the Invisible: An Interview with Lubaina Himid', *Wasafiri* no. 40 (Winter 2003), pp. 20–6.

104 Philip Hoare, *Spike Island: The Memory of a Military Hospital* (London: Fourth Estate, 2002 [2001]), p. 115.

105 Paul Weindling, 'A Virulent Strain: German Bacteriology as Scientific Racism, 1890–1920', in Ernst and Harris, *Race, Science and Medicine*, p. 221.

106 Boyarin, *Storm from Paradise*, p. 4.

107 Ibid., p. 2.
108 Kinloch Cooke in *Empire Record* quoted in 'Labour and the Aliens Bill', *Jewish Chronicle*, 6 January 1905.
109 *Jewish Chronicle*, 13 January 1905.
110 *Southampton Times*, 22 April 1905.
111 Ivor Weintroub, 'The Jews of Southampton', unpublished manuscript, no date, Southampton Hebrew Congregation archives.

8

Memory at the margins, matter out of place: hidden narratives of Jewish settlement and movement in the inter-war years

Introduction

It was tucked away 'back of the walls', the seedy, seamy side of a seafaring centre. Canal Walk reeked of danger – and, indeed, of unindentifiable smells – a darkened, bumpy, narrow street packed with tiny tumbledown stores: butchers, drapers, twine-sellers, a homemade-sweets shop, a stewed-eel-and-pie shop, a primitive amusement arcade. Many of the places were run by immigrants, especially European Jews. It was a subculture straight out of a Dickens novel, the kind of street that mothers forbade their children to visit. If you did go there, the word about town was that you had better make sure that the fingers on your wallet were your own.[1]

This melodramatic urban scene could have been drawn from a 1930s crime novel with a Sexton Blake-style hero 'slumming it' in the mean alleyways of the East End, uncovering the ethnic intrigue behind the brutal murder of a local girl of 'low repute'. In fact, it is taken from Mark Lewisohn's *Funny Peculiar: The True Story of Benny Hill* (2002) and describing an area in Southampton popularly known as the Ditches.

While it is possible to criticise Lewisohn for the overly lurid image he conjures up which, as will be shown, borrows heavily from earlier descriptions of Canal Walk, much of the factual detail is accurate. Indeed, Lewisohn in this one paragraph has revealed, or, more tellingly, exposed a communal experience forgotten within the dominant narratives of both local and Jewish history. There is a much wider significance of such amnesia, confirming again the analysis of Doreen Massey that 'The identity of places is very much bound up with the *histories* which are told of them, *how* those histories are told, and which history turns out to be dominant.'[2] First, however, it is necessary to explain how the Jewish presence in streets such as the Ditches emerged in the inter-war period before exploring the meanings and symbolism that were attached to them.

In the 900-year span of this study there have been particular places and times where the Jewish presence has been more conspicuous in their settlement and resettlement in England from the medieval period onwards. Such visibility was generally because of the concentration of Jews in certain locations, often linked to their place in the local economy. Until the early twentieth century, however, the Jews of Southampton were neither numerous enough nor sufficiently focused in particular occupations and residential areas to be a specific visual feature of the town's topography. Post-expulsion, for example, the memory of medieval Anglo-Jewry in Southampton was limited to a particular house, rather than a major street as was the case in Winchester.[3] Similarly, after the readmission of the Jews, Southampton differed from its neighbour Portsmouth and the associations frequently made in the eighteenth and nineteenth centuries between The Point and The Hard and the Jewish presence. In 1773, when Southampton was enjoying a renaissance as a fashionable spa town, the *Hampshire Chronicle* reported on a ball in a new hotel which featured a 'Jew pedlar, Tancreds, Spaniards, sailors, nosegay-girls and ballad-singers'.[4] In contrast, however, to this imagined cosmopolitanism, the reality was that there were very few Jews living in or passing through eighteenth-century Southampton. Their paucity of numbers in the town was marked in comparison to its neighbour Portsmouth, where the Jewish community was experienced and encountered on an everyday level. Even in the 1890s and 1900s in Southampton, while east European Jewish transmigrants increased rapidly in numbers, they were largely isolated in the port area and cut off from the rest of the town's residential and commercial districts. Their prominence was further obscured in this port town by being part of a wider population of transmigrants and other temporary residents such as foreign sailors and itinerant workers. In 1888, Amrit Lal Roy, an Indian 'student turned tourist', linked Southampton with London and Liverpool in its cosmopolitan atmosphere and outlook, but this was in reference to the docks rather than the town as a whole.[5] Before 1900, there was nothing approximating to a visible east European Jewish sub-community in Southampton as had been the case in Portsmouth from the mid-nineteenth century onwards. In Southampton, the Jewish-owned commercial enterprises were largely in the respectable shopping streets of the town and were dispersed – Emanuel's, in High Street, as was noted in Chapter 5, had become the most famous and prominent. That spatial invisibility was, however, to change just before, during and after the First World War when a new Jewish trading community emerged, and one that was very different to its predecessors.

In the period from the 1900s until the later 1930s, the Jewish population of Southampton more than tripled. According to the *Jewish Year Book*, in 1905 there were twenty Jewish families in the town and in 1934 this had grown to sixty-five – a growth from around 100 individuals to over 300.[6] Most of this increase was due to inward migration from other parts of Britain, most notably the East End of London. It reflected, as a pull factor, the growth of Southampton whose population increased from just over 100,000 to over 175,000 from 1901 to 1931.[7] It also represented the push factor – the economic misery and intense competition within primary immigrant settlement areas such as the East End. While the fledgling Jewish communities of Basingstoke and Aldershot struggled to survive in the inter-war period, elsewhere in Hampshire those in Portsmouth and Bournemouth followed Southampton in receiving further influxes of east European origin Jews, many of whom had initially settled in London. It was Southampton Jewry, however, because of the late settlement of these new arrivals, that was particularly and perhaps uniquely transformed in the inter-war years. It is for this reason that the bulk of this chapter will be devoted to this dynamic and unique south coast community.

New arrivals

David Cesarani has suggested that

> The belief in upward social mobility is cherished in Anglo-Jewry today, but it is substantially a myth. The inter-war years saw some dramatic cross-class mobility registered unambiguously by occupational and geographical change. But for a more significant section of the Jewish population, the experience was one of statis or sideways movement. Occupations and addresses changed, but this only gave an illusion of genuine social mobility.[8]

Cesarani points to migration from the East End to other London districts, and to similar processes in other major cities of settlement such as Manchester, Leeds and Liverpool, emphasising that the move to 'adjacent inner-suburbs such as Hackney, Chapeltown and Hightown ... did not [necessarily] signify upward social mobility'. He concludes that the 'Jewish route to the [middle-class] suburbs was long, hard and devious'.[9] This contribution will confirm Cesarani's analysis but add to it another layer of evidence relating to the economic desperation and marginality of first- and second-generation east European Jews in Britain. These Jews were not simply in motion *within* the major cities of primary settlement – their mobility extended into other urban locations, including towns such as Southampton which are not, in popular memory, normally associated with having possessed an east European

Jewish milieu. Indeed, it must be emphasised that the struggle to make ends meet led to a geographical restlessness that has yet to be fully understood in the existing historiography of twentieth-century British Jewry.

On the surface, Southampton, as a fast-developing port, as well as an industrial and commercial centre, would appear as an obvious magnet to those trying to move away from economically depressed areas of Britain. In this respect, of particular relevance to the Jewish experience was the East End of London where, contrary to widespread contemporary assumptions, Jewish poverty was at a higher level than the local population as a whole. *The New Survey of London Life and Labour* estimated that, at the end of the 1920s, 13.7 per cent of Jewish East Enders were in poverty, compared with 12.1 per cent for the area as a whole.[10] And as Harold Pollins points out, 'this was before the depression was at its deepest'.[11] The classic Jewish immigrant trades such as tailoring, shoe-making and furniture-making were particularly vulnerable to seasonal and long-term decline through increasing global competition. Thus many Jews, especially the younger generation, either tried their luck in these trades in new locations or in different occupations, especially those involving self-employment.

But Southampton's image as a prosperous gateway to a more affluent south was deceptive. Indeed, its mixed economic and social reality surprised J. B. Priestley as he embarked from the port on his classic *English Journey* (1934).[12] While escaping the worst ravages of inter-war depression, Southampton was still a poor town with major problems of overcrowding and seasonal labour with its major sources of wealth coming from outside.[13] Many of the Jewish newcomers to Southampton eked out a living in the lock-up shops of Canal Walk. Jim Bellows, who grew up a few streets away, remembers them clearly:

> Along the top right-hand side of 'The Ditches' was a line of small shops built against the old town wall. These shops were just three or four feet deep and displayed their wares on shutters which, when lowered, turned into counters. They sold a a variety of clothes, towels, curtains and such. These shops were kept by Jewish people and were the only shops open on a Sunday.[14]

These lock-ups were, in reality, closer to market stalls than shops and required minimal capital and were cheap to rent. Business concerns came and went and most disappeared without leaving much trace. One of these was a dress shop run by two women, Rachel Solomons and Sophie Noah, both of families of east European origin. Their story was perhaps typical of those who settled in Southampton in the inter-war period, consisting of frequent movement and the requirement of entrepreneurial risk-taking to make a living. It also reflected the economic activity of Jewish women, in spite of huge family commitments.[15] Sophie was born in the East End in 1892 and married a Russian-born widower, Abraham Noah. Abraham had three children from his first marriage and a son and daughter with Sophie. With these five children Abraham and Sophie moved to Southampton in 1925. Abraham had not gone through the laborious and relatively expensive task of gaining naturalisation and thus Sophie, on marriage, lost her British citizenship. On 16 June 1925, therefore, she registered with Southampton Borough Police as an alien – under the Aliens Order, 1920, all permanent changes of residence had to be officially recorded.[16] Sophie's daughter, who was a small child when her parents moved to Southampton, recalls that the dress shop was 'not particularly successful' and it soon closed down.[17] Sophie's certificate of alien registration indicates that they left Southampton on the SS *Andes* in 1927 before returning to the port fourteen months later. It must be assumed that the family had tried their luck abroad and had returned to England, this time moving to Stoke Newington in the north-east of London. Her business partner, Rachel, born in 1900, was married in Southampton in 1928 and she and her husband moved to Manchester shortly after.[18] In these cases scraping out a living, even in the cheap and basic premises of Canal Walk, had proved impossible and both women, with their husbands, were forced eventually to try their luck elsewhere in Britain, especially in other areas of Jewish settlement.

In 1983 the Southampton Hebrew Congregation celebrated the 150th anniversary of its formal establishment with a visit of the Chief Rabbi, Immanuel Jakobovits. Sidney Weintroub, its President, marked the occasion by producing a short hand-written history of Southampton's Jewry. Contained within it were two sentences relating to the Jewish trading community of the inter-war years:

> Before World War II most of the members of the Congregation were private shopkeepers, many in Canal Walk and the lower part of the town. The blitz of 1940 destroyed most of their shops and they, like others, left the town.[19]

Weintroub, who came to Southampton in the early 1930s, was right to highlight the finality brought by German bombing to the commercial premises of Canal Walk. Yet the blitz was only the final part of a process of decline – failed businesses and slum demolition in the later 1930s had already altered the dynamics of Canal Walk and dimished the local Jewish population. By the Second World War, the total of the Southampton Hebrew Congregation had fallen to 250 and would decline thereafter.[20]

It is significant in itself that contemporaries referring to Weintroub's narrative of Southampton Jewry in 1983 failed to mention his comments on the Canal Walk-linked community. Lacking permanence of presence, or the reassuring motif of Jewish economic success, they were difficult to place in official memory and thus subject to the active process that is amnesia. To Weintroub, however, as a committed second-generation Jew born in Manchester of east European origin, they would have been the essence of Southampton Jewry in the inter-war period. As we will see, to many local non-Jews, too, memory of the Canal Walk community was still vivid as late as the last decades of the twentieth century.

In his 1980s history, Weintroub commented that in contemporary Southampton, only one shop now bore the name of that inter-war Jewish trading community – Millet's.[21] In contrast to the lock-up shops of Canal Walk, Millet's, a drapery business, in the inter-war years was large and in a prominent and prestigious position in Above Bar. The premises were destroyed in the blitz in 1941 and the business did not return to Southampton until 1958.[22] The Millet family were of Galician origin and came to Southampton in the 1890s having first settled in London. The company that still bears the family name is now a major retailer and 'one of the high street's best-known names, offering quality [outdoor] products ... in over 280 stores nationwide'.[23] Yet rather than fundamentally query the model of Jewish economic marginality as exemplified by the Canal Walk business of Rachel Solomons and Sophie Noah, the experiences of the Millets shows that for every success there were, at least initially, many more failures. By the start of the twentieth century there were four inter-related Millet families within Southampton, and most of the businesses they set up, almost all in the poorest parts of town, including Canal Walk, lasted only a few years. Itinerant hawk pedlars in the first instance, the Millet siblings and their partners set up enterprises as drapers, haberdashers and second-hand clothes dealers. These businesses depended on the poorest of customers and were thus particularly prone to bankruptcy. Indeed, it seems that the only Millets that were successful in Southampton most likely came to the town with some capital – as early as the 1901 census the family were listed as employing a servant.[24] They thus would have represented the small number of east European Jews who were not penniless. These were the so-called *alrightniks*, the most famous of whom was Michael Marks of Marks and Spencer fame.[25]

The Millet families consisted of eleven siblings. Their patterns of movement can be traced through the census which reveals the transient nature of the Jewish experience before the First World War. The children of these siblings were born in London, Dublin, Bristol, Southampton and Le Havre.[26] Three Millet brothers initially came to England and the other siblings followed in classic chain migration fashion. It was within Southampton that the pattern of economic marginality and business failure – their earlier ventures in London, Dublin and Bristol had failed – was partially overcome. The end of the Boer War provided the opportunity for selling government surplus uniform and kit and in the words of a descendant, 'Max [one of the brothers], the commercial genius of the family, had the vision to see that he could sell it on on civvy street at a tremendous profit'.[27] East European Jewish immigrants, with their strong connection to the clothing and boot trade, were ideally and fortunately situated for this business opportunity. In Portsmouth as well, and in other provincial communities, army surplus shops provided the possibility of economic mobility for the new Jewish arrivals and their descendants, a form of entrepreneurship that has not yet received attention in the existing historiography.[28] Even then, the limited opportunities in Southampton, as well as sibling rivalry, meant that only one branch of the Millet family would remain in Southampton. Peter Millet's haberdasher's shop in Canal Walk, for instance, first appeared in the local trade directory in 1901. It then reduced in size and had disappeared by the end of 1909, thus conforming to the general pattern of business failure and marginality in this singular street.[29] Indeed almost all the Millet siblings, continuing their pattern of restlessness, left Southampton before 1914 and settled across England in towns including Bristol, Nottingham, Leicester, Birmingham and Croydon as well as Portsmouth and Gosport in Hampshire.[30]

Constructing the Ditches

Whether economically successful or otherwise, Southampton Jewry, including its Hebrew Congregation, was transformed both in numbers and in nature by this east European influx. The religiosity of the community was changed, marked by a greater orthodoxy reflecting the recent roots of the newcomers. For example, in 1919, it was decided to build a *mikveh*, or ritual bath, which was, in the words of the Polish-born religious leader of the congregation, Reverend Gordon, 'a most essential thing to our community'.[31] Part of the everyday life in eastern Europe, a *mikveh* would have been regarded as a (largely) unnecessary luxury to the settled and assimilated Jewish population of Southampton during the nineteenth century. In the secular sphere, after 1918 the greater size and commitment of the community also enabled a flourishing of cultural Jewishness including literary events and sport – in 1921, for example, the Southampton Jewish Cricket Club was formed.[32] Such activities extended into the political realm with a stronger Jewish diasporic identity emerging and manifest through more vocal support of Jews in distress abroad than had been the case before the war.[33] It was also reflected in the strengthening of Zionism within the community. In 1919 it was resolved to merge the local Zionist Society with the Southampton Hebrew

Congregation.[34] Similar tendencies were apparent elsewhere in Britain, including elsewhere in Hampshire. In Portsmouth, Ian Mikardo remembered how in 1922 a meeting was called at the synagogue 'for the purpose of setting up a Portsmouth Zionist Society. An audience of a hundred or so turned up, mostly of the fairly recent immigrants of the Portsea ghetto'.[35] Earlier, further to the west of Southampton, a special meeting of the Bournemouth Hebrew Congregation was summoned in November 1917 to record 'heartfelt gratitude to His Majesty's Government for their declaration in favour of the establishment in Palestine of a National Home for the Jewish People'.[36] The link between British Zionism and suburbanisation in the inter-war period, especially in London, has been highlighted by the movement's historian,[37] but its significance in forging provincial Jewish identities at this time also requires recognition.

It would be misleading to present this vibrant Jewish community as being without conflict. Indeed, in 1931 the police were called for protection after a disagreement following a committee meeting.[38] Some of the older, more anglicised members clearly were uneasy about the religious and political direction the expanded community was taking and, as elsewhere in Britain, tension existed between first- and second-generation Jews, the latter being drawn to the attractions of the secular world.[39] In 1925, when discussions about building a *mikvah* were still ongoing, one committee member of the Southampton Hebrew Congregation wondered whether social facilities for the youth of the community might not be more useful from a practical perspective, 'as our younger children only loiter about the town, and have nowhere that they can come and meet and get more sociable and know what we are'.[40] Nevertheless, such friction reflected the dynamism of the community during the 1920s. While the transformation of Southampton Jewry through the arrival of east European Jews followed the general pattern of British Jewry as a whole, it was a metamorphosis which notably occurred later than the major points of migrant settlement such as London, Manchester, Leeds and Glasgow. As has been noted, even Southampton's south coast rival, Portsmouth had transmogrified with its influx of East End Jewish tailors as the pre-war naval race escalated. For the period from 1883 to 1903, for example, of those marrying in the synagogue in Portsmouth, the most common occupation of their fathers was merchantry (11) closely followed by tailoring and outfitting (10), but in the next twenty-year period the equivalent figures were 31 tailors and 20 merchants. By the start of the First World War, Portsmouth Jewry had become numerically dominated by east European Jews in classic immigrant occupations whereas in Southampton such changes in the composition of the community were far less pronounced.[41] It was also now a much smaller and less status-driven community than that emerging in Bournemouth.

Ronald Hayman was born in 1932 and his father, owner of a Jewish hotel in this seaside resort, was President of the Bournemouth Hebrew Congregation during the 1930s. Hayman remembers going to the synagogue for a *Shabbos* service and the caretaker handing over a 'shiny black silk hat' to his father:

> Daddy adjusted it in the mirror and then we made our entrance ... With eyes averted upwards as if his chanting were a rope that led straight up to Heaven, the bearded cantor would pretend not to notice as we marched past the platform he was standing on to open the door of the presidential box and sit down on the red velvet seat in front of him next to the treasurer and the secretary.[42]

And relatively small (and later) though it was compared to the larger Jewish communities in Britain, the new interwar migrant Jewish community in Southampton became particularly prominent through its visibility in a singular street in the town.

Portsmouth Jewry in the Napoleonic era and beyond developed a notoriety linked to crime and violence in this roughest of seaports. In literature and popular discourse they were connected to particular places – the Hard and the Point – which, now gentrified, were then infamous for prostitution and disorder.[43] In a twentieth-century context, the Ditches brought forth similar associations within Southampton. Just as the East End was both a geographical area and a symbol of London's dangerous 'other', so the Ditches was to Southampton as much an imagined place as a physical reality. What makes it intriguing as a site of contested collective memory is that it had a direct connection to all major developments in Southampton's history from the medieval period onwards. Rather than simply a small street in the heart of a major town, the Ditches had many layers of meanings attached to it. The naming and renaming of this street involved inclusion and exclusion, remembering and forgetting. The Ditches/Canal Walk was a place of evocation, bringing to mind again Walter Benjamin's musings on Paris in his *Arcades Project* that 'we hold a world in the names of old streets, and to read the name of a street is like undergoing a transformation.'[44]

In the inter-war period, 'Townsman', or E. A. Mitchell, was the leading populariser of Southampton's history. Theatre critic of the local paper, the *Southern Daily Echo*, he used his literary skills to produce intriguing vignettes of the town's past.[45] Canal Walk featured prominently in his publications. The street became a test case through which Mitchell could explore the relationship between Southampton 'then' and 'now'. The excitement as well as the dilemmas of flux in Mitchell's narratives of Southampton through the ages could be explored with reference to Canal Walk/the Ditches. Ultimately Mitchell's search for a usable and rejuvenating past by constructing a sense of continuity and tradition were realised through his topographical imaginings of this particular and peculiar place.

The Ditches were linked to the fortifications of the medieval town and had the dual function of defence and acting as the town's rubbish dump. Rather than dwell on its less savoury function, which, by the sixteenth century had become a public nuisance,[46] Mitchell only connected the Ditches to its more illustrious role in helping to protect from invasion what was one of the major medieval ports in England.[47] In the late eighteenth century a canal, attempting to connect Southampton to Winchester, was partially built and ran through the Ditches. Unsuccessful and abandoned as a commercial venture, as early as 1800 it was parodied in the *Gentleman's Magazine*:

> Southampton's wise sons found the River so large,
> Tho' 'twould carry a ship, 'twould not carry a barge
> But soon this defect their sage noddles supply'd,
> For they cut a snug *ditch* to run close by its side.[48]

Business failure though it was, the abandoned canal nevertheless provided a pleasant walk connecting the docks to the south with the semi-rural outskirts of the Georgian spa town to the north. Its role as a pathway to an idyllically imagined pastoral Southampton was highlighted by Mitchell by including a sketch from the first half of the nineteenth century drawn by the prominent local artist, Thomas Gray Hart. Hart portrayed the Ditches literally as a romantic bridge to the countryside of old times complete with ruined medieval towers and walls.[49] Neighbouring Canal Walk was Orchard Lane, which, as was noted in the *Civic Survey* of Southampton in 1931, through its nomenclature, 'preserve[d] the memory of a rural past'.[50]

In the early nineteenth century the canal was filled in and by the 1850s 'respectable' businesses with dwellings above them were built in what became a street, Canal Walk. It was only at the beginning of the twentieth century that the lock-up shops developed fully and the nature of Canal Walk was transformed. In the process of development from the late eighteenth century onwards, almost all physical traces of the medieval origins and spa town evolution of this area of Southampton were removed. It was a loss that clearly upset Mitchell. The critic/historian was one of the first to actively campaign for the saving of Southampton's physical historical heritage, a frustrating and lonely pursuit in a town that had little interest and put few resources into preserving and representing its past. Indeed, the landmark Southampton Civic Survey of 1931 commented that the 'state of affairs [with regard to museums] can only be described as "backward" for a city of such importance'.[51]

The social transformation and 'decline' of what became Canal Walk was symptomatic to Mitchell of the deterioration of Southampton as a whole and its disinterest in its own history. As late as the 1860s, he reflected, 'it was [still] an attractive quarter'. He quoted a man brought up in Canal Walk who could remember 'watching the fashions go by' and his mother picking fruit in the back yard. Mitchell was dissatisfied with its current status and took refuge in its perceived Elysian past: 'It is a curiously challenging panoroma that one sees with the mind's eye if one traces back in imagination the history of Canal Walk'. To emphasis the point further, and thereby not needing to make explicit his contemporary distaste, he stressed that 'There is no doubt that at one time Canal Walk was one of the pleasantest parts of Southampton.' He gave substance to this by including a sketch of Canal Walk which, although drawn in 1915, reflected its more salubrious commercial past in the mid-nineteenth century, with the background dominated by two tall and flourishing trees.[52]

Mitchell was constructing a somewhat romanticised past for Canal Walk and Southampton as a whole. A later appreciation of Mitchell referred to his full identification with Southampton although he was born in London and only came to the town in 1913.[53] The same, however, cannot be said of those who made the street economically viable. In spatial terms, both physically and metaphorically, Canal Walk was situated in between worlds. The old dock area of Southampton to the south of Canal Walk was in many ways self-contained, especially as the docks were privately owned and had no public access. Here there were shops catering specifically for the docks and the floating maritime population. The writer Laurie Lee, as a young man coming from the Gloucestershire countryside, was disappointed not to see the sea in the Hampshire port, but instead 'a muddy river which they said was Southampton Water'. In contrast,

> Southampton Town … came up to all expectations, proving to be salty and shifty in turns, like some ship-jumping sailor who'd turned his back on the sea in a desperate attempt to make good on the land. The streets near the water appeared to be jammed with shops designed more for entertainment than profit, including tattoists, ear-piercers, bump-readers, fortune-tellers, whelk-bars and pudding-boilers.[54]

Further up town was the main shopping area of High Street and East Street, with the tendency in both these thoroughfares since the First World War towards larger concerns. Shops in these major streets catered for a wide range of people from both inside and outside the town. Canal Walk's premises had a different constituency, firstly consisting of those living in the district, secondly adjacent working-class districts such as Northam with its strong dock and seafaring connections, including streets that were literally decimated by the sinking of the *Titanic* in 1912, and finally the floating population of Southampton, the sailors, and an important category in any port, prostitutes.[55] It is here that the Benny Hill connection is made – his father had a shop selling surgical appliances and rubber goods in Canal Walk offering contraceptive devices to sailors and prostitutes.[56]

Canal Walk was undoubtedly cosmopolitan in inter-war Southampton – aside from the Jews, there were Italian shops, Chinese laundries, and amongst its customers were lascars and many other foreign sailors. Violence and drunkenness were also not unknown. Its various attractions made it a colourful place to visit, especially on a Saturday night. The adolescent Tommy Cooper began his career as a magician-comedian by entertaining at Chiari's cafe and ice-cream parlour in Canal Walk. Chiari, an Italian immigrant, was also an artist and amateur magician:

> He fascinated Tommy with the tricks he knew and taught him several … When [he] couldn't afford the price of a cup of tea, Tommy would be allowed to perform for the patrons in lieu of payment.[57]

Yet for many, the importance of Canal Walk was more mundane. Maie Hodgson was, in her words, a 'child of the Ditches'. To Hodgson, Canal Walk was home, a place she felt safe in and the various shopkeepers were people she grew up with: 'With this mixture of Jewish and Italian neighbours combined in later years with a sort of fair-ground element then added together with family businesses like ours, the Ditches certainly exuded a real cosmopolitan atmosphere.'[58]

The Jewish shops of the Ditches also served an important function as an alternative to the expensive and increasingly standardised shops of High Street and East Street. The oral testimony of Mrs G, an elderly lady brought up a docker's daughter in Chapel, provides an account that while not without its racialisation, also highlights the crucial economic role played by the Canal Walk shops:

> [It was] lined with Jew shops with all the latest tip-top clothes. They'd be at the door and well, floggin' the stuff you know. I think you could get a beautiful suit there for about sixpence, if you'd stay long enough to argue with 'em … We all used to buy our clothes there. You'd go one week and perhaps buy the one part of yer rigout. You'd buy it bit by bit. As much as you could afford … It was threepence down on it … We all used to buy our clothes like that.[59]

Similarly, Jim Bellows recalled the Jewish businesses and how for 'eleven pence and three farthings I could buy a pullover there and go to Sunday School looking tidy'.[60]

The Jewish shops of Canal Walk, therefore, were economically marginal businesses catering for economically marginal customers. The Southampton Council rate books show that as a whole, the shops in Canal Walk were paying a fraction of the rateable value of those in Below Bar and East Street. Even then, the Jewish lock-up shops were paying half the rates of other shops in Canal Walk.[61] Survival was borderline, and, as we have seen in the case of Rachel Solomons and Sophie Noah, many went to the wall. Indeed, while the neighbourliness of Canal Walk should not be dismissed, nor should its poverty and violence be forgotten. Policeman, John Arlott, later the voice of cricket in England, recalls the reality of the street in the 1930s: 'Colourful it was, but not always salubrious.'[62] In 1931 Southampton Civic Society sponsored a survey of the town. A pioneer study of urban development and planning, it highlighted two inner-city slum areas. One was within the Town Ward with Canal Walk at the heart of it. Congested and unhealthy, most of the buildings were condemned as 'not really fit for human habitation at all' and partly cleared in the later 1930s.[63]

Although J. B. Priestley does not specifically name Canal Walk in *English Journey*, one of the most important pieces of social commentary in inter-war Britain, he clearly had visited its neighbourhood. First, however, Priestley remarked that

> We hear a good deal about Southampton's comparative prosperity; and [High Street] is the symbol of it ... The pavement on each side was crowded with neat smiling people ... and the mile of shops seemed to be doing a brisk trade. Here at last was a town that had not fallen under the evil spell of our times.[64]

But Priestley's England was full of complexities and contradictions,[65] and two pages later in *English Journey* he turned off High Street to find himself 'in some very poor quarters'.[66] These were the Town Ward slums and Priestley was even more disgusted by the shops that serviced them. Priestley is hard to categorise – a man of the people capable of intense snobbery, a radical with international sympathies but also an English nationalist.[67] There is also a strong racialisation to *English Journey* and within it Priestley's ambiguities are exposed further. There was a deep sympathy towards persecuted German Jewry and a sense of nostalgia for the German Jews of his hometown Bradford. Alongside these, however, was at best a patronising attitude and often irritation towards east European Jews and other less 'desirable' immigrants. His class-racial snobbery and prejudices are blatant when describing what was, with little doubt, Canal Walk:

> The small shop flourishes in this quarter ... Even after you have given yourself the strongest dose of individualistic sentiment, it is hard to look at these small shops with anything but disgust or to find good reasons why they should not be promptly abolished. They are slovenly, dirty and inefficient.[68]

What slum clearance had not finished, the blitz completed in 1940. By the end of the war there was little physical trace left of Canal Walk. Nevertheless, it has been noted that the street featured prominently in Sotonian autobiographical practice, whether written or oral. For those from working-class backgrounds, Canal Walk was remembered as a place where everyday goods could be purchased (or had on credit) from its cosmopolitan shopkeepers far cheaper than the rest of Southampton. For others, perhaps of a more prosperous background, it offered goods not available elsewhere and a place, in daytime at least, that was excitingly different with a frisson of danger adding further spice to the experience of a visit. For Eric Gadd, a 'tram-ride with Mum from the suburbs' to shop in the Ditches was 'a treat', enabling a sampling of its 'teeming cosmopolitan buzz'.[69] Recalling, over half a century later, such trips during and after the First World War, Gadd remembered vividly the entrance to Canal Walk

> with its tiny shops and booths, its picturesque traders, its wide variety of merchandise and its cosmopolitan customers, many strolling in from the ships in nearby dockland. Here one saw sallow skins, brown skins, black skins, yellow skins; flashing eyes and gleaming teeth; turbans and fezzes; earrings and gaudy sashes. Often the air was filled with a babble of strange tongues.[70]

In contrast to those like Maie Hodgson who grew up in the Ditches and took its diversity for granted, for middle-class outsiders the street provided an enticing otherness, representing the fear and fascination resulting from an orientalist discourse. Brian Lawrence was older than Eric Gadd when he visited the Ditches before the First World War. Like Gadd, the memories remained with him powerfully many decades later, although his testimony closes by revealing a greater self-reflexivity when confronting his earlier responses to its 'strangeness':

> A picturesque touch was often added by the lascars from the troopships, who did much of their shopping here; they seemed to like these haunts, perhaps reminiscent of bazaars back home. Their often odd mixture of oriental and accidental costume, and the occasional overheard snatches of unintelligible speech, could add an exotic note which almost suggested, to the young imagination, a visit to 'foreign parts'.[71]

By the 1970s, both Gadd and Lawrence regretted the passing of this world within a world and wrote nostalgically of Canal Walk. To Gadd, 'Sadly, though the name may still be read upon a side wall, most of this thoroughfare and all of its vibrant, earthy character have long disappeared. Here were constant chatter, endless movement. Here the wise shopper made sure that the fingers on his wallet were his own.'[72] Lawrence went further and perceptively noted that the street and all it stood for was now subject to increasing amnesia: 'Those of us who saw and remember may regret the passing of these symbols of an earlier way of life; it is hard to realise that to the younger generation who have succeeded us they are not even a memory.'[73] It was left to an exceptionally talented local historian, Elsie Sandell, to ensure that the memory of Canal Walk/the Ditches was not totally forgotten at a collective level in Southampton.

After 1945, Elsie Sandell replaced 'Townsman' or E. A. Mitchell as the popular historian of Southampton. In her *Southampton Cavalcade* (1953) she commented that 'Many thousands of Southampton folk remember the Ditches, or Canal Walk, of pre-war days. It had closely packed little shops leaning forward on the narrow stone flagged footwalk'.[74] Sandell shared Mitchell's desire and enthusiasm to preserve the physical remnants of Southampton's past. Both were internationalist in outlook, although it manifested itself religiously in the case of Mitchell, and politically with Sandell and her work for, amongst others, the United Nations. Sandell, however, was a far more progressive interpreter of the past and had the foresight and confidence to confront contemporary history, as well as the experiences of marginalised groups such as minorities and women. As was said of her at her funeral, 'She knew that history is never past and that life to be lived to the full must be lived in the past and the future as well as the present'.[75] Sandell, like Mitchell, connected Canal Walk to Southampton's spa days and related how in the late eighteenth century it was 'fraught with many elegant and picturesque views'.[76] Yet she also relished its re-flourishing in the inter-war period when 'There was something almost continental in the look of it all and many a foreign name was written over the doors'. In stark contrast to Priestley, she listed positively the various outlets – there were 'confectioners, public houses, fruiterers, music dealers, fried fish shops, cats' meat purveyors, butchers, mouse-trap makers and many another trader' – and concluded that 'Canal Walk was, in fact, an epitome of the shopping life of a busy port'.[77] She, like Gadd and Lawrence, felt its loss in post-war Southampton which to her made 'one realise yet again the wholesale devastation of so much of our town'.[78]

Sandell, in her prolific writings on historic Southampton, could best be described as a cautious cosmopolitan. Since her death in 1974, she has been largely forgotten and neglected, paralleled by a similar amnesia at a collective level of Southampton's past diversity. This has included the Jews of Southampton, especially at their most numerous around Canal Walk in the inter-war period. For example, although the Southampton contribution to the national 'Port Cities' web-based archive is a rich source of many aspects of its past, it is relatively weak in illustrating past ethnic diversity. There is, unfortunately, no material directly relating to its Jewish community and only five entries under the heading 'immigration' of any type.[79] Rather than a case of special pleading, inclusion of the Jewish presence in Canal Walk would not just show the diversity of Southampton but also reveal the process of identity formation in a modern port town. A sense of place, space, and concepts of 'home' are all crucial in memory work whether individual or collective. As Doreen Massey highlights

> The description, definition and identification of a place is … always inevitably an intervention not only into geography but also, at least implicitly, into the re(telling) of the historical constitution of the present. It is another move in the continuing struggle over the delineation and characterisation of space-time.[80]

In this study of Canal Walk the importance of shops and businesses, which often connect the global, national and local, has been particularly emphasised.[81] In Portsmouth, Charlotte Street and its 'many side streets and alleys that made up this colourful area', fulfilled a similar function to Canal Walk.[82] Charlotte Street in the 1880s was described by the local priest as the 'main thoroughfare which the Dockyard men mostly use in reaching their homes … with the far-off scent of the sea coming over the mud of the harbour … sailors everywhere, sometimes fighting, sometimes courting [in] this poor little district … Charlotte Street was, from end to end, an open fair'.[83] From the 1900s onwards, Jewish traders became prominent in this notorious area. They made a big impression on Vera Sparkes who grew up in Portsmouth:

> My earliest recollections of Charlotte Street were when I was a very young child [during the inter-war years and] all the small shops that ran from Commercial Road practically the whole length of Charlotte Street. There was an extraordinary number, at least it seemed to me then as a child. These small shops were kept by immigrants, which I believe from information gathered since were Polish and Russian Jews … They had unpronounceable names but took new names when they became naturalised citizens.[84]

Vera Sparkes was not mistaken. As early as 1910 a Portsmouth Jewish Naturalisation Society was formed 'with the object of enabling foreign residents to become British subjects' and to give instruction in English.[85]

Yet it is only through the fragments of testimony collected by a local Workers' Educational Association, including those of Vera Sparkes, that the Jewishness of Charlotte Street has subsequently been remembered. Along with Queen Street, where the synagogue was located, it was the heart of a 'highly visible community firmly established within the maritime and commercial setting of the city'. It has been suggested that 'Supplies to ships' messes and provision of uniform and other clothing to the fleet were competitive areas where Jewish traders excelled. Most Jews lived within easy walking distance of the synagogue and were served with Jewish food and other shops within the area'. The economic foundation of this community was undermined when the navy 'develop[ed] its own central sources of supply' and in 1936 the synagogue moved to Southsea.[86]

The area was redeveloped after 1945, leaving few remnants of its Jewish past. Thereafter an amnesia in the world of Portsmouth's official heritage has developed over the town's past Jewish visibility in Charlotte Street and Queen Street, mirroring that in Southampton with Canal Walk.

In respect to such ignored or suppressed memories of past diversity and ethnic dynamism, it will be helpful, in bringing this chapter to a close, to return again to Benny Hill. The comic, through his father's business, grew up amongst the Yiddish-speaking east European Jewish shopkeepers of Canal Walk and came to love their culture, whether articulated through food, language or humour. Early in his career he changed his name from Alfred to Benny, wanting 'a stage name with a kosher ring to it'.[87] The particular reference point was the American comedian, Jack Benny, and his principal biographer suggests that Benny Hill believed that it 'would do him no harm to be thought of as Jewish'.[88] Many argue that Benny Hill produced offensive and outdated humour which relied on essentialised and stereotypical characters. It is for this reason that one of the most successful television comedians of the twentieth century at a global level has been deliberately marginalised since his death in the 1980s and has become 'the forgotten man'.[89] There is, as yet, no memorial to him in Britain, not even in Southampton, the place in which he grew up and spent much of his life: the 'city fathers seem embarrassed by the association'.[90] Yet a different reading of Benny Hill is possible, one that is informed by the cosmopolitanism of Canal Walk and the cultural hybridity and fluidity that it reflected which was part of his everyday family world. His brother relates how in an early theatre performance Benny Hill provided a spoof of 'two popular tenors of the time. One was so Jewish you could not believe it; the other so Irish he was practically green all over. Benny combined the Yiddisher schmaltz and the Irish blarney to hilarious effect.'[91] Playing with 'ethnic' categories continued throughout his career — here is Benny Hill as his Chinese character, Chow-Mein, feigning exasperation at fellow comic, Des O'Connor: 'Oy vey, we got a right meshuggenah here.'[92]

There is a serious final point to be made. The dismissal of Benny Hill, the most famous, or infamous person linked to Canal Walk, is at one with the forgetting of the street's migrant past, including its vibrant Jewish community. Yet two of Britain's most innovative comedians in the twentieth century — Benny Hill and Tommy Cooper — were inspired by the liveliness and heterogeneity of Canal Walk. Anthropologist Mary Douglas has suggested that 'if uncleanness is matter out of place, we must approach it through order. Uncleanness or dirt is that which must not be included if a pattern is to be maintained.'[93] Benny Hill and the diversity typified by Canal Walk, or Charlotte Street in Portsmouth, have become, in the world of memory and the desire for homogeneous purity, such 'matter out of place'.

Notes

1   Mark Lewisohn, *Funny Peculiar: The True Story of Benny Hill* (London: Sidgwick & Jackson, 2002), p. 7.

2   Doreen Massey, 'Places and Their Pasts', *History Workshop Journal* no. 39 (Spring 1995), p. 186.

3   John Davies, *A History of Southampton* (Southampton: Gilbert, 1883), p. 456.

4   *Hampshire Chronicle*, 20 September 1773.

5   A. L. Roy, *Reminiscences England and America* (1888), quoted by Rozina Visram, *Asians in Britain: 400 Years of History* (London: Pluto Press, 2002), pp. 113, 116.

6   Figures from *Jewish Year Book 5668–9* (London: Greenberg, 1907), p. 196 and *Jewish Chronicle*, 1 June 1934.

7   Percy Ford, *Work and Wealth in a Modern Port: An Economic Survey of Southampton* (London: George Allen & Unwin, 1934), p. 25.

8   David Cesarani, 'A Funny Thing Happened on the Way to the Suburbs: Social Change in Anglo-Jewry Between the Wars, 1914–1945', *Jewish Culture and History* vol. 1 no. 1 (1998), p. 5.

9   Ibid., pp. 9, 22.

10 H. Llewellyn Smith (ed.), *New Survey of London Life and Labour* vol. 6 (London: P. S. King, 1934), p. 287.

11 Harold Pollins, *Economic History of the Jews in England* (East Brunswick, New Jersey: Associated University Presses, 1982), p. 185.

12 J. B. Priestley, *English Journey* (London: Heinemann, 1934), Chapter 1 'To Southampton'.

13 Ford, *Work and Wealth in a Modern Port*, p. 23.

14 Jim Bellows, *My Southampton in the Twenties and Thirties* (Bradford on Avon, Wilts: ELSP, 2001), pp. 66–7.

15 More generally see Rickie Burman, 'Jewish Women and the Household Economy in Manchester, c.1890–1920', in David Cesarani (ed.), *The Making of Modern Anglo-Jewry* (Oxford: Blackwell, 1990), pp. 57–75.

16 Copy of Sophie Noah's Certificate of Registration, Aliens Order, 1920, in the possession of the author.

17 Letter of Frances Jacobs (née Noah), to the author, 13 May 2002.

18 Family information provided by Frances Jacobs, 13 May 2002.

19 Sidney Weintroub, unpublished manuscript history of the Southampton Hebrew Congregation archives (SHC), no date.

20 See *Jewish Year Book 1945–6* (London: Jewish Chronicle, 1945), p. 193.

21 Weintroub, unpublished history, SHC archives.

22 *Southern Evening Echo*, 21 November 1958.

23 Taken from its website, www.leeds-uk.com/shopping/millets.htm, accessed 15 December 2006.

24 1901 census; *Kelly's Trade Directories for Southampton*, 1898 to 1939.

25 For the *alrightniks*, see Bill Williams, '"East and West" in Manchester Jewry, 1850–1914', in David Cesarani (ed.), *The Making of Modern Anglo-Jewry*, pp. 24–6.

26 1901 census entries for Southampton: 38, 45 and 102 Northam Road and 26, Derby Road.

27 Email communication to the author from Richard Cooper, 5 December 2006.

28 There is no mention, for example, in Pollins, *Economic History* or in Andrew Godley,

Jewish Immigrant Entrepreneurship in New York and London 1880–1914: Enterprise and Culture (Basingstoke: Palgrave, 2001).

29 *Kelly's Directory* for Southampton, 1901–1910.

30 Email communication to the author from Richard Cooper, 8 December 2006.

31 See SHC minutes, 12 January 1919 and 22 February 1925. Due to financial restraint and the opposition of the town authorities, the mikveh was never constructed. More generally see Sharman Kadish, *Building Jerusalem: Jewish Architecture in Britain* (London: Vallentine Mitchell, 1996), pp. 105–33.

32 *Jewish Chronicle*, 29 July 1921.

33 See, for example, SHC minutes 8 June and 6 July 1919 concerning relief for and protests on behalf of victims of Polish massacres.

34 SHC minutes, 6 April 1919.

35 Ian Mikardo, *Back-Bencher* (London: Weidenfeld and Nicolson, 1988), p. 35.

36 Harry Ellis, 'Minute by Minute – A Chronological History 1905–2005', in *Bournemouth Hebrew Congregation Centenary 1905–2005: A Celebration* (Bournemouth: Bournemouth Hebrew Congregation, 2005), p. 18.

37 David Cesarani, 'The Transformation of Communal Authority in Anglo-Jewry, 1914–1940', in David Cesarani (ed.), *The Making of Modern Anglo-Jewry*, p. 137.

38 SHC minutes, 5 March 1931.

39 Rosalyn Livshin, 'The Acculturation of the Children of Immigrant Jews in Manchester, 1890–1930', in Cesarani (ed.), *The Making of Modern Anglo-Jewry*, pp. 79–96.

40 SHC minutes, 22 February 1925.

41 Aubrey Weinberg, *Portsmouth Jewry* (Portsmouth: Portsmouth City Council, 1985), p. 17 and Mikardo, *Back-Bencher*, Chapters 1 and 2.

42 Ronald Hayman, *Secrets: Boyhood in a Jewish Hotel 1932–1954* (London: Peter Owen, 1985), p. 34.

43 Tony Kushner, 'A Tale of Two Port Jewish Communities: Southampton and Portsmouth Compared', in David Cesarani (ed.), *Port Jews* (London: Frank Cass, 2002), pp. 93–4 and Geoffrey Green, *The Royal Navy & Anglo-Jewry 1740–1820* (London: Geoffrey Green, 1989), passim.

44 Walter Benjamin, *The Arcades Project* (Cambridge, MA: Harvard University Press, 1999), translated by Howard Eiland and Kevin Mclaughlin), p. 833.

45 See his obituary in *Southern Daily Echo*, 1 November 1939.

46 Davies, *A History of Southampton*, pp. 107–8.

47 'Townsman', *Southampton: Occasional Notes* (Southampton: Southern Newspapers, 1938), pp. 70–1 and *Southern Daily Echo*, 1 July 1939.

48 *Gentleman's Magazine* vol. LX (September 1800), p. 877.

49 Townsman, *Southampton: Occasional Notes*, p. 70.

50 Elisabeth Withycombe, 'Some Southampton Street – and Place – Names', in Percy Ford (ed.), *Southampton: A Civic Survey* (London: Oxford University Press, 1931), p. 17.

51 F. Stevens, 'Museums and Libraries', in Ford (ed.), *Southampton: A Civic Survey*, p. 83.

52 Townsman, 'Occasional Notes', *Southern Daily Echo*, 1 July 1939.

53 A. G. K. Leonard, 'The Man Who Was "Townsman"', *Southern Evening Echo*, 15 April 1953.

54 Laurie Lee, *As I Walked Out One Midsummer Morning* (London: Andre Deutsch, 1969), p. 18.

55 O. H. T. Rishbeth, 'Land Utilization', in Ford (ed.), *Southampton: A Civic Survey*, pp. 33–5 and Ford, *Work and Wealth in a Modern Port*, pp. 48–56.

56   Lewisohn, *Funny Peculiar*, pp. 7–8.
57   John Fisher, *Tommy Cooper: Always Leave Them Laughing* (London: HarperCollins, 2006), pp. 35–6.
58   Maie Hodgson, *Child of the Ditches* (Southampton: [no publisher], 1992), p. 16.
59   Southampton City Heritage Oral history collection, 'Chapel and Northam', C0008.
60   Bellows, *My Southampton*, p. 67.
61   Southampton City Archive, SC51/144 (2), Rent Book, April 1922–March 1923.
62   John Arlott, 'Yesterday in Southampton', *Hampshire* vol. 3 no. 6 (April 1963), p. 16.
63   F. W. Cuthbertson, 'Housing' in Ford (ed.), *Southampton: A Civic Survey*, p. 65.
64   Priestley, *English Journey*, pp. 12–13.
65   See John Baxendale, '"I Had Seen a Lot of Englands": J. B. Priestley, Englishness and the People', *History Workshop Journal* no. 51 (2001), pp. 87–111.
66   Priestley, *English Journey*, p. 16.
67   Baxendale, '"I Had Seen a Lot of Englands"', passim.
68   Priestley, *English Journey*, p. 17.
69   Eric Gadd, 'Beside the Park … ', *Hampshire* vol. 26 no. 4 (February 1986), pp. 47, 48.
70   Eric Gadd, 'Happiest Days?', *Hampshire* vol. 22 no. 2 (December 1981), p. 55.
71   Brian Lawrence, 'Southampton's Edwardian Barrow Boys', *Hampshire* vol. 12 no. 1 (November 1971), p. 47.
72   Eric Gadd, *Southampton in the 'Twenties* (Southampton: Paul Cave, 1979), p. 18.
73   Lawrence, 'Southampton's Edwardian Barrow Boys', p. 47.
74   Elsie M.Sandell, *Southampton Cavalcade* (Southampton: G. F. Wilson, 1953), p. 67.
75   Revd John Williams quoted in *Southern Evening Echo*, 17 July 1974.
76   Elsie Sandell, 'Old East Street and Its People', *Southern Daily Echo*, 11 June 1954.
77   Sandell, *Southampton Cavalcade*, p. 67.
78   Ibid.
79   For the PortCities website, see www.portcities.org.uk, accessed November 2004.
80   Massey, 'Places and Their Pasts', p. 190.
81   See Russell King, 'Migrations, Globalization and Place', in Doreen Massey and Pat Jess (eds), *A Place in the World? Places, Cultures and Globalization* (Oxford: Oxford University Press, 1995), p. 30.
82   Stephen Pomerey, introduction to *Memories of Charlotte Street* (Portsmouth WEA Local History Group: Portsmouth, 2001 [1993]), p. 1.
83   Robert Dolling, *Ten Years in a Portsmouth Slum* (London: Swan Sonnenschein, 1896), pp. 10–11.
84   Testimony in *Memories of Charlotte Street*, p. 9. See also pp. 31 and 41.
85   *Hampshire Telegraph*, 5 February and 30 September 1910.
86   Weinberg, *Portsmouth Jewry*, p. 17.
87   Leonard Hill, *Saucy Boy: The Life Story of Benny Hill* (London: Grafton Books, 1990), p. 117.
88   Lewisohn, *Funny Peculiar*, p. 105.
89   Ibid., pp. 436–9.
90   Ibid., p. 438.
91   Hill, *Saucy Boy*, p. 156.
92   Lewisohn, *Funny Peculiar*, pp. 422–3.
93   Mary Douglas, *Purity and Danger: An Analysis of the Concepts of Pollution and Taboo* (London: Routledge, 1996 [1966]), p. 41.

Conclusion

Sander Gilman has asked us to

> imagine a new Jewish history written as the history of the Jews at the frontier, a history with no center; a history marked by the dynamics of change, confrontation, and accommodation; a history which focuses on the present and in which all participants are given voice.[1]

This study, covering the presence – in body or image – of Jews in a geographical area hardly touched by existing historiography, has attempted such a history, juxtaposing the past with the present through the processes of memory and forgetting. Gilman has in mind particular kinds of Zionist historiography and the separation of Galut and Diaspora which 'predispose[s] a model of center and periphery and condemn[s] the periphery to remain "marginal"'.[2] But one can go further, and point to the hierarchies within the study of the Jewish diaspora itself in which certain countries and regions are seen to possess less significance than others. In this respect, British Jewish history has been regarded as being of minor importance, and its provincial experiences even more so. Yet the histories revealed in *Anglo-Jewry since 1066* show the richness of previously neglected Jewish communities from the medieval era onwards. They show that the 'global is everywhere and already, in one way or another, implicated in the local'.[3] Moreover, this study has confirmed Gilman's proposition that when 'the center/periphery model is suspended, the frontier becomes the space where the complex interaction of the definitions of self and Other are able to be constructed'. Gilman continues, that

> Once we understand that the bipolar structure of center periphery maintains the separation between 'real' and 'symbolic' definitions of the Jew, the model of the frontier can lead to a new reading of Jewish history of the modern era in which the symbolic becomes a meaningful function of both internal and external identity as an extension of the network of meaning into all aspects of our understanding of the 'Jews'.[4]

At the core of this study has been the centrality of place in the construction and reconstruction of identities, Jewish and non-Jewish. Berlin-based artist, Tacita Dean, begins her study of the concept by conceding that 'Place can be difficult to locate' before concluding that the 'description of place will always reside in the detail'.[5] It is only through the micro-historical approach adopted in *Anglo-Jewry since 1066* that the command of such detail has been made possible; hence there has frequently been a focus on particular districts and even individual streets and houses within them. Such forensic topographical probing has enabled new, more inclusive narratives to emerge, and ones that run counter to the dominant myths of the past, especially that of the 'local' as self-contained and parochial.

In Thomas Hardy's *The Woodlanders* (1887), the outsider, Dr Fitzpiers, ponders why it is impossible for him to be truly part of the local Wessex landscape. To belong he

> must know all about those invisible ones of the days gone by, whose feet have traversed the fields which look so grey from his windows; recall whose creaking plough has turned those sods from time to time; whose hands planted the trees that form a crest to the opposite hill ... what bygone domestic dramas of love, jealousy, revenge, or disappointment have been enacted in the cottages, the mansion, the street or the green. The spot may have beauty, grandeur, salubrity, convenience; but if it lacks memories it will ultimately pall upon him who settles there without opportunity of intercourse with his kind.[6]

David Lodge has written that it is a 'novel especially characterised by "unity of place"' and Fitzpiers is one of several interlopers whose presence unsettles 'the traditional life of the woodland'.[7]

The case studies within *Anglo-Jewry since 1066* fall within the area of Hardy's beloved Wessex. They argue against the novelist's mystical vision (and that of those other writers such as W. H. Hudson analysed in Chapter 2) of the region as being unchanged and unchangeable until the onset of modernity, and only knowable through race memory based on generational presence from time immemorial. Art historian, Joseph Koerner, using the work of geographer Edward Casey, has suggested that 'modern myths about place change when we move from a situation of rootedness to one of itinerancy. When human society was rooted, we didn't have a sense of a place as being a place, because anything that wasn't that place wasn't in the world.'[8] In contrast, this study has placed particular emphasis on movement and flux *throughout* the past, and not simply in the modern era, and the concomitant constant making and remaking of local identities in relation to the outside world. In medieval Winchester (Hardy's Wintoncester), for example, the settlement and then removal of the Jews prompted the change in street name from Scowertenestret to Jewry Street in the early fourteenth century. Just over a decade after the expulsion, there was a local need to record the absence of the Jews. Moreover, the world of Richard of Devizes' *Cronicon* was one in which the geography could slip effortlessly from France to England (whether staid Winchester or lascivious London), to Jerusalem and the Holy Land, and from Christian to Jewish narratives. In such imaginative wanderings, Winchester could become 'the Jerusalem of the Jews'.[9] Jews, from the medieval period onwards, whether tolerated or not, were part of the locality and the local imagination and they forced consideration of a world beyond. To the Jews also, place and identity were fluid and constantly negotiated between the local and the global. Growing up in a Jewish hotel in inter-war Bournemouth, Ronald Hayman recalls the approach to the world beyond: 'One day we'd go back to Jerusalem, Daddy said. In the meantime we kept going back to Swanage and Lyme Regis.'[10]

At the extreme of such fluidity of movement were the millions of transmigrants of the nineteenth century onwards, many of whom passed through the Hampshire ports, especially Southampton. Staying sometimes just a matter of days, they contributed to the economy of the region, but the places they passed through were important to the formation of their identities as well as those around them. The transmigrant has been largely written out of history and heritage, consideration of their temporary presence being, perhaps, too unsettling for inclusion in Jewish and non-Jewish, as well as local and national narratives of the past. Paul Gilroy in his study of the Black Atlantic has urged us to be, on the level of theory, 'less intimidated by and respectful of the boundaries and integrity of modern nation states'. He thus settled as his starting point

> on the image of ships in motion across the spaces between Europe, America, Africa and the Caribbean as a central organising symbol ... The image of the ship – a living, micro-cultural, micro-political system in motion – is especially important for historical and theoretical reasons. Ships immediately focus attention on the middle passage, on the various projects for redemptive return, on the circulation of ideas and activists as well as the movement of key cultural and political artefacts.[11]

Similarly, in this study of the Jewish world, motion and with it the migration of people, ideas and artefacts has been integral to an understanding of settlement, belonging and exclusion.

And while the focus has been on the Jews, many other 'alien' groups were equally part of that process. Alwyn Ruddock, for example, highlights how in the 'Middle Ages [Southampton] was ... one of the chief centres of foreign trade in England, much frequented by alien merchants coming to the realm. Gascon and Fleming and Spaniard settled here; a prosperous Italian colony grew up, and Southampton became one of the most cosmopolitan towns in mediaeval England.'[12] Ruddock, however, writing immediately after the Second World War, was struck by how little evidence remained of that presence. The blitz had done its irretrievable damage: 'St John's church in French Street, with its tapestries and other gifts presented by the wealthy Florentines who worshipped there, has been swept away. So has the little chapel of St Nicholas, patron of sailors, where the Venetian galleymen were buried in the communal tomb of their fraternity.' Yet past neglect and indifference to the 'flourishing colonies of foreign merchants' were of equal importance as the more instant devastation and loss caused by the bombing of 1940:

> Beyond the West Gate there remains no trace of Galley Quay, once piled with bales of spices and cloth of gold, damask and velvet brought by the great galleys from Italy and Catalonia. The fine house built by Harry Huttoft, twice mayor of Hampton, still looks out on St Michael's Square, but the gold and silver plate and tapestries are gone from the panelled hall where Huttoft celebrated the marriage of his daughter with the Florentine who was to be the ruin of his family. In Bugle Street a grey stone wall and pointed window are all that remains of the turreted West Hall with its courtyard and fountain, home of a long succession of Italian merchants and their families.

All that survived now of that remarkable past, lamented Ruddock, were the street names – 'Pepper Alley, Simnel Street, Rochelle Lane and French Street'.[13]

Ruddock's phrase, 'there remains no trace', has been echoed throughout this study. Whether it be the medieval Jews of Winchester, or the early modern Port Jews of naval Portsmouth, or the pioneers of Jewish emancipation and civic contribution in nineteenth-century Portsmouth and Southampton, or the transmigrants from the *fin de siècle* to the 1920s, or the various Jewish communities that both flourished and disappeared across Hampshire from the Victorian era through to the Second World War, the conclusion has been constant: there is an absence of memory work associated with the past Jewish presence. The *processes* by which such amnesia has occurred have often been complex and locally specific. Even so, certain features across time and place are common, relating to myths of past homogeneity and the inability to conceive Jews as being an integral part of the local world. British Jews themselves have sometimes added to this neglect – blatantly, as in the case of Winchester and the removal from the city of the Jewish remains from the cemetery, or more vaguely by ignoring or downplaying the significance of provincial life and the importance of movement and migration in the Jewish experience.

The dominant theme emerging from the archaeology of memory work in this study is thus invisibility. It includes, amongst many other examples, the failure to mention Asher's inscription in Winchester Castle three years before the expulsion of the Jews (or the Jews' Tower in contemporary displays on the castle complex), the missing Jews of Southampton Cenotaph, the silence over Atlantic Park transmigrant camp, and the failure to remember the thriving east European trading communities of Charlotte Street, Portsmouth, and Canal Walk, Southampton. In all these cases, other, often Christian narratives have proved dominant and removed the possibility of recognising and remembering alternative experiences. In other cases, evidence of the Jewish past has not been destroyed or written out, but it has been subject to universalisation and the failure to recognise ethnic and religious particularity.

There are, for example, fragments of memory work associated with the two rival Emanuel families who contributed so much to the civic and commercial life of Portsmouth and Southampton in the nineteenth and early twentieth centuries. But neither the water fountain in Southsea commemorating Emanuel Emanuel or the candelabra presented to Samuel Emanuel which is now in the mayor's parlour in Southampton have any reference to the fact that these were the first Jewish mayors of their respective towns. Portraits of Samuel Emanuel and his wife, presented to him at the end of his period of office, are now hanging in Chilworth Manor Hotel, a few miles to the north of Southampton. But there is absolutely no indication of who they were and why these images of the Emanuels were created. Chosen because of their suitability as late Victoriana (even though the hotel is actually Edwardian), they remain anonymous, contrasting with the major facility rooms in the manor house named after the antisemites Hilaire Belloc and G. K. Chesterton, the former of whom helped construct the negative image of Winchester Jewry. Samuel's grandson, Charles Frederick Emanuel, died for his country in the First World War. His name *is* on Southampton's Cenotaph, but it is memory at a cost – the memorial is fundamentally Christian in nature. Another descendant of Samuel Emanuel, Charles Ansell Emanuel, died in 1947. The epigraph on his tombstone in the Jewish cemetery in Southampton is perhaps fitting for this remarkable family as a whole: 'Gone and Forgotten'.[14]

In Portsmouth, the city museum displays home-made dolls from the 1840s, representations of local pedlars.[15] While benign, there is no reference made to the Jewishness of these figures in the exhibition and an opportunity has thus been lost to explore the rich, if often troubled, history of this 'rough' Jewish seaport community of the long eighteenth century. Even Jewry Street in Winchester, the most open reference to a past Jewish presence, has only occasionally stimulated memory work. And even then it has never been within an artistic, literary or cultural frame of reference, despite the huge artistic and cultural output that the city's past has stimulated. We might contrast this situation with the work of Susan Hiller in Germany. Through

The J-Street Project Hiller has visited the 260-plus 'roads, streets and paths whose names refer to a Jewish presence' in Germany, filming and taking photographs of 'these evocative places, whether inner-city shopping streets, anonymous suburbs or secluded country roads, in an attempt to trace the absence that is explicitly named on maps and street maps'.[16] The absence of Jews clearly meant something to those in the fourteenth century who renamed the street in Winchester. Whether its nomenclature has any such resonance of absence today is highly unlikely. A lack of sensitivity to the past is also apparent in English Heritage's Medieval Merchant's House in French Street, Southampton, 'faithfully restored and furnished to look just as it did in 1290'.[17] That this date has other significance, as the year in which the Jews were expelled close by and in other ports in England, remains unstated as does the possible connection with the expulsion through the Round Table in the Great Hall in Winchester. More insidious still, is the Eleanor Garden next to the Great Hall and the celebration of the two queens who had encouraged the removal of the Jews.

Other local traces of the 'Jew' are manifested in equally problematic ways. These include the medieval host desecration as depicted in the Lady Chapel, Winchester Cathedral, and the continued portrayal of Jews as usurers to the unsuspecting 'Jack Tar' in Portsmouth.[18] In both cases there remains no attempt to contextualise where such imagery, humorous or otherwise, emerged from. Indeed, what is particularly dangerous is that nowhere are there images or representations of the Jews as part of the normal, everyday life of the localities. Jews were not saints in the periods covered by this study, and they possessed human agency, as figures of influence for good or bad. There always remains a danger of calling for positive images to counter the hostile and stereotypical and thereby leading to minority history becoming a form of defence. Equally, it would not have been too difficult to have turned this study into a form of 'ethnic cheerleading' – of Jewish contributions from Licoricia and Benedict the Gildsman in medieval Winchester through to scientist, Hertha Ayrton and her nineteenth-century literary family in Portsmouth and the economic success of the Millets emerging from twentieth-century Southampton. Instead, this study, while far from ignoring the famous, has also provided a history from below and highlighted the importance and significance of ordinary people – Jewish and non-Jewish – in making history. It has thus followed Sander Gilman's 'sense of the frontier [as] one in which all voices can be articulated'.[19] Yet the desire to rescue the previously obscure from the 'enormous condescension of posterity' has not been at the expense of romanticising the neglected.[20] Indeed, *Anglo-Jewry since 1066* has recognised conflict *within* the marginalised Jewish communities from the medieval period onwards. Critical analysis forces us to recognise that, at all points and places, factors such as wealth, religion, place of origin and gender, as well as personal animosities, were as likely to divide the Jews as unite them.

Ultimately, what is crucial is to acknowledge that whether present, absent or passing through, Jews were an integral part of the local world, and their subsequent invisibility or problematic, 'alien', representation fails to do justice to the richness of the past. Movement and diversity are not simply products of modernity: heterogeneity is the natural order of things. While rarely acknowledged, the places covered in this study were, I argue, in Ruth Gruber's phrase, 'virtually Jewish'.[21] By acknowledging and accepting that *all* places (and not just the post-Holocaust European continent) are, amongst other things, 'virtually Jewish', we can at least start to challenge the ethnic and racial certainties that are continuing and intensifying in the twenty-first century.

Notes

1 Sander Gilman, 'Introduction', in Sander Gilman and Milton Shain (eds), *Jewries at the Frontier: Accommodation Identity Conflict* (Urbana: University of Illinois Press, 1998), p. 11.

2 Ibid., pp. 1–2.

3 Doreen Massey, 'Double Articulation: A Place in the World', in A. Bammer (ed.), *Displacements: Cultural Identities in Question* (Bloomington: Indiana University Press, 1994), p. 120.

4 Gilman, 'Introduction', p. 12.

5 In Tacita Dean and Jeremy Millar, *Place* (London: Thames & Hudson, 2005), pp. 11, 178.

6 Thomas Hardy, *The Woodlanders* (London: Macmillan, 1975 [1887]), pp. 148–9.

7 David Lodge, 'Introduction', pp. 14–15 in ibid.

8 Joseph Koerner in Dean and Millar, *Place*, p. 185 referring to Edward Casey, *The Fate of Place: A Philosophical History* (Berkeley: University of California Press, 1998).

9 John Appleby (ed.), *The Chronicle of Richard of Devizes* (London: Thomas Nelson, 1963), p. 67.

10 Ronald Hayman, *Secrets: Boyhood in a Jewish Hotel 1932–1954* (London: Peter Owen, 1985), p. 41.

11 Paul Gilroy, *The Black Atlantic: Modernity and Double Consciousness* (London: Verso, 1993), p. 4.

12 Alwyn Ruddock, *Italian Merchants and Shipping in Southampton 1270–1600* (Southampton: Southampton University College Press, 1951), p. 10.

13 Ibid., pp. 9–10.

14 The Jewish cemetery has many generations of the Emanuel family buried there, though sadly the gravestones are in a poor state of repair and several have been subject to antisemitic attack.

15 See items D28 in the 'Home, Sweet Home' section of Portsmouth Museum, visited July 2007.

16 Imagery and details reproduced in Dean and Millar, *Place*, pp. 118–19.
17 *Southampton: City Visitors Guide 2006* (Southampton: Southampton City Council, 2006), p. 23.
18 See, for example, Rick Jolly, *Jackspeak: A Guide to British Naval Slang & Usage* (Liskeard, Cornwall: SAMA Books, 2006 edition [1989]), p. 241 which includes the entry *Jew's march-past* described as 'The process of examining one's wallet to ascertain either its contents, or else the damage caused by last night's run-ashore.' This book is available at many naval heritage sites.
19 Gilman, 'Introduction', p. 21.
20 E. P. Thompson, *The Making of the English Working Class* (London: Victor Gollancz, 1963), p. 12.
21 Ruth Gruber, *Virtually Jewish: Reinventing Jewish Culture in Europe* (Berkeley: University of California Press, 2002).

Index

Lightning Source UK Ltd.
Milton Keynes UK
UKOW030751280112

186207UK00001B/20/P